TAKING SIDES

Clashing Views in

Family and Personal Relationships

EIGHTH EDITION

TAKING SIDES

Clashing Views in

Family and Personal Relationships

EIGHTH EDITION

Selected, Edited, and with Introductions by

David M. Hall, Ed.D
Professional Trainer/Consultant

Connect
Learn
Succeed™

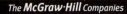

 *Connect*
Learn
Succeed™

TAKING SIDES: CLASHING VIEWS IN FAMILY AND PERSONAL RELATIONSHIPS,
EIGHTH EDITION

1 2 3 4 5 6 7 8 9 0 DOC/DOC 09

MHID: 0-07-351540-X
ISBN: 978-0-07-351540-3

Managing Editor: *Larry Loeppke*
Senior Managing Editor: *Faye Schilling*
Senior Developmental Editor: *Jade Benedict*
Editorial Coordinator: *Mary Foust*
Production Service Assistant: *Rita Hingtgen*
Permissions Coordinator: *Lenny J. Behnke*
Editorial Assistant: *Cindy Hedley*
Senior Marketing Manager: *Julie Keck*
Marketing Communications Specialist: *Mary Klein*
Marketing Coordinator: *Alice Link*
Senior Project Manager: *Erin Melloy*
Design Specialist: *Tara McDermott*
Cover Graphics: *Rick D. Noel*

Compositor: MPS Limited, A Macmillan Company
Cover Image: © Stockbyte/Getty Images/RF

Library of Congress Cataloging-in-Publication Data

Main entry under title:
    Taking Sides: clashing views on controversial issues in family and personal relationships/
    selected, edited, and with introductions by David Hall, MSW.—8th ed.

    Includes bibliographical references and index.
    1. Family—United States. 2. Interpersonal relationships. I. Hall, David, *comp.*

                                                    306.85'973

Editors/Academic Advisory Board

Members of the Academic Advisory Board are instrumental in the final selection of articles for each edition of TAKING SIDES. Their review of articles for content, level, and appropriateness provides critical direction to the editors and staff. We think that you will find their careful consideration well reflected in this volume.

TAKING SIDES: Clashing Views in FAMILY AND PERSONAL RELATIONSHIPS
Eighth Edition

EDITOR

David M. Hall
Professional Trainer/Consultant

Leon Stimpson
Professional Trainer and Consultant

William J. Taverner
Fairleigh Dickinson University

David Keller Trevaskis, Esq.
Arcadia University

Yolanda Turner, Ed.D.
Eastern University

Preface

Human beings naturally seek out relationships. Although these relationships vary depending on whether they are among family, coworkers, friends, acquaintances, or significant others, relationships with intimate others can be the most rewarding and challenging. From a public policy and social interaction perspective, they can also be the most controversial. The ways in which our personal and family relationships are understood and respected influence not only our intimate relationships but also our social relationships and livelihood. Too often in the national media, our family and relationship diversity is approached from a controversial perspective that can foster division and animosity. *Taking Sides: Family and Personal Relationships* is intended to provide thoughtful discourse, standing in sharp contrast with such divisive portrayals and rhetoric.

The eighth edition of *Taking Sides: Family and Personal Relationships* provides thoughtful discourse from diverse perspectives on some of the most controversial issues in American society today. This volume contains 17 questions with 34 thoughtful and engaging viewpoints that are designed for readers not just to reinforce but also to challenge their existing perspectives and values. Each chapter includes an *Introduction* from the editor, which provides a context for this debate. The *Introduction* may cite important statistics, pertinent history, and an overview of the debate. The *Introduction* is followed by two competing views on the controversial question. Following the competing viewpoints is a *Postscript* from the editor, which examines suggestions for further thought, research, or action on the topic posed in the chapter. The section *Internet References* provides a list of sources that will help further the reader's understanding about the topics in this volume.

Taking Sides: Family and Personal Relationships will challenge readers to examine divergent viewpoints on some of the most contentious issues in American society today. Topics relate to parenting, cyberspace, infidelity, sexual orientation, sexual decision making, and many other issues that are sensitive and often difficult to discuss openly. Each chapter will provide readers with an opportunity to reinforce what they already believe while also challenging some of their already held beliefs and convictions.

A word to the instructor   An *Instructor's Resource Guide with Test Questions* provides multiple-choice and essay questions related to this text for help with assessment of student reading. Although the *Instructor's Resource Guide with Test Questions* is tailor-made for this specific volume, educators can also reference *Using Taking Sides in the Classroom,* which provides an overview of ways in which instructors can manage discussions about divergent viewpoints within their classrooms. For an online version of *Using Taking Sides in the Classroom* and a correspondence service for *Taking Sides* adopters, please visit http://www.mhcls.com/usingts.

McGraw-Hill provides a dynamic list of titles in this series in addition to *Taking Sides: Family and Personal Relationships*. These can be used in a wide variety of courses and range from titles that relate to specific course content to those that teach students how to write and debate persuasively. If you are interested in reviewing other thought-provoking editions, please visit the Taking Sides Web site at http://www.mhcls.com/takingsides.

Acknowledgments First and foremost, let me thank McGraw-Hill's Jade Benedict. Writing and editing can be so very personal and therefore challenging when working with a publisher for the first time. However, Jade could not have been more thoughtful and collaborative throughout this process. He has been an invaluable resource in creating this edition. Jade's timely, thoughtful feedback combined with his support for my goals in creating the best edition possible have been critical to the creation of this volume. Beyond these valuable qualities, Jade knew just what to add to as well as what to remove from my plate to ensure that I was using my time in the most productive and efficient manner possible. Had it not been for Jade, this edition would never have reached publication with this level of quality.

I would also like to thank:

- Dr. Elizabeth Schroeder, the previous editor of this book. Elizabeth is a one of our nation's most respected leaders in this field. Her past work is reflected in the quality of this book, and she has acted as my mentor in working on this volume.
- William J. Taverner, Editor-in-Chief of the *American Journal for Sexuality Education,* for his generous spirit of collaboration and mentorship. I have learned so very much from Bill's intellect and creativity. It is unlikely that I would be editor of this volume had it not been for Bill.
- Ken Kratz, my friend and colleague, who helped with initial drafts of the introduction to this volume.
- Eli Green, a gifted educator and curriculum author, for serving as Contributing Editor to the *Instructor's Resource Guide* that accompanies this book.
- Sam Repko, my former student, for reminding me of the strength and resiliency of teenagers when faced with life's challenges.
- The authors featured in this edition. I am fortunate to have had the opportunity to collaborate with bright and talented scholars who have framed a powerful debate that will enhance not only learning but also public discourse.

Remember that when reading this volume, you may very well encounter viewpoints that you find challenging and even offensive. This is why I want to end by acknowledging you, the reader, for the courage to challenge your deeply held convictions in reading these chapters. It is difficult to consider positions that one finds morally wrong, but doing so leads to stronger moral and intellectual growth. Thank you for taking the time to read and interact with this book.

David M. Hall, Ed.D.
Professional Trainer and Consultant
Doylestown, PA

This book is dedicated to Annie Hall,
my spouse and life partner, for teaching
me more about healthy families and
relationships than anyone else
in this world ever could.

Contents in Brief

Contents

William J. Taverner is a nationally known sex educator and trainer who has authored a number of sexuality education manuals and is the Editor-in-Chief of the *American Journal of Sexuality Education.* Taverner argues that despite his strong support for comprehensive sexuality education, respecting the moral beliefs of the parents who choose to opt out is more important than including all students. Allyson Sandak has been a sexuality educator and trainer for a decade, as well as an adjunct professor at Montclair State University and the Editor-in-Chief of *Contemporary Sexuality,* a publication of the American Association of Sexuality Educators, Counselors, and Therapists (AASECT). Sandak argues that comprehensive sexuality education is a public health issue and that opting-out provisions are harmful to young people.

Leslie Doty Hollingsworth, an associate professor of social work at the University of Michigan, offers a history of transracial adoption that has involved primarily white adoptive parents and black or African American children. She argues that children are best served if they are adopted by families of their same racial background, and that systematic changes—such as adoption services and programs better geared toward adults of color—would enable more families to adopt children from their own backgrounds. Ezra Griffith and Rachel Bergeron, both faculty members of the Yale University School of Medicine's psychiatry department, argue that requiring racial and ethnic matching, although an appropriate effort, would leave too many children of color languishing in the foster and adoption systems. By maintaining that only in-race adoption is the best and ideal situation, they ask rhetorically, does our society actually do more to reinforce cultural stereotypes or to truly serve children needing homes?

Sarah Werthan Buttenwieser is a writer and lives in Northampton. She earned her BA at Hampshire College and her MFA from Warren Wilson College. Contributor to many magazines, newspapers, and online publications, she has a blog called "Standing in the Shadows," which can be found at http://www.valleyadvocate.com/blogs/home.cfm?uid=92. Lara Riscol is a freelance writer who explores societal conflict surrounding sexuality and family. She has been published in *The Nation, Salon, AlterNet,* and other national media outlets, and is working on a book called *Ten Sex Myths That Screw America.*

Chris Jeub, writer and president of Training Minds Ministries, is a former public school teacher with 11 children, all of whom he and his wife have home-schooled. Naming several famous home-schooled individuals, such as Winston Churchill, Benjamin Franklin, and Florence Nightingale, he argues that the home is the best environment in which to teach children, for social, academic, family strengthening, and religious reasons. Home-schooling, he maintains, frees parents to impart their own values to their children without concern for how these beliefs might clash with what is presented in the public school system. Carole Moore, a freelance writer, discusses how she weighed the options of home-schooling vs. public schooling and argues that even though home-schooling might offer some benefits to children, in the end, home-schooling provides children a distorted view of the world at large. Children will, she writes, make good decisions and bad decisions as a part of growing up, and whether they are home-schooled or public schooled is not the determining factor in whether they grow up healthy and well-adjusted.

Child developmentalists Jeanne Brooks-Gunn, Wen-Jui Han, and Jane Waldfogel assert that their findings show many types of negative effects from maternal employment on the later cognitive and educational outcomes of children. Professor of sociology and anthropology Thomas M. Vander Ven and his colleagues argue that their studies show that a mother working will have relatively little or no negative influence on the social, emotional, and behavioral functioning of her children.

UNIT 2   HOW MUCH CONTROL SHOULD PARENTS HAVE OVER THEIR CHILDREN'S LIVES?   95

Bridget E. Maher, an analyst on marriage and family issues at the Family Research Council, argues that far too much funding has gone into programs that teach young people about sexuality and contraception—programs that she asserts are ineffective. She argues that most teens say they and their peers should receive strong messages about abstinence. Sue Alford, editor and director of public information services at Advocates for Youth, argues that young people are receiving sexuality information and messages from so many sources that it is irresponsible to limit sexuality and other educators to discussing only abstinence. She maintains that the programs taught under the Abstinence Until Marriage funding often provide factually inaccurate information and hyperbolic assertions pertaining to the potential consequences of sexual relationships outside of marriage.

Professor John A. Robertson of the University of Texas at Austin's School of Law argues that preconception gender selection of infants in utero for medical purposes should be allowed, and that insufficient data exist to demonstrate that any clear harm exists in allowing parents to do so. Norman Daniels (Tufts University), Carson Strong (University of Tennessee), Mary B. Mahowald (University of Chicago), and Mark V. Sauer (Columbia University) each take one aspect of Professor Robertson's arguments to demonstrate why preconception gender selection should not be allowed, including, for example, the socioeconomic status inequity that allowing such a procedure, which likely would not be covered by health insurance, would create.

Amicur Farkas, B. Chertin, and Irith Hadas-Halpren, faculty of the Ben-Gurion University in Jerusalem, Israel, see ambiguous genitalia as a true emergency. They assert that feminizing surgery should be done on an infant with congenital adrenal hyperplasia to ensure that as an adult woman, she will have sexual functioning and be able to give birth. Paul McHugh argues that a person's sense of gender identity is biologically based–that by changing an infant's or child's body before that child has a sense of who he or she is and risking being wrong about that sex assignment can do much more damage than good.

Teresa Stanton Collett, former professor at South Texas College of Law, testifies in front of the U.S. House of Representatives in support of the federal Child Custody Protection Act. She advocates parental involvement in a minor's pregnancy, regardless of the girl's intention to carry or terminate the pregnancy. Parental involvement, Collett maintains, is not punitive; rather, it offers the girl herself additional protection against injury and sexual assault. Minors tend to have less access to information and education than adults; without this information and education, they are not able to provide truly "informed" consent, concludes Collett. Planned Parenthood Federation of America, Inc., the oldest and largest reproductive health organization in the United States, argues that parental notification and consent laws keep girls from exercising their legal right to access abortion. Notifying parents of their daughter's intent to terminate a pregnancy puts many girls at risk for severe punishment, expulsion from the home, or even physical violence. Planned Parenthood contends that just as minors have the power to give their consent for other surgical procedures, they should be able to give their own consent to terminate a pregnancy.

Joan Biskupic, legal affairs correspondent for *USA Today*, discusses the personal challenges for same-gender couples attempting to adopt in states that are not friendly to them and provides an update of legal issues and options available to lesbian and gay couples; these indicate a changing tide of acceptance toward couples of the same gender, as well as lesbian and gay individuals, adopting children. Timothy J. Dailey, senior research fellow at the Center for Marriage and Family Studies, provides an overview of state laws pertaining to adoption by lesbian or gay parents. He points to studies showing that children do much better in family settings that include both a mother and a father, and that the sexual behaviors same-sex parents engage in make them, by definition, inappropriate role models for children.

Anthony Kennedy, Associate Justice of the Supreme Court of the United States, was appointed to the Court by President Reagan in 1988. In this case, Kennedy is writing for a six-member majority that overturns a previous case, *Bowers v. Hardwick. Bowers* is overturned by Kennedy's opinion, therefore striking down state antisodomy laws. Antonin Scalia, Associate Justice of the Supreme Court of the United States, was appointed to the Court by President Reagan in 1986. Scalia writes that there are no constitutional protections from discrimination based on sexual orientation and that state sodomy laws should be upheld.

Susan Milstein is a certified health education specialist and a certified sexuality educator. She is an associate professor in the Department of Health Enhancement at Montgomery College in Maryland, as well as the lead consultant for Milstein Health Consulting. Milstein contends that while it is difficult to create a universal definition of cheating, the majority of people feel that cybersex outside of a primary relationship is cheating. Crystal Bedley argues that the anonymous nature of cybersex means that it is not cheating.

Donald Dyson is assistant professor of human sexuality education at Widener University and the national co-chair of the conference for the American Association of Sexuality Educators, Counselors and Therapists. Dyson argues that there are essential qualities of a healthy relationship and that an open relationship can be successful. Stanley Kurtz, a writer and senior fellow at the Ethics and Public Policy Center, argues that allowing for same-sex marriage will create a slippery slope, eventually leading to plural marriages. Kurtz contends that such marriages prove destructive to the institution of marriage itself.

Issue 16.   Is Pornography Harmful to Teenagers?   267

Wayne Grinwis, has been a sexual health educator for Planned Parenthood for 15 years. He is also adjunct professor in the Department of Health at West Chester University. Grinwis credits Andrea Daniels for help with this article. Grinwis argues that pornography is all right for adults, but for teenagers it can create unrealistic expectations about sex, provide a negative and inaccurate sexuality education, and increase sexual violence against women. Justin Sitron, is assistant professor of Education at Widener University. Sitron argues that pornography has no negative impact on teenagers and, in fact, has potential benefits. Sitron contends that Internet pornography can be helpful in providing teens an opportunity to see real bodies, a chance to learn about sex from seeing rather than doing, and an open door for communication with parents.

Issue 17.   Are Statutory Rape Laws Effective at Protecting Minors?   281

Sherry F. Colb, columnist and law professor, uses a case study involving a statutory rape case to raise concerns about whether rape and assault cases would be prosecuted sufficiently without statutory rape laws. Although not perfect, statutory rape laws can be assets in such rape cases as when the older partner denies the rape occurred or denies responsibility for a resulting pregnancy or infection. Marc Tunzi, a family physician, believes that statutory rape laws are ineffective because people can get around them too easily. These laws, he argues, require that an otherwise healthy relationship between two people of different ages be criminalized solely because there is some kind of sexual activity involved. As a result, medical and other licensed professionals do not want to break up these relationships that, in their professional opinion, are not problematic based on just the age difference between the two partners.

Correlation Guide

The *Taking Sides* series presents current issues in a debate-style format designed to stimulate student interest and develop critical thinking skills. Each issue is thoughtfully framed with an issue summary, an issue introduction, and a postscript. The pro and con essays—selected for their liveliness and substance—represent the arguments of leading scholars and commentators in their fields.

Taking Sides: Clashing Views in Family and Personal Relationships, 8/e, is an easy-to-use reader that presents issues on important topics such as *abstinence-until marriage, cybersex,* and *same-sex marriage.* For more information on *Taking Sides* and other *McGraw-Hill Contemporary Learning Series* titles, visit www.mhhe.com/cls.

This convenient guide matches the issues in Taking Sides: Family and Personal Relationships, 8/e, with the corresponding chapters in two of our best-selling McGraw-Hill Family Studies textbooks by Cherlin and DeGenova.

Taking Sides: Family and Personal Relationships, 8/e	Public and Private Familes: An Introduction, 6/e by Cherlin	Intimate Relationships Marriages, and Families, 7e by DeGenova
Issue 1: Should Parents Be Allowed to Opt Their Children Out of Sexuality Education Classes?	**Chapter 9:** Children and Parents	**Chapter 10:** Power, Decision Making, and Communication **Chapter 13:** Parent-Child Relationships
Issue 2: Should Adoptive Parents Only Adopt within Their Own Racial/Ethnic Group?	**Chapter 5:** Race, Ethnicity, and Families	**Chapter 11:** Family Planning and Parenting
Issue 3: Should Unhappy Couples Stay Together for the Sake of Their Children?	**Chapter 7:** Cohabitation and Marriage **Chapter 12:** Divorce **Chapter 13:** Remarriage and Stepfamilies	**Chapter 8:** Marital Relationships over the Family Life Cycle **Chapter 16:** The Family and Divorce
Issue 4: Should Parents Homeschool Their Children?	**Chapter 9:** Children and Parents	**Chapter 13:** Parent-Child Relationships
Issue 5: Do Mothers Who Work Outside the Home Have a Negative Effect on Their Children?	**Chapter 8:** Work and Families	**Chapter 9:** Work, Family Roles, and Material Resources
Issue 6: Should "Abstinence-Until-Marriage" Be the Only Message for Teens?	**Chapter 6:** Sexualities	**Chapter 6:** Love and Mate Selection

(Continued)

Taking Sides: Family and Personal Relationships, 8/e	Public and Private Familes: An Introduction, 6/e by Cherlin	Intimate Relationships Marriages, and Families, 7e by DeGenova
Issue 7: Should Parents Be Able to Select the Biological Sex of Their Children?	**Chapter 3:** Gender and Families	**Chapter 3:** Gender: Identity and Roles
Issue 8: Should Parents Surgically Alter Their Intersex Infants?	**Chapter 3:** Gender and Families	**Chapter 3:** Gender: Identity and Roles
Issue 9: Should Minors Be Required to Get Their Parents' Permission in Order to Obtain an Abortion?	**Chapter 14:** The Family, the State, and Social Policy	**Chapter 10:** Power, Decision Making, and Communication **Chapter 13:** Parent-Child Relationships **Chapter 15:** Conflict, Family Crises, and Crisis Management
Issue 10: Should Same-Sex Couples Be Able to Marry Legally?	**Chapter 14:** The Family, the State, and Social Policy	**Chapter 1:** Intimate Relationships, Marriages, and Families in the Twenty-First Century
Issue 11: Should Men Who Have Sex with Men Be Allowed to Donate Blood?	**Chapter 14:** The Family, the State, and Social Policy	
Issue 12: Should Lesbian and Gay Individuals Be Able to Adopt Children?	**Chapter 9:** Children and Parents	**Chapter 2:** Family Backgrounds and How They Influence Us
Issue 13: Should Private Sexual Acts between Gay Couples Be Legal?	**Chapter 14:** The Family, the State, and Social Policy	
Issue 14: Is Cybersex "Cheating"?	**Chapter 6:** Sexualities **Chapter 15:** Social Change and Families	**Chapter 15:** Conflict, Family Crises, and Crisis Management
Issue 15: Are Open Relationships Healthy?	**Chapter 6:** Sexualities **Chapter 15:** Social Change and Families	**Chapter 7:** Qualities of a Successful Marriage
Issue 16: Is Pornography Harmful to Teenagers?	**Chapter 6:** Sexualities	**Chapter 6:** Love and Mate Selection
Issue 17: Are Statutory Rape Laws Effective at Protecting Minors?	**Chapter 14:** The Family, the State, and Social Policy	

Introduction

Frameworks for Examining Debate

David M. Hall, Ed.D., Editor

Taking Sides: Family and Personal Relationships is released at a time when American society is reconstructing its concept of families and relationships. More children are growing up in nontraditional homes than ever before. In fact, concepts of the traditional family that were once considered a universal norm are not reflective of the diverse families that exist. These changes can be a source of societal conflict. Conversely, these changes can also be a source of societal strength and growth.

Pluralistic nations thrive by demonstrating a willingness to cooperate despite existing differences. In order for this to occur, the citizenry must engage in thoughtful and respectful discourse. In that spirit, this volume examines the diversity of views in American society as they relate to family and personal relationships to provide a context for weighing more carefully not just one's own values but also opposing values. Most readers will find that their responses to issues raised in this volume are anchored in a moral or intellectual foundation. Four such frameworks are identified in this introduction to assist the reader in providing a larger context for the issues debated in this volume.

Many readers will find themselves conducting further research on the topics raised in each chapter. Today, issues in this volume often permeate discourse in society, families, the law, and education. *Taking Sides: Family and Personal Relationships* is designed to provide an intellectual foundation for much of this discourse.

Carefully evaluate the arguments made throughout this book. Readers should be able to identify statements of fact, statements of value, and the credibility of research used to support the author's thesis. Although such evaluation is important when reading persuasive essays, higher-level thinking skills can be used to examine each chapter through a variety of frameworks.

This introduction outlines four potential frameworks: political ideology, religion, linguistics, and legal theory. Try applying one or more frameworks to the issues addressed in this book. How would you compare and contrast your conclusions for each chapter in this book? Are there areas in which competing frameworks create a conflict for you? If so, how would you reconcile these differences?

Let us now examine the four frameworks that can be used for analysis throughout this volume.

Political Ideology Framework

Many of the topics raised in this book are political and can sometimes be significant issues in campaigns and elections. The political ideology continuum contains the following stages: reactionary, conservative, liberal, and radical (see Table 1). Reactionary ideology supports going back to a previous way of doing things. Reactionaries believe that most social problems are the result of democratic excesses that favor the masses at the expense of proven traditions.

Conservative ideology believes in defending the status quo and making only small changes. Liberal ideology believes in change that guarantees greater individual rights. Radical ideology, typically the antithesis of reactionary, favors fundamental restructuring of society to ensure equality.

Table 1
Political Ideology Continuum

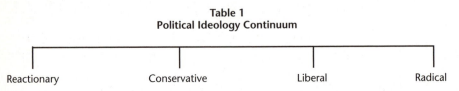

| Reactionary | Conservative | Liberal | Radical |

If the reader chooses, for example, to examine the issue of whether open relationships are healthy, a reactionary view would oppose open relationships as well as support changing marriage laws to make divorce more difficult. In fact, reactionaries would probably argue that cultural acceptance of divorce will ultimately lead to polygamy. A conservative perspective would likely oppose open relationships and same-sex marriage but support leaving divorce laws as they stand. A liberal view would likely support allowing same-sex marriage but voice opposition for polyamory. A radical perspective would favor fundamentally reconstructing the culture of marriage so that polyamory is as much the expected norm as monogamy.

The political ideology framework can be used for any topic within this book. Is your political ideology the same for adoption as it is for marriage? How about with other topics in this book? What does this comparison and contrast reveal about your overall political ideology?

Religious Framework

Many people have views about sexual orientation and gender identity that are the result of their religious upbringing. However, religious views vary not just from one religion to the next but also within certain faiths themselves. Debate over acceptance, tolerance, and rejection based on sexual orientation is dividing many places of worship. Dr. James Nelson, a Christian minister, created a continuum for religious responses to lesbian, gay, and bisexual individuals, which consists of rejecting punitive, rejecting nonpunitive, qualified acceptance, and full acceptance (see Table 2). Readers who come from a strong religious background may want to consider where their faith falls along this continuum and whether their personal views correspond with those espoused by their faith. When reading each chapter, consider how religious values may affect your views on particular issues.

Table 2
Nelson Continuum

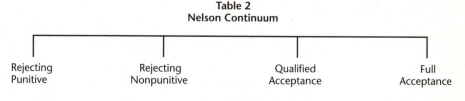

| Rejecting Punitive | Rejecting Nonpunitive | Qualified Acceptance | Full Acceptance |

A rejecting punitive place of worship would expel anyone who identifies as lesbian, gay, bisexual, or transgender. Rejecting nonpunitive values is found in places of worship where lesbian, gay, bisexual, and transgender individuals are welcome to attend but will regularly hear sermons about the immorality of their identity. Qualified acceptance is found in a place of worship in which one will never hear hatred from the pulpit and will generally feel accepted. However, if one day a gay attendee offers to teach his child's Bible study group, a committee at the church might meet and decide that gay members of the church may not teach children. Full acceptance is featured in a place of worship that holds same-sex weddings and allows for the full inclusion of all lesbian, gay, bisexual, and transgender members, including serving as clergy.

When reading Unit 3, "Being Inclusive: Lesbian, Gay, and Bisexual Individuals, Couples, and Families," try to identify whether your response has a religious foundation. Where does your school community fall on this continuum? Where does your home community fall on this continuum? What do you believe is the most ethical response on this continuum and why?

Although Nelson uses this framework in the context of religious faith and sexual orientation, it can be applied to any of the topics found in this book.

Linguistics Framework

Professor of linguistics George Lakoff utilizes a Nation as Family framework for examining political rhetoric. Lakoff argues that Americans view the nation as a family, which is evidenced by metaphors such as "founding fathers," "daughters of the American revolution," and "sending our sons off to war." Using the Nation as Family model, Lakoff contends that Republicans tend to support what he calls Strict Father Morality and that Democrats tend to support what he calls Nurturant Parent Morality. A Lakoffian framework is pertinent to this particular volume in the *Taking Sides* series, as it demonstrates that our concept of family applies not just to our personal lives but also to our sense of patriotism and national psyche.

Strict Father Morality rests upon a patriarchal system that values adherence to past moral standards to ensure future success. Strict Father Morality would not only support defining marriage as between a man and a woman but would also argue that a nation's success comes from such a traditional family structure. Conversely, Nurturant Parent Morality values independent thinking that will strengthen the family. Nurturant Parent Morality would support marriage being reconstructed to include same-sex couples as an issue of fairness and equality for all members of the familial society. Nurturant Parent Morality argues that such change will strengthen American society.

Few people fit entirely into either Strict Father or Nurturant Parent Morality. For example, a person can adhere to Strict Father Morality about social welfare programs but Nurturant Parent Morality about funding for education. Are your Nation as Family views regarding family and personal relationship issues consistent across chapters in this volume? How do your Nation as Family views on topics raised within this volume compare and contrast with your views on other issues within American society?

Legal Framework

The two primary competing legal philosophies are Orignialism and Living Constitution. This framework can be applied to any article involving law and policy. Originalism is the belief that judges should base their decisions on the original meaning of the text of the Constitution. Their understanding of the intent is based on the writings of the framers and the debates at the Constitutional Convention. In the case of constitutional amendments, advocates of Originalism would consider the writings and discussions at the time of the amendment's adoption. In contrast, Living Constitution is the belief that the Constitution was written with the intent that its interpretation would evolve in response to an ever-changing society. Those who believe in Living Constitution believe it is against the spirit and intent of the Constitution to interpret contemporary legal issues with a nineteenth-century mindset.

The Fourteenth Amendment guarantees equal protection under the law. Sexual orientation was not debated during passage of this amendment. As a result, an Originalist would argue that such protection refers only to race because the intent was to protect newly freed slaves and that it therefore categorically denies protection based on sexual orientation. However, adherents of a Living Constitution perspective argue that the equal protection guarantee was written without mention of any identity, including race, so applications of this right could be applied differently for successive generations. Supporters of the Living Constitution perspective would support extending equal protection rights based on biological sex as well as sexual orientation.

Conclusion

During early American history, someone caught having sex outside of marriage was likely to be severely punished. Within marriage, sex for procreation was typically the expected norm. In fact, married couples lacked a defined, constitutional right to contraception until the 1960s. Over the past 50 years, accepted norms of family and personal relationships have been fundamentally reconstructed. Today Americans are living in an era in which society is openly grappling with a wide variety of changes related to family and personal relationships.

The debate over rights for nontraditional families is sometimes referred to as part of a culture war. Although there is no protracted physical battle, the passion associated with many people's deeply held beliefs is at stake in the issues addressed in this volume. In some cases, individual livelihoods and even lives are threatened. The use of such a violent metaphor as *culture war* reflects the strong feelings and deep divisions that exist within American society when people discuss many of the issues addressed in this volume.

Each chapter provides an engaging examination of both sides of each issue. Readers may find that they will be challenged in some of their beliefs and that they need to conduct further research. It is important not only to read about these issues but also to work for better understanding of the diversity of views that are expressed in this volume. A willingness to consider diverse views will allow for growth and mutual collaboration, thereby strengthening America's pluralistic society.

Internet References . . .

National Adoption Center

The National Adoption Center works to expand adoption opportunities for children living in foster care throughout the United States and to be a resource to families and to agencies who seek permanent, caring homes for children.

http://www.adopt.org

National Association of Black Social Workers

The National Association of Black Social Workers was established in 1968 to "advocate and address important social issues that impact the health and welfare of the Black community." Their affiliate chapters, including student chapters, are spread throughout the United States.

http://www.nabsw.org

National Home Education Network

The National Home Education Network (NHEN) works to encourage and facilitate the grassroots efforts of state and local homeschooling organizations and individuals by providing information, fostering networking, and promoting public relations on a national level. NHEN supports "the freedom of all individual families to choose home education and to direct such education."

http://www.nhen.org/

National Association of Social Workers

The National Association of Social Workers (NASW) is the largest membership organization of professional social workers in the world. NASW works to enhance the professional growth and development of its members, create and maintain professional standards, and advance sound social policies.

http://www.naswdc.org

Parental Decision Making: What's Best for Children . . . Or What's Best for Parents?

*U*se of the oft-quoted "it takes a village to raise a child" is still met with understanding, thoughtful nods as we appreciate the concept that many people beyond the family structure play key roles in raising children. There are, however, numerous factors that contribute to, interfere with, detract from, and otherwise affect how parents raise their children. Parenting styles vary. The so-called village includes the government, which is met with open arms by some and skepticism and mistrust by others. This section examines five questions that society often asks relating to parenting issues:

- Should Parents Be Allowed to Opt Their Children Out of Sexuality Education Classes?

- Should Adoptive Parents Adopt Only within Their Own Racial/Ethnic Group?

- Should Unhappy Couples Stay Together for the Sake of Their Children?

- Should Parents Home-school Their Children?

- Do Mothers Who Work Outside of the Home Have a Negative Effect on Their Children?

ISSUE 1

Should Parents Be Allowed to Opt Their Children Out of Sexuality Education Classes?

YES: William J. Taverner, from "The Right to Pass," written for *Taking Sides: Family and Personal Relationships* (2009)

NO: Allyson Sandak, from "Let the Teachers Teach," written for *Taking Sides: Family and Personal Relationships* (2009)

ISSUE SUMMARY

YES: William J. Taverner is a nationally known sex educator and trainer who has authored a number of sexuality education manuals and is the Editor-in-Chief of the *American Journal of Sexuality Education*. Taverner argues that despite his strong support for comprehensive sexuality education, respecting the moral beliefs of the parents who choose to opt out is more important than including all students.

NO: Allyson Sandak has been a sexuality educator and trainer for a decade, as well as an adjunct professor at Montclair State University and the Editor-in-Chief of *Contemporary Sexuality,* a publication of the American Association of Sexuality Educators, Counselors, and Therapists (AASECT). Sandak argues that comprehensive sexuality education is a public health issue and that opting-out provisions are harmful to young people.

$\mathbf{S}$exuality education curricula in the public school system often attract controversy and scrutiny. Two types of sexuality education that are most often debated are comprehensive sexuality education and abstinence-only-until-marriage education. Comprehensive sexuality education includes abstinence but also contains topics such as contraception, sexual orientation, gender identity, body image, gender roles, dating violence, and human reproduction. Abstinence-only-until-marriage education is based on the belief that abstinence is the only form of protection that should be practiced by teenagers to avoid sexually transmitted infections and pregnancy. This curriculum will speak about contraception only from the perspective of its failure rate. Abstinence-only-until-marriage education, which has enjoyed significant federal funding, tends to be strongly supported by the very population most likely to opt out of comprehensive sexuality education.

States mandate some sort of sexuality education for children in their public schools, and the public school curricula offered range from abstinence-only-until-marriage education to comprehensive sexuality education. However, only a small minority of students attend a school that provides a comprehensive sexuality education program of study. Despite this reality, challenges to comprehensive sexuality education remain common. In fact, administrators and educators find that there are often challenges to sexuality education even when the curriculum falls far short of comprehensive.

Particular controversy exists within sexuality education as it may conflict with a person's religious beliefs. In fact, a number of families opt out of public education altogether because much within the system conflicts with their religious beliefs. However, most people who possess such religious convictions still send their children to public school. Considering the diversity of people who send their children to the public school system, there is an inevitable conflict between the curriculum and various families' moral values.

David Trevaskis, Esq., a distinguished lecturer in school law, explains that both sides of this issue are complicated: "In a democracy like ours, which has so many different voices, schools are a place where everyone is forced to be together. It is important that our schools provide space for these diverse values. However, schools should prohibit expressions that society cannot accept, such as racism, even if they claim that racism is a religious value. Parents should have a right to opt out of some of the curriculum. When opting out of the curriculum, this mostly arises in matters that are more elective than required. For example, a Christian Scientist cannot have their child removed from science class because medical procedures are discussed."

According to the First Amendment Center, parents have the right to remove their children from a class when the curriculum taught in school violates their religious views. The standard for schools is to determine whether the objection is sincere, and it is not the place of the school to determine whether the objection is rational. In fact, if parents are taking the time to challenge the curriculum for religious reasons, then that should be regarded as evidence of their sincerity. However, there are typically limits to the degree to which parents can opt their children out of the school curriculum.

After a school has determined that the challenge is sincere, they then must determine whether the curriculum or assignment places a "substantial burden" on the student's religious liberty. If the student can demonstrate a "substantial burden," then the school has two choices. First, it can create an alternative assignment consistent with the student's religious liberty. Second, it can demonstrate a "compelling state interest" that cannot be accomplished with an alternative assignment.

Trevaskis's comments and the First Amendment Center criteria raise an important question: How important is sexuality education? Is there a "compelling state interest" that cannot be accomplished with an alternative assignment? Should it be treated as subject matter so fundamentally important that participation should be compulsory? Should opting out be treated as a right based on a family's religious beliefs?

YES ←

William J. Taverner

The Right to Pass

"Class . . . I will now show a short sex education film. Ezekiel and Ishmael, in accordance with your parents' wishes, you may step out into the hall and pray for our souls."

—Edna Krabappel, schoolteacher on The Simpsons

I might be the last person one would expect to write an essay supporting a parent's right to opt his or her child out of sexuality education. I have spent my entire professional life advocating for comprehensive sexuality education—empowering teens with positive information and the knowledge and skills to make healthy decisions. Twice I have spoken on Capitol Hill urging Congress to support sexuality education. I have railed against federally funded abstinence-only-until-marriage programs that forbid giving young people accurate information about contraceptives and the prevention of sexually transmitted infections and that deny the existence of gay, lesbian, bisexual, and transgender people. I have written a number of manuals to help teachers teach about sexuality education. I have presented workshops and given keynotes urging teachers and schools to provide young people with complete information about sexuality. So what is the editor of the *American Journal of Sexuality Education* doing championing a cause that might be better suited to a home-schooling parent or a conservative ideologue?

Perhaps some commentators at Fox News could do a better job with this article than I. They might be very persuasive in rallying the masses, torches in hand, against the evil "sex ed industry" that wants to destroy the precious and innocent ears of our children. The one bit of information they'd leave out is perhaps the most important fact in understanding this issue, and one that the parents of the fictional Ezekiel and Ishmael surely knew: that parents have *always* had the right to take their child out of sex ed class if their values or beliefs were contrary to what is being taught in that class.

I am a parent myself. I have two great children who probably have had far more sex ed than their peers ever will have. When my older son's fifth-grade class took a field trip to a health center to learn the basics of reproduction, no other fifth-grade hand shot up as frequently as my son's in response to the health teacher's very elementary questions. In fact, few other hands were raised at all. In all honesty, my six-year-old probably would have had a better handle on the subject than most of the children in that room. Clearly, I feel strongly about the importance of sexuality education. But at the same time, I also support the right of any parent to exclude his or her child from learning this critical information at school.

Conservative pundits like to portray sexuality education as being forced upon our nation's youth. In fact, sexuality education does not exist in that many places at all. It receives $0 (yes, zero) federal dollars, in contrast to abstinence-only-until-marriage programs, which have received more than $1.5 billion over the last decade. In places where more comprehensive sexuality education *does* exist, parents are usually given the option to exclude their children from the classes. For this reason, it makes absolutely no sense when pundits demand to put an end to sexuality education. Parents *already* have the right to keep their children out of sexuality education, and it's important that they retain that right so other students can learn. What the conservative pundits are really looking for is not a parent's right to take his or her kid out of sex ed class, but to make a concerted effort to prevent *every other* child from learning this important information, too.

There are religious and cultural considerations pertaining to sexuality education and parenting that must be respected. I would hope that the children of parents who keep them out of sex ed class would have some alternative mechanisms for learning—in fact, in many cases, schools that do offer an "opt out" provision require parents to teach the same information at home.

The other little secret is that a very tiny percentage of parents actually exercise their right to opt their children out of sex ed. Research and polling data has consistently found that the overwhelming number of American parents support their children learning about sexuality education in school. This includes blue states and red states; liberals *and* conservatives; people of all religious faiths.

For those parents who are on the proverbial fence, it may be helpful to know that there there is also a mechanism for effectively "opting out" of a particular discussion within the structure of most sexuality education programs. Well-trained sexuality educators often begin their classes by establishing "ground rules," and one of the most important ground rules is the "right to pass." This means that any student can decide *not* to engage in any activity or discussion at any time, for any reason, and without needing to give the teacher an explanation. So if a student does not feel like engaging in a role play about assertive communication, s/he doesn't have to. If a student would rather not participate in a brainstorm about the qualities of a healthy relationship, s/he can sit that one out. Trained sexuality educators understand and respect the diversity of their students and their varying levels of comfort with the topic. They present opportunities for students to explore and understand their values, communicate with their parents and other important adults in their lives, and make healthy decisions. Yet all of this notwithstanding, parents still should have the right to opt their children out of these lessons should they decide to do so.

Don't get me wrong—it would be ideal if no parents denied their children life-fulfilling, and often life-saving, information that is part of sexuality education. But not every household has one or more parents or caregivers whose job it is to be a sexuality educator. The reality is that the "opt out" clause has been much more about keeping anti-sex ed advocates from withholding sex ed from every other student in places where sex ed does exist than it's been about parental rights. This is why I say, let's keep the "opt out" option and give parents the right to pass. If "opt out" provisions are removed, then anti-sex ed forces gain credibility in their assertions that parents have no options when it comes to their children learning about sexuality education. It's important that this not happen. Let parents who feel they need to do so opt their children out of sex ed, and let the rest of the kids learn.

Allyson Sandak

➜ **NO**

Let the Teachers Teach: Parents Should Not Be Allowed to Opt Their Children Out of Sex Ed

Parents and sexuality educators alike agree that parents are (or should be) the primary sexuality educators of their children. Beginning at birth, parents send messages and convey core values to their children about caring, affection, and respect; about bodies, birth, and babies; about gender roles and relationships, and so much more. These messages and values are often sent without addressing the issues directly, but rather simply by parents and other key adults modeling them. In far too many cases, sexuality-related issues at home are simply ignored—sending the message that sexuality is a topic that is not to be discussed or about which people should feel ashamed. Many parents, for a number of reasons, shy away from having conversations with their children about sexuality, leaving these young people in the dark about this very important topic.

As young people develop, they need factual information related to sexuality in addition to the emotional, social, and moral/religious support and guidance that are provided by parents. Because so many parents lack even the most basic knowledge about sexuality, school-based sexuality education is there to offer the factual information as a complement to family-based efforts. School programs not only provide critical health information and skills development to individual young people, but they also serve as an important public health tool. For this reason, sexuality education should be a required school course for grades K–12, and parents should *not* be able to opt their children out of school-based sexuality education.

What Is Sexuality Education?

Sexuality education is designed to promote sexual health, which includes assisting young people as they develop a positive view of sexuality, providing them with information they need to take care of their sexual health, and helping them acquire skills to make decisions now and in the future (SIECUS Guidelines, 2004). The American Public Health Association (2007) states that school-based sexuality education should provide youth with information and skills to make informed decisions regarding their sexual health. Further, the

National Health Education Standards (American Association for Health Education), based on established health behavior theories and models, provides a framework for school-based sexuality education that highlights the need for students to be able to

1. Comprehend concepts related to health promotion and disease prevention to enhance health.
2. Analyze the influence of family, peers, culture, media, technology, and other factors on health behaviors.
3. Demonstrate the ability to assess valid information and products and services to enhance health.
4. Demonstrate the ability to use interpersonal communication skills to enhance health and avoid or reduce health-risk behaviors.
5. Demonstrate the ability to use decision-making skills to enhance health.
6. Demonstrate the ability to use goal-setting skills to enhance health.
7. Demonstrate the ability to practice health-enhancing behaviors and avoid or reduce health risks.
8. Demonstrate the ability to advocate for personal, family, and community health.

Within all of these topics, sexual health must be seen as an integral part, as outlined below.

My work as a community sexuality educator affords me the wonderful opportunity of partnering with many local schools as they implement sexuality education. I often spend a great amount of time preparing for my programs before I even meet with a group of students. I usually meet with the principal, nurse, and health teacher to develop our program in accordance with the school, state, and national health curriculum standards. The lessons delivered are age- and developmentally appropriate and address sexuality from a comprehensive and holistic perspective. Topics can include the physical and emotional changes of puberty, healthy relationships (including friendships), goal setting, communication and decision-making skills, sexually transmitted infections (STIs), pregnancy, and prevention methods, including abstinence, condoms, and contraception.

Sexuality Education as a Public Health Issue

One of the key purposes of school-based sexuality education is to address critical public health issues. Research shows that many teens are engaging in sexual activity. In 2007, 63 percent of high school seniors reported having sexual intercourse at some point in their lives (CDC, 2007). Fifty-four percent of females and 55% of males ages 15–19 said they had engaged in oral sex with a different-sex partner (Hoff et al., 2006). Young people who are sexually active face significant health risks. Each year, there are approximately 19 million new cases of STIs in the United States, with almost half of them occurring among youth ages 15–24 (Weinstock et al., 2004). In addition, each year, almost 750,000 teens between the ages of 15 and 19 become pregnant (Guttmacher Institute, 2006). Young people are often in unhealthy or abusive relationships, homophobia abounds in school settings and beyond, and gender-based violence is on the rise. Given these statistics, along with the health, social, and financial costs that these issues bring for families and society as a whole, what parents would not want their children to learn how to be as happy and healthy as possible as they grow up? The best venue for teaching young people how to do this is at school, where they spend the vast majority of their K–12 years.

Consider other health-related issues that are addressed at school, such as drug and alcohol prevention, smoking cessation, nutrition, and more. None of these classes provide an "opt out" for parents that disagree with them. So why is this topic any different? True, it would be ideal for families to address these issues with their children at home—yet family-based education is often inconsistent, inaccurate, and sometimes nonexistent.

It is important to note that while pregnancy and STI rate reduction are key, they are not the only goals of sexuality education. One of the goals of our education system is to develop critical thinking skills among students. The goals of sexuality education are no different.

There Should Be No Sex Ed Opt-Out

Sexuality education is a critical element of health education, a core subject in any school curriculum. We would never dream of permitting parents to opt their children out of their math, English, or history classes. Even within the subject of health education, we do not allow parents to opt their children out of classes covering drug prevention, nutrition, or hygiene, despite the fact that many people have wide-ranging, diverse beliefs pertaining to these subjects. So why do we even consider this an option for sexuality education classes?

The purpose of school-based sexuality education is not to make value judgments or to exclude anyone based on their personal beliefs about sexuality, but to provide factual information and the skills needed to promote healthy behaviors. Similar to other classes that include a social perspective, sexuality education should be inclusive of all points of view. Parents don't opt their children out of political science classes because these classes present perspectives from both a conservative and liberal standpoint, though they may not be aligned with those parents' personal or family values. What these classes do is present a variety of viewpoints and perspectives, allowing students to take those perspectives into consideration within the context of their family values in order to make their own decisions. Students can become more informed citizens and critical thinkers as a result of being exposed to a variety of perspectives about issues, including sexuality.

Some parents fear that giving children access to information about sexuality will lead to or condone sexual behaviors. While this is a common concern among many parents, research indicates that quite the opposite occurs. Programs that address sexuality in a comprehensive manner delay the onset of first sexual intercourse, reduce the frequency of sexual behaviors, and reduce the number of sexual partners among students who received this type of education (Kirby, 2007). So it is clear that sexuality education does not increase sexual activity, but rather decreases it, which is great news for parents who are concerned about this issue.

Opting Out Harms Young People

The Society for Adolescent Medicine (2006) states that access to accurate and complete sexual health information, including information about HIV/AIDS, is a *basic human right*. School-based education without an opt-out policy is the only way to ensure that this need is met for *all* young people. It would be irresponsible to allow students to grow up without this vital information, particularly in light of the health risks young people face. While schools with an opt-out policy often suggest that students receive equivalent information at home, there is absolutely no guarantee that that will happen. Students are not asked to complete homework assignments that reflect their discussions with parents, and parents are not required to submit lesson plans or summaries of what was discussed.

Another reason that makes opt-out policies unrealistic is the push to make school subjects more interdisciplinary, particularly health-related subjects, which often don't get as much attention as other core subjects. There is great opportunity to educate about sexuality in other classes, outside of the confines of a health class. Students can learn about STIs in biology classes, gender roles in a history or sociology class, rates of pregnancy in a math class. Think of the challenge that would present itself if the opt-out policy applied to all of these situations. Additionally, if parents were to opt their children out of any class with a mere mention of sexuality, their children would be missing other vital information such as how the immune systems work and statistics . . . and we wouldn't want that, now, would we?

Additionally, opting children out of school-based sexuality education by no means implies that children's only source of sexuality information will come from their families. We would be remiss to turn our heads to the impact the media and peers have on adolescent sexuality, which often provide inaccurate information and send messages that differ greatly from those of schools and parents. American society has a tendency to avoid honest and frank discussions about sexuality, while sexual messages abound in our culture. Without an appropriate context for these messages (provided by schools), children can be left to navigate through the sea of mixed messages on their own.

Opting Out Is Not the Answer; Parental Involvement Is

In my experience as a community sexuality educator, both teachers and young people need parents to be involved in what their children are learning to provide moral and/or religious context for the factual information learned in school. Sexuality educators support the idea that the values-driven components of a student's sexuality education should take place at home, and by no means want to replace essential family communications.

The mere act of opting young people out of school-based sexuality education does not translate into active parental involvement in their children's education. In fact, some parents may opt their children out of sexuality education without even seeing the curriculum, basing their decision solely on their own assumptions about what might be covered in the class. The best way to address concerns that parents may have about a sexuality education program is for them to get involved and provide guidance rather than opting children out. Most schools welcome and encourage parental involvement with their sexuality education programs. This is also endorsed by Centers for Disease Control and Prevention's Division of Adolescent School Health, whose mission is to prevent serious health risk behaviors among children, adolescents and young adults. Prior to starting a series of sexuality education classes at a school, I often offer Parent Orientation sessions which provide parents with an opportunity to find out what their children will be learning, ask questions, and gain tips for communicating with their kids about the subject at home. Parents are often so appreciative of this opportunity. They feel involved and connected with their children's education and are able to learn valuable communication skills, which they can apply at home. One parent even stood up and exclaimed how proud she was of the school for offering the student education *and* for offering help to the parents along the way! In fact, one of my main reasons for providing Parent Orientations is to foster that essential parent–child communication. The opportunities for communication are plentiful: Parents can even get started by going home and saying to their children, "Hey, guess where I was tonight?" and follow up with a great conversation about what's to come in the next couple of weeks.

Conclusion

SIECUS's position on school-based sexuality education states that school-based education is meant to "complement and augment the sexuality education children receive from their families." This is exactly what we sexuality educators are going for. And many parents are thankful for this. One parent eloquently states that her children's sexuality education program at school "provides families with the ability to discuss their beliefs at home and to talk about sexuality education at home. It gives children an opportunity to think of questions" (Lawrence Journal World, 2005). This so clearly illustrates the fact that again, the goal of school-based sexuality education is not to replace vital family communication, but rather to complement it.

Why not combine forces? Schools are charged with providing factual information to students while also developing skills for healthy lifestyles such as critical thinking, communication, and decision making. But remember, parents are the primary sexuality educators of their children. Their role includes providing children with family values and morals as they relate to sexuality—putting what is learned in school into a more personal context. Unfortunately, many parents do not take this job seriously and avoid any conversation that has to do with sexuality. Let's not allow young people to be at a loss and potentially miss out on their basic human right to honest, factual, and comprehensive information, much of which can have a major impact on their health and the health of others.

References

American Public Health Association, "Sexuality Education as Part of a Comprehensive Health Education Program in K-12 School" (Policy Number 2005–10). 2007. Accessible online at http://www.apha.org/advocacy/policy/policysearch/default.htm?id=1304.

Centers for Disease Control and Prevention, "Youth Risk Behavior Surveillance—United States, 2007," *Morbidity & Mortality Weekly Report* 2008 (vol. 57[SS-4], pp. 1–131). Accessible online at http://www.cdc.gov/mmwr/PDF/SS/SS5505.pdf.

CDC Health Youth! Accessible online at http://www.cdc.gov/HealthyYouth/sexual-behaviors/index.htm.

Guttmacher Institute, "U.S. Teen Pregnancy Statistics: National and State Trends and Trends by Race and Ethnicity." 2006. Accessible online at http://www.guttmacher.org/pubs/2006/09/12/USTPstats.pdf.

Hoff, T., L. Greene, and J. Davis. *National Survey of Adolescents and Young Adults: Sexual Health Knowledge, Attitudes and Experiences.*

The Henry J. Kaiser Family Foundation, Menlo Park, CA: 2003. *National Survey of Adolescents and Young Adults,* Accessible online at http://www.kff.org/youthhivstds/upload/National-Survey-of-Adolescents-and-Young-Adults.pdf.

Kirby, D. *Emerging Answers 2007: Research Findings on Programs to Reduce Teen Pregnancy and Sexually Transmitted Diseases.* Washington, DC: National Campaign to Prevent Teen and Unwanted Pregnancy, 2007. Accessible online at http://www.thenationalcampaign.org/EA2007/EA2007_full.pdf.

National Health Education Standards. American Association for School Health. Accessible online at http://www.aahperd.org/aahe/pdf_files/standards.pdf.

"Petition Urges State Board to Let Alone Sex Ed Policy," *Lawrence Journal World* (August 3, 2005). Accessible online at http://www2.ljworld.com/news/2005/aug/03/petition_urges_state_board_let_alone_sex_ed_policy/?print.

Guidelines for Comprehensive Sexuality Education Kindergarten through 12th Grade, 3rd ed. Washington, DC: Sexuality Information and Education Council of the United States, National Guidelines Task Force, 2004.

SIECUS position statements. Available online at http://siecus.org/index.cfm?fuseaction=Page.viewPage&pageID=494&parentID=472#sexuality%20education.

Society for Adolescent Medicine. "Abstinence-Only Education Policies and Programs: A Position Paper for the Society for Adolescent Medicine," *Journal of Adolescent Health* (vol. 38, 2006, pp. 83–87).

Weinstock, H., S. Berman, & W. Cates, "Sexually Transmitted Diseases among American Youth: Incidence and Prevalence Estimates, 2000," *Perspectives on Sexual and Reproductive Health* (vol. 36, no. 1, 2004, pp. 6–10).

POSTSCRIPT

Should Parents Be Allowed to Opt Their Children Out of Sexuality Education Classes?

Public schools are bound to cause controversy over their decisions due to the pluralistic composition of our society. Although school boards have the power to determine the curriculum, the right of individual families to exercise religious liberty remains fundamental. In the case of sexuality education, the schools have designed a curriculum that is deemed in the best interest of the community. They would argue that there are public health benefits to be gained from what students will gain from the curriculum. Opponents would argue that the curriculum undermines core values that are damaging at least to their family and quite possibly to the larger society. Communities are left to balance two critical but sometimes clashing values within our society: the need to have an educated citizenry and the right to religious liberty.

After reading these two essays, how would you assess how they have addressed the legal criteria raised in the introduction? How would you evaluate whether sexuality education causes a "substantial burden" for the religious liberty of some children? How would you determine whether there is a "compelling state interest" in requiring sexuality education? Perhaps more importantly, how would you compare and contrast your moral beliefs with the legal criteria for opting out of sexuality education?

School board meetings are open to the public, and every citizen should attend at least one such meeting. These boards are typically composed of elected officials who are concerned about public sentiment, and school board members need to hear from their constituents. Readers are encouraged to attend a local school board meeting and advocate about the type of sexuality education that they believe students should receive.

Before attending your local school board meeting, conduct some research about comprehensive sexuality education and abstinence-only-until-marriage education. Remember, comprehensive sexuality education includes abstinence but also includes topics such as contraception, sexual orientation, gender identity, body image, gender roles, dating violence, and human reproduction. Abstinence-only-until-marriage education is the belief that abstinence is the only form of protection that should be practiced by teenagers to avoid sexually transmitted infections and pregnancy. Abstinence-only-until-marriage education will speak about contraception only from the perspective of its failure rate.

Once well versed in the types of sexuality education, inquire about the sexuality education curriculum offered at your school. Does it reflect your community's values? Does it reflect your values? Examine not just what is taught but also the frequency with which instruction occurs. Is the curriculum extensive enough to help children make sexual decisions that are consistent with their long-term goals in life? Then inquire about the opt-out policy that exists within the curriculum. Determine whether this policy is consistent across the curriculum.

With a deeper understanding of all of this information, attend a school board meeting and share with them the type of education that you feel young people most need. Explain to them your beliefs about the role of an opt-out provision in human sexuality education.

ISSUE 2

Should Adoptive Parents Adopt Only within Their Own Racial/Ethnic Group?

YES: Leslie Doty Hollingsworth, from "Promoting Same-Race Adoption for Children of Color," *Social Work* (vol. 43, no. 2, 1998)

NO: Ezra E. H. Griffith and Rachel L. Bergeron, from "Cultural Stereotypes Die Hard: The Case of Transracial Adoption," *The Journal of the American Academy of Psychiatry and the Law* (vol. 34, no. 3, 2006)

ISSUE SUMMARY

YES: Leslie Doty Hollingsworth, an associate professor of social work at the University of Michigan, offers a history of transracial adoption that has involved primarily white adoptive parents and black or African American children. She argues that children are best served if they are adopted by families of their same racial background, and that systematic changes—such as adoption services and programs better geared toward adults of color—would enable more families to adopt children from their own backgrounds.

NO: Ezra Griffith and Rachel Bergeron, both faculty members of the Yale University School of Medicine's psychiatry department, argue that requiring racial and ethnic matching, although an appropriate effort, would leave too many children of color languishing in the foster and adoption systems. By maintaining that only in-race adoption is the best and ideal situation, they ask rhetorically, does our society actually do more to reinforce cultural stereotypes or to truly serve children needing homes?

The practice of adopting children is nothing new; adoptions have been documented in the United States going back to the late nineteenth century. In the twentieth century, international adoptions in the United States increased at the end of World War II, a logical response to the number of children orphaned when families were uprooted or eradicated by the war's violence. This increase was also documented after the Korean and Vietnam wars, and more recently as violence continues to mar various countries worldwide and the number of children needing homes grows.

This means that many of the adults who have adopted and are currently adopting children are from a different racial or ethnic group than their adoptive children. In the most recent U.S. census, just over 17 percent of the adopted children under age 18 had adoptive parents of a different racial background than theirs (www.census.gov/prod/cen2000/doc/sf3.pdf).

Although adoption as a practice is much less stigmatized today, adopting children outside of one's own racial or ethnic group remains controversial. Some believe that raising a child in a family outside of the child's racial group impedes the child from forming a healthy identity and from coping effectively in the world. In 1972, in response to the increase in transracial adoptions, the National Association of Black Social Workers (NABSW) produced a resolution stating, in part, that "black children belong physically and psychologically and culturally in black families where they can receive the total sense of themselves and develop a sound projection of their future. Only a black family can transmit the emotional and sensitive subtleties of perceptions and reactions essential for a black child's survival in a racist society." Although this statement is specifically about black and African American children, the National Association of Social Workers (NASW)'s 2003 position statement about foster care and adoption includes all racial and ethnic backgrounds. Others argue that love is the most important component of any family, that parents of any racial or ethnic background can invest time and resources to teach their children about their racial or ethnic heritage and history and connect them with social supports to ensure that their children integrate whatever identity best fits them. It is better, these individuals argue, to give a child a home, regardless of the different racial or ethnic backgrounds of the family members, than to let a child languish in foster care. Another controversial aspect about this debate is that these same individuals argue that there is an implicit bias in the NABSW and NASW guidelines, that they assume an adoptive family that is white; there are no guidelines or discussions around placing white children with families of color.

In the following selections, Leslie Doty Hollingsworth emphasizes the importance of placing children in families of the same racial background as theirs, that that is the only way of truly providing the child with an opportunity to develop a solid, clear racial identity. Ezra Griffith and Rachel Bergeron cite research demonstrating, they assert, that children of transracial adoptions can develop strong identities and high self-esteem, the difference between their and their family's backgrounds notwithstanding.

YES ↵   Leslie Doty Hollingsworth

Promoting Same-Race Adoption for Children of Color

Opponents of policies to protect same-race adoption for children of color assert that it is necessary to lift all restrictions on transracial adoption (alternately referred to as "interracial," "interethnic," or "transethnic" adoption) of the many children of color believed to be "languishing" in foster homes, residential programs, and institutional settings. This article briefly presents the history of the transracial adoption controversy and discusses its current status; counters assertions typically used to oppose same-race adoption policies for children of color; summarizes the positions of several social work organizations regarding adoption and race; and makes recommendations for education, policy, research, and practice.

History of Transracial Adoption

The adoption of orphaned children from other countries by U.S. families began in the 1940s with the end of World War II (Simon & Alstein, 1977). A rise in the number of such adoptions accompanied later wars, including the Korean and Vietnam Wars (Silverman, 1993). In the 1960s, widespread use of artificial birth control, the legalization of abortion, and decreased social stigma associated with bearing a child outside of marriage were accompanied by a substantial decrease in healthy white infants available for adoption. There was, however, no corresponding decrease among African American and other children of color (although foreign countries began to establish rules that limited some adoptions in those countries).

It has been suggested that adoption agencies, feeling the pressure of reduced fee income, found in the availability of children of color an opportunity to increase adoption fees (McRoy, 1989). One writer (Bartholet, 1991) suggested that as the United States became accustomed to children of color from other countries in its communities, it became easier to accept the transracial adoption of African American children. By 1971 transracial adoptions had reached an annual high of 2,574 (Simon & Alstein, 1987). Responding to this increase, a 1972 meeting of the National Association of Black Social Workers (NABSW) ended with a resolution opposing transracial adoption:

> Black children belong physically and psychologically and culturally in black families where they can receive the total sense of themselves

From *Social Work*, Vol. 42, Issue 2, 1998, pp. 104–116. Copyright © 1998 by NASW Press. Reprinted by permission.

and develop a sound projection of their future. Only a black family can transmit the emotional and sensitive subtleties of perceptions and reactions essential for a black child's survival in a racist society. Human beings are products of their environment and develop their sense of values, attitudes, and self-concept within their own family structures. Black children in white homes are cut off from the healthy development of themselves as black people. (quoted in McRoy, 1989, p. 150)

In response to that resolution, and to the Indian Child Welfare Act of 1978 giving tribal courts exclusive jurisdiction over American Indian child custody proceedings, some states established policies and procedures limiting transracial adoption and requiring that serious efforts be made to place children of color with adoptive parents of their own racial or ethnic group. Agencies specializing in same-race placements were established, and many traditional agencies modified their programs in the same direction.

Some parents who had adopted transracially were offended, however, by the NABSW resolution, perceiving it as not based in truth and disagreeing with the assertion that they were not capable of parenting their adoptive children of color adequately (Hermann, 1993). White foster parents began to file legal suits to prevent children of color who were in their care from being placed with same-race adoptive parents and to be allowed to adopt the children themselves (Elias, 1991). Advocates of transracial adoption, some of them transracial adoptive parents themselves (Bartholet, 1991; Mahoney, 1991), began to speak and write publicly in its support and in opposition to same-race protective policies. Criticism of protective policies for same-race adoption has included the following assertions:

- that same-race placement policies result in retention of children in foster care for longer than necessary, which may result in delay or denial of placement for children of color and therefore in long-term harm
- that there is no systematic recruitment of white parents to correspond to that of families of color, and therefore families of color are being given unfair advantage
- that same-race policies give families of color an edge in receipt of adoption subsidies, because children of color (whom same-race parents adopt) are eligible for such subsidies by nature of their "special-needs" status
- that agencies apply differential screening criteria to prospective black parents than to prospective white families (such as socioeconomic status, age, and marital status requirements), even though these have not been ruled out as viable criteria for selection
- that empirical studies have been biased toward studying the negative aspects of transracial adoption
- that in spite of such biases, studies have failed to document a negative effect of transracial adoption in areas such as general adjustment and self-esteem and, in some instances, have indicated a possible benefit with regard to the transracial adoptee's ability to get along with and in a white world
- that there is no empirical support for the contention that parents of color do a better job at socializing their children ethnically

- that racial matching policies are in conflict with antidiscrimination legislation, such as the U.S. Constitution and Title IV of the Civil Rights Act of 1964 (Bartholet, 1991; Mahoney, 1991; National Coalition to End Racism in America's Child Care System, cited in McRoy, 1994).

A result of the opposition to same-race policies has been that "states have begun to reassess their policies which include race as a viable consideration in placement decision making" (National Coalition to End Racism in America's Child Care System, cited in McRoy, 1994). Subsequently, transracial adoptions began to increase in the early 1980s (McRoy, 1989). Bill Pierce, president of the National Council for Adoption, estimated that 12,000 children were transracially adopted in 1992 (Richman, 1993). Accurate national data on the numbers of transracial and same-race adoptions are not available because after 1971 the federal government no longer required states to maintain and report such data.

On December 22, 1995, the U.S. Department of Health and Human Services published final rules implementing the Adoption and Foster Care Analysis and Reporting System, a mandatory system of data collection on all children covered by Title IV-B of the Social Security Act, Section 427 ("Foster Care," 1997). Included are rules requiring states to collect data on all adopted children who were placed by the state child welfare agency or by private agencies under contract with the public child welfare agency. However, national adoption data are not yet available.

The recent increase in transracial adoptions has been influenced by a trend among child welfare agencies toward greater flexibility in eligibility to adopt. Such changes have included less rigidity regarding age, income, housing, family composition, and infertility examination requirements; attempts to make application procedures and agency locations and hours more convenient for prospective adopters; less emphasis on the need for matching the characteristics of child and parent (which may have facilitated same-race placements); a willingness to select single parents or those who already have birth or adopted children; openness to adoption by foster parents, caretakers, and relatives of the child; use of adoption resource exchanges; use of active and ongoing recruitment methods, often using the mass media and featuring specific children; and expansion of adoption subsidy programs (Child Welfare League of America, 1988). Although some of these changes may facilitate same-race adoptions, they have also opened the way for increases in transracial adoptions. People interested in adopting transracially typically either originally desired a white infant or preschool child and became willing to adopt a child of a different race or were the child's foster parents (Child Welfare League of America, 1988).

The Multiethnic Placement Act of 1994 prohibited agencies or entities engaged in adoption or foster care placements that receive federal assistance from "categorically deny[ing] to any person the opportunity to become an adoptive or foster parent, solely on the basis of the race, color, or national origin of the adoptive or foster parent or the child" and "from delay[ing] or deny[ing] the placement of a child solely on the basis of race, color, or national origin of the adoptive or foster parent or parents involved" (p. 4056). However, this law allowed "an agency or entity to which [the preceding applied to] consider the cultural, ethnic, or racial background of the child and the capacity of the prospective foster or adoptive parents to meet the needs of a child of this background as one of a number of factors used to determine the best interests of a child" (p. 4056).

Opponents of same-race protective policies criticized the qualification in the Multiethnic Placement Act that allowed race, culture, and ethnicity to be considered at all and the absence of penalties for failure to conform to the requirements of the act. Advocacy efforts with regard to federal and state adoption policy continued, and in August 1996 legislation was signed that modified the Multiethnic Placement Act of 1994. This legislation, which was enacted as a part of the Small Business Job Protection Act of 1996, had two sections: Section 1807 (Adoption Assistance), which allowed a tax credit to adoptive families with incomes not exceeding $75,000 of up to $5,000 ($6,000 in the case of children with "special needs") annually for qualified adoption expenses, and Section 1808 (Removal of Barriers to Interethnic Adoption), which removed the qualification provided by the earlier act and simply prevented any entity that receives federal funds from denying any person the opportunity to adopt or provide foster care and from delaying or denying the placement of a child on the basis of the race, color, or national origin of the adoptive or foster parent or the child involved.

Alternative Considerations

Given the history of transracial adoption, social workers need to be aware of alternative considerations to those that resulted in the current legislation. Delays in moving children of color out of the out-of-home care system are caused by factors other than restrictions on transracial adoption and can be resolved by actions other than lifting such restrictions. Improvements in six areas would alleviate such delays and lessen the need for transracial adoptions. First, because there are insufficient non-kin foster families of color, policies favoring adoption by foster parents are increasing the numbers of transracial adoptions. Second, there are indications that sufficient numbers of families of color are available to adopt healthy infants of color if such families are sought out and if traditional barriers to adoption are eliminated. Third, many children of color in the child welfare system are not available for adoption or have special needs. Fourth, overrepresentation of children of color in the child welfare system has been linked to disparities in services related to ethnic group. Fifth, children of color may be counted as being in foster placements when they are actually in permanent kinship care. Finally, poverty, which disproportionately affects families of color, has been associated with the abuse and neglect that often result in the out-of-home placement of children.

Policies Favoring Adoption by Foster Parents

Many children of color are placed with non-kin foster families (as many as 52 percent in California, according to Meyer & Link, cited in Barth, Courtney, Berrick, Albert, & Needell, 1994). Barth, Courtney, Berrick, Albert, and Needell noted that among the California children they studied, only two-thirds of African American children were placed in African American foster homes, and only 31 percent of Hispanic children were placed with Hispanic caregivers. (Because the figures for children of color include kinship placements, the actual proportion of placements of children of color with same-race, non-kin foster families is much lower than they found.) In contrast, 92 percent of selected white children in foster homes were placed with white foster families. The researchers noted that "when children were not placed with ethnically similar foster parents, they were almost always placed with Caucasians [and that] nearly one-half of Caucasian foster parents were caring for children of color" (Barth, Courtney, Berrick, Albert, & Needell, 1994, p. 245).

What has come to be known as the "fost adoption" program (Barth, Courtney, Berrick, & Albert, 1994) emerged in the mid-1970s (Meezan & Shireman, 1985) to promote the placement of children in foster homes with the explicit expectation that the foster parents will adopt the child if reunification with the birth parents fails. Before this program was implemented, foster placements were established in such a way that they would interfere neither with the reunification of the child with her or his birth parents nor with the permanent placement of the child in an adoptive home. Foster parents were considered temporary substitutes, and they were urged not to become attached to the child. If they did become attached, the child was often removed to another placement. With the advent of the "fost adoption" program, white foster families began to seek adoption of children of color placed in their homes, sometimes from birth, even when the children were not placed with the intention of their future adoption by those foster parents.

Thus, insufficient numbers of foster families of color reduce the likelihood that children of color will be adopted by a family of their same racial or ethnic group and gives an advantage to transracial placements. There is evidence that even children of mixed racial parentage tend to be confronted with racism or problems of racial identity while they are in placement, and researchers have recommended that these factors be considered in the selection and preparation of potential foster parents (Folaron & Hess, 1993). Increasing the numbers of available foster families of color has the potential, therefore, for increasing same-race adoptive placements (Rezendes, 1994).

Barth, Courtney, Berrick, and Albert (1994) compared children who were adopted within two years of entering foster care with children who remained in foster care for longer than two years before being adopted. Although they found no effect of ethnicity on "the odds of a timely adoption," an item consistently related to length of time until adoption was whether the child welfare worker and the foster family with whom the child was placed planned, at the time of the placement, that the child would be adopted by the family. The authors added, "the fact that an adoption is planned at the time of foster placement or that a child is under one month of age both decrease the odds that a child will stay in foster care more than two years" (p. 167). Because there was no effect for ethnicity, it can be concluded that the effect of age and planned placement occurs for children of color as well as for other children. If the pool of foster parents is less likely to contain foster parents of color, and if adoption plans continue to be made at the point of initial foster placement, especially within the context of the increased restrictions on same-race adoption protective policies, the likelihood that a child of color will be adopted by someone of her or his own race or ethnic group is diminished and the odds of a transracial adoption are increased.

Availability of Adoptive Families of Color

Evidence indicates that the number of families of color who are willing to adopt healthy infants may be sufficient if agency recruitment and eligibility policies are responsive to the cultures and lifestyles of such families. Early studies documented the failure of adoption agencies to implement culturally sensitive recruitment strategies and eligibility standards for potential adoptees of color (Day, 1979; Herzog, Sudia, Harwood, & Newcomb, 1971). Although many states and agencies took action to correct these circumstances, a recent survey by the North American Council on Adoptable Children (Gilles & Kroll, 1991) found that 83 percent of agencies in the 25 states studied acknowledged that organizational barriers continued to exist that prevented or discouraged families of color from adopting. The most frequently cited barriers were "institutional/systemic racism; lack of people of color in managerial positions; fees; 'adoption as business' mentality; communities' of color historical tendencies toward 'informal' adoption; negative perceptions of agencies and their practices; lack of minority staff; inflexible standards; general lack of recruitment activity and poor recruitment techniques; and 'word not out'" (pp. 7–8). With regard to the "adoption as business" mentality, one agency head was quoted as saying, "If your agency relied on fees, where would you place a minority kid . . . with a white family that can afford to pay, or a black family that can't?" (p. 14).

When adoption services and programs have become more responsive to families of color, such families have come forward to adopt. Haring reported in 1975 (cited in McRoy, 1989) that following changes in public and private adoption practices to encourage same-race adoptions, 70 families of color were approved for every 100 available children of color, reflecting an increase from 1971 (Herzog et al., 1971) of 39 families of color approved for every 100 children of color (and 116 white families approved for every 100 white children). More recently, a study by the North American Council on Adoptable Children (Gilles & Kroll, 1991) of 17 agencies specializing in finding same-race adoptive placements for children of color found that these agencies located same-race placements for 94 percent of their 341 African American children and 66 percent of their 38 Hispanic children; nonspecializing agencies obtained an average of 51 percent of same-race placements of 806 African American children and 30 percent of 168 Hispanic children (p. 8).

A number of sources have identified agencies that are exemplars in successfully engaging same-race adoptive families ("Adoption," 1992; Gant, 1984; Hairston & Williams, 1989; "Homes," 1993; Jackson-White, Dozier, Oliver, & Gardner, 1997; McRoy, Oglesby, & Grape, 1997). Hairston and Williams (1989) found that more than half of the 58 African American adoptive families they surveyed viewed the services they had received from exemplary national African

American adoption agencies or programs as having led to their decision to adopt. Others (Gant, 1984; Gilles & Kroll, 1991) have similarly identified agency characteristics associated with successful recruitment of same-race families.

Availability for Adoption and Special Needs

Many children in out-of-home placements either are not available for adoption or have characteristics that make them difficult to place. Thus, they should not be included in numbers of children "languishing" in the system who are considered easily adoptable. Regarding availability for adoption, the Voluntary Cooperative Information System (VCIS) (cited in Flango & Flango, 1994), using figures received from states reporting, estimated that nationally 71,000 children had a permanency plan for adoption at the end of fiscal year 1992, meaning that their child welfare workers expected that parental rights would be voluntarily or involuntarily terminated and that the children would then become eligible for adoption. Of that number, it was estimated that 17,000 adoptions had been finalized and that another 17,000 adoptions were in the process of finalization. VCIS estimated that 21,000 children were in substitute care and still awaiting a decision regarding a final disposition. (The plight of the remaining 16,000 children was not clarified by VCIS, but because they were not included in one of the three categories mentioned above, they are assumed to not be imminently available for adoption.)

Two conclusions may be drawn from these data. First, half of children in the child welfare system may not be available for adoption (21,000 in out-of-home care awaiting final disposition and 16,000 not included in the statistics). Second, there is a difference between a child's having a permanency plan for adoption and actually being available for adoption. Child welfare workers, on assessing a family, may record adoption as the permanency plan without that ever becoming a reality, leading to incorrect assumptions among the public and among policymakers that children in such instances are actually available for adoption. Although these data are not restricted to children of color, they point to the inaccurate conclusions on which policy decisions may be made. With regard to children with special needs, the Child Welfare League of America (1988) observed that "there is a surplus of potential parents seeking to adopt white infants and preschool children and a shortage of those applying for those children who are available and need families" (p. 5); available children are "minority, severely handicapped, . . . age 12 or over; and in foster care four or more years" (p. 5). Thus, although the latter children are heavily counted among those who are languishing in out-of-home care, they are not the children that potential parents are seeking to adopt. Transracial adoption laws that are more liberal would not be expected, therefore, to decrease the numbers of these children substantially.

Inequities in Services

Disparities related to ethnic group have been observed in the prevention and intervention services that children in the child welfare system receive (Barth, Courtney, Berrick, & Albert, 1994). The implication is that prevention and intervention services are associated with children's successful exit from the child welfare system, although the authors do not speak directly to this point.

Mech (cited in Gould, 1991) found that African American children "were more likely to have no contact with workers than were white or Hispanic children" (p. 64). Similarly, African American families studied in the first three months after placement of their children were found to have experienced a mean number of agency contacts of 2.9, compared with a mean of 7.2 for white families (Close, cited in Williams, 1991). In Connecticut white children and foster families received more services and supports than children and foster families of color (Fein, Maluccio, & Kluger, cited in Barth, Courtney, Berrick, & Albert, 1994).

The issue of inequities in provision of services is especially important in family preservation, the process of providing intensive services and resources to families at risk of a child's removal from the home, usually because of real or threatened abuse or neglect. Williams (1991) noted that placement was avoided in more than three-fourths of families who received family preservation services and that children were able to remain in their own homes, safely, for one year after intervention. Recent research (Fraser, Pecora, & Haapala, 1991) has suggested that family preservation services may result in fewer placements for families of color compared to white families. Among families in Washington State, only 18.2 percent (10 of 55) of families of color who received family preservation services required the out-of-home placement of children, compared with 29.8 percent (75 of 252) of white families who received these services. These results suggest that intensive services can keep children of color out of out-of-home care.

Kinship Foster Care as Permanent Care

One of the most potentially misleading elements in the argument surrounding children of color in the out-of-home care system is the presentation of foster care statistics. Such statistics seldom distinguish kinship foster placements (placement of dependent children in the homes of relatives who have been formally approved, and subsidized, as foster parents for this purpose) from non-kinship foster placements. This distinction is important. Barth, Courtney, Berrick, Albert, and Needell (1994) noted that in California, two-thirds of the growth in the foster care caseload from 1984 to 1989 could be accounted for by the rise in kinship foster care. (This increase represents children who may otherwise have been placed in group homes or residential settings.) They also cite figures indicating that in 1990 kinship foster care accounted for 48 percent of all placements in New York (Meyer & Link, cited in Barth, Courtney, Berrick, Albert, & Needell, 1994). In New York City alone, the number of children in kinship foster homes rose from 151 in April 1985 to 14,000 in June 1989 (Thornton, 1991).

Children of color are widely represented in kinship foster placements. Forty-six percent of selected children in kinship foster care in California were African American, compared with 32 percent white children, 14 percent Hispanic children, and 9 percent children of other ethnic groups (Barth, Courtney, Berrick, &

Albert, 1994). Ninety percent of kinship foster families in a Baltimore study were African American and 10 percent were white (Dubowitz, Feigelman, & Zuravin, 1993).

Two issues are important here. First, many kinship foster placements are considered permanent placements. In interviews with kinship foster parents in 20 homes, none of the children had a permanency goal of return to their parents (Thornton, 1991). In 19 of the 20 cases, the children were expected to be discharged to independent living when they became eligible (typically at age 17 or 18 years); in contrast, independent living was a goal for only 42 percent of children who were in nonrelative foster placements. When the kinship foster parents were asked "How long are you willing to provide care for your related foster child?" 100 percent of those who responded indicated they expected the children to remain with them until they were independent, until they no longer needed to be there, or as long as the foster parents were able to care for them. Similar findings were reported by Barth, Courtney, Berrick, Albert, and Needell (1994).

Second, kinship foster placements frequently do not result in formal adoption. Therefore, placement in relative foster care has consistently been linked to a corresponding decrease in the odds of adoption, especially for children of color, as if these were permanency failures. Barth, Courtney, Berrick, and Albert (1994) noted that "other things being equal, entering foster care under one year of age more than doubles a child's odds of being adopted but being placed initially in a kinship home cuts the odds by one-half" (p. 161). Thornton (1991) found that kinship foster parents were not interested in adopting the children in their care. Even when they were aware of available adoption subsidies, 85 percent of kinship foster parents stated that they would not adopt; one additional kinship foster parent stated that she would adopt only if she was pressured by the agency. Ninety-one percent of foster care case-workers indicated awareness of this mindset on the part of kinship foster parents.

The reluctance to adopt formally among African American kinship foster caregivers is based in cultural definitions of family and attitudes about family relationships. For example, the reason given by 70 percent of kinship foster parents for their unwillingness to adopt was that they already considered the child and themselves as being a part of the same family and that it was therefore unnecessary to adopt and would be confusing to the child (Thornton, 1991). They were content to maintain a grandparent-to-grandchild caregiving relationship. (In most instances, kinship foster parents are grandparents or great aunts or uncles.) Also, 30 percent of kinship foster parents were concerned that adopting the child formally would result in conflict in their relationship with the child's biological parents.

In summarizing factors associated with the likelihood of being adopted, Barth, Courtney, Berrick, and Albert (1994) asserted that kinship foster care should not be considered a substitute for adoption. At the same time, they pointed out that it must, under law (Adoption Assistance and Child Welfare Act of 1980), be understood as an option for adoption. In spite of this, foster care statistics may continue to combine relative and nonrelative foster placements, inflating the number of children who are in out-of-home care and appear to be available for adoption. If kinship foster caregivers are accepted as a part of the child's family, and the child's planned long-term placement with them considered an acceptable alternative to adoption, the numbers recorded for children who are available for or requiring adoption, especially children of color, should decrease dramatically.

Effects of Poverty

An overriding issue to be addressed is the circumstances that cause children of color to be in out-of-home placement in such large numbers. Living in poverty is one such circumstance, and it disproportionately affects children of color. Over 46 percent of all African American children lived in poverty in 1993, as did 41 percent of all Latino children; only 14 percent of white children lived in poverty (Children's Defense Fund, 1995). Fifty-six percent of children living with their mothers only were poor, compared with 12 percent of those living with married parents, and children of color were more likely than white children to live in mother-only households.

Poverty has been linked to the circumstances that result in out-of-home placements. A recently released National Incidence Study of Child Abuse and Neglect ("Survey Shows," 1996) showed that "children from families with annual incomes below $15,000 were over 22 times more likely to experience maltreatment than children from families whose incomes exceeded $30,000. They were also 18 times more likely to be sexually abused, almost 56 times more likely to be educationally neglected, and over 22 times more likely to be seriously injured" (p. 3). Children of single parents had an 87 percent greater risk of being harmed by physical neglect and an 80 percent greater risk of suffering serious injury or harm from abuse and neglect. Thus, children of color may be at greater risk of abuse and neglect, which may be associated with the inadequate resources and resulting stresses their parents confront. Poor children are at risk of permanent removal from their families simply because of their economic position in society.

The direction of public policies currently is to speed up the transracial adoption of children of color without first correcting the resource deficiencies that cause the children to be in out-of-home care. Such policies ignore the complexities of this situation and risk giving one group (those desiring to adopt a young child) an advantage while failing to protect those who are among the most vulnerable (poor children and families). Social programs originating under the Family Preservation Act of 1992 (Omnibus Budget Reconciliation Act of 1993) are examples of corrective efforts. For example, most states have programs modeled after the original Homebuilders, Inc., of Tacoma, Washington (Kinney, Madsen, Fleming, & Haapala, 1977). In such programs, child welfare workers are available to families on a 24-hour basis to provide immediate services and resources to facilitate the child's safe presence within the family. Wraparound programs (VanDenBerg & Grealish, 1996) coordinate the provision of services and resources to families, but on an ongoing rather than a time-limited basis and as a collaborative community effort. These two programs are examples of how states may invest in families in attempting to prevent their breakdown.

Social Work Organization Positions

The formal positions of social work and related organizations serve as a guide to social work practice in the context of considerations of race and ethnicity in adoption. There is some variability in these positions, and this article briefly summarizes several.

In its most recent policy statement, NASW (1997) included the following: "Placement decisions should reflect a child's need for continuity, safeguarding the child's right to consistent care and to service arrangements. Agencies must recognize each child's need to retain a significant engagement with his or her parents and extended family and respect the integrity of each child's ethnicity and cultural heritage" (p. 137). The policy statement continues, "The social work profession stresses the importance of ethnic and cultural sensitivity. An effort to maintain a child's identity and her or his ethnic heritage should prevail in all services and placement actions that involve children in foster care and adoption programs, including adherence to the principles articulated in the Indian Child Welfare Act" (p. 138). With regard specifically to principles related to adoption, the statement reads, "The recruitment of and placement with adoptive parents from each relevant ethnic or racial group should be available to meet the needs of children" (p. 140).

In the concluding paragraph to its current position statement, the National Association of Black Social Workers (1994) stated,

> In conclusion, family preservation, reunification and adoption should work in tandem toward finding permanent homes for children. Priority should be given to preserving families through the reunification or adoption of children with/by biological relatives. If that should fail, secondary priority should be given to the placement of a child within his own race. Transracial adoption of an African-American child should only be considered after documented evidence of unsuccessful same race placements has been reviewed and supported by appropriate representatives of the African-American community. Under no circumstance should successful same race placements be impeded by obvious barriers (i.e., legal limits of states, state boundaries, fees, surrogate payments, intrusive applications, lethargic court systems, inadequate staffing patterns, etc.). As such, it will be mandatory that national policies with adequate funding be adopted as part of any new legislation. (p. 4)

The most recent standards of the Child Welfare League of America (1988) include an emphasis on the preservation of the birth family:

> When children's rights to the care and protection of those who gave them birth are jeopardized, society should, through its appropriate designated agencies, provide support to birth parents to make it possible for children to remain in their own homes. Children should not be deprived of their birth parents solely because of economic need, or

the need for other forms of community assistance to reinforce parental efforts to maintain a home for them. (p. 2)

With regard to the role of the extended family, the standards read, "When children's parents are unable or unwilling to rear them, efforts should be made to have members of the extended family assume the parenting role and responsibility, providing they can offer the care and protection that the children need and that this is the desire of the birth parents" (p. 3). Finally, with regard to considerations of race and ethnicity, "Children should not be deprived of the opportunity to have a permanent family of their own by reason of age, religion, racial, or ethnic group identification, nationality, residence, or handicap" (p. 4). The standards include the clarification that federal legislation is perceived as safeguarding the rights of children.

The North American Council on Adoptable Children (NACAC) (Gilles & Kroll, 1991) has reaffirmed its original position, established in 1981, which stated as follows:

> Placement of children with a family of like ethnic background is desirable because such families are likely to provide the special needs of minority children with the strengths that counter the ill effects of racism. . . . The special needs of minority children who are of mixed ethnic background, school age, sibling groups or who have handicapping conditions should be considered in order to prevent unnecessary delays in placement. NACAC supports inclusion of multiethnic adoption as an option for children. (p. 37)

In 1988 NACAC (Gilles & Kroll, 1991), in addition to encouraging federal, state, and local officials to "fully utilize family resources in minority communities through aggressive and culturally sensitive recruitment and retention programs" (p. 38), decided to "direct [its] resources to the development, growth, and empowerment of minority adoptive parent groups" (p. 38). In 1990 it resolved the following: "Recognizing that fees charged prospective adoptive families present barriers to the most culturally appropriate placement for children in need of adoption, NACAC advocates that all child-placing agencies have as a goal working to develop alternative funding sources to cover all costs related to adoption services by working with both private and public sectors" (Gilles & Kroll, 1991, p. 38).

Five themes can be noted from among the position statements of these professional organizations regarding transracial adoption: (1) that ethnic heritage is important; (2) that children be raised preferably by their biological parents or, when not possible, by other biological relatives; (3) that economic need alone is not an acceptable reason for children to be deprived of their biological parents; (4) that efforts should be made to ensure that adoptive parents of the same race as the child are available and systemic barriers should not interfere; and (5) that placement with parents of a different race is acceptable and even preferable when the alternative means a child is deprived of a permanent home and family. It is important that social work organizations publicize these positions to their members and advocate for public policies that facilitate these themes.

Conclusions and Recommendations

Inequities exist in the eligibility and recruitment of non-kin foster families and adoptive families of color, in services provided to children and families in the child welfare system, and in the increased tendency of poor children to be in out-of-home care. Statistics on the numbers and characteristics of children of color who are in foster care and who are available for adoption may be misleading. Public policies that disallow the consideration of race and ethnicity in adoption give an advantage to families who desire to adopt transracially. At the same time, they fail to correct the circumstances that cause children of color to require out-of-home placement, and they fail to eliminate methods of maintaining or interpreting statistical data that may be misleading.

The following recommendations are made to lessen the need for transracial adoption. First, foster families of color should be actively recruited for kinship and non-kinship foster care and especially to participate in fost adoption programs, if such programs are to continue. Second, active and ongoing efforts to recruit and retain adoptive families of color should be increased so that the pool of available families equals or surpasses the numbers of children of color who are available for non-kin adoption. Third, creative strategies should continue to be developed to recruit adoptive families of color for "hard to place" children or children with special needs. Such children should continue to be placed according to their individual needs. Fourth, public policies and agency procedures should be established to require that children of color receive equitable services in all areas of the child welfare system. Fifth, statistics and outcome data relating to kinship foster care should be separated from those pertaining to nonrelative foster care; the benefits of the former as an acceptable permanent alternative to adoption should be evaluated. And sixth, policymakers should address the larger issues involved in ensuring that all children have access to the economic resources that can help them remain out of the child welfare system.

Social work has a central role to play in carrying out these recommendations. This role may include advocating in agencies for equitable (bias-free) selection; recruiting foster and adoptive families; orienting agency administrators, board members, and the general community regarding cultural definitions of "family"; conducting research that can scientifically inform public policy; participating in practices oriented to strengthening and unifying families while protecting children; and educating students and new professionals in the competent performance of such roles. A review of committee reports of the most recent adoption legislation (H. Rep. No. 104-542, 104th Congress, 2nd Sess., 1996) demonstrates that statistical data, and the way they are collected and interpreted, play a primary role in the development of public policy. It is important, therefore, that social workers be actively involved in ensuring that complete and accurate research and numerical data are disseminated to public policymakers.

A limitation of this article is that in some instances the data were derived from studies of children in out-of-home care in a limited number of states. However, the consistency of the findings and the fact that research data on these topics are limited render available data useful in interpreting the state of the field and suggest directions for future research, policy, and practice.

Finally, seeking to solve the problems associated with the overrepresentation of children of color in the child welfare system by protecting transracial adoption is simplistic and fails to protect those who are most vulnerable in this society—the children dependent on that society. A more responsible approach is to understand and eliminate the circumstances that constitute the base cause of this situation. The most recent adoption legislation (Small Business Job Protection Act of 1996) only became effective on January 1, 1997, so it is too early to determine how adoption agencies will respond. However, this will be an important area for review.

References

Adoption Assistance and Child Welfare Act of 1980, P. L. No. 96–272, [section]473, 94 Stat. 500 (1981).

Adoption—Not just for Woody and Mia. (1992, September 23). *Wall Street Journal,* p. A16.

Barth, R. P., Courtney, M., Berrick, J., & Albert, V. (1994). *From child abuse to permanency planning: Child welfare services pathways and placements.* New York: Aldine de Gruyter.

Barth, R. P., Courtney, M., Berrick, J., Albert, V., & Needell, B. (1994). Kinship care: Rights and responsibilities, services and standards. In R. P. Barth, M. Courtney, J. Berrick, & V. Albert (Eds.), *From child abuse to permanency planning: Child welfare services pathways and placements* (pp. 195–219). New York: Aldine de Gruyter.

Bartholet, E. (1991). Where do black children belong? The politics of race matching in adoption. *University of Pennsylvania Law Review, 139,* 1163–1256.

Child Welfare League of America. (1988). *Child Welfare League of America standards for adoption service.* Washington, DC: Author.

Children's Defense Fund. (1995). *The state of America's children yearbook: 1995.* Washington, DC: Author.

Courtney, M. E., Barth, R. P., Berrick, J. D., Brooks, D., Needell, B., & Park, L. (1996). Race and child welfare services: Past research and future directions. *Child Welfare, 75,* 99–137.

Day, D. (1979). *The adoption of black children.* Lexington, MA: D.C. Heath.

Dubowitz, H., Feigelman, S., & Zuravin, S. (1993). A profile of kinship care. *Child Welfare, 72,* 153–169.

Elias, M. (1991, August 15). Black kids, white parents: Debating what's best for the kids. *USA Today,* p. ID.

Flango, V. E., & Flango, C. (1994). *The flow of adoption information from the states* (Publication No. R-162). Williamsburg, VA: National Center for State Courts.

Folaron, G., & Hess, P. (1993). Placement considerations for children of mixed African American and Caucasian parentage. *Child Welfare, 72,* 113–125.

Fraser, M. W., Pecora, P. J., & Haapala, D. A. (1991). *Families in crisis: The impact of intensive family preservation services.* New York: Aldine de Gruyter.

Gant, L. M. (1984). *Black adoption programs: Pacesetters in practice.* Ann Arbor, MI: National Child Welfare Training Center.

Gilles, T., & Kroll, J. (1991). *Barriers to same race placement.* St. Paul, MN: North American Council on Adoptable Children.

Gould, K. H. (1991). Limiting damage is not enough: A minority perspective on child welfare issues. In J. E. Everett, S.S. Chipungu, & B. R. Leashore (Eds.), *Child welfare: An Africentric perspective* (pp. 58–77). New Brunswick, NJ: Rutgers University Press.

Hairston, C. F., & Williams, V. G. (1989). Black adoptive parents: How they view agency adoption practices. *Social Casework, 70,* 534–538.

Hermann, V. P. (1993). Transracial adoption: "Child-saving" or "child-snatching"? *National Black Law Journal, 13,* 147–164.

Herzog, E., Sudia, C., Harwood, J., & Newcomb, C. (1971). *Families for black children.* Washington, DC: U.S. Government Printing Office.

Homes for Black Children: Hearing of the Senate Subcommittee on Children, Family, Drugs, and Alcoholism, 103d Congress, 1st Sess. 26–68 (1993, July 15) (testimony of Sydney Duncan).

Indian Child Welfare Act of 1978, [section]1214, 95th Cong., 2d Sess. (1978).

Jackson-White, G., Dozier, C. D., Oliver, J. T., & Gardner, L. B. (1997). Why African American adoption agencies succeed: A new perspective on self-help. *Child Welfare, 76,* 239–254.

Kinney, J. M., Madsen, B., Fleming, T., & Haapala, D. A. (1977). Homebuilders: Keeping families together. *Journal of Consulting & Clinical Psychology, 45,* 667–673.

Mahoney, J. (1991). The black baby doll: Transracial adoption and cultural preservation. *University of Missouri-Kansas City Law Review, 59,* 487–501.

McRoy, R. G. (1989). An organizational dilemma: The case of transracial adoptions. *Journal of Applied Behavioral Science, 25,* 145–160.

McRoy, R. G. (1994). Attachment and racial identity issues: Implications for child placement decision making. *Journal of Multicultural Social Work, 3,* 59–74.

McRoy, R. G., Oglesby, Z., & Grape, H. (1997). Achieving same race adoptive placements for African-American children: Culturally sensitive practice approaches. *Child Welfare, 76,* 85–104.

Meezan, W., & Shireman, J. F. (1985). *Care and commitment: Foster parent adoption decisions.* Albany: State University of New York Press.

Multiethnic Placement Act of 1994, P.L. 103–382, [section]553, 108 Stat. 4057 (1995).

National Association of Black Social Workers. (1994). *Preserving African-American families: Position statement.* Detroit: Author.

National Association of Social Workers. (1997). *Social work speaks: NASW policy statements* (4th ed.). Washington, DC: NASW Press.

Omnibus Budget Reconciliation Act of 1993, P.L. 103–66, 107 Stat. 312.

Rezendes, M. (1994). Debate intensifies on adoptions across racial lines. *Boston Globe,* p. 1.

Richman, R. (1993, December 7). Transracial adoptions get vocal advocate. *Plain Dealer* (From the *Washington Post*), p. 6C.

Silverman, A. R. (1993). Outcomes of transracial adoption. *Future of Children, 3,* 104–118.

Simon, R. J., & Alstein, H. (1977). *Transracial adoption.* New York: John Wiley & Sons.

Simon, R. J., & Alstein, H. (1987). *Transracial adoptees and their families: A study of identity and commitment.* New York: Praeger.

Thornton, J. L. (1991). Permanency planning for children in kinship homes. *Child Welfare, 70,* 593–601.

VanDenBerg, J. E., & Grealish, M. (1996). Individualized services and supports through the wraparound process: Philosophy and procedures. *Journal of Child and Family Studies, 5,* 7–21.

Williams, C. C. (1991). Expanding the options in the quest for permanence. In J. E. Everett, S. S. Chipungu, & B. R. Leashore (Eds.), *Child welfare: An Africentric perspective* (pp. 266–289). New Brunswick, NJ: Rutgers University Press.

**Ezra E. H. Griffith
and Rachel L. Bergeron**

→ **NO**

Cultural Stereotypes Die Hard:
The Case of Transracial Adoption

The adoption of black children by white families, commonly referred to as transracial adoption in the lay and professional literature, is the subject of a debate that has persisted in American society for a long time.[1] On one side of the divide are those who believe that black children are best raised by black families. On the other are the supporters of the idea that race-matching in adoption does not necessarily serve the best interests of the child and that it promotes racial discrimination.[2]

Coming as it does in the midst of myriad other discussions in this country about black-white interactions, transracial adoption has occupied an important place in any debate about adoption policy. But in addition, as can be seen in language utilized by the Fifth Circuit Court in a 1977 case,[3] there is a long-held belief that since family members resemble one another, it follows that members of constructed families should also look like each other so as to facilitate successful adoption outcomes.

> [A]doption agencies quite frequently try to place a child where he can most easily become a normal family member. The duplication of his natural biological environment is part of that program. Such factors as age, hair color, eye color and facial features of parents and child are considered in reaching a decision. This flows from the belief that a child and adoptive parents can best adjust to a normal family relationship if the child is placed with adoptive parents who could have actually parented him. To permit consideration of physical characteristics necessarily carries with it permission to consider racial characteristics [Ref. 3, pp 1205–6].

In utilizing this language, the court acknowledged that transracial adoption ran counter to the cultural beliefs that many people held about the construction of families. Still, the court concluded that while the difficulties attending transracial adoption justified the consideration of race as a relevant factor in adoption proceedings, race could not be the sole factor considered. With a bow to both sides in the transracial adoption debate, the argument could only continue.

As the debate marches on, mental health professionals are being asked to provide expert opinions about whether it would be preferable for a particular

From *The Journal of the American Academy of Psychiatry and the Law,* vol. 34, no. 3, 2006, pp. 303–312 (excerpts). Copyright © 2006 by American Academy of Psychiatry and the Law. Reprinted by permission via S&S Management Services, Inc.

black child to be raised by a black family or by a family or adult of a different ethnic or racial group. There are, of course, different scenarios that may lead to the unfolding of these adoption disputes. For example, the question may arise when a black child is put up for adoption after having spent a number of months or years in an out-of-home placement. The lengthy wait of black children for an adoptive black family may understandably increase the likelihood of a transracial adoption. In another situation, the death of a biracial child's parents, one of whom was white and the other black, may lead to competition between the white and black grandparents for the right to raise the child. In a third possible context, the divorce of an interracial couple may result in a legal struggle for custody of the biracial child, with race trumpeted at least as an important factor if not the crucial factor to be considered in the decision about who should raise the child. Mental health professionals should therefore make an effort to stay abreast of the latest developments around this national debate if they intend to provide an informed opinion about the merits or problems of a potential transracial adoption.

We have already alluded to two significant factors that have played a role in the evolution of adoption policy concerning black children, particularly with respect to the question of whether race-neutral approaches make sense and whether transracial adoption is good practice. One factor has been judicial decision-making. In a relatively recent review, Hollinger[4] reminded us that, in general, racial classifications are invalidated unless they can survive the "strict scrutiny" test, which requires meeting a compelling governmental interest. Hollinger suggested that the "best-interest-of-the-child" standard commonly used in adoption practice would serve a substantial governmental interest. Such argumentation would allow the consideration of race as one element in an adoption evaluation. Following this reasoning, while race-neutral adoption may be a lofty objective, the specific needs of a particular child could legally allow the consideration of race.

The second factor to influence the evolution of adoption policy in this arena has been the academic research on transracial adoption.[5-9] This work has cumulatively demonstrated that black children can thrive and develop strong racial identities when nurtured in families with white parents. Transracially adopted children also do well on standard measures of self-esteem, cognitive development, and educational achievement. However, neither judicial decision-making nor scholarly research has settled the debate on transracial adoption policy.

In this article, we focus on a third factor that emerged as another mechanism meant to deal with transracial adoptions and the influential race-matching principle. These statutory efforts started with the Multiethnic Placement Act, which Hollinger stated "was enacted in 1994 amid spirited and sometimes contentious debate about transracial adoption and same-race placement policies."[4] We will point out that even though the statutory attempts were meant to eliminate race as a controlling factor in the adoption process, their implementation has left room for ambiguity regarding the role that race should play in adoption proceedings. Consequently, even though the statutes were intended to eliminate adoption delays and denials because of race-matching, they may have allowed the continued existence of a cultural stereotype—that black children belong with black families—and may have facilitated its continued existence. This article is therefore principally about statutory attempts in the past decade to influence public policy concerning transracial adoption. Secondarily, we shall comment on potential implications of these developments for the practice of adoption evaluations.

We emphasize once again that in referring to transracial adoption, we mean the adoption of black children by white parents. This is the focus of the statutes we consider. The adoption by Americans of children from other countries (international adoptions) and other transcultural adoptions (such as the adoption of Native American children by Anglos) are explicitly outside the parameters of this article. We also do not wish to suggest that although transracial adoption has been the subject of a significant national debate it is a numerically common phenomenon. Later in this article, we review the available data on transracial adoption.

Brief Review of Race-Matching in Adoption

Feelings about who should raise a black child have run high in the United States for a long time. These feelings come from different groups for different reasons. Kennedy[1] presented a number of historical cases to illustrate this. Among the cases he described, Kennedy told the early 1900s story of a white girl who was found residing with a black family (Ref. 1, p 368). The authorities concluded that the child had been kidnapped and rescued her. They then placed her with a white family. When it was learned later that the child was black, she was returned to the black family because it was not proper for the black child to be living with a white family. This case, along with others described by Kennedy, is part of the fabric of American racism and racial separatist practices. Kennedy also pointed to the practice during slavery of considering "the human products of interracial sexual unions" as unambiguously black and the mandate that they be reared within the black slave community as an attempt to undermine any possibility of interracial parenting (Ref. 1, pp 367–8).

Whites have not been the only ones to support the stance of race-matching—the belief that black or white children belong with their own group. In 1972, the National Association of Black Social Workers (NABSW) stated unambiguously that white families should never be allowed to adopt black children.[10] The NABSW opposed transracial adoption for two main reasons: the Association claimed that transracial adoption prevents black children from forming a strong racial identity, and it prevents them from developing survival skills necessary to deal with a racist society.

Since its 1972 statement, the NABSW has remained steadfast in its opposition to transracial adoption. In testimony before the Senate Committee on Labor and Human Resources in 1985, the President of the NABSW reiterated the Association's position and stated that the NABSW viewed the placement of black children in white homes as a hostile act against the black community, considering it a blatant form of race and cultural genocide.[11]

In 1991, the NABSW reaffirmed its position that black children should not be placed with white parents under any circumstances, stating that even the most loving and skilled white parent could not avoid doing irreparable harm to an African-American child.[12] In its 1994 position paper on the preservation of African-American families, the NABSW indicated that, in placement decisions regarding a black child, priority should be given to adoption by biological relatives and then to black families.[13] Transracial adoption "should only be considered after documented evidence of unsuccessful same race placements has been reviewed and supported by appropriate representatives of the African American community" (Ref. 13, p 1).

The NABSW's position was reflected in the 1981 New York case of *Farmer v. Farmer*.[14] Mr. Farmer, a black man, sought custody of his six-year-old daughter after he and his white wife divorced. He argued that his daughter, who looked black, would do better being raised by him than by her white mother and that her best interests could be achieved only by awarding custody to him, the parent with whom she would be racially identified by a racially conscious society. Three experts testified on his behalf. Each addressed the importance of racial identity problems that the child would face and the importance of her identification with her black heritage, but none would state categorically that custody of the child should be determined by her dominant racial characteristic. The judge rejected Mr. Farmer's race-based argument, finding that "between two natural parents of different races who have opted to have a child, neither gains priority for custody by reason of race alone. Nor can race disqualify a natural parent for custody" (Ref. 14, pp 589–90). He awarded custody to the mother based on the determination of the best interests of the child. In this determination race was not a dominant, controlling, or crucial factor, but was weighed along with all other material elements of the lives of the family.

Race-matching has been and remains an influential and controversial concept regarding how best to construct adoptive families. Matching, in general, has been a classic principle of adoption practice, governing non-relative adoptions for much of the 20th century. Its goal was to create families in which the adoptive parents looked as though they could be the adopted child's biological parents. Matching potential adoptive parents and children on as many physical, emotional, and cultural characteristics as possible was seen as a way of insuring against adoptive failure.[5] It was not uncommon for potential adoptive parents to be denied the possibility of adoption if their hair and eye color did not match those of a child in need of adoption.[5] Differences among family members in constructed families were seen as threats to the integration of an adopted child and the child's identification with the adoptive parents. Race, along with religion, was considered the most important characteristic to be matched, and it continued to be important even as the matching concept regarding other characteristics began to shift.[5] For example, in 1959, in its *Standards for Adoption Service* (SAS), the Child Welfare League of America (CWLA) recommended that

> . . . similarities of background or characteristics should not be a major consideration in the selection of a family, except where integration of

the child into the family and his identification with them may be facilitated by likeness, as in the case of some older children or some children with distinctive physical traits, such as race [Ref. 5, pp 3–4].

The CWLA reiterated its view in its discussion of the role of physical characteristics: "Physical resemblances should not be a determining factor in the selection of a home, with the possible exception of such racial characteristics as color" (Ref. 5, p 4). It was not until 1968 that the CWLA omitted any reference to color as a criterion for adoption: "Physical resemblances of the adoptive parents, the child or his natural parents should not be a determining factor in the selection of a home" (Ref. 5, p 6). By 1971, the CWLA considered characteristics that had been encompassed in the matching concept to be broad guidelines rather than specific criteria and the weight afforded them depended on the potential adoptive parents (i.e., their desire for a child similar to them in particular ways should be taken into consideration).[5] While not identified as a strict criterion of adoption, matching continued to be a broad principle in adoption practices. For example, the CWLA's 1988 *Standards for Adoption Service* and its 1993 statement of its children's legislative agenda reflected its belief that the developmental needs of black adopted children could best be met by black adoptive parents.[5,6]

> Children in need of adoption have a right to be placed into a family that reflects their ethnicity or race. Children should not have their adoption denied or significantly delayed, however, when adoptive parents of other ethnic or racial groups are available. . . . In any adoption plan, however, the best interests of the child should be paramount. If aggressive, ongoing recruitment efforts are unsuccessful in finding families of the same ethnicity or culture, other families should be considered [Ref. 5, p 32].

Matching, of course, continued to influence child placement decisions outside of adoption agencies, as evidenced by the comments of the Drummond court. Following that court's decision, the general rule has been that trial courts may consider race as a factor in adoption proceedings as long as race is not the sole determinant.[15,16]

Statutory Attempts at Remedies

As we previously noted, in 1972 the National Association of Black Social Workers (NABSW) issued a position paper in which the Association vehemently opposed the adoption of black children by white families.[10] The Black Social Workers had a quick and striking effect on transracial adoption policy. Following the appearance of the paper, adoption agencies, both public and private, either implemented race-matching approaches or used the NABSW position to justify already existing race-matching policies. As a result, the number of transracial adoptions were estimated to drop significantly—39 percent within one year of the publication of the NABSW statement.[17] Although robust data were lacking, it was thought that the number and length of stay of black children in out-of-home placements increased as social workers and other foster care and adoption professionals, believing that same-race placements were in the best interest of the child, searched for same-race foster and adoptive parents. Agencies and their workers had considerable discretion in deciding the role race played in placement decisions. States, while generally requiring that foster care and adoption decisions be made in the best interest of the child, varied in their directions regarding the extent to which race, culture, and ethnicity should be taken into account in making the best-interest determination.[18]

While race-matching policies were not the sole determinant of increasing numbers of black children in institutions and out-of-home placements, there was growing concern that such policies, with their focus on same-race placement and their exclusion of consideration of loving, permanent interracial homes, kept black children from being adopted.[19] Because he was concerned that race had become the determining factor in adoption placements and that children were languishing in foster care homes and institutions, Senator Howard Metzenbaum introduced legislation to prohibit the use of race as the sole determinant of placement.[19] Senator Metzenbaum believed that same-race adoption was the preferable option for a child, but he also believed that transracial placement was far preferable to a child's remaining in foster care when an appropriate same-race placement was not available.[19]

Multiethnic Placement Act

Congress passed the Howard Metzenbaum Multiethnic Placement Act (MEPA) and President Clinton signed it into law on October 20, 1994.[20] MEPA's main goals were to decrease the length of time children had to wait to be adopted; to prevent discrimination based on race in the placement of children into adoptive or foster homes; and to recruit culturally diverse and minority adoptive and foster families who could meet the needs of children needing placement.[18] In passing MEPA, Congress was concerned that many children, especially those from minority groups, were spending lengthy periods in foster care awaiting adoption placements.[19] Congress found, within the parameters of available data, that nearly 500,000 children were in foster care in the United States; tens of thousands of these children were waiting for adoption; two years and eight months was the median length of time children waited to be adopted; and minority children often waited twice as long as other children to be adopted.[21]

Under MEPA, an agency or entity receiving federal funds could not use race as the sole factor in denying any person the opportunity to become an adoptive or foster parent. Furthermore, an agency could not use race as a single factor to delay or deny the placement of a child in an adoptive or foster care family or to otherwise discriminate in making a placement decision. However, an agency could consider a child's racial, cultural, and ethnic background as one of several factors—not the sole factor—used to determine the best interests of the child.[22] MEPA stated:

> An agency, or entity, that receives Federal assistance and is involved in adoption or foster care placements may not—(A) categorically deny to any person the opportunity to become an adoptive or a foster parent, solely on the basis of the race, color or national origin of the adoptive or foster parent, or the child involved; or (B) delay or deny the placement of a child for adoption or into foster care, or otherwise discriminate in making a placement decision, solely on the basis of the race, color, or national origin of the adoptive or foster parent, or the child involved.[23]

However, MEPA also contained the following permissible consideration:

> An agency or entity . . . may consider the cultural, ethnic, or racial background of the child and the capacity of the prospective foster or adoptive parents to meet the needs of a child of this background as one of a number of factors used to determine the best interests of a child.[24]

So, under MEPA, agencies could consider a child's race, ethnicity, or culture as one of a number of factors used to determine the best interests of the child, as long as it was not the sole factor considered, and they could consider the ability of prospective parents to meet the needs of a child of a given race, ethnicity, or culture.[22]

Following the passage of MEPA, the Department of Health and Human Services (DHHS), Office of Civil Rights, provided policy guidance to assist agencies receiving federal financial assistance in complying with MEPA.[25] The guidance permitted agencies receiving federal assistance to consider race, culture, or ethnicity as factors in making placement decisions to the extent allowed by MEPA, the U.S. Constitution and Title VI of the Civil Rights Act of 1964.[25]

Under the Equal Protection Clause of the Fourteenth Amendment, laws or practices drawing distinctions on the basis of race are inherently suspect and subject to strict scrutiny analysis.[26] To pass such analysis, classifications or practices based on race have to be narrowly tailored to meet a compelling state interest.[26] The Supreme Court has not specifically addressed the question of transracial adoption. It has considered race as a factor in a child placement decision in the context of a custody dispute between two white biological parents when the mother, who had custody of the child, began living with a black man, whom she later married. The Court found the goal of granting custody on the basis of the best interests of the child to be "indisputably a substantial government interest for purposes of the Equal Protection Clause" (Ref. 27, p 433). The DHHS guidance on the use of race, color or national origin as factors in adoption and foster care placements addressed the relevant constitutional issues and indicated that the only compelling state interest in the context of child placement decisions is protecting the best interests of the child who is to be placed.[25] So, under MEPA, consideration of race or ethnicity was permitted as long as it was narrowly tailored to advance a specific child's best interests.[25] Agencies receiving federal funds could consider race and ethnicity when making placement decisions only if the agency made a narrowly tailored, individualized determination that the facts and circumstances of a particular case required the contemplation of race or ethnicity to advance the best interests of the child in need of placement.[18,25] Agencies could not assume that race, ethnicity, or culture was at issue in every case and make general policies that applied to all children.[18] The guidance also specifically prohibited policies that established periods during which same-race searches were conducted, created placement preference hierarchies based on race, ethnicity, or culture, required social workers to justify transracial placement decisions or resulted in delayed placements to find a family of a particular race, ethnicity, or culture.[18]

The DHHS policy guidance did address MEPA's permissible consideration of the racial, cultural, or ethnic background of a child and the capacity of the prospective foster or adoptive parents to meet the needs of a child of this background as one of a number of factors in the best-interest-of-the-child determination. The guidance allowed agencies to assess the ability of a specific potential adoptive family to meet a specific child's needs related to his or her racial, ethnic, or cultural background, as long as the assessment was done in the context of an individualized assessment[18,25]:

> As part of this assessment, the agency may examine the attitudes of the prospective family that affect their ability to nurture a child of a particular background and consider the family's ability to promote development of the child's positive sense of self. The agency may assess the family's ability to nurture, support, and reinforce the racial, ethnic, or cultural identity of the child, the family's capacity to cope with the particular consequences of the child's developmental history, and the family's ability to help the child deal with any forms of discrimination the child may encounter [Ref. 18, pp 9–10].

However, agencies were not allowed to make decisions based on general assumptions regarding the needs of children of a specific race, ethnicity, or culture or about the ability of prospective parents of a specific race, ethnicity, or culture to care or nurture the identity of a child of a different race, ethnicity, or culture.[18]

To increase the pool of potential foster or adoptive parents, MEPA also required states to develop plans for the recruitment of potential foster and adoptive families that reflected the ethnic and racial diversity of the children needing placement.[28] The recruitment efforts had to be focused on providing all eligible children with the opportunity for placement and on providing all qualified members of the community with an opportunity to become an adoptive or foster parent.[18] As a result, while MEPA sought in a reasonable way to recruit a broad racial and cultural spectrum of adoptive families, the law was at the same time underlining the idea that there was something special about a black child's being raised by a black family.

Those who objected to the permissive consideration of race in MEPA asserted that it allowed agencies to continue to delay adoptions of minority

children based on race concerns.[21] They also argued that race-matching policies could and did continue under MEPA. Social workers could, for example,
use race as a factor to support a finding that a transracial adoption was not in
a given child's best interest. Supporters of MEPA reached their own conclusion that it did not accomplish its goal of speeding up the adoption process
and moving greater numbers of minority children into foster care or adoption placements and that the permissive consideration of race allowed agencies legitimately to continue race-matching to deny or delay the placement of
minority children with white adoptive parents.[22] Senator Metzenbaum himself agreed with this conclusion about MEPA and worked for its repeal.[29] As we
shall see later, the arguments and counterarguments about the effectiveness of
MEPA were being made in the absence of robust data.

The Interethnic Adoption Provisions

MEPA was repealed when on August 20, 1996, President Clinton signed the
Small Business Job Protection Act of 1996. Section 1808 of the Act was entitled
"Removal of Barriers to Interethnic Adoption" (The Interethnic Adoption Provisions; IEP).[30] MEPA's permissible consideration provision was removed and
its language changed. (The words in brackets were part of MEPA and do not
appear in the IEP.)

> A person or government that is involved in adoption or foster care
> placements may not—(a) [categorically] deny to any individual the
> opportunity to become an adoptive or a foster parent, [solely] on the
> basis of race, color, or national origin of the individual, or the child
> involved; or (b) delay or deny the placement of a child for adoption or
> into foster care [or otherwise discriminate in making a placement deci-
> sion, solely] on the basis of race, color, or national origin of the adop-
> tive or foster parent, or the child, involved [Ref. 22, pp 1616–17].

Under the IEP, states were still required to "provide for the diligent recruitment of potential foster and adoptive families that reflect the ethnic and racial
diversity of children in the State for whom foster and adoptive homes are
needed."[28]

Failure to comply with MEPA was a violation of Title VI of the Civil Rights
Act of 1964[17]; failure to comply with the IEP is also a violation of Title VI.[31]
Under MEPA, an agency receiving federal assistance that discriminated in its
child placement decisions on the basis of race and failed to comply with the Act
could forfeit its federal assistance[17] and an aggrieved individual had the right to
bring an action seeking equitable relief in federal court[32] or could file a complaint
with the Office of Civil Rights. The IEP added enforcement provisions that speci-
fied graduated fiscal sanctions to be imposed by DHHS against states found to be
in violation of the law and gave any individual aggrieved by a violation the right
to bring an action against the state or other entity in federal court.[33]

The Department of Health and Human Services issued two documents
to provide practical guidance for complying with the IEP: a memorandum[34]
and a document in question-and-answer format.[35] According to the guidance,

Congress, in passing the IEP, clarified its intent to eliminate delays in adoption or foster care placements when they were in any way avoidable. Race and ethnicity could not be used as the basis for any denial of placement nor used as a reason to delay a foster care or adoptive placement.[34] The repeal of MEPA's "permissible consideration" provision was seen as confirming that strict scrutiny was the appropriate standard for consideration of race or ethnicity in adoption and foster care placements.[34] DHHS argued that it had never taken the position that MEPA's permissible consideration language allowed agencies to take race into account routinely in making placement decisions because such a view would be inconsistent with a strict scrutiny standard.[34] It reaffirmed that any decision to consider race as a necessary element in a placement decision has to be based on concerns arising out of the circumstances of the particular situation:

> The primary message of the strict scrutiny standard in this context is that only the most compelling reasons may serve to justify consideration of race and ethnicity as part of a placement decision. Such reasons are likely to emerge only in unique and individual circumstances. Accordingly, occasions where race or ethnicity lawfully may be considered in a placement decision will be correspondingly rare [Ref. 34, p 4].

The guidance again made clear that the best interest of the child is the standard to be used in making placement decisions. So, according to the guidance, the IEP prohibits the routine practice of taking race and ethnicity into consideration ("Public agencies may not routinely consider race, national origin, and ethnicity in making placement decisions" (Ref. 35, p 2)), but it allows for the consideration of race, national origin, and ethnicity in certain specific situations ("Any consideration of these factors must be done on an individualized basis where special circumstances indicate that their consideration is warranted" (Ref. 35, p 2)). Once again, such language seems to suggest that, in certain contexts, the adoptive child may well benefit from placement in a same-race family.

Table 1

Children Waiting to Be Adopted from the Public Foster Care System, by Race, by Fiscal Year

	On Sept. 30, 2002*		On Sept. 30, 2003†	
	Number	%	Number	%
Black/non-Hispanic	54,832	43	47,630	40
White/non-Hispanic	58,975	46	43,820	37
Total	127,942	100	119,000	100

*Reference 37.

†Reference 38.

The DHHS guidance seemed to frame the possibility for adoption agencies to continue the practice of race-matching.[22] For example, while warning that assessment of a prospective parent's ability to serve as a foster or adoptive parent must not act as a racial or ethnic screen and indicating that considerations of race must not be routine in the assessment function, the guidance conceded that an important aspect of good social work is an individualized assessment of a prospective parent's ability to be an adoptive or foster parent.

Thus, it allows for discussions with prospective adoptive or foster care parents about their feelings, preferences, and capacities regarding caring for a child of a particular race or ethnicity.[22,35]

Data Collection

Hansen and Simon[36] have pointed out that the Adoption and Safe Families Act (ASFA) of 1995 created an adoption incentive program that paid bonuses to states that increased the number of adoptions of children from foster care. The incentive program also provided an incentive for data collection, using a system known as the Adoption and Foster Care Analysis and Reporting System (AFCARS). States must submit data to AFCARS on each adoption in which a public child welfare agency was involved in any fashion. AFCARS issues periodic reports, and others (such as the Child Welfare League of America) use the AFCARS data to publish analytic reports from time to time. AFCARS reports may be preliminary, interim, or final as data continue to be submitted by states over many months.

Tables 1 and 2 show that in fiscal year (FY) 2002 and in FY 2003, more whites were adopted than blacks in the public foster care system. The two fiscal years show some difference between whites and blacks in terms of the comparative number of whites and blacks waiting for adoption. The data for FY 2003 show that more whites than blacks were in the foster care system. Of course, these numbers of children in the foster care system must be viewed in light of their representation in the general population. Data from the 2000

Table 2

Children Adopted from the Public Foster Care System, by Race, by Fiscal Year

	Fiscal Year 2002*		Fiscal Year 2003[†]	
	Number	%	Number	%
Black/non-Hispanic	18,957	36	16,570	33
White/non-Hispanic	27,272	52	20,940	42
Total	52,138	100	50,000	100

*Reference 37.

[†]Reference 38.

U.S. Census . . . show that of the total population under age 18 years, 68.6 percent (49,598,289) are white and 15.1 percent (10,885,696) are black. Consequently, a substantially greater proportion of blacks (.4%), in comparison to whites (.09%), were awaiting adoption in September 2003. Still, of the children awaiting adoption in September 2002, 30 percent of black children were adopted in FY 2003 in comparison to 36 percent of white children.

The AFCARS data from FY 2001 have been the subject of greater analysis, which has led to the following conclusions.[36,39] In FY 2001, mean time for adoption of black children was 18 months compared with 15 months for white children. It was also estimated that about 17 percent of black children adopted in FY 2001 were adopted transracially by white, non-Hispanic parents. This figure of transracial adoptions (about 2,500) provided for the public foster care system is not significantly above estimates given for earlier years— about 2,574 in 1971. However, the FY 2001 data do not include private sector adoptions. This has led Hansen and Simon[36] to conclude that there has been no clear increase in transracial adoptions, at least in the arena of public child welfare agency adoptions. In 2003, McFarland[40] published a report pointing out that while AFCARS is now producing robust data about public sector adoptions, information about private sector adoptions is scant.

Nevertheless, it has been estimated that in 2001, about 127,000 children were adopted in the United States,[41] including public, private, and intercountry adoptions. These adoptions arise out of the estimated 500,000 children in out-of-home placements in the United States.

Discussion

The IEP addresses individual cultural elements such as race, color, or national origin and does not address the broad role of culture in placement decisions. The DHHS guidance notes:

> There are situations where cultural needs may be important in placement decisions, such as where a child has specific language needs. However, a public agency's consideration of culture would raise Section 1808 [IEP] issues if the agency used culture as a proxy for race, color or national origin. Thus, while nothing in Section 1808 directly prohibits a public agency from assessing the cultural needs of all children in foster care, Section 1808 would prohibit an agency from using routine cultural assessments in a manner that would circumvent the law's prohibition against the routine consideration of race, color, or national origin [Ref. 35, p 2].

This raises questions about the role of cultural capacity or cultural competence of parents in adoption and foster care decisions. In response to a question regarding whether public agencies may assess the cultural capacity of all foster parents, the DHHS responded in the negative, but seemed to open the door to such assessment, at least of particular parents:

> Race, color and national origin may not routinely be considered in assessing the capacity of particular prospective foster parents to care

for specific children. However, assessment by an agency of the capacity of particular adults to serve as foster parents for specific children is the heart of the placement process, and essential to determining what would be in the best interests of a particular child [Ref. 35, p 2].

The DHHS guidance makes a similar statement regarding cultural competency:

> The term "cultural competency" as we understand it, is not one that would fit in a discussion of adoption and foster placement. However, agencies should, as a matter of good social work practice, examine all the factors that may bear on determining whether a particular placement is in the best interest of a particular child. That may in rare instances involve the consideration of the abilities of prospective parents of one race or ethnicity to care for a child of another race or ethnicity [Ref. 35, p 5].

Such language is obviously far from being lucid and specific. It grants the potential importance of considering race and cultural competence, but cautions against general and routine use of these factors, while contemplating their utility in particular situations.

In considering the best interests of a child who is being placed for adoption, DHHS is suggesting that there could be special circumstances uniquely individualized to the child that require consideration of ethnicity and race of the potential adoptive parents. Presumably this should not be done routinely and should not be seen as serving as a proxy for a consistent and mundane contemplation of ethnicity or race in the adoption context. Undoubtedly, what constitutes special circumstances in the practices of any given adoption agency is likely to be a matter of interpretation. While agencies can readily assert what their routine practices are, much may turn on how vigorously supervised are the claims that special circumstances exist with respect to a particular black child that dictate consideration of ethnicity and race in that child's case. As a practical result, while it appears no one is now allowed to claim that every black child needs a black family, it may still be reasonable and practicable to claim that a black child requires adoption by a black family, as dictated by consideration of the best interests of that child. For example, Kennedy (Ref. 1, p 416) has raised the possibility that an older child might say he or she wanted to be adopted only by a black family. Such a context could indeed make it difficult for the child's wish to be refused outright, without any consideration whatsoever.

Such reasoning is articulated starting from the point of view of the child. Giving consideration to the interests of the potential adoptive parent is another matter. In other words, what should we consider about the adoptive parent's interest in raising black children and the parent's ability to do so? The opinions about this matter remain divided. Kennedy (Ref. 1, pp 416, 434) and Bartholet[42] have proposed that prospective adoptive parents be allowed to state a preference for adopting a child from a particular ethnic group. This is, in their view, permissible race-matching that ultimately serves the best interests of the child. After all, what would be the use of forcing a family to adopt a child they really did not want? In addition, both authors also have argued that state intervention in such racial selectivity in the formation of families would be akin to imposing race-based rules on the creation of married couples. However, Banks[43] has opposed this accommodationist stance, where in practice adoption agencies would simply show prospective adoptive parents only the class of ethnic children the adoptive parent was interested in adopting. Banks thought this merely perpetuated the status quo, as white adoptive parents had little interest in black children. This would result in black children's continuing to languish in out-of-home placements, and their time spent awaiting adoption would remain prolonged.

Kennedy and Bartholet were permissive in their attitude toward the racial selectivity of prospective adoptive parents, respecting parents' choice to construct families as they wish.

There has been and continues to be strong support for the belief that black children belong with black adoptive parents. It is not only the NABSW, which has called for the repeal of the IEP,[13] that has taken this position. For example, in a 1998 letter to the Secretary of the Department of Health and Human Services, a former executive director of the Child Welfare League of America strongly disagreed with the DHHS's interpretation of MEPA/IEP, stating that prohibiting any consideration of race in adoptive and foster care placement decisions contradicts best-practice standards in child welfare:

> CWLA standards for adoption and foster care services clearly state that the best practice requires consideration of race. . . .Children in need of adoption have a right to be placed into a family that reflects their ethnicity or race. . . . These standards—calling for the explicit consideration of race in adoption and foster care placement decisions—reflect the best thinking of child welfare experts from across the country [Ref. 44, p 2].

The CWLA, in its most recent *Standards of Excellence for Adoption Services* (2000), reiterated its belief that race is to be considered in all adoptions and that placement with parents of the same race is the first choice for any child. Other placements should be considered only after a vigorous search for parents of the same race has failed:

> All children deserve to be raised in a family that respects their cultural heritage. . . . If aggressive, ongoing recruitment efforts are unsuccessful in finding families of the same race or culture as the child, other families should be considered to ensure that the child's adoptive placement is not delayed [Ref. 45, p 68].

In its most recent policy statement on foster care and adoption (2003), the National Association of Social Workers also reiterated its position that consideration of race should play a central role in placement decisions:

> Placement decisions should reflect a child's need for continuity, safeguarding the child's right to consistent care and to service arrangements. Agencies must recognize each child's need to retain a significant engagement

with his or her parents and extended family and respect the integrity of each child's ethnicity and cultural heritage [Ref. 46, p 147].

The social work profession stresses the importance of ethnic and cultural sensitivity. An effort to maintain a child's identity and his or her ethnic heritage should prevail in all services and placement actions that involve children in foster care and adoption programs [Ref. 46, p 148].

The placement of choice should be within the child's family of origin, among relatives (kinship placement) who can provide a more stable environment for the child during the period of family crisis. If no such relatives are available, every effort should be made to place a child in the home of foster parents who are similar in racial and ethnic background to the child's own family. The recruitment of foster parents from each relevant racial and ethnic group should be pursued vigorously to meet the needs of children who require placement [Ref. 46, p 150].

Others[47–49] have espoused the view that inracial adoption is the preferred option for a black child because black families inherently possess the competence to raise children with strong black identities and the ability to cope with racism. While questions of cultural competence to raise a black child often arise about prospective white adoptive parents, no such questions are posed about prospective black adoptive parents.[1] The competence of black families to raise black children is regularly referred to as though black families are culturally identical or homogeneous and all are equally competent to raise black children and equip them to live in our society.[1,50] We may all think about black cultural competence as though it is a one-dimensional concept. Indeed, we may all be referring simply to stereotypical indicators of what we think it means to be black. We may be referring to our own personal preferences for the stereotypic activities of black people: involvement in a black church; participation in a community center where black-focused programs are operating; viewing movies with a clearly black theme; reading literature authored by blacks. What is rarely considered is that some black families are drawn to rap music, others to jazz greats, and still others to traditional classical music. Indeed, some families obviously manage to exhibit an interest in all these genres of music. With respect, therefore, to even these stereotyped indicators of what it means to be black, black families vary in the degree of their attachment to the indicators. This is to say that blacks differ in their level of commitment to the salience of black-oriented culture in their individual and family lives. As a result, there is considerable cultural heterogeneity among black families. Such variability may well lead to differences in black families' ways of coping with racism.[50]

To date, the statutory attempts to deal with transracial adoptions have not been considered as spectacularly successful, especially in the case of MEPA. Nevertheless, efforts have been made to limit the routine consideration of race and ethnicity in adoption, with the result that black children may be remaining for shorter periods in undesirable out-of-home placements. (National data are not yet able to demonstrate clear trends.[36,40]) However, DHHS guidance still permits consideration of race and ethnicity in specific cases, with the apparent concession that some black children may need a black family for the realization of the child's best interests.

The burden is on forensic psychiatrists and other mental health professionals who perform adoption evaluations to point out cogently and logically two points: first, whether race is a factor that is relevant in the adoption evaluation; and second, whether there is something unique or particular about that adoption context that requires race to be considered. It will require special argumentation for the evaluator to claim that a particular black child could benefit more from placement with a black family than with a non-black family. As stated earlier, the evidence is clear that black children can do well in transracial placements. The pointed objective, therefore, in future evaluations will be to show that a particular black child has such unique and special needs that he or she deserves particular consideration for placement in a black family. It will be interesting to see whether our forensic colleagues, in striving for objectivity, will consider the factor of race in their evaluations only when something unique about that particular adoption context cries out for race to be considered so that the best-interest-of-the-child standard can be met. It seems clear that forensic professionals must be careful not to state that they routinely consider race in their adoption evaluations unless they intend to argue clinically that race is always relevant. And even then, they should be cautious about not articulating a general preference for inracial over transracial adoptions.

Despite federal statutory attempts to remove race as a controlling factor in adoption and foster care placement decisions, the debate over transracial adoption is not over. Indeed, strains of the debate are evidenced in the statutes and their implementation guidelines and the argument continues among our mental health colleagues. For example, following passage of MEPA and the IEP, a group of adoption experts from different disciplines was assembled by the Stuart Foundation to reconsider the controversies surrounding racial matching and transracial adoption. The Adoption and Race Work Group concluded that "race should not be ignored when making placement decisions and that children's best interests are served—all else being equal—when they are placed with families of the same racial, ethnic, and cultural background as their own" (Ref. 51, p 169). The Work Group decided that the research to date was insufficient, even though research has supported transracial adoption.

The ultimate outcome of the group's deliberations is perhaps the clearest indication of how difficult it is in this debate to meld passion and scholarship. The ongoing debate exemplifies Courtney's conclusion that "those with strongly held views are likely to maintain their convictions: advocates of TRA will continue to believe that the research supports their beliefs, while opponents will contend that TRA is harmful, or that the jury is still out" (Ref. 52, p 753). After two years of work analyzing racial matching and transracial adoption, the Stuart work group acknowledged that thinking about the debate in terms of those who oppose or support transracial or inracial adoptions may get us nowhere. "It may be more productive to regard the issue in terms of assessing, deciding, and documenting when the law allows us to place more or less emphasis on race and racial matching and when good social work practice calls for it" (Ref. 52, p 177). This may be a concession to the notion that, with respect to transracial adoption, cultural stereotypes die hard.

References

1. Kennedy R: Interracial Intimacies: Sex, Marriage, Identity and Adoption. New York: Pantheon Books, 2003

2. For further commentary on the debate, see: Griffith EEH, Duby JL: Recent developments in the transracial adoption debate. Bull Am Acad Psychiatry Law 19:339–50, 1991. Griffith EEH: Forensic and policy implications of the transracial adoption debate. Bull Am Acad Psychiatry Law 23:501–12, 1995

3. Drummond v. Fulton County Department of Family and Children's Services, 563 F.2d 1200 (5th Cir. 1977)

4. Hollinger JH: A Guide to the Multiethnic Placement Act of 1994 as Amended by the Interethnic Adoption Provisions of 1996. National Resource Center on Children and the Law. . . .

5. Simon RJ, Alstein H: Adoption, Race and Identity: From Infancy to Young Adulthood. New Brunswick, NJ: Transaction Publishers, 2002

6. Vroegh KS: Transracial adoptees: developmental status after 17 years. Am J Orthopsychiatry 67:568–75, 1997

7. Griffith EEH, Adams AK: Public policy and transracial adoptions of black children, in Family, Culture and Psychobiology Edited by Sorel E. Ottawa, ON, Canada: Legas Press, 1990, pp 211–33

8. Griffith EEH, Silverman IL: Transracial adoptions and the continuing debate on the racial identity of families, in Racial and Ethnic Identity: Psychological Development and Creative Expression. Edited by Harris HW, Blue HC, Griffith EEH. New York: Routledge, 1995, pp 95–114

9. Burrow AL, Finley GE: Transracial, same-race adoptions, and the need for multiple measures of adolescent adjustment. Am J Orthopsychiatry 74:577–83, 2004

10. National Association of Black Social Workers: Position Statement on Transracial Adoptions. September 1972. . . .

11. Testimony of William T Merritt, President of the National Association of Black Social Workers, Hearings Before the Committee on Labor and Human Resources, United States Senate, 99th Congress, June 25, 1985

12. Institute for Justice: Separate is not equal: striking down state-sanctioned barriers to interracial adoption. . . .

13. National Association of Black Social Workers: Preserving Families of African Ancestry. Washington, DC: NABSW, 2003

14. Farmer v. Farmer, 439 N.YS.2d 584 (N.Y Sup. Ct. 1981)

15. Farrell T, Gregor R, Payne A, *et al:* Adoption § 138 Interethnic Adoption. Am Jur 2d: 138, 2004

16. Zitter JM: Race as a factor in adoption proceedings. ALR 4th 34:167, 2004

17. Marby CR: "Love alone is not enough!" in transracial adoptions: scrutinizing recent statutes, agency policies, and prospective adoptive parents. Wayne Law Rev 42:1347–23, 1996

18. Bussiere A: A Guide to the Multiethnic Placement Act of 1994. ABA Center on Children and the Law. . . .

19. Metzenbaum HM: S. 1224—In Support of the Multiethnic Placement Act of 1993. Duke J Gender Law Policy 2:165–71, 1995

20. 42 U.S.C. § 5115a (1994)

21. Varan R: Desegregating the adoptive family: in support of the Adoption Antidiscrimination Act of 1995. J Marshall Law Rev 30:593–625, 1997

22. Campbell SB: Taking race out of the equation: transracial adoption in 2000. SMU Law Rev 53:1599–626, 2000

23. 42 U.S.C. § 5115a (a) (1)(A)-(B) (1994)

24. 42 U.S.C. § 5115a(a)(2) (1994)

25. Hayashi D: Policy Guidance on the Use of Race, Color or National Origin as Considerations in Adoption and Foster Care Placements. Washington, DC: Office of Civil Rights, Department of Health and Human Services. . . .

26. Adarand Constructors, Inc. v. Pena, 515 U.S. 200 (1995)

27. Palmore v. Sidoti, 466 U.S. 429 (1984)

28. 42 U.S.C. § 622(b)(9)

29. Statement of the Honorable Howard Metzenbaum: Testimony Before the Subcommittee on Human Resources of the House Committee on Ways and Means. Hearing on Interethnic Adoptions, September 15, 1998. . . .

30. 42 U.S.C.S. § 1996 b(l) (2003)

31. 42 U.S.C.S. § 1996 b(2) (2003)

32. 42 U.S.C.S. § 5115a(b) (1994)

33. 42 U.S.C.S. § 674(d) (2003)

34. Hayashi D: Interethnic Adoption Provisions of the Small Business Job Protection Act of 1996. Memorandum, Office for Civil Rights, Department of Health and Human Services. June 4, 1997. . . .

35. Questions and Answers Regarding the Multiethnic Placement Act of 1994 and Section 1808 of the Small Business and Job Protection Act of 1996. Office for Civil Rights, Department of Health and Human Services. . . .

36. Hansen ME, Simon RJ: Transracial Placement in Adoptions With Public Agency Involvement: What Can We Learn From the AFCARS Data? . . .

37. National Data Analysis System. . . .

38. U.S. Department of Health and Human Services, Administration for Children and Families: The AFCARS Report 10. . . .

39. The Multiethnic Placement Act. National Data Analysis System. . . .

40. McFarland MC: Adoption Trends in 2003: A deficiency of Information. National Center for State Courts, 2003. . . .

41. National Adoption Information Clearinghouse: How Many Children Were Adopted in 2000 and 2001? . . .

42. Bartholet E: Private race preferences in family formation. Yale Law J 107:2351–6, 1998

43. Banks RR: The color of desire: fulfilling adoptive parents' racial preferences through discriminatory state action. Yale Law J 107: 875–964, 1998

44. Letter from David Liederman, Former CWLA Executive Director to Donna Shalala, HHS Secretary, December 21, 1998. . . .

45. Child Welfare League of America: Standards of Excellence: Standards of Excellence for Adoption Services (Revised edition). Washington, DC: Child Welfare League of America, Inc., 2000

46. National Association of Social Workers: Foster care and adoption, in Social Work Speaks: National Association of Social Workers Policy Statements, 2003–2006 (ed 6). Washington, DC: NASW Press, 2003, pp 144–51

47. Chimezie A: Transracial adoption of black children. Social Work 20:296–301, 1975

48. Jones E: On transracial adoption of black children. Child Welfare 51:156–64, 1972

49. Bowen JS: Cultural convergences and divergences: the nexus between putative Afro-American family values and the best interests of the child. J Family Law 26:487–531, 1987–1988

50. Griffith EEH: Culture and the debate on adoption of black children by white families, in American Psychiatric Press Review of Psychiatry (vol 14). Edited by Oldham JM, Riba MB. Washington, DC: American Psychiatric Press, 1995, pp 543–64

51. Brooks D, Barth RP, Bussiere A, *et al:* Adoption and race: implementing the Multiethnic Placement Act and the Interethnic Adoption Provisions. Social Work 44:167–78, 1999

52. Courtney ME: The politics and realities of transracial adoption. Child Welfare 76:749–79, 1997

POSTSCRIPT

Should Adoptive Parents Adopt Only within Their Own Racial/Ethnic Group?

As with any discussion of race, culture, or ethnicity, presumptions, perceptions, and biases can all affect how a person forms her or his opinion about this sensitive topic.

Consider your reactions to the readings—would your views change at all if the discussion were not about two parents of the same racial or ethnic background adopting a child from a different background, but rather about a man and a woman of two different racial or ethnic background choosing to procreate together? Why or why not? In doing so, the couple is intentionally creating a child who will have a race or ethnicity that is different from—albeit a combination of—their own. If adopting outside of one's own group is okay—or not okay—with you, what about planned procreation, done within the context of a long-term committed relationship?

Also, consider your own racial or ethnic makeup—how, do you think, does this come into play as you think about your position for or against transracial adoption? If your initial response is "not at all," I encourage you to go back and think again. It is impossible for who we are not to play some kind of role, even a small one, in how we think about issues pertaining to social membership, whether it is race, ethnicity or culture, religion, sexual orientation, gender, or anything else.

Later in this edition, we will discuss adoption by same-sex parents. Keep the thoughts you had in response to this topic in mind as you read the later issue, and see whether your arguments can be applied to a same-sex couple adopting a child who may be heterosexual.

Suggested Readings

H. M. Dalmadge, *Tripping on the Color Line: Black-White Multiracial Families in a Racially Divided World* (Piscataway, NJ: Rutgers University Press, 2000).

H. Fogg-Davis, *Ethics of Transracial Adoption* (Ithaca, NY: Cornell University Press, 2001).

J. Lang, *Transracial Adoptions: An Adoptive Mother's Documentary of Racism, Injustice, & Joy* (Universe, Incorporated, 2002).

S. Patton, *Birthmarks: Transracial Adoption in Contemporary America* (New York: New York University Press, 2000).

R. J. Simon and H. Altstein, *Adoption across Borders: Serving the Children in Transracial and Intercountry Adoption* (Lanham, MD: Rowman & Littlefield Publishers, Inc., 2000).

R. J. Simon and R. Roorda, *In Their Own Voices: Transracial Adoptees Tell Their Stories* (New York: Columbia University Press, 2000).

G. Steinberg and B. Hall, *Inside Transracial Adoption* (Indianapolis: Perspectives Press, Inc., 2000).

J. J. J. Trenka, S. Y. Shin, J. C. Oparah, and S. Y. Shin, eds., *Outsiders Within: Writing on Transracial Adoption* (Cambridge, MA: South End Press, 2006).

ISSUE 3

Should Unhappy Couples Stay Together for the Sake of Their Children?

YES: Sarah Werthan Buttenwieser, from "Because Unhappy Divorces Are Not All Alike," written for *Taking Sides: Family and Personal Relationships* (2009)

NO: Lara Riscol, from "Pursuing Happiness for the Sake of Your Children," written for *Taking Sides: Family and Personal Relationships* (2009)

ISSUE SUMMARY

YES: Sarah Werthan Buttenwieser is a writer and lives in Northampton. She earned her BA at Hampshire College and her MFA from Warren Wilson College. Contributor to many magazines, newspapers, and online publications, she has a blog called "Standing in the Shadows," which can be found at http:// www.valleyadvocate.com/ blogs/home.cfm?uid=92

NO: Lara Riscol is a freelance writer who explores societal conflict surrounding sexuality and family. She has been published in *The Nation, Salon, AlterNet,* and other national media outlets, and is working on a book called *Ten Sex Myths That Screw America.*

In the United States today, 63 percent of children grow up with both biological parents. The highest divorce rates in America are found in Nevada and Arkansas, whereas the lowest divorce rates are found in Washington, DC; Massachusetts; and Pennsylvania. Divorces lead to a division of parenting responsibility as well as financial responsibility; 7.8 million Americans pay approximately $40 billion each year in child and spousal support. Although there has been a slight decline in divorces over recent years, there has been a corresponding decrease in marriage as well.

Couples today are often focused on the well-being of the children in the family. How, then, do we assess the impact of separation on children? Marriage and cohabitation laws vary across the states. These laws are often based on the belief that marriage will provide greater family and societal stability by keeping couples together. Over the last 50 years, American values related to marriage and cohabitation have changed significantly. It was not until 1967, in the case of *Loving v. Virginia,* that the U.S. Supreme Court ruled to strike down state laws forbidding interracial marriages. During more recent times, some courts have struck down state laws prohibiting cohabitation, policies intended to discourage living together out of wedlock.

The history of marriage is one that is diverse and fluid. It can be a story of extraordinary love and joy. It can also be a story of great pain and even abuse. Across time, the meaning of marriage and love has been reconstructed. What was once often a financial arrangement is today something that is much more likely to have a foundation in love. In America today, the economic necessity to remain married, or even to get married in the first place, is less than it has ever been before in this nation's history.

Considering the decrease in marriage, the challenges of separation now extend well beyond the marital relationship. Many unmarried couples with children choose to cohabit. In fact, the frequency of cohabitation with children is four times higher today than it was in 1970. With a sizable number of children born out of wedlock, the concept of parents staying together involves more than just marriage and divorce.

Clearly, concepts of family and matrimony are being reconstructed in American society. Virtually every reader has experience with these changes. It is difficult to grow up in American society today without having the personal experience of divorce or knowing someone well who comes from a divorced family. Additionally, there are many families today where two unmarried parents are raising a child. The same challenges and questions for staying together face them as face married couples.

The focus of debate in this chapter is whether couples should stay together for the sake of their children. If the reader references the Political Ideology Continuum featured in the Introduction to this book, reactionaries or conservatives would be more likely to support staying together for the sake of the children. In contrast, liberals and radicals tend to support ending the relationship if the couple thinks it is best. However, political labels tend to be limited when considering the real-life impact on personal lives. Indeed, many conservatives' marriages end in divorce while their children are young. Meanwhile, a significant number of liberals stay in their relationships for the sake of their children. In fact, the writers in this chapter prove that there are limitations when too rigidly applying the Political Ideology Continuum. Specifically, when taking a close look at Buttenwieser's article, readers will notice a sometimes liberal but often nonpolitical framework for a position that is traditionally associated with conservative values.

When reading, give consideration to how these views shared fit into the Political Ideology Continuum. Apply these views to experiences in your own world, either in your own family or the relationships of others you know well.

YES ↵   Sarah Werthan Buttenwieser

Because Unhappy Divorces Are Not All Alike

We all know that Tolstoy was right: "Happy families are all alike; every unhappy family is unhappy in its own way." And so often, unhappy couples decide that their ticket to happiness—their shot at it—begins with divorce. From divorce, there is possibility—of freedom and of love working out—the next time around. But are kids better served by parents chasing personal happiness or by parents staying together "for the children's sake"? Is divorce better for the kids, too? I say, *probably not* (with a couple of caveats).

The first caveat is critical: If anyone in a family—spouse or child—is being abused, physically or emotionally, then safety is the top priority. That's a stand-alone and nonnegotiable consideration.

The second caveat is also critical. One other stand-alone and nonnegotiable consideration is this: one spouse is homosexual (discovered or admitted to oneself after the marriage took place) and the other is not.

Here's the thing: If a couple chooses to divorce and they have children, the fact is that a healthy divorce with children requires a hell of a lot more work than a healthy marriage with children. How's that, you might wonder; isn't the point of divorce to disintegrate the marital union? Well, it's true that marriage is essentially a handy contract, and thus inherently includes a legal route to its dissolution. Children, however, come with no equally simple and clear documentation. Beyond custody and finances, and including custody and finances for that matter, there's so much shared—or very conspicuously not—between parents. Children cannot be as equally divvied up as furniture or real estate and remain emotionally intact. Children are *the* lifelong commitment parents make. Their welfare goes far beyond roof over head and food in bellies. And parents owe their children far more than those things; they owe them a version of a happy family, even if it's post-divorce and a family apart rather than a family together. Any couple contemplating divorce should think long and hard about whether they can really commit to a good divorce.

I would say to any uniquely unhappy couple to think long and hard about staying together and if at all possible, to do so. Let me add this clarification: If a couple is staying together for the children's sake, when the children fly from the less than totally happy nest, so too may the parents fly as well, without apology.

Whether in a solid, happy marriage, a primarily disappointing marriage, or a divorce, parents need to remain focused upon their children's best interests and they need to remain flexible in thought and in action in order to accommodate their children's needs. That's really the main message here.

So, must parents put their children's happiness above their own? I think, in some significant way, the answer is yes. The ideal is no, because the ideal is that everyone's happiness lines up like stars on a perfect evening, like ducks in a row, like that equation we hope is true, that "happy parent equals happy child." However, by choosing one's own adult happiness, your child's happiness does not inevitably follow. Now, parents cannot protect children from all unhappiness (nor should they; learning to deal with disappointment and unhappiness is a pretty essential part of life, indeed of a happy life). But parents should try to protect their children, and in so doing, parents should—I believe—place their children's happiness on a pedestal.

Essentially, I'm advocating that parents adhere to three considerations: (1) Remain focused upon the child or children; (2) be flexible; and (3) be willing to put your child's happiness first, if necessary.

⚬◈⚬

Full disclosure: I'm a (grown) child of divorce. I'm also contemplating this issue from within a very happy marriage (with four kids). Not that I had a choice about the divorce; although I cannot rewrite history, I think my parents' marriage required dissolution under the first, nonnegotiable caveat of emotional safety, in that my father was cheating—frequently—and for my mother, that breach was not only sad and hurtful, it was humiliating. Given that he wasn't stopping, she had no chance to stand on equal footing with him. Her self-esteem was dashed, and without that, she would not have been much of a person or parent. Although it was a protracted and ambivalent and messy split, her emotional survival really depended upon creating a life independent of my father.

From my experience, I can say that divorce, even if necessary, will likely be hard on the children. If I close my eyes, I can still picture the small, rectangular, flowery suitcase that I carried from my mother's house to my father's house during some critically formative years. The green was a bit olive-y; the reds contained a bit of magenta; the flowers were rendered with a seventies aesthetic. It had a plastic, rectangular handle and a gold-brass clasp—like a journal might—that slid into place. I absolutely hated it. Not the suitcase itself; I hated what it represented. We went back and forth at a dizzying rate. The prevailing wisdom of the time was that young children should not be separated from their mothers for very long, so we had a staccato rhythm that had us at our dad's a night, our mom's for two, our dad's again for some, our mom's, our dad's . . . working out to five days with our father out of every fourteen. Put another way, my sister—nearly three years my junior—and I were in constant motion. Divorce required that we keep track of our schedule and our stuff. More so, divorce—at least the peripatetic version I experienced—made me feel that I lacked something I truly longed for: a home. Read carefully: a home, one home, you know, of the "there's no place like home" variety. Two houses do not equal a home. Two houses are more houses, less home.

⚜

Before I launch into the stay-in-it-for-the-kids argument, let's assume you took the other path—divorce—and wanted to do right by your kids who did not ask you to marry, have them, or divorce. Because what I'm really trying to say here holds whether parents stay together or live apart; it's that parents can sabotage their children's happiness by pitting kids in the middle of seething emotions, warring tactics, and dysfunctional communication. And that's not fair. It is extremely hard to parent like a good crew team, pulling oars in unison. Unison, as in complete agreement, isn't the goal for good parenting. Don't aim for a race; try to get the rowboat across the lake in reasonable fashion.

Working backward: What makes a good divorce? In an ideal world, couples—parents—try hard to make a marriage work. In the less than ideal world, the couple try hard to make a marriage work and they are well-supported by the couples or family therapist they toiled with; they can continue to garner support from that person through the untangling of their shared lives into two more separate lives, with the large overlapping and continuing attachment of their child or children.

What I observe: The "best" divorces—for the kids—are the ones in which the parents remain, gasp, friends (in the best marriages, couples are friends, as well). Really. I have divorced friends who discuss with each other, with similar ease, their children and *their own* dating lives, and who share farm chores or "hang out" with their kids. While there are tensions—if the relationship were perfectly easy, they might still be together—they decided to override them *for the sake of their children.* Some people let the kids stay in one place and they cycle in and out of the family home, for a year or for many years, depending. As with any arrangement, that would not work for all families (nor would friendship). The idea, though, is to keep things comfortable enough that decisions aren't battles and that the adults aren't seething. Without gigantic tensions between the parents, the parents are happier and thus able to present a more unified front about the most important issues and support one another's choices (where they differ) than they could back when less than happily married.

It seems, too, that the best divorces—again, like the best marriages—have room for flexibility. A special out-of-town friend is visiting at the other house? Stay another night. A kid needs something from the other house? We'll get it. If what's needed is the other parent, we'll get the other parent. Flexibility assumes that parents can still talk to one another and thus that the kids are safe to rely upon their parents as a team.

Fast forward through holidays and birthday parties, plays, sports competitions, graduations, and weddings, births, and other family milestones; even if a couple divorce, once they have children, they are either in one another's lives through these events at the very least, or all events—those significant and lesser events—become somewhat more chopped up for the kids, at least (which parent comes to which occasion?).

A divorce that remains open—I think you could call it "warm"—assumes this underlying principle: The adults want the best not only for their children but for one another. That's the underlying principle for a good marriage, too. There's a pattern here: So much that is necessary for a good marriage is also essential for a good divorce. This probably means the best divorces do not emerge from the worst marriages.

⋯⊙⋯

I'm sure there are physics involved in these things, and that there's a point in which the momentum of one's work within a marriage no longer contributes to its forward movement. There must be some place from which a couple can split with enough positive energy left to propel it toward a reasonably happy divorce. Long before reaching that point, though, any unhappy couple—or even more specifically, each member of an unhappy couple—should seek support, through friends, through counseling, and through patience.

Parenting is a very stressful undertaking, after all. Work can be stressful. Growing into adulthood and adult responsibilities is often stressful. With so much to push through in one's life, it's no wonder that two people, each trying to push his or her way along, struggle to negotiate these challenges together. I'd also say, having reached adolescence with one child, that the early years of parenthood—sleepless nights, nap strikes, diapers, crumbs, runny noses, minute-to-minute vigilance—is grueling, wonderful, fun, and grueling. For most of us, these are not the most romantic years, and not the easiest on marriage. It's hard in a culture that's so quick-fix- and instant-gratification-oriented to counsel patience, but I do believe in weathering those periods before trying anew (because, for one thing, anew—as in blended family, for example—is not easy, either). I am not counseling anyone to just give up, though. I'd offer that, if possible, work on finding happiness within the relationship rather than seeking out the next one.

One bottom line (and not the only one) is that kids are innocent creatures, and parents really do owe their children protection and love and as great a foundation as possible. The muse I'd listen to as a parent in a troubled marriage is not Tolstoy, and it's not a romantic poet extolling the virtues of true love. It's Mick Jagger: "You can't always get what you want, but if you try sometimes, you just might find, you get what you need."

Lara Riscol

Pursuing Happiness for the Sake of Your Kids

"**M**aybe it would've been better if I could've kept us together," my mother-in-law blurted after a couple glasses of wine, talking about her ex and the father of my husband. "I just can't help but wonder if I should've done more."

Would've, could've, should've? At some time, we all wonder what might be different "if only . . . ." Especially when it comes to our babies, we want to do what's best. But as Republicans said during the 2008 presidential campaign of their VP pick's teenaged daughter being in "a family way," life happens. And it doesn't always mesh with how we see things ought to be. Despite Bristol Palin's vow to "do the right thing" by choosing motherhood and marrying her baby's dad, she and Levi Johnston split with their baby just weeks old, becoming another notch in America's belt of rising rates of teen pregnancy and record 40 percent of births out of wedlock.

Life happens, often contradicting our box of *shoulds* or the latest stats. Still, after doing the whole "first comes love, then comes marriage, then comes baby in a baby carriage," many unhappy couples face a crossroads they never dreamed of traversing. This is what makes so charged the political—as in today's flush national marriage movement to get or keep parents hitched—and personal decision for unhappy couples who have children of whether to stay together for the sake of their kids.

It depends. Who are you? Where do you come from? What do you value? What's unhappy, and when does it bleed from disillusionment to hopelessness, to your own private hell? How real are your choices?

Trapped in a dead-end relationship in today's turbulent economy, more couples say separation is a non-starter when together means meeting the bare necessities for their family. To a same-sex couple with no rights, a breakup could turn shattering, as in the legal case of a soured Vermont civil union where the "converted straight" Christian ex forbade her ex, lesbian partner—and the non-biological mom of their child—to see their daughter. Or take my gay Mexican cousins who wouldn't dream of causing any disruption to their delicate charge of providing stability to their two adopted sons who were so scarred by mom's abandonment and foster care nightmares, including being locked in a dumpster all day—even if they themselves were miserable.

Clearly, the agonizing conundrum immortalized by the Clash, "Should I Stay or Should I Go," is a luxury for those of us with children but not in dire straits. For some couples, physical, verbal, or emotional abuse is when push comes to shove no matter what. For others, the addiction of a spouse or partner when that spouse or partner is unwilling to seek help is the nonnegotiable in ending a marriage or lifetime commitment. But the line of what would or would not cause a couple to separate is fuzzy for too many, let alone the pundit distinction between unhappiness versus high conflict. So digging through the variable muck of couples on the verge who still want what's *best* for their kids, I say choose the pursuit of happiness—together or not—for self, for child.

The reality is that my mother-in-law had little choice in preserving her marital status. Her husband left for Afghanistan when my husband was just 6 years old. She concludes that he didn't want to be burdened with family. "We had three young children, and he wanted to ride a horse to China!" The reality is that she alone raised the most beautiful, grounded man in the world, and her ex—largely absent for his own boys beyond financial support—is now a routinely engaged grandpa our 6-year-old, hiking together in the Rockies and teaching him to write. And reality is that my conservative parents, married 47 years, badly damaged their children by staying together, and their grandson has asked more than once if they're alive or dead.

Maybe my husband's mom was so wistful that night about not having saved her marriage because our family glow made her so. We're blessed. We married at 30 -ish and welcomed our son eight years later. We both work from home and my sweetie, the primary breadwinner, daily nurtures and plays with our angel, from skiing, to rock climbing, to building a 6-foot autonomous robot, to packing his school lunch each morning, no matter what the client demands. Still smitten at 14 years married, we're a tight parental team in sync, with imbuing respect and gratitude, joy and dignity. My partner's parents somehow staying married wouldn't have recreated our family bliss.

Because of personal experience with defying conventional wisdom that reflexively applauds enduring marriages and decries divorce as failure, I was struck by one salon.com writer's clarity on the Bristol-Levi split. "As someone whose parents were very young, conceived me by accident, and broke up while I was still in utero, I believe sometimes the best thing you can do for your kids is be brave enough to know when to quit," wrote Mary Elizabeth Williams. "I can't speak for any other family's circumstances, but I do know that I never spent a day of my childhood in a home where the people in it didn't love each other. And I wish to God that we as a culture would get over our sanctification of staying together for the kids."

Amen. From my fundamentalist Christian upbringing, I understood intimately that once married under God, there's no exit strategy. End of story—forget happily ever after. Knowing fear, sorrow, and powerlessness, I vowed at 17 to never get married or have kids. My conviction endured for 15 years until I met my sweetie and realized I needn't remain enslaved to traditional notions of wife and mother. My push to shed baggage, build my foundation, and follow the American pursuit of life, liberty, and happiness means I now can offer beauty to my chosen family versus the ugly realism of another repeating cycle.

A range of parents and children of divorce I interviewed are unequivocal that not waiting for "death do us part" was a good thing—such as the married, child-free environmental engineer from Texas, who says of her parents' divorce, "Like rats trapped in a cage, kids feel unhappiness. My parents didn't need to live under the same roof, and we were all better off once they didn't." Or the remarried conservative Christian father of four—his, hers, and theirs— who says he's a much better father now than when living in such toxicity. "Why would I want my kid to model our crap?" says a global pharmaceutical entrepreneur based in Colorado.

Or take the twice-divorced Catholic mother, who says her mom should've left her dad, but, unable to take the plunge, her three kids all suffered tremendously. "I know couples who sleep in separate rooms and stay together for the kids. Those kids are so dysfunctional." "In relationships there should be self-sacrifice or hard work put into it, but not to the level that you hurt yourself or your children," says an Oregon small business owner and union manager, who married versions of her father. "If I were still married to his father, I'd be in survival mode and never have the pleasure of knowing my child and who he is and the man he is becoming," she says of her 17-year-old.

"In a house full of unrest and lack of love, how can anyone thrive?"

Renowned psychologist Joshua Coleman says in his introduction to *The Marriage Makeover: Finding Happiness in Imperfect Harmony*, "Contrary to the wisdom of pop psychology, it is not essential to you or your children's well-being for you to have a great marriage." Over the phone he dismisses today's relationship concept of "soulmate" as harmful. "The notion that if parents are unhappy, then their children must be unhappy is problematic. It depends on what parents are doing with their unhappiness."

Having worked with couples for 30 years, he and other liberal therapists I interviewed decry our consumer culture that sees marriage as a disposable vehicle to romantic fulfillment and personal growth—"a one-stop shopping center for all our needs—that devalues two parents in children's lives." He says research shows children overwhelmingly want their parents together, no matter what.

Though it's hard to weight research that makes such a sweeping claim when it's easy to romanticize a forever family and simpler times, especially if your parents' breakup didn't translate into healthier relationship patterns, I agree divorce shouldn't be the default switch for marital discontent. Often, reasons for divorcing aren't any more mature than reasons for getting married and having kids. I wish adults were bigger grown-ups with affairs of the heart, especially when responsible for trusting little lives.

And I respect Coleman's lifelong work giving couples tools in serenity and due diligence to preserve their family structure for the sake of their kids. Splitting isn't the only option for a broken union. "You don't want to raise your children half-time," says the remarried-with-twins Coleman, whose own divorce tore him from his daughter and stirs him to help others avoid the same loaded terrain. "Hopelessness, like happiness, is a transitory emotion."

But unlike today's powerful cottage industry of books, conservative think-tank studies, and family values groups that insists divorce categorically hurts children and society, Coleman says parents should separate if they can't move past depression, anxiety, martyrdom, hostilities, or otherwise spewing toxic fumes. "Those people should be given support if they can pull off divorce in a mature fashion. You can't stay with each other and consistently humiliate."

America's highest divorce rate in the world is a multifaceted problem. And though I agree our romantic myths too often doom relationships, especially once children enter the picture, most couples about to throw in the towel go far beyond Barbra Streisand-Neil Diamond's "You Don't Bring Me Flowers" ("you don't sing me love songs . . . you hardly talk to me anymore, when I come through the door at the end of a day"). The average couple waits six years too long before seeking help. Keep in mind, too, that as psychology professors Philip A. and Carolyn Pape Cowan, who have worked on strengthening families for 30 years, say, we're not talking about whiny couples, but unresolved conflict that spills over as violence, verbal abuse, aggression, and disgust that proves damaging to children.

"Most couples who have kids are hoping and expecting to stay together. It's that couples don't have much help maintaining a lifelong relationship and have many pressures that divide them," says Philip, who with his wife has done longitudinal intervention research with couples in transition, including couples with a new baby, couples with a first child going to school, and low-income couples with young children. Findings show ordinary parents receiving skilled support experience much less of a decline in marital satisfaction and less of an increase in child behavior problems.

"It is simply a myth repeated over and over again that 'most research shows' divorce is more harmful than sticking it out," says Philip. "It's true that if studies only ask whether the couple is married or divorced, statistics favor children of the married, but that's because they're asking the wrong question." The Cowans say, however, that such studies lack a control group, falsely comparing those divorced to happy intact versus unhappy marriages.

Coleman and others who lean toward "staying together for the sake of the kids" distinguish between unhappy versus high-conflict marriages. The Cowans, however, who like Coleman are members of the Council on Contemporary Families, say their research shows that children experience low-conflict deep freeze the same way as those experiencing fighting or high conflict. It's not family structure that matters, but the quality of the relationship. "Well-functioning marriages are good for kids, and dysfunctional marriages (divorced or intact) pose risks for kids," Philip says.

"Couples should try to make their relationships better whether married or divorced, and that's what's good for kids."

The parents of my son's wonderful best friend made a conscious decision to stay together for their only child. Although not agreeing on much, they're clear on a shared purpose of their son's well-being, which includes living on a farm and no media, pop culture, or consumer corruption. Mostly forgoing adult intimacy, both take full responsibility for their own happiness as they separately pursue deeply spiritual paths.

As child physiologist Lanning says, the goal is to get away from bad and move toward good, to get people's needs met and avoid harm. Though he recommends delaying separation until after a child is three years old to avoid abandonment issues, he says ultimately everyone has a right to a life.

And though polls show that most Americans favor divorce if parents are "very unhappy," polls also show that the vast majority sees a two-parent home as best to raise children. Mary Elizabeth Williams, author of *Gimme Shelter: My Three Years Searching for the American Dream,* found more hostility than not when, after years of therapy, she separated from the father of her two children. She spoke of friends who stopped talking to her, who couldn't deal with such a challenge to their view of the wife they thought they knew. An old college roommate who came out in her mid-30s told her, "You must feel like I felt."

In her salon.com essay, "The Cost Of Leaving: I Can't Afford to Stay in My Marriage—But How Will I Afford to Leave It?," she wrote, "I'm still not convinced that the mere possibility of mutual happiness apart from each other is a noble or practical enough goal. I worry that I am limiting my children's lives, that in addition to all the emotional baggage of not having Mom and Dad across from them at the dinner table, they will have to make all kinds of material sacrifices they didn't sign up for." She concludes, "I saw something that had been wonderful and good and loving for so long becoming twisted into something mercenary and suffocating, dwindling into a joyless splitting of the electricity bill and the groceries. . . . I couldn't save my marriage. . . . But I might be able to save, at least, the rest of our lives."

Most of the 122 readers that responded to her thoughtful vulnerability on this liberal website expressed outrage for her selfishness, including this gem, "Who the *** told you you were a human being?" One typical post read, "You signed on to have children, now you're contemplating screwing them up to save your 'happiness.' Grow up and suck it up. Most intact marriages aren't happy either."

Despite a culture that has supposedly moved from duty bound to a me-first sensibility, compassion doesn't come readily for an individual's pursuit of happiness if it means cracking open the only world a child's ever known.

"I don't give a f*** what others think. Are my kids happy? Am I treating them with respect? Am I treating the man I've been with all these years with regard?" Williams says. "There's a difference between giving kids stability and thinking you can give them permanence. I can't help thinking that if I stayed for all the wrong reasons, it would screw them up. It would certainly screw me up." And as a woman whose child comes first, I just can't see how that would be best for her kids.

POSTSCRIPT

Should Unhappy Couples Stay Together for the Sake of Their Children?

One of the ways to avoid becoming an unhappy couple is to work on entering healthy relationships and work on ensuring that a relationship remains healthy. However, this is a challenging goal, and unhealthy relationships, or even relationships that are just not right, are inevitable. Despite this fact, little time is invested in helping teenagers identify the qualities of a healthy relationship and to further develop the skills of making relationships work.

While an equal relationship is not a guarantee of a happy relationship, it is a critical component. Dating and domestic violence organizations will often cite the following qualities in a healthy relationship: negotiation and fairness, nonthreatening behavior, respect, trust and support, honesty and accountability, responsible parenting, shared responsibility, and economic partnership. In all relationships, including happy ones, it is typically necessary to work on ensuring that both individuals are treated equally and feel valued and respected within their relationship.

If separation is inevitable for a couple, it is critical to examine what can make this experience work as well as possible for the children involved. WebMD lists nine do's and don'ts in helping children with divorce. This advice can also be applied to nonmarital cohabitation as well:

- Don't confide in your children about adult concerns like your disagreements with your spouse or your money worries. Find a friend or counselor to confide in instead.
- Don't criticize your ex. If you have a dispute with your ex-spouse, don't expose your children to your conflicts and frustration.
- Don't quiz your child about the other parent or what goes on at the other parent's house. It's fine to ask general questions about your child's time there, but don't snoop.
- Don't introduce major changes in your child's life if you can help it. Try to keep to your usual family routines and community ties.
- Do continue to parent as you always have. You may feel guilty that your children have to cope with divorce, but it won't help to give them special presents or let them stay up late. They'll feel more secure if you're firm and consistent.
- Do encourage children to call the other parent when they have news or just to talk. Keep the other parent informed about school events and other activities.
- Do learn more about how to help your child cope with divorce.

- Do get help for a child having trouble coping with divorce. A young child may show regressive behavior like excessive clinginess or bedwetting, while an older child may become angry, aggressive, withdrawn, depressed, or have problems in school. A therapist can provide a safe place for your child to express his or her feelings.
- Do seek help if you and your ex can't interact without hostility. A family therapist or professional mediator can help you develop a more friendly communication style—one with fewer negative effects on your children.

How would you assess WebMD's list? What advice is most important to adhere to? What advice is most challenging to adhere to?

While there are differences regarding whether or not unhappy couples should separate for the sake of their children, there are good and bad ways to go about separation not only for the children but also for the former couple. Adhering to these guidelines can help limit the struggles associated with divorce or separation.

ISSUE 4

Should Parents Home-school Their Children?

YES: Chris Jeub, from "Home School" *Focus on the Family* (2006)

NO: Carole Moore, from "Why Home-schooling Isn't Right for Us," Scholastic.com (2006)

ISSUE SUMMARY

YES: Chris Jeub, writer and president of Training Minds Ministries, is a former public school teacher with 11 children, all of whom he and his wife have home-schooled. Naming several famous home-schooled individuals, such as Winston Churchill, Benjamin Franklin, and Florence Nightingale, he argues that the home is the best environment in which to teach children, for social, academic, family strengthening, and religious reasons. Home-schooling, he maintains, frees parents to impart their own values to their children without concern for how these beliefs might clash with what is presented in the public school system.

NO: Carole Moore, a freelance writer, discusses how she weighed the options of home-schooling vs. public schooling and argues that even though home-schooling might offer some benefits to children, in the end, home-schooling provides children a distorted view of the world at large. Children will, she writes, make good decisions and bad decisions as a part of growing up, and whether they are home-schooled or public schooled is not the determining factor in whether they grow up healthy and well-adjusted.

Education for children in the United States was not originally required; it was up to parents to decide whether and how to educate their children, including whether to send them to school. In 1850, however, Massachusetts became the first state to pass a law requiring "schooling" for children. Some of this took place in school buildings, and some was done by parents at home—but requiring that children be educated became more and more commonplace as time went on. And as early as the beginning of the twentieth century, there were proponents who believed that school-based education failed children, and that children were better off educated at home.

According to the Home School Association of California, the home-schooling that took place between then and the 1970s tended to be a bit more clandestine and to be found in rural areas. The early 1980s saw the emergence of home-schooling publications and groups that were associated specifically with conservative and religious (in particular, Christian) ideologies. Fearing the "godlessness" of public school, members of these groups received ongoing support for teaching their children at home. As we moved into the 1990s, home-schooled children in the United States increased, with a federal government survey in 1999 estimating that nearly 900,000 children are being home-schooled in this country, a number that can only have increased over the past eight years.

In your opinion, what are the benefits do children attending school with other children and being taught by a trained teacher receive that they can't receive being taught at home? What are some of the benefits, do you think, of teaching children at home, within the context of one's own family values and without the distractions of other people, noise, and social pressures? There are clear arguments on each side, some of which are expressed in the following selections.

Chris Jeub's reasoning is outlined by topic areas, in which he describes his perceptions—having been a schoolteacher himself—of the ways in which home-schooling benefits children, as well as parents, more than traditional education in a shared classroom environment. Home-schooling, he argues, gives children much more freedom to pursue individual interests, and parents much more leeway to integrate religious messages into their teaching. Carole Moore considered home-schooling very carefully and acknowledges some of the potential strengths, some of which center around safety issues for young people. In the end, however, she chose not to home-school her own child and argues that doing so creates a much more sheltered life for young people, which does not reflect the reality of the world at large.

YES ↵

Chris Jeub

Home School

Introduction

She innocently asked, "So, where do your children go to school?"

Of all casual questions one teacher could ask another, this one always creates butterflies in my stomach.

"Well, uh, my wife and I tutor them," I say. Then I try to think of something to change the subject. But I never think of anything quickly enough.

"Tutor them?" she might say, squinting her nose and ruffling her brows as if I had held a cockroach up to her face. "You mean, you home-school them?"

These situations inevitably lead to an hour-long apologetic on why we educate our kids at home. This should not surprise me. Home schooling is still unusual and a bit radical. Teachers and others in education—or in any field, for that matter—naturally question new, innovative practices.

But home education is not so rare anymore. Twenty years ago, there were roughly 15,000 home-schooled students in the United States. By 1991, the U.S. Department of Education figured there were 350,000 home schools in the U.S. and 40,000 in Canada. Today, estimates stretch over 2 million home schools nationwide.

The world of education has had to adjust to this exploding movement. There are many magazines and newspapers for home schools, numerous home-school curriculum distributors and countless home-school network and contact groups. Why do parents choose to teach their children at home?

Social Reasons

Home-schooling parents believe that children can learn basic life skills—working together, sharing, showing respect for others—without formal classroom experience. The students can develop social graces by being involved in community and church activities.

Pat Farenga, publisher of Growing Without Schooling, a catalog of home-school resources, has written: "Group experiences are a big part of education, and home schoolers have plenty of them.

They write to us about how they form or join writing clubs, book discussion groups, and local home-schooling groups. Home schoolers also take part in school sports teams and music groups [in nearby public schools], as well as in the many public and private group activities our communities provide. These young people can and do experience other people and cultures without going to school."

Our children have many church and neighborhood friends. Our community has a home-school contact group where they often get together for field trips and outings that give our kids more than enough socialization. We have gone on camping trips, facilitated soccer tournaments, traveled to speech and debate tournaments, and coordinated educational classes.

But not all socialization is necessarily good for a child. Certain social plagues like drugs, alcohol, premarital sex, violence, and gangs damage a child's growth and development. A home-school environment frees the child from the increasingly persuasive peer pressure prevalent in many schools.

The positive side of socialization—building respect and communication, getting along with and relating to others—is wonderfully fulfilled in a home-school setting. Behavioral psychologist Urie Bronfenbrenner concluded that "meaningful human contact" is best accomplished with few people.

Academic Reasons

While some parents choose to teach at home to promote positive socialization, others make the decision for academic reasons. Any teacher will agree that the smaller the class size, the more learning takes place. The one-on-one tutoring atmosphere is the healthiest, most productive and most progressive atmosphere for a student's academic success.

Take a look at some famous home-schooled students: Andrew Carnegie, Charlie Chaplin, Agatha Christie, Winston Churchill, Charles Dickens, Thomas Edison, Benjamin Franklin, Florence Nightingale, Woodrow Wilson, and the Wright brothers.

People ask how parents—especially parents with little or no post-secondary education—can teach children every discipline available to public school students. Although I have my degree in English, am I qualified to teach math or science to my kids? My wife has a business administration degree; is she able to teach the language arts? With sufficient information and dedication to the task, we certainly are.

Even if parents do not have an abundance of academic training themselves, they can find solutions to fill the gaps. For example, many home schools will team up with other home schools to exchange skills. I traded skills with another home school family by going to their house once a week to teach English to three of their sons. In return, their mom taught algebra to my two oldest daughters.

Most communities today have enrichment classes students can sign up for much like college students sign up for electives. Here in Colorado Springs, the High Plains Christian Home Educators support group has hired a full-time administrator who coordinates 60 classes for over 200 students. Cooperatives such as this are becoming more popular as home schooling grows.

But education is more than individual academic courses—more than teaching what the teacher knows or training students in a particular skill. It is actually passing on a worldview. Separating the disciplines—as if English had nothing to do with math, and science were unrelated to civics—promotes a fragmented vision of true education.

A wise man once said, "A good teacher teaches himself out of a job." When I taught English in the public schools, I was not merely repeating what I learned in college; I was teaching students to love and passionately engage in the language arts. And when I taught, I integrated all disciplines—history science, social studies, even math—into my lessons. Treating any learning discipline as separate from others misrepresents real life. Real life is interdisciplinary, and home-school instruction lends itself to a cross-disciplinary approach.

Students have the freedom to pursue their interests and strengths. They also receive the attention needed to improve skills in their more difficult learning areas. Pat Farenga explains the benefits of solitary reflection: "Children, like adults, need time to be alone to think, to muse, to read freely, to daydream, to be creative, to form a self independent of the barrage of mass culture." Granting such a time presents a struggle in traditional schools, but home schools allow such freedom.

Family Reasons

Home-school parents see their role as the single most important responsibility they carry. The family helps to build strong minds and healthy personalities.

Along with strengthening the family and setting firm foundations for kids, home-school parents discover some personal pluses. Wendy and I are now much closer to our kids, more in touch with their needs and feelings. Alicia and Alissa attended public school through first- and third-grade, respectively, until I completed college and Wendy returned home from full-time work (to unpaid full-time work).

While Alicia's grades were excellent, she needed to be home for security's sake. Alissa, on the other hand, loved the social contact at school but struggled in basic writing and reading skills. Wendy and I noticed positive changes immediately in Alicia's esteem and Alissa's academics. They both became more confident. I can only accredit this improvement to the loving and affirming atmosphere of the family.

Religious Reasons

It is no secret that public schools have not taken religion seriously. Fear of church and state laws keep some schools from even mentioning the influence of religion in American life. Instead of recognizing religion as part of our culture, civil liberties organizations have fought hard in the courts to make religion illegal in the classroom.

This has been too bad. With the exclusion of religion, many parents have felt compelled to go elsewhere—even to their own homes—to teach their children basic moral and religious truths to provide a well-rounded and liberal education.

Teaching our kids at home frees us to handle religious questions and spiritual training without worrying about public school issues. While some districts restrict the discussion of religious influence in history, literature, and science, home schools can incorporate the impact of spiritual beliefs into all curricula.

Mutual Respect

Home-schooling is being recognized by professional educators and by society as a reasonable educational option for families. Some public schools and private schools have formed alliances with home education groups and have adopted programs that suit the home education lifestyle.

Home-schooling is not so much a rebellion against public schools as it is a choice made on social, academic, family, and religious grounds. As educators and home schoolers get to know one another, we will see that we share many of the same goals for our children.

Carole Moore

Why Home-schooling Isn't Right for Us

I became interested in home-schooling a few years ago when a friend told me how much she loved it. A former cop turned writer, I approached the editor at the newspaper where I worked and convinced him to let me write a series on the topic. I interviewed dozens of home-schooling parents and students. All told, including the work on the series plus my own follow-up research, I spent over a year studying the possibility and debating whether learning at home would be best for my kids—a daughter, then age 10, and a son, age 8.

I learned that many families home-schooled because they didn't like the secular curriculum. Others complained that classes were dumbed down, which caused boredom and restlessness in bright students. A lot chose to remove their kids from what they perceived as an unhealthy social atmosphere. All were convinced they'd done the right thing.

They explained the differences in the types of home-schooling to me: Some followed rigorous religious-based curricula, while others used the same materials as their public schools. A few, called unschoolers, followed nothing but their hearts and let the kids themselves pick what they wanted to study. Many bartered with other parents on subjects requiring special expertise, such as trading French instruction for piano lessons.

The kids' education seemed balanced and academically sound, but most appealing was the bond they shared with their parents. My own daughter, anxious to grow up, nibbled at her ties to me, with her younger brother fast on her heels. I wondered if home-schooling could bring us closer.

Still, as I spoke with home-schooling families from one coast to the other, certain troubling questions bubbled to the surface—many of them familiar to me from my days in law enforcement.

Our community is nowhere near a major city. Still, my children went to elementary school with a girl whose father committed suicide in her presence, kids with both parents in prison, and youngsters who couldn't read, yet knew all the words to filthy rap songs. As a police officer, I often dealt with adolescent drug dealers, pregnant teens, and runaways—kids whose lives were out of control. Certainly the largest majority of them were enrolled in public schools, but not all. Some of the most troubled kids I dealt with came from homes where they'd been very sheltered.

I remember one teenager in particular. After years of alternately being home-schooled and attending a very strict, small, church-based school, she moved to a public school—where she spiraled out of control. She drank. She took drugs. And she had sex. Her parents were appalled; that was not how they'd raised their daughter.

Some would blame the influence of the public school system. They'd say she made friends with bad kids. And they'd be right. But that wasn't the only reason she got into so much trouble. In my opinion, her problem went much deeper: she didn't know how to handle the sudden combination of freedom and exposure to a side of life she'd never personally confronted. Her parents had talked about these things. She'd heard about them in church. But talk alone isn't a substitute for reality and the forbidden often looms sweet and tantalizing by virtue of its mystery.

Academics form only part of the equation when it comes to teaching life skills. Kids need to know how to write a persuasive essay but they also should learn about real life and, in the process, develop the skills they need to cope with it.

My daughter, who now attends a public high school, has made good choices in both her academic and social lives so far. We've talked about sex, but nothing I've ever said to her has provided as strong a deterrent to casual, early sex as the girl in her class with the ever-expanding belly. Nothing makes my daughter more aware of the effects of drugs than seeing burnt-out kids. And nothing brings home the consequences of drinking and driving more than the empty seat of a boy who did just that.

They're tough lessons, but ones she will never forget. Seeing the after-math of negative behavior with her own eyes impresses her much more than simple words or even our own good examples.

Do I like that my children are exposed to life's underbelly? Of course not. I'd much prefer to bring them up in an atmosphere of innocence and trust. But we can't raise our children in carefully controlled environments and expect them to instinctively know how to handle evil. Pretending that it doesn't exist won't make it go away.

Home-schooling would have built a wall around my kids and kept them safe—for a little while. Ultimately, they would have had to go out into the real world. Public school has exposed them to bad influences as well as good ones. I believe they're stronger for having had to make tough choices. And going through it together has strengthened our relationship, making it easier for me to start letting go of their hands.

POSTSCRIPT

Should Parents Home-school Their Children?

There is limited research available about how effective school-based education is as opposed to home-schooling much of which cannot control for the myriad factors that come into play. In schools, factors include teacher experience, school and district leadership, the socioeconomic status of the community in which the school is located, and more. In home-schooling, issues include whether a parent can afford financially to stay home and devote the time and energy necessary to home-school effectively, whether the parent(s) can facilitate a social life for their child(ren) that is comparable to their school-based peers, and whether the child(ren) can still access nonacademic activities such as organized sports, theater, and student clubs.

Ask young people who have been home-schooled whether they liked it, and you will receive a range of responses. A Web site, WikiAnswers.com., asked people to comment on what they felt the longer-term effects of home-schooling were; here is what several people had to say:

"I was home-schooled for lst–9th grade. I attended 10th and part of 11th grade. I took my proficiency test and attended community college on and off for 6 years. My younger brother was home-schooled from 1st–8th grade and attended 9th–12th grade. He did not attend college. Almost all the kids I hung out w/ were home-schooled also. We were both socially impaired by it; our parents made a point to keep us in sports and try to keep us socializing w/ other kids. But it wasn't enough. Most of our friends were also home-schooled too. Some of us turned out OK, some didn't."

"I am 30 years old now, and was home-schooled through junior high and high school. . . . Part of the answer to [the] question is this: Socialization with adults is improved, while socialization with peers is hindered. . . . There are so many social do's and don'ts that are very arbitrary and are pounded home by peer pressure, teasing, cliques, etc."

"I home-schooled through junior high and high school. I agree that there are some social disadvantages to home-schooling, but I think that they can be avoided or changed. I realized when I was 15 that I was awkward around most of my peers and so I worked really hard at changing that. If parents are careful to involve their children in social groups, the kids will be able to learn the necessary skills. I was lucky; there is a big home-schooling community where I live, with many children to interact with. . . . I am now in college and I don't have any qualms about participating in social-groups with other students, whether home-schooled or not. If done right don't think home-schooling interferes a whole lot with social skills" (from http:// www.faqfarm.com/Q/What_are_the_long-term_effects_of_home-schooling).

Do these quotes reinforce your beliefs or change your mind?

Suggested Readings

R. Barfield, *Real-Life Homeschooling: The Stories of 21 Families Who Teach Their Children at Home* (New York: Simon & Schuster Adult Publishing Group, 2002).

S. Bielick, K. Chandler, and S. P. Broughman, *Homeschooling in the United States: 1999* (2001). Accessible online at http://nces.ed.gov/programs/quarterly/Vol_3/3_3/q3-2.asp.

R. H. Davis, "Homeschooling a Personal Choice not a Movement." *Teachers College Record* (May 16, 2005). Accessible online at www.tcrecord.org/Content.asp?ContentID=11876.

P. T. Hill, "Home Schooling and the Future of Public Education." *Peabody Journal of Education* (vol. 75, no. 1&2, 2000: 20–31).

J. Kaufield, *Homeschooling for Dummies* (Hoboken, NJ: John Wiley & Sons, 2001).

C. Lubienski, "Whither the Common Good? A Critique of Home Schooling," *Peabody Journal of Education* (vol. 75, no. 1&2, 2000: 207–232).

C. Lubienski, "A Critical View of Home Education," *Evaluation and Research in Education* (vol. 17, no. 2/3, 2003: 167–178).

R. G. Medlin, "Home Schooling and the Question of Socialization," *Peabody Journal of Education* (vol. 75, no. 1&2, 2000: 107–123).

ISSUE 5

Do Mothers Who Work Outside of the Home Have a Negative Effect on Their Children?

YES: Jeanne Brooks-Gunn, Wen-Jui Han, and Jane Waldfogel, from "Maternal Employment and Child Cognitive Outcomes in the First Three Years of Life: The NICHD Study of Early Child Care," *Child Development* (July/August 2002)

NO: Thomas M. Vander Ven et al., from "Home Alone: The Impact of Maternal Employment on Delinquency," *Social Problems* (May 2001)

ISSUE SUMMARY

YES: Child developmentalists Jeanne Brooks-Gunn, Wen-Jui Han, and Jane Waldfogel assert that their findings show many types of negative effects from maternal employment on the later cognitive and educational outcomes of children.

NO: Professor of sociology and anthropology Thomas M. Vander Ven and his colleagues argue that their studies show that a mother working will have relatively little or no negative influence on the social, emotional, and behavioral functioning of her children.

Over a decade ago, former First Lady Hillary Rodham Clinton made what became an often-quoted statement from an African saying: "It takes a village to raise a child." Although there are those who would agree with this sentiment, the role of the mother—and, in particular, the child's biological mother—has received and continues to receive intense scrutiny. Even with so many members of a family or a "village," a bias exists toward the effects a mother has on her child's development—good, bad, or indifferent.

Since the 1950s, this scrutiny has focused on working women—those who work professional jobs outside of the home in addition to parenting a child or children. As some know, during World War II, thousands of women in the United States felt it was their patriotic duty to fill in for their husbands and other men who were fighting overseas in the war by working in factories and doing other jobs that traditionally had been held by men. The good news is that doing this kept many industries alive in the 1940s. The bad news for many women is that when U.S. soldiers returned stateside, the women were expected to give up their jobs and return home—and many were resistant to doing so.

In the 1960s and 1970s, the women's rights movement gave women much more support for working outside the home—although this meant that many women who did *not* want to work outside of the home, who wanted to be stay-at-home mothers, were criticized for making this choice. Some people are very invested in keeping women at home, for a range of reasons—not the least of which, they say, is that it is vitally important for a woman to be with her child during the child's early years.

Over the past 20 years, the number of women who have entered or returned to the workforce has risen from 31 percent to 59 percent. It is currently estimated that 70 percent of mothers with children who are their dependents are working today. Researchers have been curious about and explored what effects working mothers who place their children in some kind of care—whether in an organized daycare or with a nanny—have on children's early development. The results are inconclusive, although there are strong opinions on both sides of the argument—those who maintain that not having a mother at home with a child, particularly an infant, is harmful, and those who insist it is not. The "harms" range from impaired cognitive development (e.g., challenges in thought and learning processes) to delinquency (e.g., either illegal or antisocial behavior).

There are many claims that a woman who works outside of the home will not bond as effectively with her child, claims that those who disagree would say are simply a conservative viewpoint and unsubstantiated by research. They believe that the push to have women return home rather than remain in the workplace is an ongoing backlash against the feminism that paved the way for it to be acceptable for a woman to be a mother as well as a full-time professional.

What do you think? Is it enough for mothers to be home with their children in the evening and morning hours? What about the other people in their lives—like their partners or spouses or other family members? Is it important for a child to bond with any significant adult, or must that adult be the biological mother?

In the following selections, Jeanne Brooks-Gunn, Wen-Jui Han, and Jane Waldfogel argue that the data show that there are significant long-term negative effects on cognitive development for children whose mothers work outside of the home during the child's earlier years. Conversely, Thomas M. Vander Ven and his colleagues maintain that a child who is born to a mother who works outside of the home is not more likely to exhibit delinquent behavior—unless, at the very basic level, supervision of the child is an issue.

YES ← Jeanne Brooks-Gunn, Wen-Jui Han, and Jane Waldfogel

Maternal Employment and Child Cognitive Outcomes in the First Three Years of Life

The past few decades have seen an unprecedented increase in early maternal employment. The share of mothers who return to work before their child's first birthday doubled from 1976 to 1998, rising from 31% to 59% (Bachu & O'Connell, 1998). Women are now nearly as likely to be working when they have an infant as they are when they have an older preschooler (U.S. Department of Labor, Bureau of Labor Statistics, 2000). Yet, questions remain as to what the impact of this rapid shift toward early maternal employment might be. With increased attention being paid on the part of parents and policy makers to the importance of early experiences for children, establishing what links might exist between early maternal employment and child cognitive outcomes is more important than ever.

The potential impacts of early maternal employment and early child care on child development have been extensively studied (for reviews, see Belsky, 2001; Bornstein, Gist, Hahn, Haynes, & Voigt, 2001; Lamb, 1998; Shonkoff & Phillips, 2000; Weinraub & Jaeger, 1990). Most relevant to the present study are the results from (1) studies using the National Longitudinal Survey of Youth–Child Supplement (NLSY-CS) to examine the effects of early maternal employment on child outcomes, and (2) studies using the National Institute of Child Health and Human Development Study of Early Child Care (NICHD-SECC) to examine the effects of early child care on child development.

A large literature has studied the effects of early maternal employment on children's cognitive outcomes using data on children born to respondents of the NLSY-CS (for a helpful overview of this dataset, see Chase-Lansdale, Mott, Brooks-Gunn, & Phillips, 1991). Because these NLSY-CS studies are reviewed elsewhere (see, e.g., Han, Waldfogel, & Brooks-Gunn, 2001), only a brief overview is provided here. The studies that have examined the effects of first-year maternal employment separately from the effects of employment later in the preschool years have tended to find negative effects of first-year maternal employment on children's later cognitive outcomes (see, e.g., Baydar & Brooks-Gunn, 1991; Belsky & Eggebeen, 1991; Blau & Grossberg, 1992; Han et al., 2001; Hill, Waldfogel, Brooks-Gunn, & Han, 2001; Ruhm, 2000;

Waldfogel, Han, & Brooks-Gunn, 2002; but see also Harvey, 1999). An important limitation of these studies is that none have been able to control for the quality of the child-care settings in which the children of the working mothers are placed. Although the NLSY-CS contains retrospective data on the type of child care in which children are placed, it does not contain any assessment of the quality of that care. A further limitation is that none of the NLSY-CS studies have been able to control for the quality of the mothers' interactions with their children. The NLSY-CS contains no direct assessment of the sensitivity of the mother's care for the child. The NLSY-CS does contain data on one measure of the quality of the home environment, the Home Observation of the Measurement of the Environment (HOME) Scale, but it did not start administering the HOME until 1986, so for many children in the sample (children born in 1983 or earlier) this measure was not administered until they were age 3 or older and therefore no data on the earlier home environment are available.

Thus, when studies using the NLSY-CS have found that early maternal employment has negative effects on children's later cognitive outcomes, the extent to which these effects might be due to the poor quality of child care experienced by these children and/or the poor quality of their home environments has not been clear. Establishing the mechanism by which early maternal employment is linked to poorer cognitive outcomes, and the role played by child care or home environments, is critical to understanding the source of the links and also potential policy remedies.

For this reason, the present study turned to newly available data from the NICHD-SECC. This dataset is extremely well suited to address the limitations of the prior NLSY-CS studies and the questions they could not answer, because it contains data on child-care quality and the quality of children's home environment, as well as detailed data on maternal employment and child outcomes (for an excellent overview of this dataset, see NICHD Early Child Care Research Network, in press). It also contains a rich set of data on child and mother characteristics, including a measure of maternal depression, which is not available in the NLSY-CS. The NICHD-SECC dataset has not been used to study the effects of early maternal employment. It was designed as a study of the effects of early child care on child development and has been used extensively to study that topic (for results on the effects of early child care on children's development at age 54 months, see, e.g., NICHD Early Child Care Research Network, in press). . . .

Methods

Data for the present study were obtained from the NICHD-SECC, a unique longitudinal dataset that has followed 1,364 children from 10 sites around the nation since the time of their birth in 1991. (For a detailed description of the dataset, including how the sample was selected and interviewed, see NICHD Early Child Care Research Network, 2000, in press). It is important to note that some groups were excluded from the sample (e.g., mothers under 18, families who anticipated moving, infants who were multiple births or had health problems or disabilities, mothers who did not speak English, mothers with medical problems or substance-abuse problems, or families living in a dangerous neighborhood). A total of 1,525 families were deemed eligible for inclusion in the study and agreed to be interviewed; of these, 1,364 completed an interview and became participants in the study.

The NICHD-SECC conducted home visits to the children in the sample at 1, 6, 15, 24, and 36 months, supplemented by phone interviews every 3 months to track maternal employment and child-care use. The study also conducted visits to the children's child-care settings at 6, 15, 24, and 36 months (if children were in care more than 10 hr per week). In addition, the children were assessed at home and in the laboratory at ages 15, 24, and 36 months (later visits and assessments were also conducted, but those data have not yet been released for public use). . . .

Discussion

The present study took advantage of a newly available dataset, the NICHD-SECC, to examine the effects of early maternal employment on children's cognitive outcomes at ages 15, 24, and 36 months, controlling for child care (quality and type) and home environment (assessed with the HOME Scale and a rating of maternal sensitivity). The study analyzed three related sets of questions: (1) Is maternal employment in the first year of life associated with negative child cognitive outcomes in the first 3 years of life and, if so, are these effects more pronounced when mothers work full-time? (2) Are there subgroups for whom these effects are more likely to be found? and (3) To what extent are these effects mediated by quality of child care and home environment in the first 3 years of life? These analyses took as their point of departure the literature on the timing of early maternal employment, which has relied mainly on analyses of the NLSY-CS. Because this literature (with important input from developmentalists, economists, and sociologists) has been increasingly concerned with issues of selection bias and model specification, the present study included a large array of covariates that were not available in the NLSY-CS, such as measures of child care and the early home environment. It also drew extensively on the literature on the effects of early child care, in particular the recent work by the NICHD Early Child Care Research Network on the timing and intensity of early child care. The work of the NICHD Early Child Care Research Network was followed closely in terms of how the rich child-care and child-assessment data available in the NICHD-SECC dataset were utilized and also in how the factors that might mediate the effects of early maternal employment on later child outcomes were conceptualized. However, unlike the NICHD Early Child Care Research Network, the focus in the present research was on early maternal employment rather than early child care, reflecting our interest in extending and updating the prior work from the NLSY-CS as well as contributing to the literature regarding women and employment. Thus, we believe the results of the present study complement those of the NICHD Early Child Care Research Network, because it tackled essentially different questions than those addressed in that group's work.

To review the main findings, with regard to the first research question, this study found that children whose mothers worked at all by the ninth month of their life had lower scores on the Bracken [School Readiness Scale] at 36 months than did children whose mothers did not work by that time. The effects of any maternal employment by 1, 3, 6, or 12 months were also negative, although only the effect of maternal employment by 9 months was statistically significant (the effect of employment by 6 months was marginally significant at $p < .10$). This pattern of results suggests that there may be something particularly problematic about having a mother who went to work between 6 and 9 months and/or something unusual about the children whose mothers began employment at this time (which about 5% of the sample did), and the few prior studies that had examined timing effects of maternal employment within the first year (Baydar & Brooks-Gunn, 1991; Han et al., 2001) provided some support for this idea. However, it is also important to note that these results provided some evidence of negative effects of earlier employment as well. Moreover, once the intensity of employment was taken into account, larger negative effects were found, which were statistically significant for employment beginning by 6 months as well as 9 months. Specifically, the negative effect of having a mother who began employment by the ninth month was most pronounced for children whose mothers worked longer hours (30 hr or more per week) in the first year; the same was true for children whose mothers began employment by the sixth month.

The significant negative effects found on the Bracken at 36 months for any employment by the ninth month, and for employment of 30 hr or more per week by the sixth month or ninth month, were consistent with previous findings from the NLSY indicating that early maternal employment had significant negative effects on children's PPVT-R [Peabody Picture Vocabulary Test-Revised] at 36 months (see, e.g., Han et al., 2001; Waldfogel et al., 2002). The fact that these effects were strongest for European American non-Hispanic children was also consistent with prior findings from the NLSY-CS. No effects were found for early maternal employment on children's Bayley MDI [Mental Development Index] scores at 15 or 24 months. The fact that there were negative effects of early maternal employment on the Bracken at 36 months but not on the Bayley MDI in the first 2 years of life is most likely due to the different cognitive competencies tapped in the first 2 years compared with the later preschool years. The cognitive competencies tapped at 15 and 24 months may be less likely to be influenced by environmental events than those tapped later on. Studies that looked at the effects of poverty, for example, found few effects on cognition in the first 18 months of life using the Bayley MDI, but found effects when language and reasoning were assessed in the third year of life (see, e.g., Klebanov et al., 1998). In addition, competencies tapped in the first 2 years of life may not be as predictive of later functioning (McCall, 1983; McCall, Hogarty, & Hurlbut, 1972).

With regard to the second research question, the present results showed that some subgroups of children were more likely to be affected than were others. The effects of early and full-time maternal employment were larger for children whose mothers were rated as insensitive at 6 months (compared with those whose mothers were rated as sensitive), for boys (compared with girls), and for children with married parents (compared with single mothers). The finding on sensitivity was consistent with prior results from the NICHD-SECC (i.e., investigators found that children whose mothers were rated as not sensitive and were in early child care more than 10 hr per week were more vulnerable to attachment problems than were other children in care more than 10 hr per week; NICHD Early Child Care Research Network, 1997). The findings on differences by gender and by parents' marital status were consistent with prior results from the NLSY-CS (see Desai et al., 1989, on gender; Han et al., 2001, on marital status). With regard to the more negative impacts for boys, some analysts have observed that boys are more vulnerable to early stressors in general (see, e.g., Rutter, 1979; Zaslow & Hayes, 1986) and that boys may be more affected by nonmaternal child care as well (for an excellent discussion on this topic, see Bornstein et al., 2001). With regard to the more negative impacts for children of married parents, one possible explanation is that the extra income generated by the mothers' employment may be more valuable, on average, to families headed by unmarried mothers than it is to married-couple families. If so, to the extent that positive income effects offset otherwise negative effects of early maternal employment, this would explain why the observed effects of early maternal employment seemed to be more negative in married-couple families. These differences by subgroup are intriguing and warrant further research, which might shed more light on the mechanisms that underlie the effects of early maternal employment on child cognitive outcomes. In this regard, it would also be useful to conduct research on individual differences in children's vulnerability to early and full-time maternal employment.

With regard to the third research question, it was found that both child care (quality and type) and home environment (as measured by both maternal sensitivity and the HOME Scale) mattered for children's Bracken scores at 36 months. Also found was some evidence that early and full-time maternal employment was negatively associated with the quality of subsequent child care and home environments. Children whose mothers worked more than 30 hr per week by 9 months were in lower quality child-care settings at 36 months than children whose mothers worked fewer hours per week in the first year. Moreover, children whose mothers worked more than 30 hr per week by 9 months had mothers who were rated as providing less sensitive care at 36 months than children whose mothers did not work in the first year (this result is consistent with the finding of the NICHD Early Child Care Research Network, 1999, that children who spent more hours in early child care had mothers who provided less sensitive care at 36 months), although their home environments (as assessed by the HOME Scale) were not significantly different (this latter result may indicate that early and full-time maternal employment may have offsetting effects, reducing some resources due to the limitations on mothers' time available for activities with their children but increasing other resources due to the increased income available to the family through the mothers' employment). However, even after controlling for child care and home environment, a negative association was still found between full-time employment begun in the first 9 months of children's lives and the children's Bracken scores at 36 months.

Because the NICHD-SECC is an observational (rather than experimental) study, it is important to be cautious in interpreting these results. It is possible that mothers' entry into full-time work in the first 9 months did adversely affect their children's cognitive performance at age 3. If this is correct, then one could conclude that encouraging mothers who would otherwise be employed full-time to stay home or work part-time during the first year would produce children with higher Bracken School Readiness scores. However, the NICHD-SECC did not experimentally assign mothers to employment or non-employment, so it is not known from these estimates whether full-time maternal employment by 9 months was causing the lower Bracken School Readiness scores. It is possible that there were pre-existing differences between mothers who did and did not work full-time in the first 9 months of their children's lives that were not observed in the data and that mattered for children's cognitive outcomes. These differences may have had to do with characteristics of the mothers, or with the reasons that they were working. Although selection bias in the present study was controlled for to the extent possible by including a large set of covariates (several of which were not available in prior work with the NLSY-CS), clearly, further work on this topic is needed.

The results of the present study do have some implications for policy. One clear implication is the need to improve the quality of child care that children experience in the first 3 years of life. The results confirm that quality of care matters and also document that, all else equal, children whose mothers work full-time in the first year of life go on to experience poorer quality care in their first 3 years. This lower quality of care in part explains why cognitive outcomes are worse at 36 months for children whose mothers worked full-time rather than part-time in the first year of life. This suggests that improving the quality of child care used by the children of full-time working mothers might help to mitigate the observed negative effects of mothers' early and full-time employment on children's cognitive development. It is important to keep in mind that the present study examined a specific group of children who were infants and toddlers in the early 1990s, and was, therefore, situated in the context of the quality of child care available in the United States during those years. If the quality of that care was, on average, lower than the quality of care that the children's mothers would have offered had they not been working, then that "mismatch" could help to explain the negative relation between early and full-time maternal employment and cognitive development at age 36 months reported in this article. (It was not possible to control for this directly because we did not observe the care that the mother would have provided had she not been working; we only observed the care that she did provide, which may have been affected by the fact that she was employed.) Studies in other countries in which the quality of care is higher have reported different results (see, e.g., Andersson, 1989, 1992, who found that Swedish children who entered child care earlier in the first year of life had better cognitive outcomes than those who entered care later).

A second implication has to do with family leave policy. The United States currently has family leave provisions that guarantee less than 3 months of leave for new mothers as compared with an average of 10 months in the advanced industrialized nations who are members of the Organization for Economic and Community Development (OECD); the United States also differs from peer industrialized nations by not providing paid leave and by having a national law that covers less than half the private sector workforce (Kamerman, 2000; Waldfogel, 2001a). If any maternal employment by the ninth month (and maternal employment of 30 hr or more per week by the sixth or ninth month) has adverse effects on children's cognitive development, this is relevant to consideration of proposals to extend U.S. leave provisions to the 10-month OECD average, provide paid leave, and provide coverage for a larger portion of the U.S. workforce (see, e.g., Kamerman, 2000; Waldfogel, 2001a).

A third implication has to do with family-friendly policies that make it easier for mothers (and fathers) to combine work and family responsibilities. In addition to child care and family leave, such policies include flexible hours, part-time or job-sharing arrangements, and other workplace policies that might reduce the stress or fatigue experienced by working parents with young children. Although, as noted above, the United States lags behind other countries in its provision of family leave, it has at least made some progress in this area with the passage of the Family and Medical Leave Act (FMLA) in 1993. The same is not true of other family-friendly benefits for families with young children. The share of employers who provide such benefits is quite low and has not increased in recent years (Waldfogel, 2001b).

Taken together, the results of the present study illustrate the extent to which the effects of early maternal employment on children's cognitive outcomes depend crucially on both the quality of care that children receive at home and the quality of care that children receive in child care. Good-quality care at home, and good-quality child care, can go a long way toward buffering the negative links between early maternal employment and later child outcomes. Nevertheless, it is concerning that even after controlling for home-environment quality and child-care quality, full-time maternal employment by the ninth month was found to be associated with lower Bracken scores at 36 months. Until there is better understanding with regard to what causes this association and how to buffer it, it would be prudent for policy makers to go slow on measures (such as the recent Temporary Assistance to Needy Families reforms) that would require mothers to enter the labor force (full-time) early in the first year of life and to consider measures (such as proposed FMLA extensions) that would allow more mothers to choose to delay their return to the labor force and/or to work part-time until later in the first year of life. More generally, we concur with the conclusions of the recent National Academy of Sciences expert panel on the science of early development (Shonkoff & Phillips, 2000), that call for policies to improve the quality of child care, extend family leave provisions, and expand other family-friendly policies, to give parents more and better choices about how to balance their work and family responsibilities in the first year of their children's lives.

Thomas M. Vander Ven et al. ➡ **NO**

Home Alone: The Impact of Maternal Employment on Delinquency

In recent decades, American family life has been transformed dramatically. Family scholars debate the causes and consequences of these major changes, routinely clashing over whether family forms are changing for the better (Stacey 1993) or whether our most important social institution is experiencing a moral and functional freefall (Gill 1993; Poponoe 1993).

One of the most profound changes is the unprecedented number of women who have entered the paid workforce since the 1950s. Census data show that female labor force participation rose from approximately 28 percent in 1940 to close to 60 percent in 1992 (U.S. Bureau of Census 1993). This wave of women entering the labor force was accompanied by a large increase in maternal employment. While only 16 percent of all children had working mothers in 1950, close to 70 percent of all mothers with dependent children work today (Coontz 1977). Recent estimates show that over half of those with children less than one year old are employed outside the home and over 60 percent of those with children younger than six are employed (Gerson 1996).

While the mass entrance of women and mothers into the labor market might be regarded as a sign of social progress, many Americans are worried about the trend and have been for some time (Greenberger, Goldberg, Crawford, and Granger 1988). And in what may be seen as part of the "backlash" to feminist political victories (Faludi 1991), politicians, social critics, and parenting "experts" have frequently pointed to the working mother as the cause of many of our social problems.

While supporting empirical evidence is scarce, the political Right charges that feminist philosophies damage the American family by encouraging women to choose work and self-fulfillment over family obligations (Cohen and Katzenstein 1988). Additionally, noted psychologists argue that the neglected child of the working mother may suffer from an attachment disorder, which is widely believed to be a major causal factor in the production of extreme child behavior problems. One pediatrician and TV personality warns that mothers should stay home to raise their infants or risk the disruption of the critical mother-child bonding period: "if he doesn't have that through infancy, it's

From *Social Problems*, vol. 48. no. 2, May 2001, pp. 236–257 (refs. and notes omitted). Copyright © 2001 by University of California Press. Reprinted by permission via Rightslink.

hard to put it in later . . . and these kids that never get it . . . will become difficult in school, they'll never succeed in school, they'll make everybody angry, they'll become delinquents later and eventually they'll become terrorists" (see Eyer 1996:6).

Although there is no shortage of claims that maternal employment causes negative child outcomes, there is little evidence that this is the case. Recent research shows that the children of working mothers are no less attached than other children (Chira 1998) and that they experience no deficits in social, emotional, or behavioral functioning (Harvey 1999; Hoffman 1989; Parcel and Menaghan 1994). While no work and family issue attracts more scholarly attention than the potential effects of maternal employment on children's development (Barling 1990), few researchers have investigated the possible link between working mothers and delinquency.

In this context, we analyze the impact of maternal employment—of kids being left "home alone"—on delinquency using models that include different characteristics of maternal employment (e.g., hours, workplace controls), variations in maternal non-employment (e.g., welfare reliance), and child care arrangements. Our analysis is influenced by the research program of Parcel and Meneghan (1994, 1994a), who investigated the impact of various dimensions of parental work on a range of social, cognitive, and behavioral outcomes. Similarly, we test models that consider the number of hours usually employed, working conditions, and the timing of work. This more comprehensive measurement of maternal work improves upon past research on maternal employment and delinquency, where mother's work was simply divided into "working mother" and "non-working mother" categories (e.g., Glueck and Glueck 1950; Hirschi 1969; Sampson and Laub 1993).

Furthermore, in an attempt to isolate the independent effects of maternal work, we simultaneously consider the impact of maternal resources (i.e., maternal cognitive skills, maternal education, family income), child care arrangements, and marital status. By controlling for maternal resources, we are better able to isolate the independent effects of maternal employment. . . .

⚬◉⚬

Although there is a tremendous body of literature on the effects of maternal employment on child outcomes, studies on the link between maternal work and delinquency are relatively scarce. Early researchers tended to find a small positive effect of maternal employment on delinquency, which they usually assumed was the consequence of low maternal supervision (Glueck and Glueck 1950; Hirschi 1969; Nye 1963; Roy 1963; see also Sampson and Laub 1993). Most contemporary researchers found little or no connection between maternal work status and delinquency (Broidy 1995; Hillman and Sawilowsky 1991; Riege 1972; Wadsworth 1979). Other studies suggest that delinquency is less common among the children of regularly employed mothers (Farnworth 1984; West 1982; Zhao, Cao, and Cao 1997). In some cases, maternal work actually served as insulation against delinquent risks because working mothers effectively raised the family income, thus improving the living conditions of their children. Maternal employment, then, should be considered as an economic dimension of family life and may be most beneficial for children when the alternative is poverty or welfare dependency (Baca-Zinn 1989).

When examined closely, the extant literature on maternal employment and delinquency suggests that working conditions are an important factor that must be included in analytical models. Glueck and Glueck (1950), for example, found that delinquency was highest among the children of occasionally employed mothers. This finding is provocative because occasional or sporadic work may be indicative of secondary labor market employment. Employment in the secondary labor market is often erratic and coercive due to the vulnerability of the low-skilled, uneducated workers at this level (Edwards 1979). Such employment may be criminogenic if coercive workplace experiences negatively shape parenting techniques (Colvin and Pauly 1983).

In a related vein, Roy (1963) found that maternal work was related to delinquency in urban settings, but not in rural areas. This effect, also, may reflect important differences between working conditions in urban vs. rural communities. It may be that maternal work in urban centers and among minority populations is, on average, more likely to be coercive, secondary labor market work (see Haurin 1992). In light of these findings, better measures of maternal employment—including measures for workplace controls and regularity of employment (part-time vs. full-time) are needed. . . .

Methodology
Sample

In the 1960s, the United States Department of Labor hired the Center for Human Resource Research at the Ohio State University to gather longitudinal data on the labor market experiences of four representative target groups among the U.S. population (Fahey 1995). A fifth cohort of men and women between the ages of 14 and 22 was identified in 1979. Known as the National Longitudinal Survey of Youth (NLSY), this project involved a multistaged stratified random sampling that produced 12,686 subjects, 11,404 of whom were interviewed annually about their occupational, educational, familial, and childbearing experiences (see Chase-Landsdale, Mott, Brooks-Gunn, and Phillips 1991, Parcel and Menaghan 1994).

By 1994, 10,042 children of sample mothers were identified to report on their home environment, family relations, and school experiences in addition to taking a number of inventories designed to measure cognitive and socioemotional development. To investigate the relationship between maternal work and delinquency, we conduct our analysis on a sample of 707 adolescents who were between the ages of 12 and 14 in 1994. These children are the offspring of female respondents originally interviewed in 1979. Each of these respondents completed the Child Self-Administered Supplement (CSAS) in 1992 and in 1994. This self-report booklet collects information on a wide range of variables including child-parent interaction, peer relationships, and involvement in various delinquent activities. . . .

Dependent Variable: Delinquency

The 1994 CSAS includes nine highly correlated items that assess involvement in deviant and delinquent acts. Five of the items measure relatively minor to moderate acts of youth deviance: breaking parents' curfew, dishonesty (i.e., lying to a parent), school problems (i.e., parent came to school because of child behavior), truancy, and staying out all night. The other four items involve more serious acts of lawbreaking: alcohol abuse, vandalism (i.e., damaged school property on purpose), store theft, and violence (i.e., hurt some one badly enough to need bandages or a doctor). These nine items are summed to create our scale measuring youth deviance and delinquency (alpha = .78). . . .

Independent Variables

Maternal employment status. A continuous measure of hours usually worked is used in this analysis. In past studies (e.g., Parcel and Menaghan 1994, 1994a), investigators assigned missing values to work-hour variables for non-employed mothers, who were then excluded from the analysis. Thus, these studies focused on the effects of paid maternal employment among a sub-group of working mothers only. Other studies include non-employed mothers but as a dummy category that is used in equations with other dummy variables capturing increasing levels of time commitment to paid employment (e.g., part-time, full-time, overtime) (Baydar and Brooks-Gunn 1991; Muller 1995; Parcel, Nickoll, and Dufur 1996). Measuring maternal work hours via a series of dummy variables is arguably a good strategy for organizing information and for detecting non-linear effects (see Harvey 1999). As Harvey points out, however, this method is problematic because the dummy categories are formed from continuous variables so there are infinite ways one could create categories and arbitrary boundaries between categories are often created. Moreover, using continuous variables does not prevent the detection of nonlinear effects (Harvey 1999). Based on this rationale, we use a continuous measure of hours worked in our primary analysis. . . .

Occupational class.   We measure occupational class in two ways. First, following Parcel and Menaghan (1994), we construct a 19-item-based occupational complexity scale by matching occupational titles reported by NLSY respondents to job descriptions reported in the Dictionary of Occupational Titles. . . .

Our primary measure of workplace conditions is developed based on the work of Mark Colvin (Colvin 2000; Colvin and Pauly 1983). Drawing from Kohn (1977) and Edwards (1979), Colvin links the workplace controls experienced by parents to the patterns and styles of control parents exert upon children. Unskilled, non-unionized employees (Fraction I workers) are subjected to "simple control" in the workplace, which is coercive and alienating. . . .

Skilled laborers and craftspersons (Fraction II workers), who often belong to labor unions, experience greater job security, and are controlled via "technical control"—the machine-paced atmosphere of manufacturing and industrial workplaces where workers are motivated to produce by wage increases and job security. . . .

Fraction III workers are those skilled workers, technicians, salaried professionals, and supervisory staff who experience greater self-direction, job complexity, and job security in the workplace. . . .

Family income. Total family income is included in all models. By employing a family income measure, we are able to assess the impact of the mother's employment experiences while controlling for the total standard of living of each family included in the analysis. Controlling for family income helps to isolate the independent effects of occupational variables in the analysis.

Child care. Following Parcel and Menaghan (1994), we measure child care with a series of dummy variables. Dummy variables representing professional daycare settings, childcare provided by a relative (including fathers), and childcare provided by a non-relative are included. . . .

Discussion

Are the children of working mothers more likely to be delinquent than other children? According to past studies and to the results of our analysis, the answer is a qualified "No." The present study demonstrates that regardless of how this issue is examined, having a working mother has only a small and indirect effect on delinquency. This general pattern holds whether we considered maternal employment in a child's pre-school years or maternal work in adolescence. Furthermore, with the lone exception of maternal supervision, maternal employment has little influence on several known pathways to delinquency.

Like Parcel and Menaghan (1994, 1994a) and more recent findings by Harvey (1999), our research suggests that the widespread concern over the fates of working women and their children is largely unsupported. Rather than being a social problem whose untoward effects can be demonstrated empirically, the maternal employment–delinquency connection is better understood as a socially constructed problem. As a perceived social problem, the dark side of maternal employment has a long history in America. Fueled by scientific data on the link between early family processes and delinquency and by cherished popular beliefs in the sanctity of the "first relationship" (the coupling of mother and child-for decades) politicians and social commentators have pointed to modern trends in female labor participation to explain social problems such as crime. But if the unprecedented entrance of mothers into the paid workforce is related to delinquency, it must be because working mothers fail their children by depriving them of the support and discipline they need. The current study adds to the growing literature that casts doubt on these assumptions.

Our findings suggest other notable conclusions. First, it is maternal and family resources, rather than the characteristics of maternal work, that most influence some well-known pathways to delinquency in our study. Maternal AFQT [Armed Forces Qualifications Test] score, a measure of intellectual resources, affects both parental support and mother-child bonds in early childhood and in adolescence: mothers who draw from greater cognitive resources are more supportive in parenting and raise more securely attached children.

Although the AFQT measures an individual's intellectual capacity, it reflects the subject's developed abilities rather than a biologically assigned aptitude (Menaghan and Parcel 1991). The AFQT score varies with family of origin, geographic region, and years of schooling, which implies that, like maternal education, an AFQT score reflects relative social advantage or disadvantage (Maume, Cancio, and Evans 1996; Menaghan and Parcel 1991). Our findings should be interpreted as further evidence that social disadvantage is reproduced partly through its effect on parent-child relations. Consistent with this theme, our analysis found that an important family resource, family income, exerts a positive influence on warm and responsive parenting in adolescence, while welfare reliance has the opposite effect. This relationship is consistent with past research that identified economic hardship as a strain on family functioning (McLoyd 1990; Siegal 1984).

The most powerful predictors of delinquency in our analysis are maternal supervision, delinquent peer association, and school attachment. Adolescents who are supervised more closely, those who have fewer delinquent peers, and those who are more attached to school show less involvement in delinquency. This result supports a large body of research that identifies these factors as important to the production of antisocial behavioral patterns. We reiterate, here, our discovery that maternal employment had relatively little negative impact on these important pathways to delinquency.

In one instance, however, workplace controls had a small indirect effect on delinquency. Specifically, bureaucratic work controls were negatively related to maternal supervision and, thus, had a slightly positive effect on delinquency. One interpretation of this result is that professional mothers may invest more time in their careers than the average mother does, which may diminish their ability to monitor children. On the other hand, the negative effect of bureaucratic controls on supervision may not reflect a difference in time spent with children so much as a difference in parenting style. The freedom and autonomy experienced by the professional parent may translate into a parenting style characterized by less overt supervision and greater attempts to equip children with internal normative controls.

Conversely, we found that maternal work hours were indirectly related to lower involvement in delinquency, through their positive effect on supervision. Again, although the effect is small, maternal work hours is actually related to greater supervision in our sample. This may be due to the stabilizing influence of steady employment on family life. As Wilson (1996:73) has argued, a job "constitutes a framework for daily behavior and patterns of interaction because it imposes disciplines and regularities" upon a parent.

Furthermore, while no maternal employment variable is related to delinquent peer association, neighborhood disorder is. This finding is consistent with social disorganization theory (Shaw and Mckay 1942): the breakdown of informal neighborhood controls leaves children at a greater risk for being socialized in intimate delinquent peer groups. It is instructive that our analysis points to community breakdown, as it operates through delinquent peer influence, as a cause of delinquency rather than family breakdown related to the absence of a working mother.

Finally, if improving family life is a goal of crime control policy, it would make good sense to aim at addressing the structural factors that limit maternal and family resources and that contribute to community disorder. Our study suggests that policy debates should avoid ideological attacks on working mothers, which portray them as leaving their children "home alone," and concentrate instead on the economic and educational inequalities that weaken families and neighborhoods.

Note

1. Contrary to past work by Parcel and Menaghan (e.g., 1994), we did not find that mother's working conditions had a substantial impact on parenting or home environment. In their research, higher quality work was related to higher quality home environments. Whether we measured mother's working conditions with the occupational complexity scale favored by Parcel and Menaghan or our series of dummy variables representing the three fractions of the working class, we found no such effect. Our contradictory findings may be explained, in part, by the measurement of our pathway variables. As discussed earlier, many of our delinquency pathway variables are one-item measures that lack the sensitivity of the multi-item family and home variables used by Parcel and Menaghan.

POSTSCRIPT

Do Mothers Who Work Outside the Home Have a Negative Effect on Their Children?

In 2009, the cost of living has exploded to the highest levels seen to date. A family who wants more than one bedroom in a New York City apartment can expect to pay $3,600 or more per month in rent—not including gas, electricity, and other utilities. To even move into an apartment in this city, one must be able to put down an additional first and last month's rent, plus a broker's fee, which could be as high as 17 percent of a year's rent. So just to sign a lease, a person would need to have just over $10,000 in cash. This does not begin to cover the other expenses involved in raising a child.

This is just one possible scenario—but it demonstrates that in many family situations where there are two parents, both parents are working not because they think it is an important aspect of their identity or self-esteem, but because they need to in order to survive. The scenario above seems like no big deal to an investment banker on Wall Street, but it would be a huge deal to a sanitation worker and his partner, a city bus driver. For many parents, therefore, working is a necessity that is not up for discussion, not a luxury, a hobby, or part of some political agenda.

In the end, does it help to know the effects that mothers working outside of the home have on the development of their children if there is nothing a mother can do about it? What about the effects of fathers? It is interesting how biased so many cultures are toward mothers and against fathers. Although there is research looking at the effects of a mother's working on her child's development, what about the effects of a father working? What about families in which there are two mothers? Families in which there is no mother, but another adult caregiver?

There is no easy answer to this question, and there are certainly arguments for and against parents working outside of the home if they even have the capacity to entertain that argument. Regardless of how one feels about this issue, however, it is important to avoid judging a parent's decision about whether to work or stay home; guaranteed, whatever decision was made was very likely a difficult one to make!

On the Internet . . .

Sexuality Information and Education Council of the United States

The Sexuality Information and Education Council of the United States is a national organization advocating for comprehensive sexuality education, sexual health programs and services, and sexual rights.

http://www.siecus.org

For Health Freedom

For Health Freedom is a nonpartisan, nonprofit research center, or "think tank," based in Washington, DC. It does not endorse any health care treatment, product, provider, or organization, but rather aims to present the ethical and economic case for strengthening personal health freedom.

http://www.forhealthfreedom.org

Intersex Society of North America

The Intersex Society of North America is devoted to systemic change to end shame, secrecy and unwanted genital surgeries for people born with an anatomy that someone decided is not standard for male or female.

http://www.isna.org/

The American Society for Human Genetics

The American Society of Human Genetics (ASHG), founded in 1948, is the primary professional membership organization for human geneticists in the Americas, including researchers, academicians, clinicians, laboratory practice professionals, genetic counselors, nurses, and others involved in or with special interest in human genetics.

http://www.ashg.org

National Right to Life Committee

The National Right to Life Committee (NRLC) was founded in 1973 in direct response to the United States Supreme Court's decision in the *Roe v. Wade* case, which guaranteed women the right to access abortion in the first trimester of their pregnancy, with some exceptions.

http://www.nrlc.org

Planned Parenthood Federation of America

Planned Parenthood Federation of America is the nation's oldest and largest reproductive health organization, believing in "the fundamental right of each individual, throughout the world, to manage his or her fertility, regardless of the individual's income, marital status, race, ethnicity, sexual orientation, age, national origin, or residence."

http://www.plannedparenthood.org

How Much Control Should Parents Have Over Their Children's Lives?

*M*ost people can recall at one time or another being a child, and *wanting to do something their parent didn't want them to do. When they asked their parent, "Why not?" the answer that came back was, "Because I said so." Parents have an enormous amount of social control over children, from a very young age. This power extends, however, beyond decisions about who a child can play with, how long she or he can stay up at night, or whether she or he can watch television for 10 more minutes. These decisions extend into areas that can affect a child for the rest of her or his life, including health and education. How much say should parents have in these types of decisions? How much say should a young child have? A teenager?*

This section examines four particularly challenging parental decisions:

- Should "Abstinence-Until-Marriage" Be the Only Message for Teens?
- Should Parents Be Able to Select the Biological Sex of Their Children?
- Should Parents Surgically Alter Their Intersex Infants?
- Should Minors Be Required to Get Their Parents' Permission in Order to Obtain an Abortion?

ISSUE 6

Should "Abstinence-Until-Marriage" Be the Only Message for Teens?

YES: Bridget E. Maher, from "Abstinence Until Marriage: The Best Message for Teens," *Family Research Council* (2004)

NO: Sue Alford, from "What's Wrong with Federal Abstinence-Only-Until-Marriage Requirements?" *Transitions* (March 2001)

ISSUE SUMMARY

YES: Bridget E. Maher, an analyst on marriage and family issues at the Family Research Council, argues that far too much funding has gone into programs that teach young people about sexuality and contraception—programs that she asserts are ineffective. She argues that most teens say they and their peers should receive strong messages about abstinence.

NO: Sue Alford, editor and director of public information services at Advocates for Youth, argues that young people are receiving sexuality information and messages from so many sources that it is irresponsible to limit sexuality and other educators to discussing only abstinence. She maintains that the programs taught under the Abstinence Until Marriage funding often provide factually inaccurate information and hyperbolic assertions pertaining to the potential consequences of sexual relationships outside of marriage.

In 1996, President Clinton signed the welfare reform law. Attached to this law was a federal entitlement program allocating $50 million per year over a five-year period to abstinence-only-until-marriage educational programs. This Act specifies that a program is defined as "abstinence-only" education if it:

- Has as its exclusive purpose teaching the social, psychological, and health gains to be realized by abstaining from sexual activity
- Teaches that abstinence from sexual activity outside of marriage is the expected standard for all school-age children
- Teaches that abstinence from sexual activity is the only certain way to avoid out-of-wedlock pregnancy, sexually transmitted diseases, and other associated health problems

- Teaches that a mutually faithful monogamous relationship in the context of marriage is the expected standard of sexual activity
- Teaches that sexual activity outside the context of marriage is likely to have harmful psychological and physical side effects
- Teaches that bearing children out-of-wedlock is likely to have harmful consequences for the child, the child's parents, and society
- Teaches young people how to reject sexual advances and how alcohol and drug use increase vulnerability to sexual advances
- Teaches the importance of attaining self-sufficiency before engaging in sexual activity *(Section 510(b) of Title V of the Social Security Act, P.L. 104-193)*

In order to access these funds, an entity must agree to teach all of these points, not just a few. Failure to do so would result in loss of the funding.

Those who support the teaching of comprehensive sexuality education disagree with the tenets that abstinence-only-until-marriage (AOUM) supports. They present research that demonstrates how comprehensive sexuality education programs help young people to delay the onset of risky sexual behaviors, and to use contraceptives more effectively once they do start engaging in these behaviors. Some argue that AOUM is exclusionary, excluding nonheterosexual youth; is fear- and shame-based, and is wildly out of touch with the reality in which young people are living. They are quick to point out that AOUM supports have yet to provide empirical evidence that their programs "work."

AOUM supporters believe that comprehensive sexuality education programs teach "too much, too soon." They believe strongly that providing information about abstinence, along with safer sex information, confuses teens, and gives them permission to become sexually active when the potential consequences for sexual activity are much more serious.

Take a look at the language of the legislation. The language refers to "sexual activity." What does that include to you? Would you be able to support this if it included some behaviors, but not others? Are there some messages you agree with and not others? If you were an educator, would you be able to teach all eight points?

As you read these selections, think about any sexuality education classes you may have had. Do you think they should have taught you more? Less? Consider, too, young people who are already sexually active. Would abstinence messages work for them? Did a more comprehensive program "fail" them?

In the first selection, Bridget E. Maher outlines some of the negative consequences of teen sex and why abstinence is the only 100-percent-effective option for avoiding those negative consequences. She argues that more comprehensive sexuality education programs, while purporting to teach about abstinence, actually rarely, if ever, do. Sue Alford describes what she perceives to be flaws in the assertions made by AOUM proponents, such as the idea that if educators teach only abstinence, teens won't have sex. Highlighting some of the core values behind sexuality education, she asserts that teaching only about abstinence conflicts with these core values.

YES ← Bridget E. Maher

Abstinence Until Marriage: The Best Message for Teens

The federal government has provided some abstinence-until-marriage funding in recent years, but comprehensive sex education and contraception programs are vastly over-funded in comparison. In 2002, abstinence-until-marriage programs received $102 million, while teen-sex education and contraception programs received at least $427.7 million. In his last budget, President Bush proposed an increase of $33 million for abstinence-until-marriage programs, following upon his campaign promise to try to equalize funding between comprehensive sex education and abstinence programs. This is a good first step, but it still doesn't bring true parity between these programs. It's time for our government to get serious about fulfilling the president's promise to at least level the playing field with regard to funding of the positive and healthy message of abstinence-until-marriage versus that of promoting premarital sex and contraception.

Teens are greatly influenced by the messages they receive about sex in school. Unfortunately, the majority of schools teach "safe sex"—"comprehensive" or so-called "abstinence plus" programs—believing that it's best for kids to have all the information they need about sexuality and to make their own decisions about sex. Abstinence is downplayed while sexual activity and condom use are encouraged in these curriculums, because it's assumed that children are eventually going to have sex. A 2002 report by the Physicians Consortium, which investigated comprehensive sex programs promoted by the Centers for Disease Control, reveals that abstinence is barely mentioned and condom use is clearly advocated in these curriculums.

Abstinence-until-marriage programs, on the other hand, teach young people to save sex for marriage, and their message has been very effective in changing teens' behavior. Today, there are over one-thousand abstinence-until-marriage programs around the United States and one-third of public middle and high schools say that abstinence is "the main message in their sex education." Abstinence organizations do more than just tell teens to say no to unwed sex: they teach young people the skills they need to practice abstinence. Classes cover many topics including self-esteem building, self-control, decision-making, goal-setting, character education, and communication skills.

Choosing the Best, Teen-Aid, Inc., and Operation Keepsake are just a few of the many effective abstinence programs in the U.S. . . .

Teens want to be taught abstinence. Nearly all (93 percent) of teenagers believe that teens should be given a strong message from society to abstain from sex until at least after high school. A 2000 poll found that 64 percent of teen girls surveyed said sexual activity is not acceptable for high-school-age adolescents, even if precautions are taken to prevent pregnancy and sexually transmitted diseases.

Those who do not abstain from sex are likely to experience many negative consequences, both physical and emotional. Aside from the risk of pregnancy, teens have a high risk of contracting a sexually transmitted disease (STD). Each year 3 million teens—25 percent of sexually active teens—are infected with an STD. About 25 percent of all new cases of STDs occur in teenagers; two-thirds of new cases occur in young people age 15–24. Teens who engage in premarital sex are likely to experience fear about pregnancy and STDs, regret, guilt, lowered self-respect, fear of commitment, and depression. . . .

Public opinion polls show that teens value abstinence highly. Nearly all (93 percent of) teenagers believe that teens should be given a strong message from society to abstain from sex until at least after high school.[1] A 2000 poll found that 64 percent of teen girls surveyed said sexual activity is not acceptable for high-school-age adolescents, even if precautions are taken to prevent pregnancy and sexually transmitted diseases.[2] Moreover, teens who have not abstained often regret being sexually active. In 2000, 63 percent of sexually active teens said they wish they had waited longer to become sexually active.[3]

Negative Consequences of Unwed Teen Sex

Teens need to be taught to save sex for marriage, because premarital sex has many negative consequences, both physical and emotional. One of the most obvious outcomes of engaging in premarital sex is having a child outside marriage; today, one-third of all births are out-of-wedlock.[4] Teen birthrates have declined since the early 1990s, but the highest unwed birthrates are among those age 20–24, followed by those 25–29.[5] This shows that many young girls abstain from sex while they are in high school, but not afterward.

Teen unwed childbearing has negative consequences for mothers, children, and society. Unwed teen mothers are likely to live in poverty and be dependent on welfare, and only about 50 percent of them are likely to finish high school while they are adolescents or young adults.[6] Children born to teen mothers are more likely than other children to have lower grades, to leave high school without graduating, to be abused or neglected, to have a child as an unmarried teenager, and to be delinquent.[7] Teen childbearing costs U.S. taxpayers an estimated $7 billion per year in social services and lost tax revenue due to government dependency.[8] The gross annual cost to society of unwed childbearing and its consequences is $29 billion, which includes the administration of welfare and foster care programs, building and maintaining additional prisons, as well as lower education and resultant lost productivity among unwed parents.[9]

Aside from the risk of pregnancy, teens have a high risk of contracting a sexually transmitted disease (STD). Each year 3 million teens—25 percent of sexually active teens—are infected with an STD.[10] About 25 percent of all new cases of STDs occur in teenagers; two-thirds of new cases occur in young people age 15–24.[11]

Chlamydia and gonorrhea are two of the most common curable STDs among sexually active teens. According to the Centers for Disease Control, gonorrhea rates are highest among 15- to 19-year-old females and 20- to 24-year-old males, and more than 5 to 10 percent of teen females are currently infected with chlamydia.[12] If these diseases are untreated, they can lead to pelvic inflammatory disease, infertility, and ectopic pregnancy.[13] Studies have found that up to 15 percent of sexually active teenage women are infected with the human papillomavirus (HPV), an incurable virus that is present in nearly all cervical cancers.[14]

In addition to being at risk for STDs, unwed sexually active teens are likely to experience negative emotional consequences and to become both more promiscuous and less interested in marriage. Teens who engage in premarital sex are likely to experience fear about pregnancy and STDs, regret, guilt, lowered self-respect, fear of commitment, and depression.[15] Also, adolescents who engage in unwed sex at a younger age are much more likely to have multiple sex partners. Among young people between the ages of 15–24 who have had sex before age 18, 75 percent had two or more partners and 45 percent had four or more partners. Among those who first had sex after age 19, just 20 percent had more than one partner and 1 percent had four or more partners.[16] Premarital sex can also cause teens to view marriage less favorably. A 1994 study of college freshmen found that non-virgins with multiple sex partners were more likely to view marriage as difficult and involving a loss of personal freedom and happiness. Virgins were more likely to view marriage as "enjoyable." . . .[17]

"Safe Sex" or "Comprehensive Sex Education" Programs

In addition to the influence of their parents, teens are also affected by the messages on sex and abstinence that they receive in school. Unfortunately, the majority of schools teach "safe sex," "comprehensive," or so-called "abstinence plus" programs, believing that it is best for children to have all the information they need about sexuality and to make their own decisions about sex.[18] Abstinence is downplayed and sexual activity and condom use are encouraged in these curriculums, because it is assumed that kids are eventually going to have sex. A 2002 report by the Physicians Consortium, which investigated comprehensive sex programs promoted by the Centers for Disease Control, reveals that abstinence is barely mentioned and condom use is clearly advocated in these curriculums. Not only do students learn how to obtain condoms, but they also practice putting them on cucumbers or penile models. Masturbation, body massages, bathing together, and fantasizing are listed as "ways to be close" in one curriculum. . . .[19]

The Effectiveness of Abstinence-Until-Marriage Programs

Abstinence-until-marriage programs, on the other hand, teach young people to save sex for marriage, and their message has been very effective in changing teens' behavior. According to the Physicians Resource Council, the drop in teen birth rates during the 1990s was due not to increased contraceptive use among teens, but to sexual abstinence.[20] This correlates with the decrease in sexual activity among unwed teens. In 1988, 51 percent of unwed girls between the ages of 15 and 19 had engaged in sexual intercourse compared to 49 percent in 1995. This decrease also occurred among unwed boys, declining from 60 percent to 55 percent between 1988 and 1995.[21]

Today, there are over one thousand abstinence-until-marriage programs around the United States, and one-third of public middle and high schools say both that abstinence is "the main message in their sex education" and that abstinence is taught as "the only option for young people."[22] Started by non-profit or faith-based groups, these programs teach young people to save sex for marriage. However, abstinence organizations do more than just tell teens to say no to unwed sex: They teach young people the skills they need to practice abstinence. Classes cover many topics including self-esteem building, self-control, decision making, goal setting, character education, and communication skills. Sexually transmitted diseases, the realities of parenthood, and anatomy are also discussed.[23] The effectiveness of birth control may be discussed, but it is neither provided nor promoted in these programs.

Choosing the Best, an abstinence program based in Marietta, Georgia, and started in 1993, has developed curriculum and materials that are used in over two thousand school districts in 48 states. Students in public or private schools are taught abstinence by their teachers, who have been trained by Choosing the Best's staff. Appropriate for 6th through 12th graders, the curriculum teaches students the consequences of premarital sex, the benefits of abstaining until marriage, how to make a virginity pledge, refusal skills, and character education. Choosing the Best involves parents in their children's lessons and teaches them how to teach abstinence to their children. . . .

This abstinence program has contributed to lower teen-pregnancy rates in Georgia. In Columbus, Georgia, Choosing the Best's materials were used in all 8th grades for a period of four years. A study requested by the Georgia State Board of Education to examine the effectiveness of this curriculum found a 38-percent reduction in pregnancies among middle-school students in Muscogee County between 1997 and 1999. Other large school districts that did not implement Choosing the Best's program experienced only a 6-percent reduction in teen pregnancies during those same years.

Teen-Aid, Inc., based in Spokane, Washington, has been promoting abstinence until marriage and character education for over twenty years. This program seeks to teach young people the knowledge and skills they need to make good decisions and to achieve goals. Parent-child communication is a key component of the Teen-Aid curriculum, as parents are involved in every lesson. In 1999–2000, over 41,000 families in public schools, churches, and community organizations used these materials.

A 1999 study conducted by Whitworth College in Spokane, Washington, found many positive results among teens in Edinburg, Texas, who were taught the Teen-Aid curriculum. On the pretest administered to students after the course, 62 percent said "having sex as a teenager would make it harder for them to get a good job or be successful in a career," compared to 71 percent on the post test. When asked if they were less likely to have sexual intercourse before they got married, 47 percent responded yes on the pretest, compared to 54 percent after taking the course. . . .[24]

Operation Keepsake, a Cleveland, Ohio–based abstinence program started in 1988, has its "For Keeps" curriculum in 90 public and private schools in the greater Cleveland area. It is presently taught to over 25,000 students, including those in middle and high school, as well as college [freshmen]. Along with a classroom component, this program also includes peer mentoring, guest speakers, opportunities to make an abstinence pledge, and parental involvement.

Case Western Reserve University evaluated Operation Keepsake's program in 2001, finding that it is having a positive impact on adolescents' beliefs and behavior regarding abstinence. Over nine hundred 7th and 8th graders completed the pretests and post tests. According to the study, the program had "a clear and sustainable impact on abstinence beliefs" because students in the program had "higher abstinence-until-marriage values" at the follow-up survey than did those in the control group, who did not attend the abstinence program. . . .[25]

Virginity pledges are also successful in encouraging sexual abstinence among unwed teens. A 2001 study based on the National Longitudinal Study of Adolescent Health . . . found that teens who take a virginity pledge are 34 percent less likely to have sex before marriage compared to those who do not pledge, even after controlling for factors such as family structure, race, self-esteem, and religiosity. . . .[26]

Conclusion

These are only some of the many abstinence-until-marriage programs in the United States. Their success in changing young people's views and behavior regarding abstinence is due to their telling the truth about sex to young people: that it is meant to be saved for marriage and that it is possible to live a chaste life. Along with this message, they give kids the encouragement and skills they need to save themselves for marriage. . . .

Notes

1. "The Cautious Generation? Teens Tell Us About Sex, Virginity, and 'The Talk,'" National Campaign to Prevent Teen Pregnancy, April 27, 2000.

2. Ibid.

3. "Not Just Another Thing to Do: Teens Talk About Sex, Regret and the Influence of Their Parents," National Campaign to Prevent Teen Pregnancy, June 30, 2000.

4. Joyce A. Martin et al., *Births: Final Data for 2001,* National Vital Statistics Reports 51, December 18, 2002, National Center for Health Statistics, Table C.

5. Bridget Maher, *The Family Portrait: A Compilation of Data, Research and Public Opinion on the Family,* Family Research Council, 2002, p. 73, 162.

6. Rebecca Maynard, *Kids Having Kids: Economic and Social Consequences of Teen Pregnancy,* The Urban Institute, 1997, p. 2–5.

7. Ibid, p. 205–229, 257–281, Judith Levine, Harold Pollack and Maureen E. Comfort, "Academic and Behavioral Outcomes Among the Children of Young Mothers," *Journal of Marriage and Family* 63 (May 2001): 355–369 and Amy Conseur et al., "Maternal and Perinatal Risk Factors for Later Delinquency," *Pediatrics* 99 (June 1997): 785–790.

8. Rebecca A. Maynard, ed., *Kids Having Kids: A Robin Hood Foundation Special Report on the Costs of Adolescent Childbearing,* The Robin Hood Foundation, 1996, p. 19.

9. Ibid, pp. 20, 88–91.

10. The Alan Guttmacher Institute, "Teen Sex and Pregnancy," *Facts in Brief,* 1999.

11. Linda L. Alexander, ed., et al., "Sexually Transmitted Diseases in America: How Many Cases and at What Cost?" The Kaiser Family Foundation, December 1998, 8.

12. Centers for Disease Control, *Tracking the Hidden Epidemics: Trends in the United States 2000,* 4.

13. The Alan Guttmacher Institute, "Teen Sex and Pregnancy."

14. Ibid. See also the Kaiser Family Foundation, "HPV (Human Papillomavirus) and Cervical Cancer," *Fact Sheet,* July 2001.

15. Tom and Judy Lickona, *Sex, Love and You,* (Notre Dame: Ave Maria Press, 1994), 62–77.

16. Centers for Disease Control, "Current Trends: Premarital Sexual Experience Among Adolescent Women—United States, 1970–1988," *Morbidity and Mortality Weekly Report* 39 (January 4, 1991): 929–932. . . .

17. Connie J. Salts et al., "Attitudes Toward Marriage and Premarital Sexual Activity of College Freshmen," *Adolescence* 29 (Winter 1994): 775–779.

18. Tina Hoff and Liberty Greene et al., "Sex Education in America: A Series of National Surveys of Students, Parents, Teachers, and Principals," Kaiser Family Foundation, September 2000, 16.

19. The Physicians Consortium, "Sexual Messages in Government-Promoted Programs and Today's Youth Culture," April 2002.

20. Cheryl Wetzstein, "Drop in Teen Birthrates Attributed to Abstinence," *The Washington Times,* February 11, 1999, A6.

21. Joyce C. Abma and Freya L. Sonenstein, *Sexual Activity and Contraceptive Practices Among Teenagers in the United States, 1988 and 1995,* Series 23: Data from the National Survey of Family Growth, National Center for Health Statistics, Washington, D.C., April 2001, Table 1.

22. Tina Hoff and Liberty Greene et al., "Sex Education in America: A Series of National Surveys of Students, Parents, Teachers, and Principals," 14.

23. Barbara Devaney et al., "The Evaluation of Abstinence Education Programs Funded Under Title V Section 510: Interim Report," Mathematica Policy Research, Inc., April 2002, 14.

24. Raja S. Tanas, "Report on the Teen-Aid Abstinence-Education Program Fifth-Year Evaluation 1998–1999, Whitworth College, Spokane, WA, July 1999.

25. Elaine Borawski et al., "Evaluation of the Teen Pregnancy Prevention Programs Funded Through the Wellness Block Grant (1999–2000), Case Western Reserve University, March 23, 2001.

26. Peter S. Bearman and Hannah Bruckner, "Promising the Future: Virginity Pledges and First Intercourse," *American Journal of Sociology* 106 (January 2001): 859–912.

Sue Alford

→ **NO**

What's Wrong with Federal Abstinence-Only-Until-Marriage Requirements?

1. Federally mandated abstinence-only-until-marriage education jeopardizes the health and lives of young people by denying them information that can prevent unintended pregnancy and infection with sexually transmitted diseases (STDs), including HIV.

Youth need to know *how* to avoid the potential negative consequences of sexual intercourse. Every young person urgently needs accurate information about contraception and condoms. STDs and unintended pregnancy are extremely common. Consider the following:

- One-half of all new HIV infections occur among people ages 25 or less.[1]
- One-quarter of all new HIV infections occur among people under age 21.[1]
- The human papilloma virus—genital warts—is so common that experts believe three-quarters of *all* the sexually active people in the world have been infected with it.[2]
- In the 1995 National Survey of Family Growth, 28 percent of *all* women reported having had an unintended birth, and one-fifth of those women reported the birth as unwanted.[3]

2. Proponents of abstinence-only-until-marriage education assume that, if young people do not learn about contraception, they will not have sexual intercourse.

Throughout human history, people have had sexual intercourse. Often, people had to rely on contraceptive methods that were not very effective in preventing unwanted pregnancy because highly effective methods were not available. Today, highly effective methods are available to help people avoid unintended pregnancy, if they know about these methods and have access to them.

The fact that some U.S. teens report oral and/or anal intercourse while considering themselves "virgin" underscores the fact that lacking information does not prevent young people from having sexual intercourse. It may, however, prevent them from making healthy choices about sexuality.

From *Transitions*, vol. 12, no. 3, March 2001, pp. 3, 13–14. Copyright © 2001 by Advocates for Youth. Reprinted by permission.

Research shows that teenagers who receive contraceptive education in the same year that they choose to become sexually active are
about 70 percent more likely to use contraceptive methods (including condoms) and more than twice as likely to use oral contraceptives as those not exposed to contraceptive education. That is why
the National Institutes of Health recommends that, although sexual
abstinence is a desirable objective, programs must include instruction
in safer sex behavior, including condom use.[3]

2. **Proponents of abstinence-only-until-marriage education assume
that, if young people do not learn about contraception, they will not have
sexual intercourse.** Throughout human history, people have had sexual intercourse. Often, people had to rely on contraceptive methods that were not very
effective in preventing unwanted pregnancy because highly effective methods
were not available. Today, highly effective methods are available to help people
avoid unintended pregnancy, if they know about these methods and have
access to them. The fact that some U.S. teens report oral and/or anal intercourse while considering themselves 'virgins' underscores the fact that lacking
information does not prevent young people from having sexual intercourse. It
may, however, prevent them from making healthy choices about sexuality.

However, abstinence-only-until-marriage education goes further. It *dis-
courages* young people from using contraception. It encourages young people
to believe that condoms and modern methods of contraception—such as birth
control pills, injectable contraception, implants, and the intra-uterine device
(IUD)—are far less effective than they, in fact, are. Many abstinence-only-until-
marriage programs discuss modern methods of contraception *only* in terms of
failure rates (often exaggerated) and censor information about their correct use
and effectiveness. Thus, many of these programs keep young people in igno-
rance of the very facts that would encourage them to protect themselves when
they eventually become sexually active.

- By age 18, about 71 percent of U.S. youth have had sexual intercourse.[6]
- One recent study found that, by the age of 18, more than 75 percent of
  young people have engaged in various heavy petting behaviors.[7]
- Another study found that 25 to 50 percent of teens report having had
  oral sex.[8]
- A third study focusing exclusively on adolescent "virgins" (defined in
  the study as teens who had not experienced vaginal intercourse) found
  that nearly one-third of respondents reported having participated in
  masturbation with a partner. In the same study, 10 percent of teens
  who defined themselves as virgins had participated in oral intercourse
  and 1 percent had participated in anal intercourse.[9]
- Data from a nationally representative survey indicate that, in 1999,
  49.9 percent of all high school students have had sexual intercourse.

The percentage rises by grade level—38.6 percent of ninth graders have had sexual intercourse compared with 64.9 percent of seniors.[10]

- By the time young people reach age 20, about 80 percent of males and 76 percent of females have had sexual intercourse.[6]

Federal legislation does not define sexual activity when it requires sexuality education classes to teach that *abstinence from sexual activity outside of marriage is the expected standard for all school-age children.*[5] Holding hands, kissing, deep kissing, petting—each of these may be included in the disapproved category of 'sexual activity' in individual abstinence-only-until-marriage curricula. At the same time, these curricula provide no guidance about very real behaviors that put youth at risk—oral and/or anal intercourse. Yet, the reality is that almost every American teenager today has had at least one romantic relationship by the time he/she is 18, and most young people have engaged in "sexual activity." In fact, most American parents would be likely to worry about the well-being of a teenager who went through his/her entire teenage years without even one romantic relationship.

If these young people have had abstinence-only-until-marriage sexuality education, they will not know how to protect themselves and their partners from STDs and unintended pregnancy. In the end, research demonstrates that, instead of keeping young people from having sexual intercourse, abstinence-only-until-marriage programs merely keep them from having *safer* sexual intercourse.

3. Federal requirements assume that young people will not learn about sexuality from any source other than sexuality education classes.

Legislators and congressional staff do not acknowledge the world in which young people live. If they did, they would hesitate to push, as an *ultimate value,* something that is actually a *norm.* Moreover, it is a norm that is contradicted by nearly every television show, movie, popular magazine, song, or music video that young people see, hear, or read. This legislatively mandated norm is contrary to the behaviors of many adults (including members of Congress and their staff) that young people hear or read about. Young people learn about sexual expression nearly everywhere they turn in society. They do not learn about responsible, mutually respectful, sexual expression in many places—and certainly not in abstinence-only-until-marriage programs. In such programs, they learn instead about a single congressionally mandated standard that is at odds with nearly every other sexuality message they receive from the society in which they live.

Federally funded abstinence-only-until-marriage programs must teach that *a mutually faithful monogamous relationship in the context of marriage is the expected standard of human sexual activity.*[5] By contrast, a recent nationally representative poll found that 56 percent of U.S. adults agreed that sexual intercourse should be reserved for a committed, monogamous relationship, *whether or not* people are married. Only 33 percent believed that sexual intercourse should occur only within marriage.[11] Moreover, 93 percent of men and 79 percent of women report having had sexual intercourse prior to marriage.[12]

The refusal of abstinence-only-until-marriage proponents to accept the reality of young people's lives also creates a vacuum for youth as to what constitutes "sexual activity." Indications are emerging that many youth engage in unprotected sexual activities, such as oral and anal intercourse, while avoiding coitus (vaginal-penile intercourse). Abstinence-only-until-marriage programs cannot even address these issues because they shrink from discussing specific sexual behaviors.

Comprehensive sexuality education rests upon certain core values, including

- Every individual has dignity and self-worth.
- Sexual relationships should never be coercive or exploitative.
- All sexual decisions have effects or consequences.
- Every person has the right and the obligation to make responsible sexual choices.[13]

Comprehensive sexuality education encourages young people to complement these values with the values of their parents, society, and culture and to define and clarify the values by which they can live fulfilling, satisfying lives. Comprehensive sexuality education does not supplant family values; rather, it provides young people with the tools to integrate these values into their lives and daily decision-making.

When a teen identifies his/her own values and the norms that are consonant with those values, that teen is unlikely to fall back on doing something because "everyone is doing it" or to engage in activities just to circumvent an arbitrarily imposed standard. A vital developmental component in comprehensive sexuality education is encouraging teens to think and teaching them *how* to think rather than *what* to think. It is a component that is missing in abstinence-only-until-marriage education, which prefers to tell teens *what* to think and distrusts their ability to think for themselves.

4. Federally funded abstinence-only-until-marriage education too often provides young people with medically inaccurate information.

Abstinence-only-until-marriage education provides no information about contraception and condoms other than failure rates. Moreover, it often provides inaccurate information, even about failure rates. In asserting that condoms are ineffective, abstinence-only-until-marriage education usually relies on studies that either pre-date today's highly effective latex condoms or that are not scientific in their research and analysis and, thus, are not published in peer-reviewed journals. Another tactic of proponents of abstinence-only-until-marriage education is to link condom failure with sexually transmitted infections that may occur in areas of the body that condoms do not cover and, thus, *could not* protect. For example, recent abstinence-only arguments against using the condom to prevent HIV infection have focused on the inability of condoms to protect one totally against human papillomavirus (genital warts).[14] What opponents fail to mention, however, is that genital warts may be transmitted across portions of the anatomy (such as the upper thighs, lower abdomen, the groin, testicles, labia majora, or anus) that condoms do not cover.[2]

Second, federal guidelines require abstinence-only-until-marriage programs to teach that *sexual activity outside of marriage is likely to have harmful psychological and physical effects.*[5] First, consider the assertion about harmful physical effects of sexual activity outside of marriage. Certainly, sexual intercourse can result in unplanned pregnancy, STDs, and/or HIV infection. But these results are not necessarily "likely." Moreover, these negative physical consequences are not linked to marital status and may occur inside or outside of marriage. It is precisely to protect against negative physical consequences that comprehensive sexuality education provides young people with information on contraception and condoms.

Next, consider the claim about negative psychological effects of sexual activity outside of marriage. There is simply no sound public health or medical data to support this assertion. Most people have had sexual relations prior to marriage with absolutely no negative psychological consequences. For example, one study reported that, when premarital sexual intercourse is satisfying, it positively affects the relationship for both males and females.[15] The largest study ever undertaken of adult sexual behavior found that more than 90 percent of men and more than 70 percent of women recall wanting their first sexual intercourse to happen when it did.[12]

Sexuality is a natural, normal, and positive component of life. Comprehensive sexuality education can address issues in a positive, helpful manner that encourages young people to make responsible and safe decisions that protect their sexual health.

Notes

1. Centers for Disease Control & Prevention. *Young People at Risk for HIV Infection.* Atlanta, GA: The Centers, 1999.

2. Marr L. *Sexually Transmitted Diseases: A Physician Tells You What You Need to Know.* Baltimore, MD: Johns Hopkins University Press, 1998.

3. National Center for Health Statistics. *Fertility, Family Planning, and Women's Health: New Data from the 1995 National Survey of Family Growth* [Vital & Health Statistics, Series 23, no. 19]. Hyattsville, MD: U.S. Dept. of Health & Human Services, 1997.

4. National Institutes of Health. *Consensus Development Conference Statement.* Rockville, MD: The Institutes, 1997.

5. Welfare Reform Act of 1996 (P.L. 104-193).

6. Alan Guttmacher Institute. *Sex and America's Teenagers.* New York: The Institute, 1994.

7. Roper Starch Worldwide. *Teens Talk about Sex: Adolescent Sexuality in the '90s.* New York: SIECUS, 1994.

8. Newcomer S, Udry J. Oral sex in an adolescent population. *Archives of Sexual Behavior* 1985; 14:41–46.

9. Schuster MA, Bell RM, Kanouse DE. The sexual practices of adolescent virgins: genital sexual activities of high school students who have never had vaginal intercourse. *American Journal of Public Health* 1996; 86: 1570–1576.

10. Centers for Disease Control & Prevention. Youth risk behavior survey, American high school students, 1999. *Morbidity & Mortality Weekly Report* 2000; 49(SS-5).

11. Hickman-Brown Public Opinion Research. *Overview of Research Results.* Report to Advocates for Youth and SIECUS. Washington, DC: Advocates for Youth, 1999.

12. Michael RT *et al. Sex in America: A Definitive Survey.* Boston: Little, Brown & Company, 1994.

13. National Guidelines Task Force. *Guidelines for Comprehensive Sexuality Education.* New York: SIECUS, 1994.

14. Wetzstein C. Unfamiliar sexual disease has no cure, spreads easily. *Washington Times,* Nov. 7, 2000.

15. Cate RM, et al. Sexual intercourse and relationship development. *Family Relations* 1993 (April):162.

POSTSCRIPT

Should "Abstinence-Until-Marriage" Be the Only Message for Teens?

In the United States, there are just under 900,000 teenage pregnancies every year. There are also as many as 4 million new cases of sexually transmitted infections (STIs) among the same age group annually in the United States.

Each side of the sexuality debate is working with what they consider to be a logical presumption. For AOUM proponents, the surest way to avoid an unintended pregnancy or STI is to not do anything sexually until a committed, monogamous relationship—which, to them, is only acceptable within the context of marriage. If people do not engage in the behaviors, they cannot be exposed to the negatives. Because AOUM supporters also believe that marriage is a commitment that is accompanied by a promise of monogamy, or sexual exclusivity, it is, for them, the only appropriate choice for teens.

For comprehensive sexuality education proponents, the logic is that sexual exploration is a normal part of adolescents' development. They believe that the "just say no" approach to sexual behaviors is as unrealistic as it is unhealthy. Rooted in education, social learning, and health belief theories, comprehensive sexuality education programs believe that youth can make wise decisions about their sexual health if given the proper information.

Society will likely never reach consensus on this issue. With AOUM program funding budgeted at an all-time high of $241.5 million for fiscal year 2007, and federal legislation supporting comprehensive sexuality education sitting stagnant in the house for nearly two years, however, the debate will certainly continue.

ISSUE 7

Should Parents Be Able to Select the Biological Sex of Their Children?

YES: John A. Robertson, from "Preconception Gender Selection," *The American Journal of Bioethics* (Winter 2001)

NO: Norman Daniels, from "It Isn't Just the Sex . . ."; **Carson Strong**, from "Can't You Control Your Children?"; **Mary B. Mahowald**, from "Reverse Sexism? Not to Worry"; and **Mark V. Sauer**, from "Preconception Sex Selection: A Commentary," *The American Journal of Bioethics* (Winter 2001)

ISSUE SUMMARY

YES: Professor John A. Robertson of the University of Texas at Austin's School of Law argues that preconception gender selection of infants in utero for medical purposes should be allowed, and that insufficient data exist to demonstrate that any clear harm exists in allowing parents to do so.

NO: Norman Daniels (Tufts University), Carson Strong (University of Tennessee), Mary B. Mahowald (University of Chicago), and Mark V. Sauer (Columbia University) each take one aspect of Professor Robertson's arguments to demonstrate why preconception gender selection should not be allowed, including, for example, the socioeconomic status inequity that allowing such a procedure, which likely would not be covered by health insurance, would create.

Biological sex is determined by the male sperm cell, hundreds of millions of which are present in semen after ejaculation. Among the chromosomes a sperm cell will contain is a sex chromosome, typically either an "X" chromosome or a "Y" chromosome. A woman's egg carries an "X" sex chromosome. When a sperm and egg meet, they create the chromosomal blueprint for the sex of the offspring of any resulting pregnancy. If a man's sperm carries an "X" chromosome, the resulting "XX" baby will typically be a girl. If it carries a "Y" chromosome, the baby will typically be a boy. A man can also contain no sex chromosome, resulting in an "XO" baby, an extra "Y" chromosome, resulting in an "XYY" baby, and other chromosomal differences that result in a range of biological sex variations, usually referred to as "intersex" conditions. These will be discussed more in Issue 8.

Many people believe that parents cannot currently select the biological sex of their children, yet preconception sex selection (PSS) has existed since the 1970s. Technology has been developed to determine whether a sperm carries either an X or a Y chromosome and implant it accordingly, although doing so is not always reliable, is an invasive medical procedure, and can be quite costly. It has been understood, therefore, that cases involving PSS have typically been done to avoid some kind of genetic disease that can be linked to either an X or a Y chromosome. Like with any medical procedure, however, there are those who may be able to access it for other reasons, and those who may not.

Why else would some people choose to select the sex of their children? For some families, having a first-born child who is either a boy or a girl is important to them. Others who know they plan to only have one child may have a strong preference for that child to be a boy or a girl. Still others may have a child of one sex and wish to ensure gender variance within their family. Regardless of the reason, one concern that medical practitioners have is about parents who carry an erroneous preconceived notion that having a girl or boy will yield a particular type of child. What happens, for example, when a father who wants a son so that he can teach him sports, only to end up with a son who hates sports? When a mother who looks forward to taking her daughter shopping and for manicures ends up with a daughter who is an outstanding athlete? Adults, they say, connect sex (biology) to gender (how we express our biological sex), when the manners in which a child expresses her or his femaleness or maleness can be quite broad.

In the following selections, John Robertson outlines the arguments both for and against PSS, concluding that there is no ethical reason against it. He disagrees that a potential exists for the practice of PSS for gender variance in the family alone could potentially be sexist, and argues that, as long as parents keep the well-being of their child(ren) in mind, they should be able to have the family composition they wish. Norman Daniels, Carson Strong, Mary B. Mahowald, and Mark V. Sauer each address one aspect of Robertson's arguments to demonstrate why preconception gender selection should not be allowed unless there is a medically necessary reason to do so.

YES ↵   John A. Robertson

Preconception Gender Selection

Advances in genetics and reproductive technology present prospective parents with an increasing number of choices about the genetic makeup of their children. Those choices now involve the use of carrier and prenatal screening techniques to avoid the birth of children with serious genetic disease, but techniques to choose nonmedical characteristics will eventually be available. One nonmedical characteristic that may soon be within reach is the selection of offspring gender by preconception gender selection (PGS).

Gender selection through prenatal diagnosis and abortion has existed since the 1970s. More recently preimplantation sexing of embryos for transfer has been developed (Tarin and Handyside 1993; The Ethics Committee of the American Society of Reproductive Medicine 1999). Yet prenatal or preimplantation methods of gender selection are unattractive because they require abortion or a costly intrusive cycle of in vitro fertilization (IVF) and embryo discard. Attempts to separate X- and Y-bearing sperm for preconception gender selection by sperm swim-up or swim-through techniques have not shown consistent X- and Y-sperm cell separation or success in producing offspring of the desired gender.

The use of flow cytometry to separate X- and Y-bearing sperm may turn out to be a much more reliable method of enriching sperm populations for insemination. Laser beams passed across a flowing array of specially dyed sperm can separate most of the 2.8% heavier X- from Y-bearing sperm, thus producing an X-enriched sperm sample for insemination. Flow cytometry has been used successfully in over 400 sex selections in rabbit, swine, ovine, and bovine species, including successive generations in swine and rabbit (Fugger et al. 1998). A human pregnancy was reported in 1995 (Levinson, Keyvanfar, and Wu 1995).

The United States Department of Agriculture (USDA), which holds a patent on the flow cytometry separation process, has licensed the Genetics and IVF Institute in Fairfax, Virginia, to study the safety and efficacy of the technique for medical and "family balancing" reasons in an institutional review board-approved clinical trial. In 1998 researchers at the Institute reported a 92.9% success rate for selection of females in 27 patients, with most fertilizations occurring after intrauterine insemination (Fugger et al. 1998). A lower success rate (72%) was reported for male selection.

At this early stage of development much more research is needed to establish the high degree of safety and efficacy of flow cytometry methods of PGS that would justify widespread use. With only one published study of outcomes to date, it is too soon to say whether the 92% success rate in determining female gender will hold for other patients, much less that male selection will reach that level of efficacy. Animal safety data have shown no adverse effect of the dye or laser used in the technique on offspring, but that is no substitute for more extensive human studies (Vidal et al. 1999). In addition, if flow cytometry instruments are to be used for sperm separation purposes, they may be classified as medical devices that require U.S. Food and Drug Administration (FDA) approval. Finally, the holder of the process patent—the USDA—will have to agree to license the process for human uses.

If further research establishes that flow cytometry is a safe and effective technique for both male and female PGS, and regulatory and licensing barriers are overcome, then a couple wishing to choose the gender of their child would need only provide a sperm sample and undergo one or more cycles of intrauterine insemination with separated sperm. A clinic or physician that offers assisted reproductive technologies (ART) and invests in the flow cytometry equipment could run the separation and prepare the X- or Y-enriched sperm for insemination, or it could have the sperm processed by a clinic or firm that has made that investment. Flow cytometry separation would not be as cheap and easy as determining gender by taking a pill before intercourse, but it would be within reach of most couples who have gender preferences in offspring.

Demand for Preconception Gender Selection

Unknown at present is the number of people who have offspring gender preferences robust enough to incur the costs and inconvenience of PGS. Although polls have often shown a preference for firstborn males, they have not shown that a large number of couples would be willing to forego coital conception in order to select the gender of their children. If PGS proves to be safe and effective, however, it may be sought by two groups of persons with gender preferences.

One group would seek PGS in order to have a child of a gender different from that of a previous child or children. A preference for gender variety in offspring would be strongest in families that have already had several children of one gender. They may want an additional child only if they can be sure that it will be of the gender opposite to their existing children. Couples who wish to have only two children might use PGS for the second child to ensure that they have one child of each gender. If social preferences for two-child families remain strong, some families may use PGS to choose the gender of the second child.

A second group of PGS users would be those persons who have strong preferences for the gender of the first child. The most likely candidates here are persons with strong religious or cultural beliefs about the role or importance of children with a particular gender. Some Asian cultures have belief systems that strongly prefer that the firstborn child be a male. In some cases the preference reflects religious beliefs or traditions that require a firstborn son to perform funeral rituals to assure his parents' entrance into heaven (for a discussion of son preferences in India and China, see Macklin 1999, 148–151). In others it simply reflects a deeply embedded social preference for males over females. The first-child preference will be all the stronger if a one-child-per-family policy is in effect, as occurred for a while in China (Greenlagh and Li 1995, 627). While the demand for PGS for firstborn children is likely to be strongest in those countries, there has been a sizable migration of those groups to the United States, Canada, and Europe. Until they are more fully assimilated, immigrant groups in Western countries may retain the same gender preferences that they would have held in their homelands.

Other persons with strong gender preferences for firstborn children would be those who prize the different rearing or relational experiences they think they would have with children of a particular gender. They may place special value on having their firstborn be male or female because of personal experiences or beliefs. Numerous scenarios are likely here, from the father who very much wants a son because of a desire to provide his child with what he lacked growing up, to the woman who wants a girl because of the special closeness that she thinks she will have with a daughter (Belkin 1999).

The Ethical Dilemma of Preconception Gender Selection

The prospect of preconception gender selection appears to pose the conflict—long present in other bioethical issues—between individual desires and the larger common good. Acceding to individual desires about the makeup of children seems to be required by individual autonomy. Yet doing so leads to the risk that children will be treated as vehicles of parental satisfaction rather than as ends in themselves, and could accelerate the trend toward negative and even positive selection of offspring characteristics. The dilemma of reconciling procreative liberty with the welfare of offspring and families will only intensify as genetic technology is further integrated with assisted reproduction and couples seek greater control over the genes of offspring.

Arguments for Preconception Gender Selection

The strongest argument for preconception gender selection is that it serves the needs of couples who have strong preferences about the gender of their offspring and would not reproduce unless they could realize those preferences. Because of the importance of reproduction in an individual's life, the freedom to make reproductive decisions has long been recognized as a fundamental moral and legal right that should not be denied to a person unless exercise of that right would cause significant harm to others (Robertson 1994, 2–12). A corollary of this right, which is now reflected in carrier and prenatal screening practices to prevent the birth of children with genetic disease, is that prospective parents have the right to obtain preconception or prenatal information about the genetic characteristics of offspring, so that they may decide in a particular case whether or not to reproduce (Robertson 1996, 124–135).

Although offspring gender is not a genetic disease, a couple's willingness to reproduce might well depend on the gender of expected offspring. Some couples with one or more children of a particular gender might refuse to reproduce if they cannot use PGS to provide gender variety in their offspring or to have additional children of the same gender (E. F. Fugger, personal communication to author). In other cases they might have such strong rearing preferences for their firstborn child that they might choose not to reproduce at all if they cannot choose that child's gender. Few persons contemplating reproduction may fall into either group; but for persons who strongly hold those preferences, the ability to choose gender may determine whether they reproduce.

In cases where the gender of offspring is essential to a couple's decision to reproduce, the freedom to choose offspring gender would arguably be part of their procreative liberty (Robertson 1996, 434). Since respect for a right is not dependent on the number of persons asserting the right, they should be free to use a technique essential to their reproductive decision unless the technique would cause the serious harm to others that overcomes the strong presumption that exists against government interference in reproductive choice. Until there is a substantial basis for thinking that a particular use of PGS would cause such harms, couples should be free to use the technique in constituting their families. The right they claim is a right against government restriction or prohibition of PGS. It is not a claim that society or insurers are obligated to fund PGS or that particular physicians must provide it.

Arguments Against Preconception Gender Selection

There are several arguments against preconception gender selection. Although such methods do not harm embryos and fetuses or intrude on a woman's body as *prenatal* gender selection does, they do raise other important issues. One concern is the potential of such techniques to increase or reinforce sexism, either by allowing more males to be produced as first or later children, or by paying greater attention to gender itself. A second concern is the welfare of children born as a result of PGS whose parents may expect them to act in certain gender specific ways when the technique succeeds, but who may be disappointed if the technique fails. A third concern is societal. Widely practiced, PGS could lead to sex-ratio imbalances, as have occurred in some parts of India and China due to female infanticide, gender-driven abortions, and a one-child-per-family policy (Sen 1990). Finally, the spread of PGS would be another incremental step in the growing technologization of reproduction and genetic control of offspring. While each step alone may appear to be justified, together they could constitute a threat to the values of care and concern that have traditionally informed norms of parenting and the rearing of children.

Evaluation of Ethical and Social Issues

Concerns about sex-ratio imbalances, welfare of offspring, and technologizing reproduction may be less central to debates over PGS than whether such practices would be sexist or contribute to sexism. If the number of persons choosing PGS is small, or the technique is used solely for offspring gender variety, sex-ratio imbalances should not be a problem. If use patterns did produce drastic changes in sex ratios, self-correcting or regulatory mechanisms might come into play For example, an over-abundance of males would mean fewer females to marry, which would make being male less desirable, and provide incentives to increase the number of female births. Alternatively, laws or policies that required providers of PGS to select for males and females in equal numbers would prevent such imbalances. A serious threat of a sex-ratio imbalance would surely constitute the compelling harm necessary to justify limits on reproductive choice.

It may also be difficult to show that children born after PGS were harmed by use of the technique. Parents who use PGS may indeed have specific gender role expectations of their children, but so will parents who have a child of a preferred gender through coitus. Children born with the desired gender after PGS will presumably be wanted and loved by the parents who sought this technique. Parents who choose PGS should be informed of the risk that the technique will not succeed, and counseled about what steps they will take if a child of the undesired gender is born. If they commit themselves in advance to the well-being of the child, whatever its gender, the risk to children should be slight. However, it is possible that some couples will abort if the fetus is of the undesired gender. PGS might thus inadvertently increase the number of gender-selection abortions.

Finally, technological assistance in reproduction is now so prevalent and entrenched that a ban on PGS would probably have little effect on the use of genetic and reproductive technologies in other situations. With some form of prenatal screening of fetuses occurring in over 80% of United States pregnancies, genetic selection by negative exclusion is already well-installed in contemporary reproductive practice. Although there are valid concerns about whether positive forms of selection, including nonmedical genetic alteration of offspring genes, should also occur, drawing the line at all uses of PGS will not stop the larger social and technological forces that lead parents to use genetic knowledge to have healthy, wanted offspring. If a particular technique can be justified on its own terms, it should not be barred because of speculation of a slippery slope toward genetic engineering of offspring traits (for an analysis of the slippery-slope problem with genetic selection, see Robertson 1994, 162–165).

Is Gender Selection Inherently Sexist?

A central ethical concern with PGS is the effect of such practices on women, who in most societies have been subject to disadvantage and discrimination because of their gender. Some ethicists have argued that any attention to gender, male or female, is per se sexist, and should be discouraged, regardless of whether one can show actual harmful consequences for women (see Grubb and Walsh 1994; and Wertz and Fletcher 1989). Others have argued that there are real differences between male and female children that affect parental rearing experiences and thus legitimate nonsexist reasons for some couples to prefer to rear a girl rather than a boy or vice versa, either as a single child or after they have had a child of the opposite gender.

To assess whether PGS is sexist we must first be clear about what we mean by sexism. *The Compact OED* (1991, 1727) defines sexism as "the assumption that one sex is superior to the other and the resultant discrimination practised against members of the supposed inferior sex, especially by men against women." By this definition, sexism is wrong because it denies the essential moral, legal, and political equality between men and women. Under this definition, if a practice is not motivated by judgments or evaluations that one gender is superior to the other, or does not lead to discrimination against one gender, it is not sexist.

Professor Mary Mahowald, an American bioethicist writing from an egalitarian feminist perspective, makes the same point with a consequentialist twist:

> Selection of either males or females is justifiable on medical grounds and *morally defensible in other situations* [emphasis added] so long as the intention and the consequences of the practice are not sexist. Sexist intentions are those based on the notion that one sex is inferior to the other; sexist consequences are those that disadvantage or advantage one sex vis-à-vis the other. (2000, 121)

In my view, the *OED* definition, modified by Mahowald's attention to consequences, is a persuasive account of the concept of sexism. If that account is correct, then not all attention to the biologic, social, cultural, or psychological differences between the sexes would necessarily be sexist or disadvantage females. That is, one could recognize that males and females have different experiences and identities because of their gender, and have a preference for rearing a child of one gender over another, without disadvantaging the dispreferred gender or denying it the equal rights, opportunities, or value as a person that constitutes sexism.

If this conjecture is correct, it would follow that some uses of PGS would clearly be sexist, while others would clearly not be. It would be sexist to use PGS to produce males because of a parental belief that males are superior to females. It would be nonsexist to use PGS to produce a girl because of a parental recognition that the experience of having and rearing a girl will be different than having a boy. In the latter case, PGS would not rest on a notion of the greater superiority of one gender over another, nor, if it occurred in countries that legally recognize the equal rights of women, would it likely contribute to sexism or further disadvantage women. As Christine Overall, a British feminist bioethicist, has put it, "sexual similarity or sexual complementarity are morally acceptable reasons for wanting a child of a certain sex" (1987, 27; quoted in Mahowald 2000, 117).

Psychological research seems to support this position. It has long been established that there are differences between boys and girls in a variety of domains, such as (but not limited to) aggression, activity, toy preference, psychopathology and spatial ability (Maccoby and Jacklin 1974; Gilligan 1980; Kimura and Hampson 1994; Feingold 1994; Collaer and Hines 1995; and Halpern 1997). Whether these differences are primarily inborn or learned, they are facts that might rationally lead people to prefer rearing a child of one gender rather than another, particularly if one has already had one or more children of a particular gender. Indeed, Supreme Court Justice Ruth Bader Ginsburg, a noted activist for women's rights before her appointment to the Supreme Court, in her opinion striking down a male-only admissions policy at the Virginia Military Institute (*United States v. Virginia*, 116 S. Ct. 2264 [1996]), noted that:

> Physical differences between men and women . . . are enduring: "[T]he two sexes are not fungible; a community made up exclusively of one [sex] is different from a community composed of both." . . . "Inherent differences" between men and women, we have come to appreciate, remain cause for celebration.

Some persons will strongly disagree with this account of sexism and argue that any attention to gender difference is inherently sexist because perceptions of gender difference are themselves rooted in sexist stereotypes. They would argue that any offspring gender preference is necessarily sexist because it values gender difference and thus reinforces sexism by accepting the gendered stereotypes that have systematically harmed women (Grubb and Walsh 1994; and Wertz and Fletcher 1989, 21). According to them, a couple with three boys who use PGS to have a girl are likely to be acting on the basis of deeply engrained stereotypes that harm women. Similarly, a couple's wish to have only a girl might contribute to unjustified gender discrimination against both men and women, even if the couple especially valued females and would insist that their daughter receive every benefit and opportunity accorded males.

Resolution of this controversy depends ultimately on one's view of what constitutes sexism and what actions are likely to harm women. Although any recognition of gender difference must be treated cautiously, I submit that recognizing and preferring one type of childrearing experience over the other can occur without disadvantaging women generally or denying them equal rights and respect. On this view, sexism arises not from the recognition or acceptance of difference, but from unjustified reactions to it. Given the biological and psychological differences between male and female children, parents with a child of one gender might without being sexist prefer that their next child be of the opposite gender. Similarly, some parents might also prefer that their firstborn or only child be of a particular gender because they desire a specific rearing and companionship experience.

If it is correct that using PGS for offspring diversity is sexist, then those who deny that biological gender differences exist, or who assume that any recognition of them always reinforces sexism or disadvantages women, will not have carried the burden of showing that a couple's use of PGS for offspring gender variety or other nonintentionally sexist uses is so harmful to women that it justifies restricting procreative choice. Until a clearer ethical argument emerges, or there is stronger empirical evidence that most choices to select the gender of offspring would be harmful, policies to prohibit or condemn as unethical all uses of nonmedically indicated PGS would not be justified.

The matter is further complicated by the need to respect a woman's autonomy in determining whether a practice is sexist. If a woman is freely choosing to engage in gender selection, even gender-selection abortion, she is exercising procreative autonomy. One might argue in response that the woman choosing PGS or abortion for gender selection is not freely choosing if her actions are influenced by strong cultural mores that prefer males over females. Others, however, would argue that the straighter path to equal rights is to respect female reproductive autonomy whenever it is exercised, even if particular exercises of autonomy are strongly influenced by the sexist norms of her community (Mahowald 2000, 188).

Public Policy and Preconception Gender Selection

Because of the newness of PGS and uncertainties about its effects, the best societal approach would, of course, be to proceed slowly, first requiring extensive studies of safety and efficacy, and then at first only permitting PGS for increasing the gender variety of offspring in particular families. Only after the demographic and other effects of PGS for gender variety have been found acceptable should PGS be available for firstborn children.

However, given the close connection between parental gender preferences for offspring and reproductive choice, public policies that bar all non-medical uses of PGS or that restrict it to choosing gender variety in offspring alone could be found unconstitutional or illegal. If there are physical, social, and cultural differences between girls and boys that affect the rearing or relational experiences of parents, individuals and couples would have the right to implement those preferences as part of their fundamental procreative liberty. The risk that exercising rights of procreative liberty would hurt offspring or women—or contribute to sexism generally—is too speculative and uncertain to justify infringement of those rights.

The claim of a right to choose offspring gender is clearest in the case of PGS for gender variety. If flow cytometry or other methods of PGS are found to be safe and effective, there would be no compelling reason to ban or restrict their nonmedical use by persons seeking gender variety in the children they rear. Couples with one child or several children of a particular gender might, without being sexist or disadvantaging a particular gender, prefer to have an additional child of the opposite gender. ART clinics should be free to proceed with PGS for offspring variety in cases where couples are aware of the risk of failure and have undergone counseling that indicates that they will accept and love children of the dispreferred gender if PGS fails. Clinics providing PGS should also ask couples to participate in research to track and assess the effects of PGS on children and families.

The use of PGS to determine the gender of firstborn children is a more complicated question. The choice to have one's first or only child be female has the least risk of being sexist, because it is privileging or giving first place to females, who have traditionally been disfavored. The use of PGS to select firstborn males is more problematic because of the greater risk that this choice reflects sexist notions that males are more highly valued. It is also more likely to entrench male dominance. The danger of sexism is probably highest in those ethnic communities that place a high premium on male offspring, but it could exist independently of those settings.

Yet restricting PGS to offspring gender variety and firstborn females may be difficult to justify. Given that individuals could prefer to have a boy rather than a girl because of the relational and rearing experiences he will provide, just as they might prefer a girl for those reasons, it might be difficult to show that all preferences for firstborn males are sexist. Nor could one easily distinguish firstborn male preferences when the couple demanding them is of a particular ethnic origin. Although the risk that firstborn male preferences would be sexist is greatest if the PGS occurred in a country in which those beliefs prevailed, the chance that PGS would contribute to societal sexism lessens greatly if the child is reared in a country that legally protects the equal status of women and men.

If prohibitions on some or all nonmedical uses of PGS could not be justified and might even be unconstitutional, regulation would have to take different forms. One form would be to deny public or private insurance funding of PGS procedures, which would mean that only those willing to pay out-of-pocket would utilize them. Another form would be for the physicians who control access to PGS techniques to take steps to assure that it is used wisely. If they comply with laws banning discrimination, physician organizations or ART clinics could set guidelines concerning access to PGS. They might, for example, limit its use to offspring gender variety or firstborn female preferences only. As a condition of providing services, they might also require that any couple or individual seeking PGS receive counseling about the risks of failure and commit to rear a child even if its gender is other than that sought through PGS. Although such guidelines would not have the force of statutory law, they could affect the eligibility of ART clinics to list their ART success rates in national registries and could help define the standard of care in malpractice cases.

Conclusion

The successful development of flow cytometry separation of X- and Y-bearing sperm would make safe, effective, and relatively inexpensive means of nonmedical preconception gender selection available for selecting female, if not also male, offspring. The nonmedical use of PGS raises important ethical, legal, and social issues, including the charge that any or most uses of PGS would be sexist and should therefore be banned or discouraged. Assessment of this charge, however, shows that the use of PGS to achieve offspring gender variety and (in some cases) even firstborn gender preference, may not be inherently sexist or disadvantaging of women. Although it would be desirable to have extensive experience using PGS to increase the variety of offspring gender before extending it to firstborn gender preferences, it may not be legally possible to restrict the technique in this way. However, practitioners offering PGS should restrict their PGS practice to offspring gender variety until further debate and analysis of the issues has occurred. In any event, physicians offering

PGS should screen and counsel prospective users to assure that persons using PGS are committed to the well-being of their children, whatever their gender.

A policy solution that gives practitioners and patients primary control without direct legal or social oversight, although not ideal, may be the best way to deal with new reprogenetic techniques. Society should not prohibit or substantially burden reproductive decisions without stronger evidence of harm than PGS now appears to present. Ultimately, the use of PGS and other reprogenetic procedures will depend on whether they satisfy ethical norms of care and concern for children while meeting the needs of prospective parents.

**Norman Daniels, Carson Strong,
Mary B. Mahowald, and Mark V. Sauer**

 **NO**

It Isn't Just the Sex . . .

John Robertson argues that preconception sex selection (PSS) should remain a moral and legal prerogative of parental family planning, provided certain other conditions are met, including caveats about harms to others. If sound, his argument also applies to parental prerogatives to select offspring having any one of a family of traits that have properties and effects similar to sex (or sex selection). Bringing out this more general formulation will help us evaluate his argument.

Suppose, as Robertson does with regard to flow cytometry, that a specific sex-selection technology exists and has the following properties:

A. It is safe;
B. It imposes no harm on any fetus (because it is preconception);
C. It has quantifiably high reliability;
D. There is parental demand for using the technique (even though other techniques are much cheaper and more enjoyable); and
E. Some parents would not reproduce if they could not use it.

Now suppose that we also have techniques for preconception selection of traits other than sex, such as height, greater immune capacities, calmer temperament, or better memory, and that these techniques also have properties A–E. Property E may now seem more problematic than when it was applied only to sex selection. Robertson imagines a family that has several children of one gender and would rather not reproduce again unless it could raise a child of a different gender. Similarly, we can imagine parents refusing to reproduce further unless they can have a much taller or much calmer child—one different from the ones they already have.

Exactly what role does property E play in Robertson's argument? Property E does clearly show the strength of the parental preference, but strength of preference seems irrelevant to establishing that we have a right to gender or other trait selection. For Robertson, the point of property E seems to be this: if the parents would not reproduce at all unless they could have a child with a particular gender or other trait, then state prohibitions on gender or other trait selection technologies interfere with their basic moral and legal liberty to make reproductive choices, unless, of course, there are harms to others that the prohibition is aimed at preventing. In contrast, if parents prefer to select for a particular trait but would choose to reproduce even if they could not—that is,

From *The American Journal of Bioethics*, Vol. 1, no. 1, Winter 2001, pp. 15–16. Copyright ©
2001 by Routledge/Taylor & Francis Group. Reprinted by permission via Rightslink. www.
informaworld.com.

if property E is missing—then the state has not interfered with their liberty to make reproductive choices if it prohibits use of trait selection technologies.

Robertson's appeal to property E seems misguided. Consider Table 1:

Table 1

Agents	First Choice	Second Choice	Third Choice
Ben and Lily	gender selection	take chances	no offspring
Max and Sophie	gender selection	no offspring	(take chances?)

Property E is present for Max and Sophie but not Ben and Lily. If gender selection is denied either couple, they get their second choice. The prohibition on sex selection affects both couple's reproductive choices in the same way. Perhaps it seems worse for Max and Sophie because they are then "driven" to have no children, whereas Ben and Lily still reproduce, but the result in both cases is determined by each couple's choice in the absence of their first choice. Property E thus seems to do no work in the argument, and I believe it should be dropped.

Perhaps what motivates Robertson's appeal to E is a narrow (perhaps legally constrained) interpretation of reproductive liberty: it is a negative right against government interference with the choice to reproduce or not. Given this narrow interpretation, we might still be able to derive a right against interference with some cases of gender selection if property E did the work that I have argued it fails to do. Since property E fails to do what this alternative requires, we have two options. We can adopt and justify a broader interpretation of reproductive liberties, one that provides a right against interference with reproductive choices about trait selection, provided there are no harms to others. Alternatively, we can retain the narrow interpretation of reproductive liberty but argue for an additional, broader (negative) right of parents to pursue what they think is best for their children (and their families) through the selection, shaping, and development of the traits of their offspring. This broader right will include means other than reproductive choices (Buchanan et al. 2000, 187–191).

Much of Robertson's paper focuses on the reasons for thinking that gender selection either poses no harm to others or poses harms that can be countered in ways that infringe less on liberty than would prohibitions on gender selection. The disjunction of conditions (F–H) that Robertson's argument appeals to as constraints on gender selection constrains selection for other traits as well.

F. Neither individual cases of selection, nor the aggregate effect of many such selections, imposes (nonspeculative) harms on others;
G. Where there is a potential harm to others, it will correct itself in a reasonable time period (as in some cases of gender ratio imbalance); or
H. Any potential harm to others can be eliminated through regulation that does not directly infringe on basic reproductive liberties.

Robertson should have emphasized more the way in which the estimate of harms, and thus the justification of a liberty to select a trait, is sensitive to empirical facts about a society. He correctly argues that the case of family gender balancing does not by itself reinforce sexist beliefs or practices. When societies have a strong gender bias, permitting preconception sex selection beyond family balancing would reinforce existing biases and might lead to sex ratio imbalances. Under these conditions, permitting sex selection would require rigorous regulation of the grounds for selection. Robertson fails to emphasize the ways in which such regulations would appear to many as intrusions into basic parental liberties and how politically difficult it might be to sustain them.

One kind of harm Robertson does not mention, perhaps because it is not raised by gender selection, is the competitive or positional disadvantage that might result from allowing trait selection for certain traits, but financing them only through out-of-pocket payments. Advantages in wealth will then lead to the further transmission of advantage through access to trait selection. Fairness issues must be addressed in this case (for a discussion of these issues, see Buchanan et al. 2000, chs. 5–6).

Reference

Buchanan, A., D. Brock, N. Daniels, and D. Wikler. 2000. *From chance to choice: Genetics and justice*. New York: Cambridge University Press.

♥

Can't You Control Your Children?

In his paper "Preconception Gender Selection" (PGS), John Robertson (2001) discusses two issues: What limitations, if any, should the government impose on use of PGS? And what restrictions, if any, would be justifiable for physicians to impose on prospective parents who request PGS? For both issues, the focus is on PGS for parental preference, as opposed to prevention of sex-linked diseases The issue requires the use of our constitutional law framework. According to that framework, procreative liberty is a *fundamental* right, which entails that government restrictions must be justified by compelling state interests. Meeting the test of being "compelling" requires especially strong reasons for infringing procreative liberty; according to Robertson, meeting the test typically requires showing that substantial harm to others would occur. The second issue does not require the constitutional framework. Here the question is whether some individuals—either individual physicians or groups of physicians—are justified in refusing to carry out patients' requests for PGS. In arguing that it is ethically justifiable for physicians to refuse such requests, it is not necessary to show that there are compelling reasons for the refusal. It is only necessary to show that the arguments for refusing are better than the arguments for carrying out the requests.

Unfortunately, this basic difference between constitutional and professional ethical argumentation is not clearly acknowledged in Robertson's article.

Throughout the paper he appeals to the more demanding constitutional frame-work, even where the less demanding framework for professional ethical jus-tifiability is all that is required. For example, he argues that PGS for offspring diversity is ethically permissible, despite the objection of some ethicists that it is sexist. He concludes his argument by stating:

> If this view is correct, then those who deny that biological gender dif-ferences exist, or who assume that any recognition of them always reinforces sexism or disadvantages women, will not have carried the burden of showing that a couple's use of PGS for offspring gender vari-ety or other nonintentionally sexist uses is so harmful to women that it justifies restricting procreative choice. Until a stronger basis for finding harm to others from PGS exists, policies to prohibit or substantially restrict its use would not be justified.

Here Robertson appeals to the test of substantial harm. Later he advocates phy-sician guidelines that permit PGS for gender diversity, but the only arguments for such guidelines that can be found in the paper appeal, like this one, to the test of substantial harm. This blurring of constitutional and professional eth-ics argumentation creates a problem in trying to justify physician guidelines. Robertson seems to approve of guidelines that permit PGS for gender diversity because objections to such guidelines do not meet the demanding "compel-ling reasons" test. But objections to physician guidelines simply do not have to meet this high standard.

This problem is significant because there are important arguments bear-ing on the issue of physician guidelines that Robertson does not address. In particular, in discussing concerns about the genetic control of offspring, he does not present those concerns in a particularly forceful form. As a result, his paper does not engage those issues very well. There are at least two concerns that should be discussed, and although they overlap, I believe it is useful to distinguish between them. First, there are concerns about the genetic enhance-ment of offspring. Second, there are concerns about parental genetic control of offspring characteristics irrespective of whether the purpose of the control is properly labeled "enhancement" (as in the case of control for offspring diver-sity, eye and hair color, or various other possibilities).

Let me begin with the first set of concerns, which is relevant to the issue of physician response to requests for PGS for firstborn male offspring. I want to emphasize that sex selection is not itself a form of enhancement. To claim otherwise is to imply that one gender is superior to the other. However, it is obvious that in our male-dominated society, being male confers advantages upon a person. Parents who seek genetically to enhance the ability of off-spring to succeed in life could easily reason that being male would enhance that ability. When physicians allow PGS for firstborn male offspring, they are at least in some circumstances allowing parents who think this way to pur-sue their vision of genetic enhancement. Those who would want additional forms of genetic enhancement in the future could point to this as a precedent; we would *already* be a distance down the proverbial slippery slope. Let me mention two arguments that have been given to explain why we should be wary of the genetic enhancement of offspring. First, such technologies likely would not be available to all, but would be skewed among different socio-economic and ethnic groups. The economically advantaged would be better able to afford the costs of the technology. Because enhancement can improve the offspring's opportunities, unequal access to it would exacerbate current social and economic inequities (for a similar argument in the context of germ-line genetic modification, see Zimmerman 1991). Second, allowing parents to choose enhancements might erode our opposition to state-sponsored programs that promote (or carry out) enhancements of offspring. There is wide concern that abuses might occur, as has happened in all previous eugenics programs, or that efforts would be made to redesign human nature, resulting in more harm than benefit (Wertz and Fletcher 1989; Anderson 1989).

It should be acknowledged that enhancement could have positive consequences, as well. In some cases, it might promote the happiness of parents and children and the quality of family life. Also, it has been pointed out that we do not have sufficient information to assess the risks and benefits of positive eugenics, and that we should not assume that it is automatically wrong (Munson and Davis 1992). Admittedly, it is difficult to predict the long-term consequences of enhancement. However, the arguments against enhancement of offspring raise concerns significant enough to suggest that we should not proceed with enhancement without a better understanding of where it might take us (Strong 1997, 143–144). These considerations, in addition to the argument from sexism, provide important reasons why, for now at least, physicians should not carry out requests for PGS for firstborn male offspring.

The concern about parental control of offspring characteristics applies to all uses of PGS, including its use for offspring diversity and for firstborn female offspring based on a parental desire for the rearing and companionship experiences that would be involved. There is a legitimate worry that genetic control of offspring characteristics, if it becomes common and is applied to many characteristics, would alter parent-child relationships and that children would become more like "products" (Botkin 1990; Strong 1997, 143–144). When offspring characteristics are under parental control (whether they are properly labeled "enhancement" or not), parents might be less willing to accept the shortcomings of their children. Such designing might undermine a child's ability to have self-esteem. Less parental tolerance of children's imperfections might result in less compassion for the handicapped. Also, there would be a greater tendency to blame parents for their children's imperfections. The question, "Can't you control your children?" might take on a darker meaning. Children themselves might blame their parents, and this could harm family relationships. These sorts of considerations suggest that we should be more wary about proceeding with PGS than Robertson would have us be. It is not necessary to have compelling reasons for physician refusal to carry out requests for PGS based on parental gender preferences. It is only necessary to have good reasons. Concerns about what we might be doing to our future seem to justify a cautionary approach. They support the view that, for now at least, physicians should not carry out any requests for PGS for parental preference.

References

Anderson, W. F. 1989. Human gene therapy: Why draw a line? *Journal of Medicine and Philosophy* 14:681–693.

Botkin, J. R. 1990. Prenatal screening: Professional standards and the limits of parental choice. *Obstetrics and Gynecology* 75:875–880.

Munson, R., and L. H. Davis. 1992. Germ-line gene therapy and the medical imperative. *Kennedy Institute of Ethics Journal* 2:137–158.

Robertson, J. A. 2001. Preconception gender selection. *American Journal of Bioethics,* 1(1) 2–9.

Strong, C. 1997. *Ethics in reproductive and perinatal medicine: A new framework.* New Haven: Yale University Press.

Wertz D. C, and J. Fletcher 1989. Fatal knowledge? Prenatal diagnosis and sex selection. *Hastings Center Report* 19:21–27.

Zimmerman, B. K. 1991. Human germ-line therapy: The case for its development and use. *Journal of Medicine and Philosophy* 16:593–612.

❧

Reverse Sexism? Not to Worry

I concur with John Robertson that preconception sex selection (PSS) would be morally objectionable if it were sexist, and that it is not necessarily sexist (any more than post conception sex selection is necessarily sexist).[1] I disagree, however, that PSS is morally permissible on grounds of procreative liberty or the right to reproduce. Further, I believe that PSS is more likely than not to be sexist in its intent or in its consequences. Robertson appears to think otherwise.

According to Robertson, procreative liberty is the "freedom to reproduce or not to reproduce in the genetic sense." It also includes the freedom to gestate "whether or not there is a genetic connection to the resulting child" (Robertson 1996, 22–23). He deploys this definition in support of PSS by arguing that a couple who wish to have a biologically related child only if the child is of one sex rather than the other are deprived of their "fundamental right" to reproduce if PSS is not available to them. This argument erroneously assumes that the right to reproduce implies the right to reproduce a child of a specific kind. As Rebecca Dresser observes, "helping people to have children is different from helping them to have a particular kind of child" (Dresser 2001). It would be as wrong to say a couple have a fundamental right to reproduce a child who is a clone of one of them or to reproduce a child who has the same disabilities that they have. Although Robertson may affirm procreative liberty in these situations also, neither right is implied by the right to reproduce.

In *Children of Choice,* Robertson (1996, 22) acknowledges that the right to reproduce is separable from the right to raise a child, but he does not fully examine the implications of that separability for sex selection. This leaves me wondering how he might respond to scenarios not addressed in his article. Would he defend the right to reproduce a child of the desired sex solely on grounds of that right even if the reproducing person had no intention of raising the child? Would a sperm "donor," for example, be entitled to flow cytometry so as to ensure, or to maximize the chance, that any embryo developed from his gametes is male?[2] Would a potential egg "donor" be entitled to require that embryos formed from her gametes be transferred to the recipient only if they are determined to be female? Or would a woman who desires to gestate the genetic offspring of another be entitled to exclude some embryos from that offer on grounds of their sex? In none of these cases is the rationale for sex selection necessarily sexist. But as Robertson defines it, the right to reproduce entails the right to sex selection in all of these cases, as well as those where the right to reproduce is exercised by those who intend to raise the child.

Neither does the right not to reproduce imply the right to terminate a pregnancy at any point during gestation for any reason. *Roe v. Wade* (410 U.S. 113 [1973]) allows the states to proscribe abortion after viability only if the pregnant woman's health is not threatened by continuation of the pregnancy. The rationale for this caveat is not simply procreative freedom but the woman's right to avoid harm to herself. Even those who, like me, do not agree with Robertson's claim that the right to reproduce includes the right to PSS, may support PSS on this basis. We may argue, for example, that the anticipation of social stigmatization or ostracization may provide moral justification for PSS by individuals in particular cultural milieux. However, this is not equivalent to justification of permissive policies for PSS.

In addition to his affirmation of procreative liberty, Robertson apparently supports permissive policies for PSS because such policies are unlikely to be sexist in their intent or consequences. In contrast, I think that sexist intent and sexist consequences are more likely than not to be associated with the social and legal permissibility of PSS. Neither Robertson nor I have empirical data to buttress our positions, in part because intent is difficult if not impossible to verify in most cases. The mere fact that individuals prefer to have a boy or girl as a first, only, or additional child does not count as evidence of sexism. But sexist consequences are evident in situations where sex selection is practiced, despite its illegality, because the preponderance of boys in such situations shows that in general, male children are more valued than female children.

Even if male children are more valued for morally defensible reasons such as economic security or to avoid discriminatory or oppressive practices towards son-less women and their daughters, this constitutes complicity in sexism. Individuals themselves may not have sexist reasons for PSS, but their practice inevitably supports the view that one sex is inferior to the other. On an individual level, sexism may also be practiced by those who choose to have female children—if the intent or consequences of their choices are based on the notion that men are inferior to women. If and when a preponderance of female children in the general population shows them to be more valued than male children, we may then need to worry that the permissibility of PSS has led to "reverse sexism." Present circumstances lend little weight to that worry.

References

Dresser, R. 2001. Cosmetic reproductive services and professional integrity. *American Journal of Bioethics,* 1(1):11–12.

Mahowald, M. B. 2000. *Genes, women, equality.* New York: Oxford University Press.

Robertson, J. A. 1996. *Children of choice: Freedom and the new reproductive technologies.* Princeton: Princeton University Press.

Notes

1. My own views on sex selection, whether it is practiced prior to conception, prenatally or postnatally, are developed in Mahowald (2000, 115–121).

2. I put the term "donor" in quotation marks to call attention to the fact that the literal meaning of the term, i.e., one who gives a gift, is typically inapplicable in this context. In most cases, those who provide gametes to others are vendors rather than donors. Whether gamete providers are in fact donors or vendors, however, their right to reproduce does not imply a right to select the sex of their genetic offspring.

‧◉‧

Preconception Sex Selection: A Commentary

Gender selection of offspring created through assisted reproductive technology (ART) has been hotly debated since the inception of the method of in vitro fertilization (IVF). Given the broad range of innovation enjoyed throughout the development of IVF, it should not be surprising that couples would ask whether or not predetermination of gender is possible. Thus, early on, attempts at controlling outcomes began through the development of techniques that would preferentially select the desired sex of the embryo. What has never been universally agreed upon, however, is what, if any, situation should warrant attempts to manipulate the gender of the offspring.

The issue of sex selection through prenatal determination is one of the more difficult subjects facing clinicians. Ultimately physicians must decide whether or not to offer services; such decisions are based largely on the soundness of the medical and ethical practice. Today, couples choosing to select the gender of their children have essentially three options:

1. to terminate a pregnancy already established after the sex has been determined by chorionic villus sampling or amniocentesis;
2. to undergo preimplantation genetic diagnosis (PGD) by embryonic biopsy prior to embryo transfer; or
3. to alter the population of inseminated sperm so as to increase the likelihood of achieving a pregnancy of the desired sex.

Karyotyping a fetus or embryo is inherently invasive, expensive, and potentially dangerous to the mother and/or the pregnancy. However, it is the only way to guarantee that the sex of the embryo is the one desired by the mother.

Manipulating the insemination is appealing since the intervention occurs prior to conception, and avoids most issues involving abortion. From this perspective, sperm separation techniques would appear to have a decisive advantage over traditional methods. Unfortunately, to this date all techniques involving sperm separation are flawed since none guarantee success. As John Robertson points out, at best between 8% and 18% of pregnancies will result in the "wrong sex" even using flow cytometry to separate sperm of X and Y genotype. It is this fact of life that troubles most of us responsible for "assisting" in the creation of these lives. What happens to the pregnancies of the wrong sex? I would guess that many would choose to abort. As noted, "paying greater attention to gender" than to the importance of the life itself in many ways perverts the original intent of helping the infertile to conceive. Knowing that we live in a sexist world, there can be no doubt that many (mostly female) embryos would be terminated in the name of "procreative liberty."

All agree that the right of the individual to reproduce is fundamental. What isn't always clear is whether or not the pursuit of reproductive interventions requires regulation. Society and individuals speaking on behalf of the unborn have an equal right to object to gender selection when performed without clear medical justification. Physicians and patients with genetic diseases generally agree that the avoidance of X-linked illness is a valued reason for gender selection, whether through invasive or noninvasive means. However, "family balancing" is a politically correct euphemism that does little to diminish the valid concerns related to societal sexism.

The flow cytometry method has been neither clinically tested nor approved by the U.S. Food and Drug Administration. Yet, it has been discussed in the international press and news media and profiled as a treatment option in the medical literature. Naturally patients are inquiring as to its efficacy even though the procedure remains largely unavailable. Typically, the debate over whether or not it should be used is obscured by debate over the clinical success of the method.

Unfortunately, throughout the history of reproductive medicine, sensational press has often dictated medical practice. Many techniques in ART were introduced in this manner (e.g., intracytoplasmic sperm injection, cryopreservation, assisted hatching, and blastocyst culturing). Even IVF itself was equally unorthodox in its development and presentation. With respect to preconception sex selection, I agree with Robertson's assessment as to the need to "proceed slowly." In order for individuals to give informed consent, more needs to be known of the long-term effects, both medical and psychosocial, of flow cytometry. More importantly, I believe ethics committees at each institution should discuss how best to implement policy related to gender selection, and physicians should abide by these recommendations.

The Ethics Committee at Columbia University believes gender selection should not be performed except in instances in which a clear medical indication exists (e.g., a known genetic X-linked carrier status). Undoubtedly, many will disagree with that opinion. However, public debate is good for the field, and each physician should take a clear stand prior to introducing yet another untested procedure.

POSTSCRIPT

Should Parents Be Able to Select the Biological Sex of Their Children?

The idea of being able to select a child's biological sex is as fascinating as it is controversial. It is also nothing new. Throughout the late nineteenth and early twentieth centuries, people discussed and debated genetic engineering of children in order to eliminate so-called "undesirable" traits. Initially referring to disease, eugenicists (those who study or espouse the improvement of the human race through controlled selective breeding—www.dictionary.com) were often accused of racism, sexism, and other biases. What one person thinks would improve the human race others would see as tantamount to annihilation or extinction. Hitler's campaign to create a superior human race during World War II is a clear example of these concepts gone frighteningly awry.

For some, the argument for PGS is about rights—people have the fundamental right to control their reproductive potential in all ways, including whether and when to have a child, and what sex their child will be. Others oppose PGS because if sex selection takes place for any other reason other than medical necessity, society is opening a Pandora's box of ethical issues that would be impossible to close.

Take, for example, any other traits that human beings possess. What if there were a test to determine eye color of a child, and prospective parents decided that they wanted their child's eyes to match theirs? Should they be able to genetically alter their child to reflect that? What about another physical characteristic like height?

What about something that is not physical, yet still in-born—our sexual orientation, or the gender(s) of the people to whom we are attracted physically or romantically? There is a fascinating fictional movie called *The Twilight of the Golds* in which a woman finds that she is pregnant and takes a genetic test that determines within a certain percentage of certainty that the child that she will have will be gay. The movie centers around whether she will choose to carry the pregnancy to term or end it through having an abortion. Clearly, the different ways people might wish to affect their children can be endless, and endlessly controversial.

In 2001, the ethics committee of the American Society for Reproductive Medicine (ASRM) released a position statement in which they discussed PCG selection for medical and nonmedical reasons. The ASRM stresses that medical professionals must inform that the only current method of PCG selection available (separating X-bearing and Y-bearing sperm cells) is still an experimental procedure. If it were to become safer and eventually approved for PCG selection so that parents could select the gender of their children, the ASRM believes that PCG selection should only be offered:

- In clinic settings
- To couples who are seeking gender variety in their families
- If the couples are made fully aware of the risks of failure
- To couples who state that they would fully accept a child of a different sex should the PCG process fail
- To couples after counseling that their expectations of what it may be like to have a child of a particular gender may not match the eventual reality
- To couples who are given the opportunity to participate in a research study so that medical professionals can continue to track such issues as safety as effectively as possible

As the medical world continues to advance in leaps and bounds, this debate is far from over—in fact, we probably cannot even imagine how far it will reach in the years to come.

Suggested Readings

M. Darnovsky, "Revisiting Sex Selection: The Growing Popularity of New Sex Selection Methods Revives An Old Debate," *GeneWatch* (vol. 17, no. 1, January/February 2004). Accessible online at http://www.gene-watch.org/genewatch/articles/17-1 darnovsky.html.

M. Darnovsky, "Sex Selection Moves to Consumer Culture—Ads For 'Family Balancing' in *The New York Times*," *Genetic Crossroads: The Newsletter of the Center for Genetics and Society* (vol. 33, August 20, 2003). Accessible online at http://www.genetics-and-society.org/newsletter/archive/33.html#II.

D. King, "Eugenic Tendencies in Modern Genetic," in B. Tokar, ed., *Redesigning Life?* (New York: Zed Books, 2001).

R. Mallik, "A Less Valued Life: Population Policy and Sex Selection in India," The Center for Gender and Health Equity, 2002. Accessible online at www.genderhealth.org/pubs/MallikSexSelectionIndiaOct2002.pdf.

R. McDougall, "Acting Parentally: An Argument Against Sex Selection," *Journal of Medical Ethics* (vol. 31, no. 10, 2005).

P. Moore and L. Moore, *Baby Girl or Baby Boy: Choose the Sex of Your Child* (Tallahassee, FL: Washington Publishers, 2004).

J. Savulescu and E. Dahl, "Sex Selection and Preimplantation Diagnosis: A Response to the Ethics Committee of the American Society of Reproductive Medicine," *Human Reproduction* (vol. 15, no. 9, September 2000).

R. Shettles and D. M. Rorvik, *How to Choose the Sex of Your Baby* (New York: Broadway Books, 2006).

I. Simoncelli, "Preimplantation Genetic Diagnosis and Selection: From Disease Prevention to Customized Conception," *Different Takes: The Newsletter on Population and Development Program at Hampshire College* (no. 24, Spring 2003). Accessible online at http://www.genetics-and-society.org/resources/cgs/200303_difftakes_simoncelli.pdf.

ISSUE 8

Should Parents Surgically Alter Their Intersex Infants?

YES: Amicur Farkas, B. Chertin, and Irith Hadas-Halpren, from "One-Stage Feminizing Genitoplasty: Eight Years of Experience with Forty-Nine Cases," *The Journal of Urology* (June 2001)

NO: Paul McHugh, from "Surgical Sex," *First Things* (November 2004)

ISSUE SUMMARY

YES: Amicur Farkas, B. Chertin, and Irith Hadas-Halpren, faculty of the Ben-Gurion University in Jerusalem, Israel, see ambiguous genitalia as a true emergency. They assert that feminizing surgery should be done on an infant with congenital adrenal hyperplasia to ensure that as an adult woman, she will have sexual functioning and be able to give birth.

NO: Paul McHugh argues that a person's sense of gender identity is biologically based—that by changing an infant's or child's body before that child has a sense of who he or she is and risking being wrong about that sex assignment can do much more damage than good.

$\mathbf{T}$he term *intersex* is often more recognizable by its historical term, *hermaphrodite,* a term still used by many medical professionals. In Greek mythology, Hermaphroditus was the son of Hermes and Aphrodite. A nymph named Salmacis fell in love with Hermaphroditus, but he did not feel the same. Salmacis prayed that they would never be separated—so when Hermaphroditus swam in her stream, she combined with him to create a person with male and female characteristics in one body. Most individuals born with ambiguous or mixed genitalia and chromosomal structures prefer to be called intersex rather than hermaphrodite, the latter of which is considered by many intersex individuals to be negative. However, some intersex individuals have reclaimed the word *hermaphrodite* to describe themselves, just as members of other minority groups have reclaimed epithets as a way of asserting their power.

It is estimated that every year in the United States, approximately 65,000 babies are born with ambiguous genitalia. However, reliable statistics on the true incidence of intersexuality are limited. Although attention to intersexuality and the medical, psychological, and social issues relating to intersexual individuals have increased dramatically over the last 10 years, disagreement still exists on how parents should respond when they are told that their infant has ambiguous genitalia.

Support for surgical sex assignment is rooted in the work of psychologist John Money. In 1967, Money conducted an experiment in gender identity involving an infant whose genitalia were not ambiguous at birth but deformed severely by a botched circumcision. In this now notorious case, Money maintained that gender identity was fluid for the first few months of life. Money asserted that by completing the castration, providing the child with hormones, and raising the child as a girl, the child would "become" female. At the time, the case received a lot of attention and was declared a success when, at follow-up, Money noted that the then-nine-year-old girl was adjusting "normally."

About 30 years later, two other researchers, Milton Diamond and Keith Sigmundson, found that the child with whom Money had worked ended up depressed and confused by her strong feelings that she was actually male. Once the truth was revealed to her, she was extremely relieved. Her parents arranged for the surgeries and other treatments that would enable her to transition back to male. As an adult male, he lived with his wife and their children, whom he adopted.

As you read the selections, consider the reasoning behind each argument. There is the so-called locker-room viewpoint—that adolescents have a tough enough time navigating through adolescence; why make it even harder by subjecting them to further torment in the locker room where their ambiguous genitalia would be revealed? There are also parents who believe that children should remain intact until they are older and can decide for themselves what, if anything, to do about their ambiguous genitalia.

In the first selection, Amitur Farkas, B. Chertin, and Irith Hadas-Halpren provide a detailed description of what they call "feminizing" surgery. They believe that having this type of surgery is best for patients to ensure both cosmetic contentment and satisfactory intercourse. Paul McHugh argues that a person's sense of gender identity is biologically based—that by changing an infant's or child's body before that child has a sense of who he or she is, and risking being wrong about that sex assignment, can do much more harm than good.

YES ↵

Amicur Farkas, B. Chertin,
and Irith Hadas-Halpren

One-Stage Feminizing Genitoplasty: Eight Years of Experience with Forty-Nine Cases

T he neonate with sexual ambiguity represents an enigmatic but true emergency in pediatric urology. In recent years several techniques of 1-stage feminizing genitoplasty have been described. Successful reconstruction depends on accurate preoperative recognition of the anatomy while the main area of interest is the location of the vaginal opening into the urogenital sinus and its relationship to the pelvic floor and external sphincter mechanism. Passerini-Glazel, and Gonzales and Fernandes described their techniques of 1-stage feminizing genitoplasty. The primary features of both techniques are the use of preputial skin in combination with the distal part of the urogenital sinus to construct a vaginal introitus and to avoid the frequent complications associated with previous types of operations, such as vaginal stenosis and injury of the urethral sphincter. We retrospectively analyzed the results of our modification of these techniques.

Materials and Methods

Between 1991 and 1998, 49 patients underwent 1-stage feminizing genitoplasty at our department. All patients were referred following complete evaluation of gender, and chromosomal and biochemical data by pediatric endocrinologists. Of the 49 patients, 44 had congenital adrenal hyperplasia (CAH) due to 21-hydroxylase deficiency in 33 and 11-hydroxylase deficiency in 11, 3 were true hermaphrodites, and 2 were adolescents with different degrees of the androgen insensitivity syndrome. All patients with CAH and the true hermaphrodites had 46 XX karyotype, and those with androgen insensitivity syndrome had 46 XY karyotype. The true hermaphrodites and androgen insensitivity syndrome patients were referred to us after surgical removal of the contradictory gonads and internal duct structure before the genitoplasty. Mean age was 0.9 ± 0.3 years the patients with CAH and 13 ± 2.3 of the remainder. Before surgical correctional patients underwent transabdominal pelvic ultrasound only to provide information for surgical decision making regarding status of the internal genitalia, length and anatomical position of the vagina, and whether the vaginal junction with the urogenital sinus was

From *Journal of Urology,* vol. 1 65, June 2001, pp. 2341–2346. Copyright © 2001 by Elsevier Ltd. Reprinted by permission.

distal or proximal to the pelvic floor. The ultrasound technique and results have been reported previously.

The patients with CAH underwent panendoscopy as an initial and integral step of the feminizing genitoplasty. The communication of the vagina and urogenital sinus was localized using a 10Fr pediatric cytoscope. In the majority of cases, the cystocope was passed into the vaginal cavity. At that point the telescope was removed from the sheath and a 6Fr silicone Foley catheter was inserted into the vaginal cavity through the cytoscope sheath and its balloon was inflated to 2 cc. The cytoscope sheath was then pulled back and the catheter was clamped at the distal end of the urogenital sinus to avoid balloon deflation. The distal end of the catheter was cut off to enable complete removal of the cystoscope sheath. In some cases with a small vaginal opening, a Fogarty catheter was used with the cytoscope inserted only as far as the opening and not into the vaginal cavity. After the cytoscope was removed, an 8 to 10Fr silicone Foley was inserted into the bladder in the conventional manner. Of the 44 patients with CAH, 41 had vaginal confluence at the level of the verumontanum and 3 had high vaginal confluence according to Powell types II and III classification. The patients were placed in an exaggerated lithotomy position and surgery was performed via the perineal approach by a senior urologist (A. F.) or under his personal supervision.

The operation begins with vertical incisions of the phallic skin on ventral and dorsal surfaces and degloving of the phallus circumferentially. The ventral incision is extended to the bottom of the labioscrotal folds in a Y shape and then terminates in an inverted U-shaped perineal flap to provide good exposure of the urogenital sinus. The urogenital sinus including the vagina and urethra is then completely mobilized *en bloc* from the corporeal bodies. The dissection is done between the 2 crura of corpora cavernosa and mobilization continues below the lower rami of the pubis. Thereafter the dissection between the lateral and posterior walls of the sinus, including the vagina and the anterior rectal wall, is completed circumferentially so the posterior wall of the vagina can be brought to the perineum without tension.

At this point clitoroplasty is performed using the technique of Kogan et al. The plane of cleavage is developed between the corpora and dorsal neurovascular bundle via Buck's fascia, taking care to preserve the tunica of the corporeal body. Subsequently resection of the corpora is performed from the glans to the proximal part passing the bifurcation. The stumps of the corpora are placed and sutured by running 5-zero polyglactin sutures below the pubic bone. The proximal phallic skin sutured to the preputial skin and left around the glans clitoris corona creates a preputial hood. To avoid rectal injury and bleeding from the spongiosal tissue, traction 5-zero polyglactin sutures are placed on the urogenital sinus to bring the deeper structures to a more superficial level. All of this part of the procedure is done during meticulous palpation of the balloon of the Foley or Fogarty catheter, which is inserted into the vagina and serves as a guide during dissection.

The posterior vaginal wall is opened over the balloon between the traction sutures, and the connection between the vagina and urogenital sinus is closed from the internal surface of the vagina. The vagina is opened into an adequate caliber to prevent future stenosis. The previously dissected posterior inverted U is sutured to the dorsal vaginal wall. The redundant distal part of the urogenital sinus is partially opened on the dorsal surface, leaving a long enough urethra. The inverted open strip of epithelium is sutured to the anterior and lateral vaginal walls, enabling creation of a wet and wide introitus. The preputial and phallic skin is completely split down the midline sutured around the clitoris and to the lateral epithelial edges of the aforementioned urogenital strips to create the labia minora. The lateral labioscrotal skin can be brought down and sutured to the corners between the posterior U flap and lateral skin to form the labia majora. . . .

Results

Mean operating time was 145 minutes (range 120 to 180) and average hospitalization period was 4 to 5 days. Preoperative ultrasound provided the correct data regarding vaginal and internal genitalia anatomy in all of our cases, and the exact communication between the vagina and urogenital sinus was demonstrated in 41 of 44 (93%) with CAH. In 1 patient anterior rectal wall injury occurred intraoperatively and was immediately closed without further complications. The only immediate postoperative complication was mild wound infection of the buttock area in 3 cases. Mean followup was 4.7 ± 2.6 years. In 1 case total clitoris loss was later observed, and 2 patients presented with repeat clitoromegalia due to inadequate androgen suppression. All patients who underwent our modification of genitoplasty have had successful cosmetic and early functional results. In those cases with CAH who reached puberty, repeat examinations showed normal menstruation, a wet and wide introitus, and no evidence of fibrosis or scarring of the perineum. In the smaller girls we were able to calibrate the vaginal opening easily with a 20 to 22Fr bougie. No patient had urinary tract infection, and to date all patients are continent including those with a high vagina. None of the girls with CAH has yet achieved intercourse age and, therefore, we have no information regarding sexual satisfaction, possibility of vaginal delivery and psychosocial aspects of these forms of intersexuality. Both patients with partial AIS who presented initially with a small phallus and adequate vagina are now 18 and 22 years old, and report satisfactory sexual intercourse experiences.

Discussion

Existence of ambiguous genitalia is an emergency situation necessitating a team approach, which can provide quick identification of the genetic sex and biochemical profile. One of the most common causes of genital ambiguity is CAH, and today several surgical techniques are available for reconstruction. Feminizing genitoplasty should provide an adequate opening for the vagina into the perineum, create a normal-looking wet introitus, fully separate the urethral orifice from the vagina, remove phallic erectile tissue while preserving glandular innervation and blood supply, and prevent urinary tract complications.

Successful reconstruction depends on good knowledge of the anatomy of the urogenital sinus, particularly the location of the communication of the vagina to the urogenital sinus in relation to the pelvic floor and rectum. The surgeon must know whether the vagina is long enough to reach the perineum without any tension through a perineal approach and without compromising the pelvic floor and urethral continence mechanism. To provide the necessary information, we perform only ultrasound in our patients.

The optimal time for genitoplasty is controversial. A few authors advise neonatal genitoplasty because of the presence of neonatal hypertrophy of the external and internal genitalia due to maternal and placental hyperstimulation with estrogens, and apparent easy vaginal mobilization.

In contrast, others suggest deferring definitive reconstruction of the intermediate and high vagina until after puberty. To spare our patients and parents the anxiety, we endeavor to perform genitoplasty at around age 6 months when the child reaches 5 to 6 kg, as the risk of anesthesia at this age is negligible. Modern anesthesiology produces negligible risks in neonates and recently we started to operate on patients at age 3 months.

Historically, genital reconstruction in patients with CAH involved a 2-stage operation. At stage 1, simple amputation or reduction of the clitoris was performed in the neonatal period with the vaginoplasty being postponed until an older age. Currently, many authors recommend 1-stage genitoplasty, which can be done early in life using the perineal approach in the majority of cases, even those with high vaginal confluence. We had no difficulty reaching the posterior wall of the vagina of those patients in the exaggerated lithotomy position via the perineal approach, especially as we made no effort to dissect and separate its communication with the urogenital sinus as described originally by Passerini-Glazel. Preservation of the megaloclitoris is advantageous once 1-stage genitoplasty is performed, as it enables easy dissection and *en bloc* mobilization of the urogenital sinus. The remaining redundant phallic and preputial skin after removal of the erectile tissue provides excellent material for reconstruction of the introitus and labia. Those cases referred to our hospital after clitorectomy or clitorous reduction were more challenging for reconstruction and are not included in this report.

Endoscopy is a crucial step in genitoplasty, which identifies the anatomy and enables insertion of a Foley or Fogarty catheter into the vagina through the communication to the urogenital sinus. We inserted the 10Fr cystoscope into the vagina so that a Foley catheter could be inserted into the vagina via the cystoscope sheath. The balloon of the Foley catheter that is used in the majority of our cases was bigger than that of the Fogarty catheter. This maneuver enables easier and safer localization of the posterior vaginal wall and prevents rectal injury.

Since 1989 different modifications of feminizing genitoplasty have become popular and replaced the classical Hendren and Crawford technique, decreased the percent of vaginal stenosis to negligible levels, and improved the cosmetic appearance of the external genitalia. We have improved a few steps of the previously reported operations. Complete mobilization of the urogenital sinus *en bloc* including the vagina and urethra makes it possible to bring the sinus to the perineum and avoid the difficult step of dissection between the anterior vagina wall and overlying urethra and bladder neck. The connecting fistula between the urethra and vagina is closed from the internal surface of the vagina after opening the posterior vaginal wall. It is difficult to evaluate the failure and existence of a new fistula in small girls but to date no fistula has occurred in our adolescent and adult patients. Rink and Adams and Passerini-Glazel mention that fibrosis is the main reason for vaginal stenosis. The fact that we use the healthy posterior vaginal wall to create the vaginal opening instead of the distal fibrotic vaginal portion, which creates the fistula to the sinus, also prevents further stenosis. We use the inverted distal open strip of the urogenital sinus to create a wet introitus, which at the end of the operation has nearly a 320-degree circumference of epithelial tissue or preputial skin and, therefore, prevents vaginal stenosis.

One of the most important goals of feminizing genitoplasty is to provide sexual satisfaction and normal vaginal delivery. Our patients who have reached puberty have normal appearing external genitalia and clitoris. Only 2 patients had repeat clitomegalia due to inadequate androgen suppression, necessitating reoperation to reduce the glandular part of the clitoris. Since none of our children has yet reached the age of sexual relations and childbearing, we cannot assess these results of our technique. However, both XY patients with AIS who underwent identical feminizing genitoplasty are now 18 and 22 years old, and report normal and satisfactory intercourse.

Conclusions

Our modification of feminizing genitoplasty enables nearly all children presenting with ambiguous genitalia, 1-stage reconstruction early in life with good cosmetic and functional results. Undoubtedly the outcome of vaginoplasty should be reevaluated later.

Paul McHugh   ➡ **NO**

Surgical Sex

When the practice of sex-change surgery first emerged back in the early 1970s, I would often remind its advocating psychiatrists that with other patients, alcoholics in particular, they would quote the Serenity Prayer, "God, give me the serenity to accept the things I cannot change, the courage to change the things I can, and the wisdom to know the difference." Where did they get the idea that our sexual identity ("gender" was the term they preferred) as men or women was in the category of things that could be changed?

Their regular response was to show me their patients. Men (and until recently they were all men) with whom I spoke before their surgery would tell me that their bodies and sexual identities were at variance. Those I met after surgery would tell me that the surgery and hormone treatments that had made them "women" had also made them happy and contented. None of these encounters were persuasive, however. The post-surgical subjects struck me as caricatures of women. They wore high heels, copious makeup, and flamboyant clothing; they spoke about how they found themselves able to give vent to their natural inclinations for peace, domesticity, and gentleness—but their large hands, prominent Adam's apples, and thick facial features were incongruous (and would become more so as they aged). Women psychiatrists whom I sent to talk with them would intuitively see through the disguise and the exaggerated postures. "Gals know gals," one said to me, "and that's a guy."

The subjects before the surgery struck me as even more strange, as they struggled to convince anyone who might influence the decision for their surgery. First, they spent an unusual amount of time thinking and talking about sex and their sexual experiences; their sexual hungers and adventures seemed to preoccupy them. Second, discussion of babies or children provoked little interest from them; indeed, they seemed indifferent to children. But third, and most remarkable, many of these men-who-claimed-to-be-women reported that they found women sexually attractive and that they saw themselves as "lesbians." When I noted to their champions that their psychological leanings seemed more like those of men than of women, I would get various replies, mostly to the effect that in making such judgments, I was drawing on sexual stereotypes.

Until 1975, when I became psychiatrist-in-chief at Johns Hopkins Hospital, I could usually keep my own counsel on these matters. But once I was given authority over all the practices in the psychiatry department, I realized

From *First Things*, November 2004, pp. 34–38. Copyright © 2004 by Institute on Religion and Public Life. Reprinted by permission.

that if I were passive, I would be tacitly co-opted in encouraging sex-change surgery in the very department that had originally proposed and still defended it. I decided to challenge what I considered to be a misdirection of psychiatry and to demand more information both before and after their operations.

Two issues presented themselves as targets for study. First, I wanted to test the claim that men who had undergone sex-change surgery found resolution for their many general psychological problems. Second (and this was more ambitious), I wanted to see whether male infants with ambiguous genitalia who were being surgically transformed into females and raised as girls did, as the theory (again from Hopkins) claimed, settle easily into the sexual identity that was chosen for them. These claims had generated the opinion in psychiatric circles that one's "sex" and one's "gender" were distinct matters, sex being genetically and hormonally determined from conception, while gender was culturally shaped by the actions of family and others during childhood.

The first issue was easier and required only that I encourage the ongoing research of a member of the faculty who was an accomplished student of human sexual behavior. The psychiatrist and psychoanalyst Jon Meyer was already developing a means of following up with adults who received sex-change operations at Hopkins in order to see how much the surgery had helped them. He found that most of the patients he tracked down some years after their surgery were contented with what they had done and that only a few regretted it. But in every other respect, they were little changed in their psychological condition. They had much the same problems with relationships, work, and emotions as before. The hope that they would emerge now from their emotional difficulties to flourish psychologically had not been fulfilled.

We saw the results as demonstrating that just as these men enjoyed cross-dressing as women before the operation so they enjoyed cross-living after it. But they were no better in their psychological integration or any easier to live with. With these facts in hand, I concluded that Hopkins was fundamentally cooperating with a mental illness. We psychiatrists, I thought, would do better to concentrate on trying to fix their minds and not their genitalia.

Thanks to this research, Dr. Meyer was able to make some sense of the mental disorders that were driving this request for unusual and radical treatment. Most of the cases fell into one of two quite different groups. One group consisted of conflicted and guilt-ridden homosexual men who saw a sex-change as a way to resolve their conflicts over homosexuality by allowing them to behave sexually as females with men. The other group, mostly older men, consisted of heterosexual (and some bisexual) males who found intense sexual arousal in cross-dressing as females. As they had grown older, they had become eager to add more verisimilitude to their costumes and either sought or had suggested to them a surgical transformation that would include breast implants, penile amputation, and pelvic reconstruction to resemble a woman.

Further study of similar subjects in the psychiatric services of the Clark Institute in Toronto identified these men by the auto-arousal they experienced in imitating sexually seductive females. Many of them imagined that their displays might be sexually arousing to onlookers, especially to females. This idea, a form of "sex in the head" (D. H. Lawrence), was what provoked their first adventure in dressing up in women's undergarments and had eventually led them toward the surgical option. Because most of them found women to be the objects of their interests, they identified themselves to the psychiatrists as lesbians. The name eventually coined in Toronto to describe this form of sexual misdirection was "autogynephilia." Once again I concluded that to provide a surgical alteration to the body of these unfortunate people was to collaborate with a mental disorder rather than to treat it.

This information and the improved understanding of what we had been doing led us to stop prescribing sex-change operations for adults at Hopkins—much, I'm glad to say, to the relief of several of our plastic surgeons who had previously been commandeered to carry out the procedures. And with this solution to the first issue, I could turn to the second—namely, the practice of surgically assigning femaleness to male newborns who at birth had malformed, sexually ambiguous genitalia and severe phallic defects. This practice, more the province of the pediatric department than of my own, was nonetheless of concern to psychiatrists because the opinions generated around these cases helped to form the view that sexual identity was a matter of cultural conditioning rather than something fundamental to the human constitution.

Several conditions, fortunately rare, can lead to the misconstruction of the genito-urinary tract during embryonic life. When such a condition occurs in a male, the easiest form of plastic surgery by far, with a view to correcting the abnormality and gaining a cosmetically satisfactory appearance, is to remove all the male parts, including the testes, and to construct from the tissues available a labial and vaginal configuration. This action provides these malformed babies with female-looking genital anatomy regardless of their genetic sex. Given the claim that the sexual identity of the child would easily follow the genital appearance if backed up by familial and cultural support, the pediatric surgeons took to constructing female-like genitalia for both females with an XX chromosome constitution and males with an XY so as to make them all look like little girls, and they were to be raised as girls by their parents.

All this was done of course with consent of the parents who, distressed by these grievous malformations in their newborns, were persuaded by the pediatric endocrinologists and consulting psychologists to accept transformational surgery for their sons. They were told that their child's sexual identity (again, his "gender") would simply conform to environmental conditioning. If the parents consistently responded to the child as a girl now that his genital structure resembled a girl's, he would accept that role without much travail.

This proposal presented the parents with a critical decision. The doctors increased the pressure behind the proposal by noting to the parents that a decision had to be made promptly because a child's sexual identity settles in by about age two or three. The process of inducing the child into the female role should start immediately, with name, birth certificate, baby paraphernalia, etc. With the surgeons ready and the physicians confident, the parents were faced with an offer difficult to refuse (although, interestingly, a few parents did refuse this advice and decided to let nature take its course).

I thought these professional opinions and the choices being pressed on the parents rested upon anecdotal evidence that was hard to verify and even harder to replicate. Despite the confidence of their advocates, they lacked substantial empirical support. I encouraged one of our resident psychiatrists, William G. Reiner (already interested in the subject because prior to his psychiatric training he had been a pediatric urologist and had witnessed the problem from the other side), to set about doing a systematic follow-up of these children—particularly the males transformed into females in infancy—so as to determine just how sexually integrated they became as adults.

The results here were even more startling than in Meyer's work. Reiner picked out for intensive study cloacal exstrophy, because it would best test the idea that cultural influence plays the foremost role in producing sexual identity. Cloacal exstrophy is an embryonic misdirection that produces a gross abnormality of pelvic anatomy such that the bladder and the genitalia are badly deformed at birth. The male penis fails to form and the bladder and urinary tract are not separated distinctly from the gastrointestinal tract. But crucial to Reiner's study is the fact that the embryonic development of these unfortunate males is not hormonally different from that of normal males. They develop within a male-typical prenatal hormonal milieu provided by their Y chromosome and by their normal testicular function. This exposes these growing embryos/fetuses to the male hormone testosterone—just like all males in their mother's womb.

Although animal research had long since shown that male sexual behavior was directly derived from this exposure to testosterone during embryonic life, this fact did not deter the pediatric practice of surgically treating male infants with this grievous anomaly by castration (amputating their testes and any vestigial male genital structures) and vaginal construction, so that they could be raised as girls. This practice had become almost universal by the mid-1970s. Such cases offered Reiner the best test of the two aspects of the doctrine underlying such treatment: (1) that humans at birth are neutral as to their sexual identity, and (2) that for humans it is the postnatal, cultural, nonhormonal influences, especially those of early childhood, that most influence their ultimate sexual identity. Males with cloacal exstrophy were regularly altered surgically to resemble females, and their parents were instructed to raise them as girls. But would the fact that they had had the full testosterone exposure in utero defeat the attempt to raise them as girls? Answers might become evident with the careful follow-up that Reiner was launching.

Before describing his results, I should note that the doctors proposing this treatment for the males with cloacal exstrophy understood and acknowledged that they were introducing a number of new and severe physical problems for these males. These infants, of course, had no ovaries, and their testes were surgically amputated, which meant that they had to receive exogenous hormones for life. They would also be denied by the same surgery any opportunity for fertility later on. One could not ask the little patient about his willingness to pay this price. These were considered by the physicians advising the parents to be acceptable burdens to bear in order to avoid distress in childhood about malformed genital structures, and it was hoped that they could follow a conflict-free direction in their maturation as girls and women.

Reiner, however, discovered that such re-engineered males were almost never comfortable as females once they became aware of themselves and the world. From the start of their active play life, they behaved spontaneously like boys and were obviously different from their sisters and other girls, enjoying rough-and-tumble games but not dolls and "playing house." Later on, most of those individuals who learned that they were actually genetic males wished to reconstitute their lives as males (some even asked for surgical reconstruction and male hormone replacement)—and all this despite the earnest efforts by their parents to treat them as girls.

Reiner's results, reported in the January 22, 2004, issue of the *New England Journal of Medicine,* are worth recounting. He followed up sixteen genetic males with cloacal exstrophy seen at Hopkins, of whom fourteen underwent neonatal assignment to femaleness socially, legally, and surgically. The other two parents refused the advice of the pediatricians and raised their sons as boys. Eight of the fourteen subjects assigned to be females had since declared themselves to be male. Five were living as females, and one lived with unclear sexual identity.

The two raised as males had remained male. All sixteen of these people had interests that were typical of males, such as hunting, ice hockey, karate, and bobsledding. Reiner concluded from this work that the sexual identity followed the genetic constitution. Male-type tendencies (vigorous play, sexual arousal by females, and physical aggressiveness) followed the testosterone-rich intrauterine fetal development of the people he studied, regardless of efforts to socialize them as females after birth.

Having looked at the Reiner and Meyer studies, we in the Johns Hopkins Psychiatry Department eventually concluded that human sexual identity is mostly built into our constitution by the genes we inherit and the embryogenesis we undergo. Male hormones sexualize the brain and the mind. Sexual dysphoria—a sense of disquiet in one's sexual role—naturally occurs amongst those rare males who are raised as females in an effort to correct an infantile genital structural problem. A seemingly similar disquiet can be socially induced in apparently constitutionally normal males, in association with (and presumably prompted by) serious behavioral aberrations, amongst which are conflicted homosexual orientations and the remarkable male deviation now called autogynephilia.

Quite clearly, then, we psychiatrists should work to discourage those adults who seek surgical sex reassignment. When Hopkins announced that it would stop doing these procedures in adults with sexual dysphoria, many other hospitals followed suit, but some medical centers still carry out this surgery. Thailand has several centers that do the surgery "no questions asked" for anyone with the money to pay for it and the means to travel to Thailand. I am disappointed but not surprised by this, given that some surgeons and medical centers can be persuaded to carry out almost any kind of surgery when pressed by patients with sexual deviations, especially if those patients find a psychiatrist to vouch for them. The most astonishing example is the surgeon in England who is prepared to amputate the legs of patients who claim to find sexual excitement in gazing at and exhibiting stumps of amputated legs.

At any rate, we at Hopkins hold that official psychiatry has good evidence to argue against this kind of treatment and should begin to close down the practice everywhere.

For children with birth defects, the most rational approach at this moment is to correct promptly any of the major urological defects they face, but to postpone any decision about sexual identity until much later, while raising the child according to its genetic sex. Medical caretakers and parents can strive to make the child aware that aspects of sexual identity will emerge as he or she grows. Settling on what to do about it should await maturation and the child's appreciation of his or her own identity.

Proper care, including good parenting, means helping the child through the medical and social difficulties presented by the genital anatomy but in the process protecting what tissues can be retained, in particular the gonads. This effort must continue to the point where the child can see the problem of a life role more clearly as a sexually differentiated individual emerges from within. Then as the young person gains a sense of responsibility for the result, he or she can be helped through any surgical constructions that are desired. Genuine informed consent derives only from the person who is going to live with the outcome and cannot rest upon the decisions of others who believe they "know best." . . .

Much of the enthusiasm for the quick-fix approach to birth defects expired when the anecdotal evidence about the much-publicized case of a male twin raised as a girl proved to be bogus. The psychologist in charge hid, by actually misreporting, the news that the boy, despite the efforts of his parents to treat him and raise him as a girl, had constantly challenged their treatment of him, ultimately found out about the deception, and restored himself as a male. Sadly, he carried an additional diagnosis of major depression and ultimately committed suicide.

I think the issue of sex-change for males is no longer one in which much can be said for the other side. But I have learned from the experience that the toughest challenge is trying to gain agreement to seek empirical evidence for opinions about sex and sexual behavior, even when the opinions seem on their face unreasonable. One might expect that those who claim that sexual identity has no biological or physical basis would bring forth more evidence to persuade others. But as I've learned, there is a deep prejudice in favor of the idea that nature is totally malleable.

Without any fixed position on what is given in human nature, any manipulation of it can be defended as legitimate. A practice that appears to give people what they want—and what some of them are prepared to clamor for—turns out to be difficult to combat with ordinary professional experience and wisdom. Even controlled trials or careful follow-up studies to ensure that the practice itself is not damaging are often resisted and the results rejected.

I have witnessed a great deal of damage from sex-reassignment. The children transformed from their male constitution into female roles suffered prolonged distress and misery as they sensed their natural attitudes. Their parents usually lived with guilt over their decisions—second-guessing themselves and somewhat ashamed of the fabrication, both surgical and social, they had imposed on their sons. As for the adults who came to us claiming to have discovered their "true" sexual identity and to have heard about sex-change operations, we psychiatrists have been distracted from studying the causes and natures of their mental misdirections by preparing them for surgery and for a life in the other sex. We have wasted scientific and technical resources and damaged our professional credibility by collaborating with madness rather than trying to study, cure, and ultimately prevent it.

POSTSCRIPT

Should Parents Surgically Alter Their Intersex Infants?

Regardless of whether parents choose to alter their child's ambiguous genitalia or whether they choose to let their child decide later in life whether or not to have surgery, the experience of having an infant with ambiguous genitalia usually takes parents by surprise. For many parents, especially those who have little or no information about ambiguous genitalia, the experience can be quite alarming to them. Other parents struggle with the decisions but in the end feel good about the choices they make.

The support for assigning a sex surgically seems to be based in a portion of society's strong viewpoints on the role penis size plays in not just being able to define a child as male but also in a male child's sense of his own "maleness." In fact, nearly all infants born with ambiguous genitalia whose biological sex is determined surgically are made female because, quite simply, the surgery is better and easier. Moreover, parents and medical professionals alike struggle with the implications of a male child born with a micropenis. It is clear that some adults are motivated strongly by trying to avoid embarrassment for their male child. It would be better, they feel, to create a girl rather than leave an intact boy with an "inferior" penis.

Thirty years ago, the standard operating procedure was to select a biological sex at birth based on genital appearance alone. Today, with greater capacity for chromosomal and other types of testing, many medical professionals and associations are taking a much more conservative approach to dealing with a child born with ambiguous genitalia. Diamond and Sigmundson suggest the following guidelines for working with infants with ambiguous genitalia:

- **A complete physical is necessary.** This includes, they suggest, taking a thorough history of the patient's family. The physical should look not just at the external genitalia but also at the internal systems as they exist, at genetic structures, and at the endocrine system. They argue that many cases of intersexuality go undetected. This can avoid surprises and additional challenges later in the child's life.
- **Parents should be given full information on intersexuality and start being counseled immediately.** Intersexuality is among many conditions where medical professionals often withhold information until the final outcome and conclusions are drawn. Diamond and Sigmundson recommend full disclosure from the onset and immediate and ongoing counseling to help parents understand what intersexuality is, that they are not alone, and that many people with ambiguous genitalia grow up to live happy lives.

- **Medical professionals need to respect confidentiality, even within the hospital setting.** While giving the family the clear message that having an intersex child is nothing to be embarrassed about, medical professionals must be careful about not treating the family as a novelty.
- **Assign sex based on the most likely outcome.** This is an important distinction to make for parents who may have felt ambivalent about having a child of one sex versus the other. If they are disappointed with a child of one sex and would prefer to have the other, they must understand clearly that having an intersex child is not an opportunity for sex selection and that there is a potentially disastrous outcome if the assignment is based on desire for a son or daughter rather than the child's true nature.

Above all, Diamond and Sigmundson discourage medical professionals and parents from opting for genital surgery for cosmetic rather than medical reasons.

Suggested Readings

Lenore Abramsky, Sue Hall, Judith Levitan, and Theresa M. Marteau, "What Parents Are Told After Prenatal Diagnosis of a Sex Chromosome Abnormality: Interview and Questionnaire Study." Accessible online at http://www.bmj.com/cgi/content/full/322/7284/463.

John Colapinto, *As Nature Made Him: The Boy Who Was Raised as a Girl* (HarperCollins Publishing, 2000).

M. Diamond and K. Sigmundson, "Management of Intersexuality: Guidelines for Dealing With Individuals With Ambiguous Genitalia," *Archives of Pediatrics and Adolescent Medicine* (June 10, 2002).

Alice Domurat Dreger, ed., *Intersex in the Age of Ethics* (University Publishing Group, 1999).

Anne Fausto-Sterling, "The Five Sexes, Revisited," *Sciences* (July 2000).

Anne Fausto-Sterling, *Sexing the Body: Gender Politics and the Construction of Sexuality* (Basic Books, 2000).

Melissa Hendricks, "Into the Hands of Babes," *Johns Hopkins Magazine* (September 2000).

Katherine A. Mason, "The Unkindest Cut: Intersexuals Launch a Movement to Stop Doctors From 'Assigning' Sex With a Scalpel," *New Haven Advocate* (March 29, 2001).

John Money, "Ablatio Penis: Normal Male Infant Sex-Reassigned as a Girl," *Archives of Sexual Behavior* (1975).

E. Nussbaum, "A Question of Gender," *Discover* (January 2000).

ISSUE 9

Should Minors Be Required to Get Their Parents' Permission in Order to Obtain an Abortion?

YES: Teresa Stanton Collett, from Testimony Before the Subcommittee on the Constitution, Committee on the Judiciary, U.S. House of Representatives (September 6, 2001)

NO: Planned Parenthood Federation of America, Inc., from "Fact Sheet: Teenagers, Abortion, and Government Intrusion Laws," Planned Parenthood Federation of America, Inc. (August 1999)

ISSUE SUMMARY

YES: Teresa Stanton Collett, former professor at South Texas College of Law, testifies in front of the U.S. House of Representatives in support of the federal Child Custody Protection Act. She advocates parental involvement in a minor's pregnancy, regardless of the girl's intention to carry or terminate the pregnancy. Parental involvement, Collett maintains, is not punitive; rather, it offers the girl herself additional protection against injury and sexual assault. Minors tend to have less access to information and education than adults; without this information and education, they are not able to provide truly "informed" consent, concludes Collett.

NO: Planned Parenthood Federation of America, Inc., the oldest and largest reproductive health organization in the United States, argues that parental notification and consent laws keep girls from exercising their legal right to access abortion. Notifying parents of their daughter's intent to terminate a pregnancy puts many girls at risk for severe punishment, expulsion from the home, or even physical violence. Planned Parenthood contends that just as minors have the power to give their consent for other surgical procedures, they should be able to give their own consent to terminate a pregnancy.

In 1973, the U.S. Supreme Court decision *Roe v. Wade* guaranteed a woman's right to access abortion without restriction during the first trimester. The decision did not mention, however, the age of the woman seeking the abortion. A number of individual states, therefore, have statutes that require a girl under the age of 18 to receive either one or both parents' or legal guardians' consent in order to obtain an abortion, or to notify one or both parents.

A later Supreme Court decision, *Belotti v. Baird,* upheld the rights of states to place these restrictions on girls—provided there is an option for a "judicial bypass." This means that a girl can appear before a judge and either demonstrate that she is mature enough to make the decision to have an abortion or explain why notifying her parents would be detrimental to her. As the *Belotti* decision says, "[if] the court decides the minor is not mature enough to give informed consent, she must be given the opportunity to show that the abortion is in her best interest. If she makes this showing, the court must grant her bypass petition." Confidentiality is guaranteed so that a girl's parents do not know that she has gone to court. Currently, 35 states have laws on their books about obtaining consent from or notifying at least one parent. Of these, 9 are currently not enforced. Twenty-eight states provide for a judicial bypass.

Any discussions around abortion rights are rooted in the fundamental support for or opposition to abortion itself. It can be challenging, therefore, to separate the question of abortion from the question of whether minors can make an informed decision. Even adults who consider themselves to be pro-choice may support an adult woman's right to choose whether to carry or terminate a pregnancy, while feeling differently about girls under the age of 18 being able to make this decision for themselves. Others are clear on their belief that abortion is wrong regardless of the circumstance or age of the girl or woman involved. And still others believe that any girl or woman, regardless of age, is able and has the right to make this personal decision for herself. Many encourage girls considering abortion to talk with their parent(s) or another trusted adult. However, the reality is that many girls know that doing so would create a significant conflict in their family setting.

Specific to the debate around parental notification is the issue of someone other than a parent facilitating an abortion for a girl under the age of 18. Supporters of parental notification laws believe that such legislation would prevent this from happening. Opponents agree that it would and that it would be wrong to prosecute a family member for helping a niece or granddaughter under the age of 18 obtain an abortion.

In the following selections, Teresa Stanton Collett uses her knowledge of laws in different states to demonstrate what she feels is widespread support for parental involvement laws, focusing in particular on the Child Custody Protection Act. Planned Parenthood Federation of America, Inc., believes that because minors are able to access other medical care without parental consent, an abortion procedure should be no exception.

YES

Teresa Stanton Collett

Prepared Testimony of Teresa Stanton Collett

UNITED STATES HOUSE OF REPRESENTATIVES
Committee on the Judiciary
Subcommittee on the Constitution
Congressman Steve Chabot, Subcommittee Chair
September 6, 2001

. . . I am honored to have been invited to testify on H.R. 476, the "Child Custody Protection Act." . . . My testimony represents my professional knowledge and opinion as a law professor who writes on the topic of family law, and specifically on the topic of parental involvement laws. It also represents my experience in assisting the legislative sponsors of the Texas Parental Notification Act during the legislative debates prior to passage of the act, and as a member of the Texas Supreme Court Subadvisory Committee charged with proposing court rules implementing the judicial bypass created by the Texas act. . . .

It is my opinion that the Child Custody Protection Act will significantly advance the legitimate health and safety interests of young girls experiencing an unplanned pregnancy. It will also safeguard the ability of states to protect their minor citizens through the adoption of effective parental involvement statutes. . . .

Parental Rights to Control Medical Care of Minors

Just this past year, in a case involving the competing claims of parents and grandparents to decisionmaking authority over a child, the United States Supreme Court described parents' right to control the care of their children as "perhaps the oldest of the fundamental liberty interests recognized by this Court." In addressing the right of parents to direct the medical care of their children, the Court has stated:

> Our jurisprudence historically has reflected Western civilization concepts of the family as a unit with broad parental authority over minor children. Our cases have consistently followed that course; our constitutional system long ago rejected any notion that a child is "the mere creature of the State" and, on the contrary, asserted that parents generally "have the right, coupled with the high duty, to recognize and

From *U.N. Convention on the Rights of the Child* by Teresa Stanton Collett, 2001.

prepare [their children] for additional obligations." *Surely, this includes a "high duty" to recognize symptoms of illness and to seek and follow medical advice. The law's concept of the family rests on a presumption that parents possess what a child lacks in maturity, experience, and capacity for judgment required for making life's difficult decisions.*

It is this need to insure the availability of parental guidance and support that underlies the laws requiring a parent be notified or give consent prior to the performance of an abortion on his or her minor daughter. The national consensus in favor of this position is illustrated by the fact that there are parental involvement laws on the books in forty-three of the fifty states. Of the statutes in these forty-three states, eight have been determined to have state or federal constitutional infirmities. Therefore the laws of thirty-five states are in effect today. Nine of these states have laws that empower abortion providers to decide whether to involve parents or allow notice to or consent from people other than parents or legal guardians. These laws are substantially ineffectual in assuring parental involvement in a minor's decision to obtain an abortion. However, parents in the remaining twenty-six states are effectively guaranteed the right to parental notification or consent in most cases.

Widespread Public Support

There is widespread agreement that as a general rule, parents should be involved in their minor daughter's decision to terminate an unplanned pregnancy. This agreement even extends to young people ages 18 to 24. To my knowledge, no organizations or individuals, whether abortion rights activists or pro-life advocates, dispute this point. On an issue as contentious and divisive as abortion, it is both remarkable and instructive that there is such firm and long-standing support for laws requiring parental involvement.

Various reasons underlie this broad and consistent support. As Justices O'Connor, Kennedy, and Souter observed in *Planned Parenthood v. Casey*, parental consent and notification laws related to abortions "are based on the quite reasonable assumption that minors will benefit from consultation with their parents and that children will often not realize that their parents have their best interests at heart." This reasoning led the Court to conclude that the Pennsylvania parental consent law was constitutional. Two of the benefits achieved by parental involvement laws include improved medical care for young girls seeking abortions and increased protection against sexual exploitation by adult men.

Improved Medical Care of Minors Seeking Abortions

Medical care for minors seeking abortions is improved by parental involvement in three ways. First, parental involvement laws allow parents to assist their daughter in the selection of a healthcare provider. As with all medical procedures, one of the most important guarantees of patient safety is the professional competence of those who perform the medical procedure or administer the medical treatment. In *Bellotti v. Baird,* the United States Supreme Court acknowledged the superior ability of parents to evaluate and select appropriate abortion providers.

For example, the National Abortion Federation recommends that patients seeking an abortion confirm that the abortion will be performed by a licensed physician in good standing with the state Board of Medical Examiners, and that he or she have admitting privileges at a local hospital not more than twenty minutes away from the location where the abortion is to occur. A well-informed parent seeking to guide her child is more likely to inquire regarding these matters than a panicky teen who just wants to no longer be pregnant.

Parental involvement laws also insure that parents have the opportunity to provide additional medical history and information to abortion providers prior to performance of the abortion.

> The medical, emotional, and psychological consequences of an abortion are serious and can be lasting; this is particularly so when the patient is immature. An adequate medical and psychological case history is important to the physician. Parents can provide medical and psychological data, refer the physician to other sources of medical history, such as family physicians, and authorize family physicians to give relevant data.

Abortion providers, in turn, will have the opportunity to disclose the medical risks of the various procedures to an adult who can advise the girl in giving her informed consent to the procedure ultimately selected. Parental notification or consent laws insure that the abortion providers inform a mature adult of the risks and benefits of the proposed treatment, after having received a more complete and thus more accurate medical history of the patient.

The third way in which parental involvement improves medical treatment of pregnant minors is by insuring that parents have adequate knowledge to recognize and respond to any post-abortion complication that may develop. In a recent ruling by a Florida intermediate appellate court upholding that state's parental involvement law, the court observed:

> The State proved that appropriate aftercare is critical in avoiding or responding to post-abortion complications. Abortion is ordinarily an invasive surgical procedure attended by many of the risks accompanying surgical procedures generally. If post-abortion nausea, tenderness, swelling, bleeding, or cramping persists or suddenly worsens, a minor (like an adult) may need medical attention. A guardian unaware that her ward or a parent unaware that his minor daughter has undergone an abortion will be at a serious disadvantage in caring for her if complications develop. An adult who has been kept in the dark cannot, moreover, assist the minor in following the abortion provider's instructions for post-surgical care. Failure to follow such instructions can increase the risk of complications. As the plaintiffs' medical experts conceded, the risks are significant in the best of circumstances. While abortion is less risky than some surgical procedures, abortion complications can result in serious injury, infertility, and even death.

Abortion proponents often claim that abortion is one of the safest surgical procedures performed today. However, the actual rate of many complications is simply unknown. At least one American court has held that a perforated uterus is a "normal risk" associated with abortion. Untreated, a perforated uterus may result in an infection, complicated by fever, endometritis, and parametritis. "The risk of death from postabortion sepsis [infection] is highest for young women, those who are unmarried, and those who undergo procedures that do not directly evacuate the contents of the uterus. . . . A delay in treatment allows the infection to progress to bacteremia, pelvic abscess, septic pelvic thrombophlebitis, disseminated intravascular coagulophy, septic shock, renal failure, and death."

Without the knowledge that their daughter has had an abortion, parents are incapable of insuring that the minor obtain routine post-operative care or of providing an adequate medical history to physicians called upon to treat any complications the girl might experience.

Increased Protection From Sexual Assault

In addition to improving the medical care received by young girls dealing with an unplanned pregnancy, parental involvement laws are intended to afford increased protection against sexual exploitation of minors by adult men. National studies reveal that "[a]lmost two thirds of adolescent mothers have partners older than 20 years of age." In a study of over 46,000 pregnancies by school-age girls in California, researchers found that "71%, or over 33,000, were fathered by adult post-high-school men whose mean age was 22.6 years, an average of 5 years older than the mothers. . . . Even among junior high school mothers aged 15 or younger, most births are fathered by adult men 6–7 years their senior. *Men aged 25 or older father more births among California school-age girls than do boys under age 18.*" Other studies have found that most teenage pregnancies are the result of predatory practices by men who are substantially older.

Abortion providers have resisted any reporting obligation to insure that men who unlawfully impregnate minors are identified and prosecuted. Just [recently] a lawsuit was filed in Arizona alleging that Planned Parenthood failed to report the sexual molestation of a twelve-year-old leading to her continued molestation and impregnation. If true, this conduct is consistent with the position of many abortion providers who argue that encouraging medical care through insuring confidentiality is more important than insuring legal intervention to stop the sexual abuse. While seemingly well intentioned, this reasoning fails since the ultimate result of this approach is to merely address a symptom of the sexual abuse (the pregnancy) while leaving the cause unaffected. The minor, no longer pregnant, then returns to the abusive relationship, with no continuing contact with an adult (other than the abuser) knowing of her plight. The clinic won't tell, the police and parents don't know, and the girl, still under the abuser's influence, is too confused or afraid to tell. . . .

States adopting parental involvement laws have come to the reasonable conclusion that secret abortions do not advance the best interests of most minor girls. This is particularly reasonable in light of the fact that most teen pregnancies are the result of sexual relations with adult men, and many of these relationships involve criminal conduct. Parental involvement laws insure that parents have the opportunity to protect their daughters from those who would victimize their daughters again and again and again. The Child Custody Protection Act would insure that men cannot deprive these minors of this protection by merely crossing state lines.

Effectiveness of Judicial Bypass

In those few cases where it is not in the girl's best interest to disclose her pregnancy to her parents, state laws generally provide the pregnant minor the option of seeking a court determination that either involvement of the girl's parent is not in her best interest, or that she is sufficiently mature to make decisions regarding the continuation of her pregnancy. This is a requirement for parental consent laws under existing United States Supreme Court cases, and courts have been quick to overturn laws omitting adequate bypass.

Opponents of the Child Custody Protection Act have argued that its passage would endanger teens since parents may be abusive and many teens would seek illegal abortions. This is a phantom fear. Parental involvement laws are on the books in over two-thirds of the states, some for over twenty years, and there is no case where it has been established that these laws led to parental abuse or to self-inflicted injury. Similarly, there is no evidence that these laws have led to an increase in illegal abortions.

It [is] often asserted that parental involvement laws do not increase the number of parents notified of their daughters' intentions to obtain abortions, since minors will commonly seek judicial bypass of the parental involvement requirement. Assessing the accuracy of this claim is difficult since parental notification or consent laws rarely impose reporting requirements regarding the use of judicial bypass. The Idaho parental consent law enacted in 2000 is one of the few exceptions to this general rule. Based upon the reporting required under that law, no abortions obtained by minors were pursuant to a judicial bypass. From September 1, 2000 through April 3, 2001, thirty-three minors have been reported as obtaining an abortion in Idaho. Thirty-one of these abortions were performed after obtaining parental consent. One minor was legally emancipated and did not need parental consent, and one report did not indicate the nature of the consent obtained prior to performance of the abortion.

Obtaining comparable information in states having parental involvement laws with no mandatory reporting requirement is difficult. State agencies will not accumulate such information absent a legislative mandate. Nonetheless, it is safe to say that the use of judicial bypass to avoid parental involvement varies significantly among the states. While commonly used in Massachusetts, judicial bypass is seldom used in many states. In 1999, 1,015 girls got abortions in Alabama with a parent's approval and 12 with a judge's approval, according to state health department records. Indiana also has few bypass proceedings according to an informal study. In Pennsylvania, approximately 13,700 minors obtained abortions from 1994 through 1999.

Of these only about seven percent or 1,000 girls bypassed parental involvement via court order. Texas implemented its Parental Notification Act in 2000. During the state legislative hearings, the Texas Family Planning Council submitted a study indicating that a parent accompanied 69% of minors seeking abortions in Texas. After passage of the Texas Parental Notification Act, 96% of all minors seeking an abortion in Texas involved a parent.

Conclusion

By passage of the Child Custody Protection Act, Congress will protect the ability of the citizens in each state to determine the proper level of parental involvement in the lives of young girls facing an unplanned pregnancy.

Experience in states having parental involvement laws has shown that, when notified, parents and their daughters unite in a desire to resolve issues surrounding an unplanned pregnancy. If the minor chooses to terminate the pregnancy, parents can assist their daughters in selecting competent abortion providers, and abortion providers may receive more comprehensive medical histories of their parents. In these cases, the minors will more likely be encouraged to obtain post-operative check-ups, and parents will be prepared to respond to any complications that arise.

If the minor chooses to continue her pregnancy, involvement of her parents serves many of the same goals. Parents can provide or help obtain the necessary resources for early and comprehensive prenatal care. They can assist their daughters in evaluating the options of single parenthood, adoption, or early marriage. Perhaps most importantly, they can provide the love and support that is found in the many healthy families of the United States.

Regardless of whether the girl chooses to continue or terminate her pregnancy, parental involvement laws have proven desirable because they afford greater protection for the many girls who are pregnant due to sexual assault. By insuring that parents know of the pregnancy, it becomes much more likely that they will intervene to insure the protection of their daughters from future assaults.

In balancing the minor's right to privacy and her need for parental involvement, the majority of states have determined that parents should know before abortions are performed on minors. This is a reasonable conclusion and well within the states' police powers. However, the political authority of each state stops at its geographic boundaries. States need the assistance of the federal government to insure that the protection they wish to afford their children is not easily circumvented by strangers taking minors across state lines.

The Child Custody Protection Act has the unique virtue of building upon two of the few points of agreement in the national debate over abortion: the desirability of parental involvement in a minor's decisions about an unplanned pregnancy, and the need to protect the physical health and safety of the pregnant girl. I urge members of this committee to vote for its passage.

➡ **NO**

Fact Sheet: Teenagers, Abortion, and Government Intrusion Laws

Of all the abortion-related policy issues facing decision-makers in this country today, parental consent or notification before a minor may obtain an abortion is one of the most difficult. Few would deny that most teenagers, especially younger ones, would benefit from adult guidance when faced with an unwanted pregnancy. Few would deny that such guidance ideally should come from the teenager's parents. Unfortunately, we do not live in an ideal world. For a variety of reasons, including fear of parental maltreatment or abuse, teenagers frequently cannot tell their parents about their pregnancies or planned abortions.

In the 34 states with laws in effect that mandate the involvement of at least one parent in the abortion decision, teenagers who cannot tell their parents must either travel out of state or obtain approval from a judge—known as a "judicial bypass" procedure—to obtain an abortion. The result is almost always a delay that can increase both the cost of the abortion and the physical and emotional health risk to the teenager, since an earlier abortion is a safer one (Paul et al., 1999).

Currently, anti-choice members of Congress are seeking to make it even more difficult for minors living in states with mandatory parental involvement laws to obtain an abortion with the so-called "Child Custody Protection Act" (CCPA). The bill would make it a federal crime to transport a minor across state lines for an abortion unless the parental involvement requirements of her home state had been met. If the bill were enacted, persons convicted would be subject to imprisonment, fines, and civil suits (H. R. 1755, 2003; S. 851, 2003).

Requiring Parental Consent for Abortion Is Not Consistent with State Laws Regulating a Range of Medical Services for Minors

Proponents of mandated parental involvement contend that parents have a right to decide what medical services their minor children receive. However, states have long recognized that many minors have the capacity to consent to their own medical care and that, in certain critical areas such as mental health, drug and/or alcohol addiction, treatment for sexually transmitted infections (STIs), and pregnancy, entitlement to confidential care is a public health necessity (Donovan, 1998).

- Twenty-one states and the District of Columbia grant all minors the authority to consent to contraceptive services. Approximately eleven other states grant most minors this authority (AGI, 2004a).
- Thirty-four states and the District of Columbia authorize a pregnant minor to obtain prenatal care and delivery services without parental consent or notification (AGI, 2004b).
- All 50 states and the District of Columbia give minors the authority to consent to the diagnosis and treatment of sexually transmitted infections (AGI, 2004c).
- Many of these laws allow minors to give consent to treatments that involve greater medical risk than a first-trimester abortion, such as surgical interventions during pregnancy and cesarean sections. Nevertheless, many of these same states require parental consent for abortion.

Most Teenagers Having Abortions Already Involve Their Parents, Even When Not Required to Do So by Law, and Many Have Compelling Reasons to Seek Confidential Services

A minority of teenagers do not involve their parents. Overwhelmingly, they make this decision for compelling reasons. A 1991 study of unmarried minors having abortions in states without parental involvement laws found that

- Sixty-one percent of the respondents reported that at least one of their parents knew about their abortion.
- Of those minors who did not inform their parents of their abortions, 30 percent had histories of violence in their families, feared the occurrence of violence, or were afraid of being forced to leave their homes.
- Minors who did not tell their parents were also disproportionately older (aged 16 or 17) and employed.
- Among the respondents who did not inform their parents of their pregnancies, all consulted someone in addition to clinic staff about their abortions, such as their boyfriend (89 percent), an adult (52 percent), or a professional (22 percent) (Henshaw & Kost, 1992)

Lack of Confidential Reproductive Health Care Harms Teenagers

Evidence suggests that lack of confidentiality in accessing sexual health care services severely delays or even curtails minors' use of those services. A survey of abortion patients around the U.S., conducted by the Alan Guttmacher Institute (AGI), found that 63% of minors who were having later abortions (after 16 weeks' gestation) cited fear of telling their parents as reason for the delay (Torres & Forrest, 1988). In August 2002, the *Journal of the American Medical Association* published a study of minors seeking sexual health care services at

Planned Parenthood health centers in Wisconsin. Nearly half (47%) of the respondents reported that they would discontinue use of all Planned Parenthood services if their parents were notified that they were seeking prescription contraceptives. An additional 12% would delay or discontinue using specific sexual health care services if parental notification were required. But only 1 percent said they would stop having vaginal intercourse (Reddy et al., 2002).

Experience shows that teenagers who cannot involve their parents in their abortion services suffer harm in states with mandatory parental consent and notice laws. Whether they travel to other states or obtain judicial approval, the results are the same: delays that can greatly increase both the physical and emotional health risks as well as the costs.

- While nationwide most minors seeking judicial approval receive it, the process is unwieldy and, most importantly, time-consuming. Court proceedings in Minnesota routinely delayed abortions by more than one week, and sometimes up to three weeks (ACLU, 1986). . . .
- Studies conducted in Pennsylvania and Alabama found that the vast majority of courts in those states were unprepared to implement the judicial bypass. Some court officials had not even heard of the laws, despite the fact that they had been in effect for several years (Silverstein, 1999; Silverstein and Speitzel, 2002).
- The manner in which each state enforces its judicial bypass laws is erratic. In Minnesota, the federal district court found that the state courts "denied only an infinitesimal proportion of the petitions brought since 1981" (ACLU, 1986). A study in Massachusetts found that only 9 of the 477 abortion requests studied had been denied (Yates & Pliner, 1988). However, an Ohio report found that the percentage of waivers denied ranged from 100 percent to 2 percent, depending on the county in which the petition was filed (Rollenhagen, 1992).

Some states go as far as to require the involvement of both parents. These statutes ignore the realities of teenagers' lives.

- In 2000, approximately 19 million children under the age of 18 lived with only one parent. Nearly 3 million more lived with neither parent (U.S. Census Bureau, 2001a). . . .
- Millions of children live with a single parent subsequent to divorce. In 2000, 54 percent of single parents with children under the age of 18 were divorced or separated (U.S. Census Bureau, 2001b). A study found that one-third of divorced fathers had no contact with their children during the previous year (Doherty et al., 1998).
- In Minnesota, more than one-quarter of the teenagers who sought judicial bypass were accompanied by one parent, who was most often divorced or separated. According to the federal district court that reviewed Minnesota's law, many of the custodial parents feared that notification would "bring the absent parent back into the family in an intrusive and abusive way" (*Hodgson v. Minnesota*, 1986).

Moreover, even if a teenager is able and willing to involve one or both parents, the procedures required by some state parental consent or notification laws make compliance impossible or difficult.

- Requiring that teenagers either obtain notarized evidence that parents have been notified or present a death certificate for a deceased parent may present impossible logistical barriers, lead to breaches of confidentiality for parents and teenagers, or cause serious delay.
- A requirement that the physician personally locate and notify the parents could easily both delay the procedure and increase the cost.

The Child Custody Protection Act Harms Minors

In April 2003, the CCPA was reintroduced in the House of Representatives and the Senate. The bill would make it a federal crime to transport a minor across state lines to obtain abortion services without fulfilling the parental consent or notice requirements of her home state. In 1998, the House of Representatives passed the bill by a vote of 276 to 150, but President Clinton threatened to veto it, and the Senate never took it up for consideration (Eilperin, 1999). In 1999, the House Judiciary Committee passed the CCPA, defeating five proposed amendments, including those that would create exceptions for grandparents, siblings, aunts and uncles, and clergy who assist minors in obtaining abortions (Superville, 1999). That year, the legislation passed in the full House of Representatives again, this time by a vote of 270 to 159. However, the Senate again failed to take it up for consideration. Although, if passed, the Act would only affect a small percentage of women seeking abortion services—minors account for fewer than 1 in 10 abortions performed—the impact of the Act would be dramatic.

- The CCPA would subject criminal penalties to anyone—a grandparent, adult sibling, member of the clergy, or medical professional—who assists a minor in traveling across state lines to receive an abortion without the parental consent or notification required by her home state.
- CCPA makes such assistance a crime even if confidential abortions are legal in the state where the abortion is to be performed and even if that state allows the accompanying grandparent or adult sibling to give lawful consent for the minor's abortion.
- CCPA thus isolates young women from the trusted friends and relatives who can assist them in time of crisis.
- The CCPA makes criminals out of family members and friends even in emergency situations when the minor needs an immediate abortion to protect her health.
- The CCPA potentially requires a minor to satisfy differing legal requirements in two states: the state she comes from and the state where she is to have the abortion. If those two states both have parental consent or notice requirements, the minor may have to seek waivers from judges in two states, further delaying her abortion and raising its costs and health risks.
- Because 87% of U.S. counties lack an abortion provider (Finer & Henshaw, 2003), CCPA will increase the burdens on the many young women who must cross state lines simply to access the *nearest* abortion provider.

- The CCPA also raises a number of other constitutional and legal questions, particularly those related to issues of federalism. The legislation effectively nullifies the laws of those states that allow physicians to provide confidential services to minors who enter the states for abortion and deprives individuals of their right to cross state lines to obtain lawful services. Such intervention by the federal government would be unprecedented, and raises serious implications for states, and individuals' rights (Saul, 1998).

Cited References

ACLU—American Civil Liberties Union Foundation Reproductive Freedom Project. (1986). *Parental Consent Laws: Their Catastrophic Impact on Teenagers Right to Abortion.* New York: ACLU.

AGI—Alan Guttmacher Institute. (2003a, accessed May 28). *Minors Access to Contraceptive Services* [Online]. . . .

————. (2004b, accessed July 29). *Minors' Access to Prenatal Care. State Policies in Brief.* [Online]. . . .

————. (2004c, accessed July 29). *Minors' Access to STD Services* [Online]. . . .

CDC—Centers for Disease Control and Prevention. (2003, accessed May 28). *Unmarried Childbearing* [Online]. . . . *Child Custody Protection Act,* H. R. 1755, 108th Cong., 1st Sess. (2003).

————, S.851, 108th Cong., 1st Sess. (2003).

Doherty, William J., et al. (1998). "Responsible Fathering: An Overview and Conceptual Framework." *Journal of Marriage and the Family,* 60(2), 277–292.

Donovan, Patricia. (1998). "Teenagers' Right to Consent to Reproductive Health Care." *Issues in Brief.* Washington, DC: Alan Guttmacher Institute.

Eilperin, Juliet. (1999, July 1). "House Acts to Bar Interstate Transport of Teens to Evade Abortion Laws." *Washington Post,* p. A06.

Henshaw, Stanley K. (1998). "Abortion Incidence and Services in the United States, 1995–1996." *Family Planning Perspectives,* 30(6), 263–270 & 287.

Henshaw, Stanley K. & Kathryn Kost. (1992). "Parental Involvement in Minors' Abortion Decisions." *Family Planning Perspectives,* 24(5), 196–207 & 213.

Hodgson v. Minnesota, 648 F. Supp. 756 (D. Minn. 1986).

Paul, Maureen, *et al.* (1999). *A Clinician's Guide to Medical and Surgical Abortion.* New York: Churchill Livingstone.

Reddy, Diane M., *et al.* (2002). "Effect of Mandatory Parental Notification on Adolescent Girls' Use of Sexual Health Care Services." *Journal of the American Medical Association,* 288(6), 710–14.

Rollenhagen, Mark. (1992, June 18). "Clinics Fight Notification Rule By Filing Suit." *Plain Dealer,* p. 1C.

Saul, Rebekah. (1998). "The Child Custody Protection Act: A 'Minor' Issue at the Top of the Anti-abortion Agenda." *Guttmacher Report on Public Policy,* 1(4), 1–2 & 7.

Silverstein, Helena. (1999). "Road Closed: Evaluating the Judicial Bypass Provision of the Pennsylvania Abortion Control Act." *Law & Social Inquiry,* 24 (Winter), 73–96.

Silverstein, Helena & Leanne Speitel. (2002). "'Honey, I Have No Idea': Court Readiness to Handle Petitions to Waive Parental Consent for Abortion." *Iowa Law Review,* 88(1), 75–120.

Superville, Darlene. (1999, June 23, accessed 1999, July 1). "Teen Abortion Bill Clears House Committee." [Online]. *Associated Press.*

U.S. Census Bureau. (2001a, accessed 2003, May 28). *Household Relationship and Living Arrangements of Children under 18 Years: March 2000* [Online]. . . .

———. (2001b, accessed 2003, May 28). *One-Parent Family Groups with Own Children Under 18: March 2000* [Online]. . . .

Yates, Suzanne & Anita J. Pliner. (1988). "Judging Maturity in the Courts: The Massachusetts Consent Statute." *American Journal of Public Health,* 78(6), 646–649.

POSTSCRIPT

Should Minors Be Required to Get Their Parents' Permission in Order to Obtain an Abortion?

The abortion debate, like many other controversies, is often viewed in extremes. One is pro-choice, or one is antichoice. There is no gray area in between. At the same time, however, introducing a minor into the discussion often alters the discussion—particularly the younger the girl is who is seeking the abortion. In some cases, the younger a girl is, the more protection adults may feel she needs. In other cases, the younger she is, the more likely some abortion opponents might be to make an exception, citing a preference for the "necessary evil" of abortion over letting a 14-year-old girl become a parent.

An important factor to keep in mind is the fact that not everyone has sexual intercourse by choice. Although many abortion opponents will make an exception for pregnancies that are caused by rape or incest, others maintain that a pregnancy is a pregnancy and that no potential life should be punished, even if it were conceived in a violent manner. If a state law requires that a parent be notified, and the parent who is notified is the one who caused the pregnancy, then parental notification may have stopped an abortion only to put a girl's safety or life in jeopardy. On the other hand, in cases of incest, parental notification could help to bring rape or incest—which are all too frequently hidden or kept private—out into the open so that it will not happen again, and the perpetrator, if known, can be arrested and the abuse stopped.

Legislating personal decisions is, as always, a slippery slope. How far do we go? How do laws legislating one behavior or type of procedure affect others? For example, parental consent is currently not required in order for a minor to obtain birth control. Controversy remains around one particular type of birth control, Emergency Contraception, formerly known as the "morning-after" pill. Emergency Contraception is not an abortion; it prevents pregnancy from happening. In fact, if a woman is pregnant without knowing it, has unprotected intercourse, and then takes Emergency Contraception, her pregnancy should not be affected by the Emergency Contraception. At the same time, however, because one of the ways in which Emergency Contraception works is by preventing a fertilized egg from implanting, those who believe that life begins at conception argue that Emergency Contraception is the same thing as abortion. Therefore, the door that is open to parental notification and consent laws remains open to support for parental notification or consent before Emergency Contraception can be dispensed. This in turn could lead to legislation requiring parental notification or consent for birth control pills and condoms.

In an ideal world, people would not have sex before they are old enough and established enough in their lives to be able to manage the potential consequences of being in a sexual relationship. In an ideal world, abortion would not be necessary because no pregnancy would be unplanned or come as the result of rape or incest. People, regardless of age, have unprotected sex or use contraception incorrectly. People, regardless of age, are raped and sexually abused. Women, regardless of age, have pregnancies that may need to be terminated for medical reasons. In some households, the revelation of an unplanned pregnancy can result in violence against the pregnant teen and/or her partner.

Is there a solution between these two extremes that could enable parents to show their care and support of their adolescents while at the same time letting them make their own decisions? Where do your feelings about abortion in general come into play in your thoughts on this matter?

Suggested Readings

American Civil Liberties Union, *Parental Involvement Laws*. Fact sheet available online at http://www.aclu.org/issues/reproduct/parent_ inv.html.

Focus on the Family, "Talking Points for Laws Requiring Parental Involvement in Minor Abortions," *Citizen Link* (2000). Available online at http://www.family.org/cforum/research/papers/a0012619.html.

David J. Garrow, *Liberty and Sexuality: The Right to Privacy and the Making of Roe v. Wade* (University of California Press, 1998).

Deborah Haas-Wilson, "The Impact of State Abortion Restrictions on Minors' Demand for Abortions," *Journal of Human Resources* (vol. 31, no. 1, January 1999).

N. E. H. Hull and Peter Charles Hoffer, *Roe v. Wade: The Abortion Rights Controversy in American History* (University Press of Kansas, 2001).

NARAL, *Government-Mandated Parental Involvement in Family Planning Services Threatens Young People's Health*. Fact sheet available online at http://www.naral.org/mediaresources/fact/parental.html.

Annette Tomal, "Parental Involvement Laws and Minor and Non-Minor Teen Abortion and Birth Rates," *Journal of Family and Economic Issues* (vol. 20, no. 2, Summer 1999).

Internet References . . .

Child Rights Information Network

The Child Rights Information Network (CRIN) is a global network that dissemi-
nates information about the Convention on the Rights of the Child and child
rights among non-governmental organizations, U.N. agencies, intergovernmen-
tal organizations, educational institutions, and other child rights experts.

http://www.crin.org/

Planned Parenthood Federation of America

Planned Parenthood Federation of America is the oldest and largest voluntary
reproductive health organization in the United States.

http://www.plannedparenthood.org

Eagle Forum's Mission

Eagle Forum's Mission enables conservative and pro-family men and women to
participate in the process of self-government and public policy making.

http://www.eagleforum.org/

UNICEF

UNICEF is mandated by the U.N. General Assembly to advocate for the protection of children's rights, to help meet their basic needs, and to expand their
opportunities to reach their full potential.

http://www.unicef.org/

UNIT 3

Being Inclusive: Lesbian, Gay, and Bisexual Individuals, Couples, and Families

*N*ot too long ago, the words "lesbian" and "gay" appearing in front of the word "marriage" and "families" would have been considered an oxymoron. For some people, they still do. Others see diverse family structures as social progress. There are a number of issues that remain in the news today relating specifically to the rights of lesbian and gay individuals to have legal and social recognition in the context of family and relationships. This unit examines four of these questions:

- Should Same-Sex Couples Be Allowed to Marry Legally?

- Should Men Who Have Sex with Men Be Allowed to Donate Blood?

- Should Lesbian and Gay Individuals Be Allowed to Adopt Children?

- Should Private Sexual Acts between Gay and Lesbian Couples Be Legal?

ISSUE 10

Should Same-Sex Couples Be Allowed to Marry Legally?

YES: Human Rights Campaign, from *Answers to Questions About Marriage Equality* (HRC's FamilyNet Project, 2004)

NO: Peter Sprigg, from *Questions and Answers: What's Wrong with Letting Same-Sex Couples 'Marry'?* (Family Research Council, 2004)

ISSUE SUMMARY

YES: The Human Rights Campaign (HRC), America's largest lesbian and gay organization, outlines the current disparities American lesbian and gay couples experience because they are not allowed to marry legally, as well as the logistical considerations involved in granting same-sex couples the right to marry.

NO: Peter Sprigg, director of the Center for Marriage and Family Studies at the Family Research Council, outlines why nonheterosexual relationships do not carry with them the same validity as heterosexual relationships, and therefore should not be allowed to marry legally.

The past few years have seen the topic of same-sex marriage rush into the forefront of the news and other media. As of October 2004, the only state in the United States allowing same-sex marriage is Massachusetts, although this is being challenged by those opposed to same-sex marriage by changing the state's Constitution. Same-sex couples in other states are challenging current laws by suing for the right to marry legally. As of 2006, New Jersey's State Supreme Court ruled that same-sex couples have a constitutional right to receive the same state benefits, protections, and obligations as different-sex married couples, leaving the naming of same-sex committed relationships to the state legislature, which voted at the end of that year to call them "civil unions." This, too, is being contested by proponents who believe that calling same-sex marriage anything other than marriage perpetuates the same principles of "separate but equal" that was all too familiar to African American individuals until the civil rights movement in the 1960s.

On the other side of the debate, eight additional states in 2006 voted to amend their state's constitutions to define marriage as being exclusively between a man and a woman: Idaho, Colorado, South Dakota, Virginia, Tennessee, South Carolina, Wisconsin, and Alabama.

As of the writing of this piece, Iowa, Maine, Massachusetts, Connecticut, and Vermont are the only states to have a marriage license or refer to their union as a marriage, the benefits are the same as they would be for a heterosexual marriage. These unions are not, however, recognized in any other state. This is due in great part to the Defense of Marriage Act, which was signed into law in 1996 by President Bill Clinton. This Act says that no state is required to recognize a same-sex union and defines marriage as being between a man and a woman only. Therefore, same-sex unions that are legal in one state do not have to be recognized as legal in another. Over 30 states have passed legislation saying they would not recognize a same-sex union that took place in another state.

Those who oppose same-sex marriage believe that marriage is, and always has been, between a man and a woman. They believe that a key part of marriage for many heterosexual couples is reproduction or another type of parenting arrangement, such as adoption. In those cases, they believe that any child should have two parents, one male and one female. Many do not oppose granting domestic partner benefits to same-sex partners, or even, in some cases, civil unions. They do, however, believe that if lesbian and gay couples were allowed to marry and to receive the legal and social benefits thereof, it would serve only to further erode the institution of marriage as it is currently defined, which, in the United States, boasts one divorce for every two marriages.

Supporters of same-sex marriage believe that if lesbian and gay couples wish to make a lifetime commitment, they should be afforded the same rights, privileges, and vocabulary as heterosexual couples. Although some would be as happy with the term "civil union," accompanied by equal rights, others believe that making marriage available to all is the only way to go. Some lesbian and gay couples who are in committed, loving relationships resent that they have fewer rights than a heterosexual couple in which there is alcohol or drug abuse or domestic violence.

An argument that is raised in this debate is that granting same-sex couples the right to marry would open the door for adult pedophiles to petition to marry the children with whom they engage in their sexual relationships. Most lesbian and gay individuals and their supporters find this offensive, as well as an invalid comparison. What do you think?

In the following selections, both the Human Rights Campaign and Peter Sprigg raise the most common questions pertaining to same-sex marriage. The Human Rights Campaign enumerates the rights that are not currently available to same-sex couples in long-term committed relationships, and maintains that granting equal rights to these couples is good not only for them but also for society as a whole. One of the concerns Peter Sprigg raises pertains to the expectation that a purpose of heterosexual marriage is to raise children, and that a same-sex couple is a harmful setting in which to do that.

YES ↵   Human Rights Campaign

Answers to Questions About Marriage Equality

Why Same-Sex Couples Want to Marry

Many same-sex couples want the right to legally marry because they are in love—either they just met the love of their lives, or more likely, they have spent the last 10, 20 or 50 years with that person—and they want to honor their relationship in the greatest way our society has to offer, by making a public commitment to stand together in good times and bad, through all the joys and challenges family life brings.

Many [same-sex] parents want the right to marry because they know it offers children a vital safety net and guarantees protections that unmarried parents cannot provide.

And still other people—both gay and straight—are fighting for the right of same-sex couples to marry because they recognize that it is simply not fair to deny some families the protections all other families are eligible to enjoy.

Currently in the United States, same-sex couples in long-term, committed relationships pay higher taxes and are denied basic protections and rights granted to married heterosexual couples. Among them:

- **Hospital visitation.** Married couples have the automatic right to visit each other in the hospital and make medical decisions. Same-sex couples can be denied the right to visit a sick or injured loved one in the hospital.
- **Social Security benefits.** Married people receive Social Security payments upon the death of a spouse. Despite paying payroll taxes, gay and lesbian partners receive no Social Security survivor benefits—resulting in an average annual income loss of $5,528 upon the death of a partner.
- **Immigration.** Americans in binational relationships are not permitted to petition for their same-sex partners to immigrate. As a result, they are often forced to separate or move to another country.
- **Health insurance.** Many public and private employers provide medical coverage to the spouses of their employees, but most employers do not provide coverage to the life partners of gay and lesbian employees. Gay employees who do receive health coverage for their partners must pay federal income taxes on the value of the insurance.

From *Human Rights Campaign Foundation's FamilyNet Project* (www.hrc.org). Copyright © 2004 by Human Rights Campaign. Reprinted by permission.

- **Estate taxes.** A married person automatically inherits all the property of his or her deceased spouse without paying estate taxes. A gay or lesbian taxpayer is forced to pay estate taxes on property inherited from a deceased partner.
- **Retirement savings.** While a married person can roll a deceased spouse's 401(k) funds into an IRA without paying taxes, a gay or lesbian American who inherits a 401(k) can end up paying up to 70 percent of it in taxes and penalties.
- **Family leave.** Married workers are legally entitled to unpaid leave from their jobs to care for an ill spouse. Gay and lesbian workers are not entitled to family leave to care for their partners.
- **Nursing homes.** Married couples have a legal right to live together in nursing homes. Because they are not legal spouses, elderly gay or lesbian couples do not have the right to spend their last days living together in nursing homes.
- **Home protection.** Laws protect married seniors from being forced to sell their homes to pay high nursing home bills; gay and lesbian seniors have no such protection.
- **Pensions.** After the death of a worker, most pension plans pay survivor benefits only to a legal spouse of the participant. Gay and lesbian partners are excluded from such pension benefits.

Why Civil Unions Aren't Enough

Comparing marriage to civil unions is a bit like comparing diamonds to rhinestones. One is, quite simply, the real deal; the other is not. Consider:

- Couples eligible to marry may have their marriage performed in any state and have it recognized in every other state in the nation and every country in the world.
- Couples who are joined in a civil union in Vermont (the only state that offers civil unions) have no guarantee that its protections will even travel with them to neighboring New York or New Hampshire—let alone California or any other state.

Moreover, even couples who have a civil union and remain in Vermont receive only second-class protections in comparison to their married friends and neighbors. While they receive state-level protections, they do not receive any of the *more than 1,100 federal benefits and protections of marriage.*

In short, civil unions are not separate but equal—they are separate *and* unequal. And our society has tried separate before. It just doesn't work. . . .

Answers to Questions People Are Asking

I Believe God Meant Marriage for Men and Women.
How Can I Support Marriage for Same-Sex Couples?
Many people who believe in God—and fairness and justice for all—ask this question. They feel a tension between religious beliefs and democratic values that has been experienced in many different ways throughout our nation's history. That

is why the framers of our Constitution established the principle of separation of church and state. That principle applies no less to the marriage issue than it does to any other.

Indeed, the answer to the apparent dilemma between religious beliefs and support for equal protections for all families lies in recognizing that marriage has a significant religious meaning for many people, but that it is also a legal contract. And it is strictly the legal—not the religious—dimension of marriage that is being debated now.

Granting marriage rights to same-sex couples would *not* require Christianity, Judaism, Islam, or any other religion to perform these marriages. It would not require religious institutions to permit these ceremonies to be held on their grounds. It would not even require that religious communities discuss the issue. People of faith would remain free to make their own judgments about what makes a marriage in the eyes of God—just as they are today.

Consider, for example, the difference in how the Catholic Church and the U.S. government view couples who have divorced and remarried. Because church tenets do not sanction divorce, the second marriage is not valid in the church's view. The government, however, recognizes the marriage by extending to the remarried couple the same rights and protections as those granted to every other married couple in America. In this situation—as would be the case in marriage for same-sex couples—the church remains free to establish its own teachings on the religious dimension of marriage while the government upholds equality under law.

It should also be noted that there are a growing number of religious communities that have decided to bless same-sex unions. Among them are Reform Judaism, the Unitarian Universalist Association and the Metropolitan Community Church. The Presbyterian Church (USA) also allows ceremonies to be performed, although they are not considered the same as marriage. The Episcopal Church and United Church of Christ allow individual churches to set their own policies on same-sex unions.

"This Is Different from Interracial Marriage. Sexual Orientation Is a Choice."

. . . Decades of research all point to the fact that sexual orientation is not a choice, and that a person's sexual orientation cannot be changed. Who one is drawn to is a fundamental aspect of who we are.

In this way, the struggle for marriage equality for same-sex couples is just as basic as the fight for interracial marriage was. It recognizes that Americans should not be coerced into false and unhappy marriages but should be free to marry the person they love—thereby building marriage on a true and stable foundation.

"Won't This Create a Free-For-All and Make the Whole Idea of Marriage Meaningless?"

Many people share this concern because opponents of gay and lesbian people have used this argument as a scare tactic. But it is not true. Granting same-sex couples the right to marry would in no way change the number of people who could enter into a marriage (or eliminate restrictions on the age or familial relationships of those who may marry). Marriage would continue to recognize the highest possible commitment that can be made between two adults, plain and simple. . . .

"I Strongly Believe Children Need a Mother and a Father."

Many of us grew up believing that everyone needs a mother and father, regardless of whether we ourselves happened to have two parents, or two *good* parents.

But as families have grown more diverse in recent decades and as the researchers have studied how these different family relationships affect children, it has become clear that the *quality* of a family's relationship is more important than the particular *structure* of families that exist today. In other words, the qualities that help children grow into good and responsible adults—learning how to learn, to have compassion for others, to contribute to society and be respectful of others and their differences—do not depend on the sexual orientation of their parents but on their parents' ability to provide a loving, stable, and happy home, something no class of Americans has an exclusive hold on.

That is why research studies have consistently shown that children raised by gay and lesbian parents do just as well on all conventional measure of child development, such as academic achievement, psychological well-being and social abilities, as children raised by heterosexual parents.

That is also why the nation's leading child welfare organizations, including the American Academy of Pediatrics, the American Academy of Family Physicians, and others, have issued statements that dismiss assertions that only heterosexual couples can be good parents—and declare that the focus should now be on providing greater protections for the 1 million to 9 million children being raised by gay and lesbian parents in the United States today. . . .

"How Could Marriage for Same-Sex Couples Possibly Be Good for the American Family—or Our Country?"

. . . The prospect of a significant change in our laws and customs has often caused people to worry more about dire consequences that could result than about the potential positive outcomes. In fact, precisely the same anxiety arose when some people fought to overturn the laws prohibiting marriage between people of different races in the 1950s and 1960s. (One Virginia judge even declared that "God intended to separate the races.")

But in reality, opening marriage to couples who are so willing to fight for it could only strengthen the institution for all. It would open the doors to more supporters, not opponents. And it would help keep the age-old institution alive.

As history has repeatedly proven, institutions that fail to take account of the changing needs of the population are those that grow weak; those that recognize and accommodate changing needs grow strong. For example, the U.S. military, like American colleges and universities, grew stronger after permitting African Americans and women to join its ranks.

Similarly, granting same-sex couples the right to marry would strengthen the institution of marriage by allowing it to better meet the needs of the true diversity of family structures in America today. . . .

"Can't Same-Sex Couples Go to a Lawyer to Secure All the Rights They Need?"

Not by a long shot. When a gay or lesbian person gets seriously ill, there is no legal document that can make their partner eligible to take leave from work under the federal Family and Medical Leave Act to provide care—because that law applies only to married couples.

When gay or lesbian people grow old and in need of nursing home care, there is no legal document that can give them the right to Medicaid coverage without potentially causing their partner to be forced from their home—because the federal Medicaid law only permits married spouses to keep their home without becoming ineligible for benefits.

And when a gay or lesbian person dies, there is no legal document that can extend Social Security survivor benefits or the right to inherit a retirement plan without severe tax burdens that stem from being "unmarried" in the eyes of the law.

These are only a few examples of the critical protections that are granted through more than 1,100 federal laws that protect only married couples. In the absence of the right to marry, same-sex couples can only put in place a handful of the most basic arrangements, such as naming each other in a will or a power of attorney. And even these documents remain vulnerable to challenges in court by disgruntled family members.

"Won't This Cost Taxpayers Too Much Money?"

No, it wouldn't necessarily cost much at all. In fact, treating same-sex couples as families under law could even save taxpayers money because marriage would require them to assume legal responsibility for their joint living expenses and reduce their dependence on public assistance programs, such as Medicaid, Temporary Assistance to Needy Families, Supplemental Security Income disability payments, and food stamps.

Put another way, the money it would cost to extend benefits to same-sex couples could be outweighed by the money that would be saved as these families rely more fully on each other instead of state or federal government assistance.

For example, two studies conducted in 2003 by professors at the University of Massachusetts, Amherst, and the University of California, Los Angeles, found that extending domestic partner benefits to same-sex couples in California and New Jersey would save taxpayers millions of dollars a year.

Specifically, the studies projected that the California state budget would save an estimated $8.1 million to $10.6 million each year by enacting the most comprehensive domestic partner law in the nation. In New Jersey, which passed a new domestic partner law in 2004, the savings were projected to be even higher—more than $61 million each year.

(Sources: "Equal Rights, Fiscal Responsibility: The Impact of A.B. 205 on California's Budget," by M. V. Lee Badgett, Ph.D., IGLSS, Department of Economics, University of Massachusetts, and R. Bradley Sears, J.D., Williams Project, UCLA School of Law, University of California, Los Angeles, May 2003, and "Supporting Families, Saving Funds: A Fiscal Analysis of New Jersey's

Domestic Partnership Act," by Badgett and Sears with Suzanne Goldberg, J.D., Rutgers School of Law-Newark, December 2003.)

"Where Can Same-Sex Couples Marry Today?"

In 2001, the Netherlands became the first country to extend marriage rights to same-sex couples. Belgium passed a similar law two years later. The laws in both of these countries, however, have strict citizenship or residency require-ments that do not permit American couples to take advantage of the protec-tions provided.

In June 2003, Ontario became the first Canadian province to grant marriage to same-sex couples, and in July 2003, British Columbia followed suit—becoming the first places that American same-sex couples could go to get married.

In November 2003, the Massachusetts Supreme Judicial Court recog-nized the right of same-sex couples to marry—giving the state six months to begin issuing marriage licenses to same-sex couples. It began issuing licenses May 17, 2004.

In February 2004, the city of San Francisco began issuing marriage licenses to same-sex couples after the mayor declared that the state constitution for-bade him to discriminate. The issue is being addressed by California courts, and a number of other cities have either taken or are considering taking steps in the same direction.

Follow the latest developments in California, Oregon, New Jersey, New Mexico, New York and in other communities across the country. . . .

Other nations have also taken steps toward extending equal protections to all couples, though the protections they provide are more limited than mar-riage. Canada, Denmark, Finland, France, Germany, Iceland, Norway, Portugal, and Sweden all have nationwide laws that grant same-sex partners a range of important rights, protections, and obligations.

For example, in France, registered same-sex (and opposite-sex) couples can be joined in a civil "solidarity pact" that grants them the right to file joint tax returns, extend social security coverage to each other and receive the same health, employment, and welfare benefits as legal spouses. It also commits the couple to assume joint responsibility for household debts.

Other countries, including Switzerland, Scotland, and the Czech Repub-lic, also have considered legislation that would legally recognize same-sex unions.

"What Protections Other Than Marriage Are Available to Same-Sex Couples?"

At the federal level, there are no protections at all available to same-sex cou-ples. In fact, a federal law called the "Defense of Marriage Act" says that the federal government will discriminate against same-sex couples who marry by refusing to recognize their marriages or providing them with the federal pro-tections of marriage. Some members of Congress are trying to go even further by attempting to pass a Federal Marriage Amendment that would write dis-crimination against same-sex couples into the U.S. Constitution.

10 FACTS

1. Same-sex couples live in 99.3 percent of all counties nationwide.
2. There are an estimated 3.1 million people living together in same-sex relationships in the United States.
3. Fifteen percent of these same-sex couples live in rural settings.
4. One out of three lesbian couples is raising children. One out of five gay male couples is raising children.
5. Between 1 million and 9 million children are being raised by gay, lesbian, and bisexual parents in the United States today.
6. At least one same-sex couple is raising children in 96 percent of all counties nationwide.
7. The highest percentages of same-sex couples raising children live in the South.
8. Nearly one in four same-sex couples includes a partner 55 years old or older, and nearly one in five same-sex couples is composed of two people 55 or older.
9. More than one in 10 same-sex couples include a partner 65 years old or older, and nearly one in 10 same-sex couples is composed of two people 65 or older.
10. The states with the highest numbers of same-sex senior couples are also the most popular for heterosexual senior couples: California, New York, and Florida.

These facts are based on analyses of the 2000 Census conducted by the Urban Institute and the Human Rights Campaign. The estimated number of people in same-sex relationships has been adjusted by 62 percent to compensate for the widely-reported undercount in the Census. . . .

At the state level, only Vermont offers civil unions, which provide important state benefits but no federal protections, such as Social Security survivor benefits. There is also no guarantee that civil unions will be recognized outside Vermont. Thirty-nine states also have "defense of marriage" laws explicitly prohibiting the recognition of marriages between same-sex partners.

Domestic partner laws have been enacted in California, Connecticut, New Jersey, Hawaii, and the District of Columbia. The benefits conferred by these laws vary; some offer access to family health insurance, others confer co-parenting rights. These benefits are limited to residents of the state. A family that moves out of these states immediately loses the protections.

Peter Sprigg  **NO**

Questions and Answers: What's Wrong with Letting Same-Sex Couples "Marry?"

What's Wrong with Letting Same-Sex Couples Legally "Marry?"
There are two key reasons why the legal rights, benefits, and responsibilities of civil marriage should not be extended to same-sex couples.

The first is that homosexual relationships are not marriage. That is, they simply do not fit the minimum necessary condition for a marriage to exist—namely, the union of a man and a woman.

The second is that homosexual relationships are harmful. Not only do they not provide the same benefits to society as heterosexual marriages, but their consequences are far more negative than positive.

Either argument, standing alone, is sufficient to reject the claim that same-sex unions should be granted the legal status of marriage.

Let's Look at the First Argument.
Isn't Marriage Whatever the Law Says It Is?
No. Marriage is not a creation of the law. Marriage is a fundamental human institution that predates the law and the Constitution. At its heart, it is an anthropological and sociological reality, not a legal one. Laws relating to marriage merely recognize and regulate an institution that already exists.

But Isn't Marriage Just a Way of Recognizing People
Who Love Each Other and Want to Spend Their Lives Together?
If love and companionship were sufficient to define marriage, then there would be no reason to deny "marriage" to unions of a child and an adult, or an adult child and his or her aging parent, or to roommates who have no sexual relationship, or to groups rather than couples. Love and companionship are usually considered integral to marriage in our culture, but they are not sufficient to define it as an institution. . . .

Why Should Homosexuals Be Denied the Right to Marry Like Anyone Else?
The fundamental "right to marry" is a right that rests with *individuals,* not with *couples.* Homosexual *individuals* already have exactly the same "right" to

From *Family Research Council*, Issue No. 256, 2004, pp. 173–179. Copyright © 2004 by Family Research Council. Reprinted by permission.

marry as anyone else. Marriage license applications do not inquire as to a person's "sexual orientation.". . .

However, while every individual person is free to get married, *no* person, whether heterosexual or homosexual, has ever had a legal right to marry simply any willing partner. Every person, whether heterosexual or homosexual, is subject to legal restrictions as to whom they may marry. To be specific, every person, regardless of sexual preference, is legally barred from marrying a child, a close blood relative, a person who is already married, or a person of the same sex. There is no discrimination here, nor does such a policy deny anyone the "equal protection of the laws" (as guaranteed by the Constitution), since these restrictions apply equally to every individual.

Some people may wish to do away with one or more of these longstanding restrictions upon one's choice of marital partner. However, the fact that a tiny but vocal minority of Americans desire to have someone of the same sex as a partner does not mean that they have a "right" to do so, any more than the desires of other tiny (but less vocal) minorities of Americans give them a "right" to choose a child, their own brother or sister, or a group of two or more as their marital partners.

Isn't Prohibiting Homosexual "Marriage" Just as Discriminatory as Prohibiting Interracial Marriage, Like Some States Used to Do?

This analogy is not valid at all. Bridging the divide of the sexes by uniting men and women is both a worthy goal and a part of the fundamental purpose of marriage, common to all human civilizations.

Laws against interracial marriage, on the other hand, served only the purpose of preserving a social system of racial segregation. This was both an unworthy goal and one utterly irrelevant to the fundamental nature of marriage.

Allowing a black woman to marry a white man does not change the definition of marriage, which requires one man and one woman. Allowing two men or two women to marry would change that fundamental definition. Banning the "marriage" of same-sex couples is therefore essential to preserve the nature and purpose of marriage itself. . . .

How Would Allowing Same-Sex Couples to Marry Change Society's Concept of Marriage?

As an example, marriage will open wide the door to homosexual adoption, which will simply lead to more children suffering the negative consequences of growing up without both a mother and a father.

Among homosexual men in particular, casual sex, rather than committed relationships, is the rule and not the exception. And even when they do enter into a more committed relationship, it is usually of relatively short duration. For example, a study of homosexual men in the Netherlands (the first country in the world to legalize "marriage" for same-sex couples), published in the journal *AIDS* in 2003, found that the average length of "steady partnerships" was not more than 2 < years (Maria Xiridou et al., in *AIDS* 2003, 17:1029–1038).

In addition, studies have shown that even homosexual men who are in "committed" relationships are not sexually faithful to each other. While infidelity among heterosexuals is much too common, it does not begin to compare to the rates among homosexual men. The 1994 National Health and Social Life Survey, which remains the most comprehensive study of Americans' sexual practices ever undertaken, found that 75 percent of married men and 90 percent of married women had been sexually faithful to their spouse. On the other hand, a major study of homosexual men in "committed" relationships found that only seven out of 156 had been sexually faithful, or 4.5 percent. The Dutch study cited above found that even homosexual men in "steady partnerships" had an average of eight "casual" sex partners per year.

So if same-sex relationships are legally recognized as "marriage," the idea of marriage as a sexually exclusive and faithful relationship will be dealt a serious blow. Adding monogamy and faithfulness to the other pillars of marriage that have already fallen will have overwhelmingly negative consequences for Americans' physical and mental health. . . .

Don't Homosexuals Need Marriage Rights So That They Will Be Able to Visit Their Partners in the Hospital?

The idea that homosexuals are routinely denied the right to visit their partners in the hospital is nonsense. When this issue was raised during debate over the Defense of Marriage Act in 1996, the Family Research Council did an informal survey of nine hospitals in four states and the District of Columbia. None of the administrators surveyed could recall a single case in which a visitor was barred because of their homosexuality, and they were incredulous that this would even be considered an issue.

Except when a doctor limits visitation for medical reasons, final authority over who may visit an adult patient rests with that patient. This is and should be the case regardless of the sexual orientation or marital status of the patient or the visitor.

The only situation in which there would be a possibility that the blood relatives of a patient might attempt to exclude the patient's homosexual partner is if the patient is unable to express his or her wishes due to unconsciousness or mental incapacity. Homosexual partners concerned about this (remote) possibility can effectively preclude it by granting to one another a health care proxy (the legal right to make medical decisions for the patient) and a power of attorney (the right to make all legal decisions for another person). Marriage is not necessary for this. It is inconceivable that a hospital would exclude someone who holds the health care proxy and power of attorney for a patient from visiting that patient, except for medical reasons.

The hypothetical "hospital visitation hardship" is nothing but an emotional smokescreen to distract people from the more serious implications of radically redefining marriage.

Don't Homosexuals Need the Right to Marry Each Other in Order to Ensure That They Will Be Able to Leave Their Estates to Their Partner When They Die?

As with the hospital visitation issue, the concern over inheritance rights is something that simply does not require marriage to resolve it. Nothing in current law prevents homosexual partners from being joint owners of property such as a home or a car, in which case the survivor would automatically become the owner if the partner dies.

An individual may leave the remainder of his estate to whomever he wishes—again, without regard to sexual orientation or marital status—simply by writing a will. As with the hospital visitation issue, blood relatives would only be able to overrule the surviving homosexual partner in the event that the deceased had failed to record his wishes in a common, inexpensive legal document. Changing the definition of a fundamental social institution like marriage is a rather extreme way of addressing this issue. Preparing a will is a much simpler solution.

Don't Homosexuals Need Marriage Rights So That They Can Get Social Security Survivor Benefits When a Partner Dies?

. . . Social Security survivor benefits were designed to recognize the non-monetary contribution made to a family by the homemaking and child-rearing activities of a wife and mother, and to ensure that a woman and her children would not become destitute if the husband and father were to die.

The Supreme Court ruled in the 1970s that such benefits must be gender-neutral. However, they still are largely based on the premise of a division of roles within a couple between a breadwinner who works to raise money and a homemaker who stays home to raise children.

Very few homosexual couples organize their lives along the lines of such a "traditional" division of labor and roles. They are far more likely to consist of two earners, each of whom can be supported in old age by their own personal Social Security pension.

Furthermore, far fewer homosexual couples than heterosexual ones are raising children at all, for the obvious reason that they are incapable of natural reproduction with each other. This, too, reduces the likelihood of a traditional division of labor among them.

Survivor benefits for the legal (biological or adopted) *children* of homosexual parents (as opposed to their partners) are already available under current law, so "marriage" rights for homosexual couples are unnecessary to protect the interests of these children themselves. . . .

Even If "Marriage" Itself Is Uniquely Heterosexual, Doesn't Fairness Require That the Legal and Financial Benefits of Marriage Be Granted to Same-Sex Couples—Perhaps Through "Civil Unions" or "Domestic Partnerships"?

No. The legal and financial benefits of marriage are not an entitlement to be distributed equally to all (if they were, single people would have as much reason to consider them "discriminatory" as same-sex couples). Society grants benefits to marriage because marriage has benefits for society—including, but not limited to, the reproduction of the species in households with the optimal household structure (i.e., the presence of both a mother and a father).

Homosexual relationships, on the other hand, have no comparable benefit for society, and in fact impose substantial costs on society. The fact that AIDS is at least ten times more common among men who have sex with men than among the general population is but one example. . . .

Isn't It Possible That Allowing Homosexuals to "Marry" Each Other Would Allow Them to Participate in Those Benefits as Well?

Opening the gates of "marriage" to homosexuals is far more likely to change the attitudes and behavior of heterosexuals for the worse than it is to change the lifestyles of homosexuals for the better. . . .

What About the Argument That Homosexual Relations Are Harmful? What Do You Mean by That?

Homosexual men experience higher rates of many diseases, including:

- Human Papillomavirus (HPV), which causes most cases of cervical cancer in women and anal cancer in men
- Hepatitis A, B, and C
- Gonorrhea
- Syphilis
- "Gay Bowel Syndrome," a set of sexually transmitted gastrointestinal problems such as proctitis, proctocolitis, and enteritis
- HIV/AIDS (One Canadian study found that as a result of HIV alone, "life expectancy for gay and bisexual men is eight to twenty years less than for all men.")

Lesbian women, meanwhile, have a higher prevalence of:

- Bacterial vaginosis
- Hepatitis C
- HIV risk behaviors
- Cancer risk factors such as smoking, alcohol use, poor diet, and being overweight . . .

Do Homosexuals Have More Mental Health Problems as Well?

Yes. Various research studies have found that homosexuals have higher rates of:

- Alcohol abuse
- Drug abuse
- Nicotine dependence
- Depression
- Suicide

Isn't It Possible That These Problems Result from Society's "Discrimination" Against Homosexuals?

This is the argument usually put forward by pro-homosexual activists. However, there is a simple way to test this hypothesis. If "discrimination" were the cause of homosexuals' mental health problems, then one would expect those problems to be much less common in cities or countries, like San Francisco or the Netherlands, where homosexuality has achieved the highest levels of acceptance.

In fact, the opposite is the case. In places where homosexuality is widely accepted, the physical and mental health problems of homosexuals are greater, not less. This suggests that the real problem lies in the homosexual lifestyle itself, not in society's response to it. In fact, it suggests that increasing the level of social support *for* homosexual behavior (by, for instance, allowing same-sex couples to "marry") would only increase these problems, not reduce them. . . .

Haven't Studies Shown That Children Raised by Homosexual Parents Are No Different from Other Children?

No. This claim is often put forward, even by professional organizations. The truth is that most research on "homosexual parents" thus far has been marred by serious methodological problems. However, even pro-homosexual sociologists Judith Stacey and Timothy Biblarz report that the actual data from key studies show the "no differences" claim to be false.

Surveying the research (primarily regarding lesbians) in an *American Sociological Review* article in 2001, they found that:

- Children of lesbians are less likely to conform to traditional gender norms.
- Children of lesbians are more likely to engage in homosexual behavior.
- Daughters of lesbians are "more sexually adventurous and less chaste."
- Lesbian "co-parent relationships" are more likely to end than heterosexual ones.

A 1996 study by an Australian sociologist compared children raised by heterosexual married couples, heterosexual cohabiting couples, and homosexual cohabiting couples. It found that the children of heterosexual married couples did the best, and children of homosexual couples the worst, in nine of the thirteen academic and social categories measured. . . .

Do the American People Want to See "Marriages" Between Same-Sex Couples Recognized by Law?

No—and in the wake of the June 2003 court decisions to legalize such "marriages" in the Canadian province of Ontario and to legalize homosexual sodomy in the United States, the nation's opposition to such a radical social experiment has actually grown.

Five separate national opinion polls taken between June 24 and July 27, 2003 showed opponents of civil "marriage" for same-sex couples outnumbering supporters by not less than fifteen percentage points in every poll. The wording of poll questions can make a significant difference, and in this case, the poll with the most straightforward language (a Harris/CNN/Time poll asking "Do you think marriages between homosexual men or homosexual women should be recognized as legal by the law?") resulted in the strongest opposition, with 60 percent saying "No" and only 33 percent saying "Yes."

Even where pollsters drop the word "marriage" itself and use one of the euphemisms to describe a counterfeit institution parallel to marriage, we see a decline in public support for the homosexual agenda. The Gallup Poll, for instance, has asked, "Would you favor or oppose a law that would allow homosexual couples to legally form civil unions, giving them some of the legal rights of married couples?"

This question itself is misleading, in that it downplays the legal impact of "civil unions." Vermont, the only U.S. state to adopt "civil unions" (under coercion of a state court), actually gives all "of the legal rights of married couples" available under state law to people in a same-sex "civil union"—not just "some." But despite this distortion, a 49-percent-to-49-percent split on this question in May 2003 had changed to opposition by a margin of 58 percent to 37 percent when the *Washington Post* asked the identical question in August 2003.

Even the percentage of Americans willing to declare that "homosexual relations between consenting adults" (never mind homosexual civil "marriage") "should be legal" dropped from 60 percent to only 48 percent between May and July of 2003. The biggest drop in support, a stunning 23 percentage points (from 58 percent to 35 percent), came among African Americans— despite the rhetoric of pro-homosexual activists who seek to frame the issues of "gay rights" and same-sex unions as a matter of "civil rights." . . .

POSTSCRIPT

Should Same-Sex Couples Be Allowed to Marry Legally?

Part of this discussion is that marriage is a civil right, not an inherent or moral one. Those supporting marriage rights for lesbian and gay couples cite the struggles of the civil rights movement of the 1960s in their current quest for equality for all couples. Among the points they make is that up until 1967, it was still illegal in some states for people of different races to marry. Many opponents find the idea of comparing same-sex marriage to the civil rights struggles of the 1960s and earlier is offensive, that it is like comparing apples and oranges. Many of these individuals believe that sexual orientation is chosen, rather than an inherent part of who one is—unlike race, which is predetermined. Most sexuality experts, however, agree that although we do not know for sure what "causes" a person to be heterosexual, bisexual, or homosexual, it is clear that it is determined very early in life, perhaps even before we are born. Regardless, is marriage a civil right? A legal right? An inherent right?

ISSUE 11

Should Men Who Have Sex with Men Be Allowed to Donate Blood?

YES: Bob Roehr, from "The Gift of Life: Gay Men and U.S. Blood Donation Policy," *Liberty Education Forum* (2006)

NO: Marc Germain and Graham Sher, from "Men Who Have Had Sex with Men and Blood Donation: Is It Time to Change Our Deferral Criteria?" *Journal of the International Association of Physicians in AIDS Care* (July/September 2002)

ISSUE SUMMARY

YES: Journalist and medical writer Bob Roehr believes that the blood donation policy that continues to ban men who have sex with other men is irrational because it discriminates based on a behavior, not on risk factors. Why, for example, is a heterosexual woman who has unprotected intercourse with many male partners allowed to donate blood, but a man who is in a monogamous relationship with only one other man in which they use condoms consistently is not?

NO: Dr. Marc Germain, medical director of microbiology and epidemiology at Héma-Québec, and Graham Sher, chief executive officer of the Canadian Blood Services, cite data that show a small increase in risk of transmitting HIV between men who have sex with other men and argue that even this small increase merits restricting who can donate blood in order to serve the safety of the greater society. The expectation of the people receiving a blood donation that their blood will be disease-free outweighs, they say, the rights of those who are seen as high risk for HIV and other transfusion-transmitted diseases.

The practice of attempting blood transfusions can be traced to as early as the late fifteenth century in Europe, where even the most rudimentary attempts were done poorly and unsuccessfully. Learning, however, that this could be seen as a way of saving a person's life, scientists and medical professionals did not give up, and the first known blood transfusion took place in the United States in 1795. In 1932, the first blood bank was established in Russia, and in 1947, the American Association of Blood Centers was opened.

According to the New York Blood Center (www.nybloodcenter.org/press/factsheets/index.do?sid0=8&sid1=41&page_id=88), approximately 38,000 pints of red blood cells are transfused in the United States every day to accommodate the transfusions that are needed every three seconds. To keep the blood supply safe, prospective donors are asked a long series of questions so that people who may know even before their blood is taken that there is any reason why they should not donate blood will be excluded.

When the human immunodeficiency virus (HIV) was discovered, it was believed to exist only in gay men. Initially called "gay-related immune disorder," medical professionals quickly discovered that anyone who has HIV can pass it to someone else through blood, semen, vaginal fluids, or breast milk. That notwithstanding, gay men are still seen as the primary risk group for HIV, despite statistics showing that, worldwide, HIV is being found much more commonly in heterosexual populations. As a result, the screening procedure for blood donation asks specifically whether a male prospective donor "has had sexual contact with another male, even once, since 1977." This means, basically, that gay men have not been allowed to donate blood for several decades.

Supporters of this ban argue that even as the face of HIV changes, men who have sex with men are at high risk of contracting HIV and therefore transmitting it to others. Opponents to the ban argue that the ban itself and the screening question is too broad—what, for example, does "sexual contact" mean? What if a man has only had nonpenetrative sex? Or if he has had penetrative intercourse, what if he has always used latex condoms?

In the following selections, Bob Roehr argues that behaviors, not sexual orientation, should determine whether someone is at risk for HIV—that plenty of men who have sex with other men practice safer sex and are at lower risk than their heterosexual counterparts. Marc Germain and Graham Sher counter by pointing out that even when there is lower risk, the risk exists—and that with HIV still being a relatively young disease, there is much to learn. It is therefore not worth putting the general population at risk for contracting HIV just to allow this particular population to donate blood.

YES ↵

Bob Roehr

The Gift of Life: Gay Men and U.S. Blood Donation Policy

Introduction

The U.S. Food and Drug Administration (FDA) establishes and administers policy with regard to all blood products used within the United States. The purpose is to ensure availability and uniformly high standards that guarantee safety and minimize the possibility of transmission of blood-borne infectious diseases in those blood products. About 14 million units of blood will be donated in the U.S. in 2001.

Most people who have not yet gone through the screening process to donate blood are surprised to learn that there are pages of exclusionary factors that may keep one from making a donation. Writing in the November/December 2000 edition of *GMHC Treatment Issues,* published by the Gay Men's Health Crisis in New York City, Derek Link listed some of the top 52 reasons for not being able to donate blood. And at least one more has been added since that date. The net result of these exclusionary screening procedures is that an estimated 30–40 percent of the American public is prohibited from donating blood for one reason or another.

The system relies on screening at three different levels in order to minimize the possibility of disease transmission through blood products. It encourages certain individuals, such as gay men, to self-select and not even show up to donate; it administers an elaborate questionnaire and on paper rejects those who may be at risk of carrying a blood-borne disease; finally, it submits every unit of blood that is drawn to an elaborate series of chemical tests for HIV, hepatitis B and C, syphilis, and other infections. That process takes about three days to perform.

Blood found to carry any of these infectious agents is removed from the system and destroyed. Donors are notified that their blood tested positive for specific infections, counseled as to what that means, and are encouraged to see their physician.

None of these efforts are failsafe, but the redundancy of overlapping systems has proven remarkably effective. So much so that the American Red Cross states in one of its "Frequently Asked Questions" prepared for consumers: "The risk of not getting a blood transfusion when it's needed is infinitely greater than the risk of infection from receiving one."

Most of the blood that is donated comes from a loyal 5 percent of the population that donates repeatedly throughout the year. But that group of repeat donors has been slowly shrinking, while the development of new medical procedures has increased the need for blood. The need has outpaced supply so that seasonal shortages and emergency appeals have become annual rituals in most major American cities.

History & Science

The current blood donation policy excludes all men who have had sex with another man since 1977. It is important to understand the context within which the ban was adopted, and how that context has changed over the ensuing years.

What came to be known as AIDS was identified in the United States in the early 1980s, first as a disease that affected gay men. As early as 1983 they were asked to refrain from donating blood. The FDA adopted the current policy in 1985, soon after HIV was identified as the virus that causes AIDS, and a test was developed to identify the antibody to that virus in blood. It was thought that HIV was not present or at least not widely prevalent in the United States prior to 1977, which explains why that date was chosen.

No one challenges the fact that people who know that they are HIV-positive should refrain from donating blood. And most people, including gays, believed that the draconian policy made sense in light of the devastating nature of HIV infection; the then limited epidemiological data and knowledge of how HIV is transmitted; and the relatively crude tools available to detect the virus in blood. Those conditions have changed substantially since 1985, but the policy has not.

The most recent research concludes that there is virtually no risk of transmission of HIV through oral sex, regardless of which end of the transaction one is on. Data from heterosexual couples in Uganda indicates that those with a sufficiently low viral load only rarely transmit HIV through vaginal sex. And proper, consistent use of condoms and lubricant is highly effective in preventing transmission of the virus when engaging in either vaginal or anal sex.

What policymakers have been most worried about is the window of time between the point of infection with HIV and when screening tests can detect that infection in a blood donation of that person. The early laboratory tests that screened blood for HIV looked for antibodies to the virus, which take several weeks, and in some individuals several months, to develop. Blood policymakers worried that during this window, HIV-tainted blood might slip through the screening mechanism.

This is where conditions have changed most dramatically since 1985—the window has closed to the point where it is barely open. The nucleic acid test (NAT) has become the standard by which all blood donations are screened in the U.S. It amplifies and looks for small fragments of HIV RNA in pooled samples from 512 units of donated blood at a time. It is virtually foolproof, able to detect HIV in pooled blood within 12 days of infection, says the FDA. If the technology is used on individual rather than large pooled samples, NAT can detect HIV within 4–5 days, according to testimony before the FDA by Michael Busch, MD, with the Blood Centers of the Pacific.

Another simple screening technique already in place is likely to catch many of these very early infections even before donors roll up their sleeves. Standard procedure calls for taking the temperature of every donor and turning away those with a fever as an indication of some sort of infection, even a common cold. Primary HIV infection often will result in such a fever. There also is some evidence supporting the view that the form of virus during this very early stage of infection may not be very capable of transmission to a third party.

The gay ban differs from every other blood policy exclusion in two significant ways. First, it is based on a person's status rather than acts that put them at risk for infection. Second, it reflects a double standard where the same risky acts performed by heterosexuals brings a temporal restriction that generally is limited to 12 months, while a gay man is banned for life.

Thus monogamous gay couples in stable long-term relationships, who have little risk of recent HIV infection, are barred from donating blood. However, a single heterosexual female who is dating around may be allowed to donate blood, or at worst will be deferred from doing so for a year after her sexual pattern stabilizes.

The discriminatory character of this policy has long been noted both outside the FDA and within it. Justification for the policy became increasingly difficult as blood screening technology improved and the chance of a tainted unit slipping through declined. Most experts in the field understand these changes since 1985 and have been willing to modify the de facto lifetime ban on gay men donating blood.

Reconsideration

The FDA professional staff administers policy, but that policy is set through public comment, the most visible portion of which is the consultation mechanism of an advisory committee meeting in public session. It is an opportunity for professional experts and the interested public to participate in the rule-making process. The FDA uses it to solicit input, educate the general and targeted publics, and often to take some of the heat on controversial policy issues. A solid consensus recommendation from an advisory committee inevitably is embraced by the agency, while a divided committee sometimes is overruled. Regardless, the final decision on all policy rests with the FDA.

The September 14, 2000 meeting of the FDA Blood Products Advisory Committee (BPAC) was a watershed event in reconsidering the policy of blood donations by gay men. For purposes of discussion, the FDA proposed changing the ban on donation by men who have had sex with another man from 1977 to a more flexible standard of having had sex with another man within the last five years.

By posing the question, and through its presentation in suggesting such a relaxation, the FDA professional staff indicated that it was predisposed to loosening the policy. There also was a strong suggestion that the FDA was willing to go farther in changing restrictions, but that their proposal was a compromise made with the hope of gaining support from those most opposed to any change.

FDA medical officer Andrew Dayton, MD, presented a worse-case scenario model of how many additional units of HIV-contaminated blood might slip through by relaxing the standard to a five-year deferral of donations. He estimated the risk at "around 1 in 750,000" units.

In reviewing data from hospitals in New York that process their own blood, Dayton found that even though they process just 10 percent of the volume of blood drawn, they produced 80 percent of the errors in the region. "He concluded, inappropriate release [of tainted blood] primarily due to non-automated blood handling systems, remains the biggest problem," far exceeding any risk from letting gay men donate blood.

At the BPAC meeting, the American Association of Blood Banks (AABB) went farther than the FDA and called for "modifying the deferral time period for male to male sexual contact to 12 months" to make it "consistent with those for other high risk sexual exposures." It has held that position since 1997.

By changing the policy, "The potential donor will be directed to focus on recent rather than remote risk behaviors and should have better recall for answers to the screening questions," said Louis Katz, MD, in speaking for the AABB. The organization represents professionals and facilities responsible for virtually all of the collection and more than 80 percent of the transfusion of the nation's blood supply.

America's Blood Centers (ABC) reinforced that same message. The association of 75 not-for-profit, community-based blood centers collects nearly half of the nation's blood each year. Executive vice president Celso Bianco, MD, said, "I believe that we would not see a real difference between the five year and the one year" deferral standard.

He called the current policy counterproductive because "the question focuses attention on events that occurred more than twenty years ago instead of events that occurred within the currently known window period of days or weeks" when the technology may not detect early HIV infection.

"Like risks should be treated alike," said Adrienne Smith, MD, in testifying on behalf of the Gay and Lesbian Medical Association and other gay organizations. "This maxim exposes the central flaw in the current donor deferral policy which tolerates a wide range of risks associated with heterosexual sex while imposing a zero tolerance attitude toward MSMs [men having sex with men], regardless of the risk associated with individual behavior."

"By focusing on the source of the risk rather than the size of the risk, the current policy stigmatizes gay men." Smith urged a revised policy and screening questionnaire that focuses on recent behaviors and risks.

Only the American Red Cross (ARC) opposed changing the policy. It collects nearly half of the nation's blood. Rebecca Haley, MD, called changing the deferral question "a public health issue, not a social policy issue. . . . Modifying the MSM deferral criterion to five years would result in a small but measurable increase in the possibility that infectious blood might be released."

"Until data are available to show that changing the MSM deferral criterion will not elevate the risk to the nation's blood supply, we cannot support this change," said Haley. . . .

Motivations

A recounting of events over the last few years clearly indicates that opposition to changing the policy on blood donation by gay men does not come from the FDA staff, the association representing professionals in the field, or the association representing agencies that collect about half of the blood in the United States. Opposition to changing the policy comes primarily, one is tempted to say solely, from the American Red Cross, which wields a de facto veto over the process. . . .

Changing Policy

Attempts to modify the current policy that bans donation of blood by gay men should start by proposing to amend the policy to a 12-month deferral, the same policy as with other risky behavior. It is the policy advocated by the American Association of Blood Banks and America's Blood Centers.

But the community should not stop there; it should seek parity with heterosexuals at all levels based upon the element of risky behavior.

Couples in monogamous, long-term relationships where both are HIV-negative should be held to the same standards, whether heterosexual or homosexual.

Consideration should be given to removing oral sex as a category of risky behavior.

The consistent use of condoms in anal sex, and whether the donor is exclusively insertive or receptive (top or bottom) are also factors worthy of consideration in reexamining the policy.

Alternative handling of a blood donation also should be explored. It may make sense, and be cost effective, to segregate blood from higher risk donors and screen them individually or in smaller pools.

Gay organizations may want to organize recruitment drives for first-time donors, perhaps where donors are prescreened for pathogens weeks before being allowed to donate, or where the initial donation receives special handling. After that initial donation has cleared screening, the donor will be entered into the standard registry and mainstreamed, as it were, into the donor network.

Regardless the course taken, it seems likely that internal and external pressure will have to be brought to bear on the American Red Cross for it to abandon its lone opposition to changing the policy. Even if the FDA decides to modify the policy, the ARC can always undercut it by maintaining its own, stricter policy. The most effective public argument in moving the ARC is likely to be one of identifying their position as one adopted for strictly for financial reasons, to save processing costs, while discriminating against a segment of American society when there is no valid scientific reason to do so.

Marc Germain and
Graham Sher

➡ **NO**

Men Who Have Had Sex with Men and Blood Donation: Is It Time to Change Our Deferral Criteria?

Men who have had sex with other men even once, since 1977, are permanently deferred as blood donors. This policy was put in place several years ago when it was recognized that men who have sex with men (MSM) represented a group at risk for HIV. The policy is not unique to the United States and Canada, since most industrialized countries apply the same rule, or one that is very similar. Many have expressed the view that such a policy, while it may have been justified in the early days of the HIV epidemic, is now overly cautious and has the unfortunate effect of stigmatizing gay men who would donate blood.

According to some, the policy is biased because it appears to be based on a person's sexual preferences rather than the sexual practices and partners that might put someone at risk for infection. It is also seen as setting a double standard by which certain behaviors in heterosexuals only bring a temporary deferral, while male-to-male sex entails lifetime exclusion.

The American Association of Blood Banks (AABB), an independent organization that represents the transfusion community, endorses a relaxation of the current deferral policy for MSM.[1] The AABB argues that highly sophisticated tests are now used to screen blood donations for HIV and other transfusion transmitted diseases (TTDs), making it unnecessary to apply such a restrictive policy. It suggests imposing a temporary deferral of one year for male-to-male sex, similar to deferrals that are applied for other activities at risk for TTDs. In theory, asking donors to focus on the recent past might also improve their ability to recall events that are more relevant to the risk posed by window-period donations. This revised policy would also have the benefit of increasing the pool of eligible donors.

Not surprisingly, this question of MSM and blood donations is rather controversial, and it has been the object of heated debates for a number of years and in various jurisdictions. While recognizing the following discussion will most certainly not put an end to the argument, it represents our personal opinions and positions on this issue, not that of the organizations we represent.

All blood donations are tested for the presence of antibody and/or antigen of transfusion-transmitted infections, including hepatitis C virus (HCV),

From *Journal of the International Association of Physicians in AIDS Care*, Vol. 1, No. 3, 2002, pp. 86–88. Copyright © 2002 by Sage Publications. Reprinted by permission via Rightslink.

HIV, hepatitis B virus (HBV), syphilis, and human T-lymphotrophic virus (HTLV). In recent years, nucleic acid testing (NAT) for HCV and HIV has been added to the traditional arsenal of serological tests, as an attempt to reduce the risk of transfusing blood collected from donors who might be in the early phase of infection.[2] The transfusion industry has also been transformed into a highly regulated environment, in which processes are highly controlled and safeguards are put in place to make sure that these screening tests are being performed and documented with the highest possible level of proficiency.[3]

Given all that, one may ask whether current tests are more than sufficient as a way of safeguarding the blood supply. Why bother screening donors on the basis of their self-reported risk factors, if testing has become so effective? One obvious answer is the health questionnaire currently remains our only line of defense against certain TTDs, such as malaria and Chagas disease, but also for other conditions that may be detrimental to transfusion recipients or to the donors themselves. If only for this reason, the health questionnaire will always remain a necessary step in the donor screening process. The second reason is, even with the advent of nucleic acid testing, there remains the possibility that some donors will test negative if they donate during the window period of early infection. Recent experience has shown that this can happen even with all donations being subjected to NAT.[4,5] This is due to the intrinsic limit that nucleic acid tests have in their ability to detect infections in the earliest phase of viremia.

It is widely agreed, even with the most sensitive screening assays in place, donors should be deferred temporarily if they report recent behaviors that put them at risk for certain TTDs. Why impose a permanent deferral for behaviors that may have happened only once or a few times in the distant past in the case for male-to-male sex? The transfusion community remains divided on this particular issue.

Some argue the goal of the donor interview is not only to exclude donors who are in the window period of infection, but also to reduce as much as possible the prevalence of TTDs in the donor population, even if screening tests can easily detect such donors. The main contention is there should be an effort to reduce as much as possible the number of infected donations that come into the system in the first place because of potential failures of the overall screening process. Since the prevalence of HIV is much higher in MSM in comparison with the general population, a more inclusive deferral policy should be applied to this group of people. In fact, other groups at higher risk for TTDs, such as intravenous drug users and those who accept money or drugs in exchange for sex, are also permanently deferred for similar reasons. In spite of the apparent discrepancy in the level of stringency that is imposed on the MSM population in comparison with other groups at risk for TTDs, the proponents of the current policy believe that it remains a sensible risk reduction strategy. Is this a legitimate argument?

Published data shows that the process of screening blood donations is fallible. Testing errors can produce false-negative test results.[6] Clerical and administrative errors may lead to the inappropriate release of infectious blood components.[1] Such errors are now extremely rare because of the increasing level of control in the process of screening and handling donations. On the other hand, one cannot assume that these mishaps never happen. Blood products sometimes need to be transfused on an emergency basis, prior to laboratory screening for transmissible diseases. One of us (M.G.) conducted an analysis in which the impact of a relaxation of the current deferral policy for MSM was modelled, taking into consideration these various factors.[7] The results showed, if 12-month abstinent MSM were allowed to donate blood, the additional number of HIV-positive donations that would escape detection and find their way into the inventory would be extremely small, in the order of 1:11,000,000. Consider the following to put this estimate in perspective. With current test procedures, the residual risk of acquiring HIV from a blood transfusion is estimated at 1:1,000,000, at worst.[2] The risk of changing to a 12-month deferral policy for male-to-male sex represents less than 10 percent of that current risk. A more lenient deferral policy for MSM would also have the benefit of increasing the number of eligible donors by about 1 percent. This is small but maybe not insignificant, considering the difficulties recruiting and retaining a stable number of active blood donors.

With these numbers in hand, what should be done about the current deferral policy for MSM? Given today's paradigm in blood safety, even the minuscule increment in risk that would result from the revised policy appears unjustified and undesirable to many, especially to those in need of blood. Even the prospect of a positive impact on the availability of blood donors does not appear to make a difference to those who are exquisitely concerned about blood safety. In this context, it becomes very difficult for those who manage and regulate the blood system to make a strong argument in favor of a change in the MSM deferral policy, considering the perspective of those in need of blood products.

In November 2001, Canadian Blood Services and Héma-Québec hosted a consensus conference that addressed the broader question of blood donor screening based on reported risk factors for TTDs. Not surprisingly, the controversial question of male-to-male sex and blood donation was one of the issues that triggered the conference. A panel of experts and stakeholders was asked to reflect on these issues and produce a consensus statement that could guide the policy makers in their decision-making process. In that statement, which will soon be published in its totality along with the proceedings from the conference, the panel did not make any specific recommendation concerning the MSM deferral policy. However, the panel did provide some guidelines as to the scientific, societal, and ethical principles upon which the donor screening process should be based. It was agreed that certain constraints could be imposed on individuals when a significant risk exists, on condition that the risk can be effectively mitigated by such constraints. In addition, the economic costs and the burdens to certain individuals or groups of individuals should be reasonable when compared with the benefits that these constraints will bring to society in general. Finally, these restrictions should be fairly distributed among the general population.

Without trying to second-guess the consensus panel, it is our opinion that the current MSM deferral policy adheres to these principles, albeit tenuously in some respects. We firmly believe that a temporary deferral of male-to-male sex will always remain a minimum requirement to safeguard the blood supply, as long as sexually transmitted diseases and the HIV epidemic continue to disproportionately afflict the MSM population. On the other hand, we also believe that the calculable margin of safety that is gained by the current policy is extremely small when compared to a policy that would only impose a temporary deferral for male-to-male sex. This safety margin also comes with the cost of having to defer a fairly large number of men who could potentially contribute safe donations to a blood supply that is periodically difficult to sustain. This balance between safety increments (even marginal ones) and adequacy of the donor base will continue to challenge the transfusion industry, including operators, regulators, and stakeholders. Prior to any change to the current policy regarding MSM being promoted or imposed, there should be a very clear consensus that such a change is both justified and necessary. This consensus must be broadly based, and should not only come from those who feel unjustly treated by the current policy. In seeking such consensus, we believe that if priority should be given anywhere, it should be to the opinion of those who have the most to lose or to gain from this change, namely the transfusion recipients themselves. This is reasonable, given the rights of recipients of blood transfusions to expect their therapeutic intervention to be optimally safe.

References

1. Blood Products Advisory Committee. Gaithersburgh, MD, September 14–15, 2000. . . .

2. Busch MP. Closing the windows on viral transmission by blood transfusion. In: Stramer SL, ed. Blood safety in the new millennium. Bethesda, MD: American Association of Blood Banks, 2001. Pp. 33–54.

3. Quality Systems. In: Vengelen-Tyler V, ed. Technical Manual. 13th ed. Bethesda, MD. American Association of Blood Banks, 1999. Pp. 1–36.

4. Schüttler CG, Caspari G, Jursch CA, Willems WR, Gerlich WH, Schaefer S. Hepatitis C virus transmission by a blood donation negative in nucleic acid amplification tests for viral RNA. Lancet 2000;355(9197):41–42.

5. Delwart E, Kalmin N, Jones S, Ladd D, Tobler L, Tsui R, Busch M. First case of HIV transmission by an RNA-screened blood donation. 9th Conference on Retroviruses and Opportunistic Infections. Seattle, WA, February 24–28, 2002. (Abstract 768-W).

6. Busch MP, Watanabe KK, Smith JW, Hermansen SW, Thomson RA. False-negative testing errors in routine viral marker screening of blood donors. For the Retrovirus Epidemiology Donor Study. Transfusion 2000;40(5):585–589.

7. Germain M, Delage G. Men who have sex with men (MSM) and blood donation: a risk-benefit assessment of adopting a less stringent deferral policy. VII European Congress of the International Society of Blood Transfusion. Paris, France, July 15–18, 2001. Abstract in Transfus Clin Biol 2001 June;8 Suppl 1:198s.

POSTSCRIPT

Should Men Who Have Sex with Men Be Allowed to Donate Blood?

The debate about whether men who have sex with men can donate blood has become more and more heated as the HIV pandemic has gone on and it has been demonstrated, clearly, that as a group they are not putting themselves at risk—only those who have unprotected sex with partners they do not know well are. Yet at the same time, news reports continue to demonstrate that men who have sex with men may be engaging in anal intercourse—a behavior that, if they are not using latex condoms, is extremely high risk for transmitting HIV due to the lack of natural lubrication in the rectum. The chances of even slight tears inside the rectum, introducing blood into the rectum as well as creating openings, highlights the ongoing existence of such a risk.

Then again, sexuality education professionals have been seeing an increase in the number of different-sex young people who are having unprotected anal sex. More concerned with avoiding pregnancy than sexually transmitted infections (STIs), are these young people not also putting themselves at equally high risk?

Among the reasons why this remains so controversial is that it is so difficult to know who has an STI, including HIV, and who does not. Considering that so many STIs, including HIV, can be asymptomatic, it is nearly impossible to tell whether a prospective sex partner is infected without asking her or him. And even if that person is HIV+ (or has any STI), what is the likelihood that he or she will be honest, if doing so would mean that this sexual encounter might not take place?

So, does this policy protect the general public, or discriminate? If you were desperate for a blood transfusion, would you be willing to have blood donated to you by a gay man? What if you knew that he had only had one partner for the last 20 years? Or if he'd always used a latex condom? Would you be more or less likely to accept blood from a heterosexual person who had had many sex partners but never used a condom in her or his life?

Suggested Readings

The Associated Press, *Scientists Reject Easing Ban on Gay Male Blood Donors* (September 14, 2000). Accessible online at http://archives.cnn.com/2000/HEALTH/AIDS/09/14/blood.gaymen.ap.

S. Bodzin, "Students Press to End Ban on Gay Male Blood Donors: College Activists Take Plea Directly to the Red Cross," *Los Angeles Times* (July 11, 2005). Accessible online at http://www.boston.com/news/nation/articles/2005/07/11/students_press_to_end_ban_on_gay_male_blood_donors.

Express Gay News, "Russia, France Said to Lift Bans on Blood Donations by Gay Men: Australia May Be Next," *Express Gay News* (July 17, 2006). Accessible online at http://www.washblade.com/thelatest/thelatest.cfm? blog_id=8186.

M. Germain, R.S. Remis, and G. Delage, "The Risks and Benefits of Accepting Men Who Have Had Sex with Men as Blood Donors," *Transfusion* (vol. 43, no. 1, January 2003).

M. Hutchens, "Washington State U. Blood Centers Ban Gay Men from Donating," *Daily Evergreen* (Washington State University) (October 9, 2002). Accessible online at http://www.highbeam.com/doc/1P1-68618278.html.

A. Keegan, "FDA to Revisit Bans on Blood Donors: Prohibition on Donations from Gay Men May Be Up for Review This Week," *Southern Voice* (March 6, 2006). Accessible online at http://www.sovo.com/thelatest/thelatest.cfm?blog_id=5431.

D. Link, "Should Gay Men Be Allowed to Donate Blood?" *GMHC Treatment Issues* (November/December 2000). Accessible online at www.thebody.com/gmhc/issues/novdec00/blood.html.

E. Resnick, "Blood Donation Ban Puts the Red Cross in a Hot Spot." *Gay People's Chronicle* (August 26, 2005). Accessible online at www.gaypeopleschronicle.com/stories05/august/0826053.htm.

ISSUE 12

Should Lesbian and Gay Individuals Be Allowed to Adopt Children?

YES: Joan Biskupic, from "Same-Sex Couples Redefining Family Life in USA," *USA Today* (February 17, 2003)

NO: Timothy J. Dailey, from "State of the States: Update on Homosexual Adoption in the U.S." *Family Research Council* (no. 243, 2004)

ISSUE SUMMARY

YES: Joan Biskupic, legal affairs correspondent for *USA Today*, discusses the personal challenges for same-gender couples attempting to adopt in states that are not friendly to them and provides an update of legal issues and options available to lesbian and gay couples; these indicate a changing tide of acceptance toward couples of the same gender, as well as lesbian and gay individuals, adopting children.

NO: Timothy J. Dailey, senior research fellow at the Center for Marriage and Family Studies, provides an overview of state laws pertaining to adoption by lesbian or gay parents. He points to studies showing that children do much better in family settings that include both a mother and a father, and that the sexual behaviors same-sex parents engage in make them, by definition, inappropriate role models for children.

Currently, there are thousands of children awaiting adoption. In many cases, there are strict requirements as to who can and cannot adopt. In one country, for example, a heterosexual couple must be married for at least four years—and if they already have one child, they can only adopt a child of a different gender. Most countries do not allow same-sex couples or openly lesbian or gay individuals to adopt children.

In the United States, same-sex couples can adopt in a number of ways. Some will adopt as single parents, even though they are in a long-term, committed relationship with another person, because the state or agency does not permit same-sex couples to adopt together. Others will do what is called "second parent" adoption—where one partner is the biological parent of the child, and the other can become the other legal parent by going through the court system. In other cases, the biological parent must terminate her or his own rights so that there can be a "joint adoption." Both parents jointly adopt the child and become equal, legal parents. This applies to unmarried different-sex couples, too.

There are a range of feelings about who should or should not parent children. Some individuals feel that children should be raised by a man and a woman who are married, not by a gay or lesbian individual or couple. Starting with the premise that homosexuality is wrong, they feel that such a relationship is an inappropriate context in which to raise children. For some of these opponents of lesbian and gay parenting, homosexuality is defined by behaviors. Because they fear that sexual orientation and behaviors can be learned, they also fear that a child raised by a lesbian or gay couple will be more likely to come out as lesbian or gay her- or himself.

Other people do not believe that a person's sexual orientation determines her or his ability to parent. Whether a person is raised by one parent, two men, two women, or a man and a woman is less important than any individual's or couple's ability to love, support, and care for a child. They oppose the concept that a heterosexual couple in which there is abuse or where there are inappropriate sexual boundaries would be considered preferable to a lesbian or gay couple in a long-term, committed relationship who care for each other and their children. They point to the fact that most lesbian, gay, and bisexual adults were raised by heterosexual parents. Therefore, they believe, being raised by a lesbian or gay couple will not create lesbian, gay, or bisexual children, any more than being raised by a heterosexual, married couple would guarantee heterosexuality.

Some state laws support same-sex couples' right to adopt children, and some do not. In eight states, (New Jersey, California, Connecticut, Massachusetts, New York, Illinois, Pennsylvania, and Vermont) as well as Washington, D.C., for example, joint or second parent adoption is currently available. In Utah, married heterosexual couples are given priority for foster or adoptive children, and in Mississippi, there is a law that outright bans a same-sex couple from being able to adopt children.

As you read this issue, think about what you think the characteristics of a good parent are. Can these characteristics be found only in heterosexual relationships, or can they be fulfilled by a same-sex relationship? Does the gender of a same-sex relationship affect your feelings on the subject? For example, do you find two women raising a child more or less threatening than two men?

In the following selections, Joan Biskupic discusses the assertive steps that lesbian, gay, and bisexual individuals have made to gain footage in the legal arena when it comes to adoption rights. She provides an overview of individual state statutes pertaining to adoption by same-gender couples, citing an increased focus on creating "functional" parents—regardless of the gender(s) of the parents involved. Timothy J. Dailey asserts that gay men are sexually promiscuous and are therefore poor role models and parents for children. Lesbians, he believes, are ineffective parents because they are raising a child without the presence and influence of a father figure, which theorists, he maintains, argue is vital to the psychosocial development of children, male and female.

YES ↵

Same-Sex Couples Redefining Family Law in USA

Donna Colley and Margaux Towne-Colley, a lesbian couple bringing up a son in Omaha, face an ongoing dilemma.

They could stay in Nebraska, where Colley has a satisfying job as a lawyer, the couple own a home and are close to their neighbors. It's also where state law does not allow both women to be legal parents to Grayson, a blond, blue-eyed toddler who was delivered by Towne-Colley after she was artificially inseminated with sperm from an anonymous donor.

That leaves the couple with another option: Leave Nebraska and build a new life in one of about a dozen states that recognize same-sex couples as parents.

Such legal status isn't just symbolic. Because Colley can't be a legal parent to 16-month-old Grayson under Nebraska law, the child would not be entitled to government benefits if Colley were to become disabled or die. The boy would not be guaranteed support payments from Colley if the two women were to split up. And if Towne-Colley were to die, Colley wouldn't automatically receive custody of the boy.

Legal analysts say the choice they face is typical of the forces that are transforming family law across America. Gay and lesbian couples increasingly are going to court seeking to adopt children, acquire rights as parents, take on shared last names, and secure a range of benefits similar to those enjoyed by heterosexual couples.

Nearly three years after Vermont approved civil unions for homosexual couples, the evolving acceptance of such couples nationwide is reflected in recent court decisions in which judges have looked not only at biology when determining who is a "parent," but at the roles people play in households. Many judges are saying sexual orientation shouldn't matter in deciding what makes a family. A few conservative groups are fighting the tide, without much success.

Recent cases in Pennsylvania and Delaware symbolize the new age in family law, and judges' increasing flexibility in defining parental roles. Courts in those states ordered lesbians to pay child support for children they had been rearing with their partners before the couples split up.

"People are recognizing that these non-traditional families are here to stay, and courts are finding ways to support the children," says Susan Becker, professor at the Cleveland-Marshall College of Law at Cleveland State University.

From *USA Today Newspaper*, February 18, 2003. Copyright © 2003 by USA Today, a division of Gannett Co., Inc. Reprinted by permission via Rightslink.

But as Colley and Towne-Colley's situation suggests, the rules aren't the same for everyone.

State laws—and local attitudes—vary widely when it comes to adoption, child support, domestic partnerships, and other issues that affect same-sex couples. Courts, laws, and government policies in conservative states in America's heartland and in the South generally are less tolerant of efforts to give gay and lesbian couples the same rights as heterosexuals:

- Nebraska's Supreme Court last year refused to allow a lesbian to formally adopt the boy whom she and her partner (the birth mother) are rearing. Such "second parent" adoptions, which allow a second adult to assume responsibility for a child without the biological parent losing any rights, are legal for gay and lesbian couples in California, Connecticut, Delaware, Illinois, Massachusetts, New Jersey, New York, Pennsylvania, Vermont and the District of Columbia. In a dozen other states, some local courts have backed such arrangements.
- Four states—Texas, Oklahoma, Kansas, and Missouri—still ban sex between consenting homosexual adults, although the laws are rarely enforced. The U.S. Supreme Court on March 26 will consider a challenge to Texas' law.
- Eight states and about three dozen cities and counties—mostly on the East and West coasts—now provide benefits for the partners of their gay and lesbian public employees, gay-rights advocates say.

No group tracks all cases involving gay and lesbian family issues. But those on both sides of the debate over whether gay and lesbian parents should be granted more rights agree that homosexuals' increasing aggressiveness on family issues has won them gains in courts and beyond.

"In the past, when gay and lesbian couples tried to adopt, they really couldn't identify themselves as gay," says Michele Zavos, a Washington, D.C., lawyer who specializes in gay family law. "Now, they can, either when going through a second-parent adoption or with an agency." . . .

Gay-rights advocates say it's all a reflection of the rising profile of gay men and lesbians in politics, the workplace, and everyday life. "People know now that gay and lesbian relationships are not exceptional," says Patricia Logue, a lawyer in Chicago for the Lambda Legal Defense and Education Fund. "Now, we're seeing what the political winds will bear in each state."

"I Am a Stranger to My Child"

Same-sex couples and their families have become hot topics for TV shows, movies, and media reports in recent years. The increasing openness of same-sex couples, fueled by the successes of the gay-rights movement, has made it seem as though there has been an explosion of such families.

But firm numbers are difficult to come by. The U.S. Census Bureau did not collect figures on same-sex couples until 2000, so there are no reliable statistics on the growth in such households. The 2000 Census found 1.2 million people living in households with unrelated adults of the same sex, but analysts say that figure is low because it was derived from a part of the Census form that some people ignored.

Similarly, estimates of children of gay or lesbian parents vary widely. Judges have cited various reports that put the number of children living with at least one gay or lesbian parent at 6 million to 12 million.

"The sheer number of support groups, magazines, and Web sites for gay and lesbian parents suggests that the number is significant," says Denver lawyer Kim Willoughby, who specializes in issues regarding same-sex couples.

Advances in reproductive technology, including artificial insemination, egg donation, and in-vitro fertilization, have given gay men and lesbians ways to become parents beyond adoption.

Although it has become easier for same-sex couples to work with private adoption agencies, they sometimes do not disclose their sexual orientation, making reliable statistics about such adoptions difficult. Gay men or lesbians who adopt foreign children typically have one partner adopt as an individual and the other partner initiate a second-parent adoption later.

After Towne-Colley, 38, got pregnant two years ago, she and Colley, 43, planned to return briefly to Vermont, where they had a civil union ceremony in 2000. (Towne added Colley's name to hers that year.) They wanted Grayson to be born there because the state would allow both women to be listed as parents on his birth certificate. But they were still in Nebraska in October 2001, when Grayson was born nine weeks early.

Working around Nebraska law, the couple drafted wills, a parenting agreement, and other papers that spell out their responsibilities for Grayson. "We are trying to do everything we can to tie ourselves together legally and bind me to our son," says Colley, whose salary and benefits provide for the family.

Still, Colley says, "under the law, I am a stranger to my child." For now, she and Towne-Colley are staying in Nebraska and not challenging its parenting laws. They are mindful of last year's state Supreme Court decision against a lesbian couple and say they don't want to risk an adverse ruling.

Amy Miller, a lawyer for the ACLU of Nebraska, represented the lesbian couple whose case went to Nebraska's high court. The court said state law forbids a second adult from adopting a child unless the birth mother (in this case, one of the partners) gives up her rights to the child.

Miller says her unidentified clients wanted to make sure that if the birth mother died, their 3-year-old son, Luke, could receive Social Security and other benefits tied to her partner. After they lost in court, they moved to Portland, Ore. Thanks to a second-parent adoption there, Miller said, they both are Luke's legal parents.

In Cincinnati, Cheryl, 41, and Jennifer, 36, are rearing a 2-year-old boy who is the product of an egg harvested from Cheryl, fertilized by sperm from an anonymous donor, and implanted in Jennifer.

The couple, who agreed to be interviewed if only their first names were used, say they might seek shared parental rights. But they know that Ohio courts often reject such efforts. They say moving out of state is not an option. "This is just as much our state as anyone else's," Cheryl says.

Focusing on "Functional" Parents

Ohio has been a battleground for the new generation of family law cases. The state Supreme Court has handed victories to those on both sides of the issue.

During the past year, the court endorsed shared last names for gay and lesbian couples but rejected second-parent adoptions for homosexuals. In Cleveland Heights, voters gave health benefits to gay and lesbian partners of city employees. An effort to reverse the move through a referendum failed. . . .

But Duke University law dean Katharine Bartlett says judges have struggled with nontraditional families since divorce rates jumped three decades ago. "Courts aren't trying to contribute to the demise of traditional families. But they recognize the reality of families today and 'functional' parents."

That was evident in a Pennsylvania case in December. The state Superior Court affirmed a trial judge's order that a lesbian should pay support for five children she had been bringing up with her ex-partner. That case followed one in Delaware in which a judge ordered a woman to pay support for a son that her former partner had through in-vitro fertilization.

But providing for children isn't always the overriding factor in such cases. Last year in Idaho, a local magistrate denied a gay man, Theron McGriff, custody of his two children from a marriage to a woman. The magistrate said McGriff, 38, couldn't visit them if he continued to live with another man. Idaho's Supreme Court agreed to hear McGriff's appeal.

"Sexual orientation should be irrelevant," says Shannon Minter, McGriff's attorney "Unless you're living under a rock, you know the way people live has changed."

Timothy J. Dailey   ➡ **NO**

State of the States: Update on Homosexual Adoption in the U.S.

The legal status of homosexual adoption varies from state to state, and is constantly changing due to court decisions and new state laws addressing the issue. Further complicating the issue are gay activist organizations that present misleading accounts of court rulings and laws reflecting unfavorably on homosexual parenting.

States That Specifically Prohibit Gay Adoption

Three states, Florida, Mississippi, and Utah, have passed statutes specifically prohibiting homosexual adoption. The advocates of gay adoption downplay the Utah statute, asserting that it was not intended to prevent adoption by homosexuals. Liz Winfeld, writing in the *Denver Post,* discusses claims that the Utah law was aimed squarely at homosexuals: "Not true. Utah disallows any unmarried person from adopting regardless of gender or orientation."[1] . . .

In fact, the Utah law was enacted specifically to close loopholes in Utah adoption laws that were being taken advantage of by homosexual couples seeking to adopt children. . . .

The ensuing fight led to the legislature passing a statute barring homosexual adoptions. . . .

States That Specifically Permit Gay Adoption

USA Today reports that seven states, including California, Connecticut, Illinois, Massachusetts, New Jersey, New York, Vermont, and the District of Columbia permit homosexuals to adopt.[2] However, at present, the inclusion of California on this list is inaccurate.

States That Permit Second-Parent Adoption

Homosexual couples have adopted children through "second-parent" adoption policies in at least twenty states. There is no evidence that homosexuals in the remaining states are permitted to adopt children, a fact admitted by the gay activist Human Rights Campaign (HRC): "In the remaining 24 states, our research has not revealed any second-parent adoptions."[3]

At least one state has reversed its policy of permitting second-parent adoptions. In November 2000, the Superior Court of Pennsylvania ruled that same-sex couples cannot adopt children.[4] In addition, a court decision in California has reversed that state's policy of permitting homosexuals to adopt children. On October 25, 2001, the 4th District Court of Appeal (San Diego) ruled that there was no legal authority under California law permitting second-parent adoptions.[5] . . .

Homosexual Households in the United States

There are widely varying and unsubstantiated claims about the numbers of children being raised in gay and lesbian households. . . .

- The U.S. Census Bureau reports that there are 601,209 (304,148 male homosexual and 297,061 lesbian) same-sex unmarried partner households, for a total of 1,202,418 individuals, in the United States.[6] If one million children were living in households headed by homosexual couples, this would mean that, on average, *every* homosexual household has at least one child.
- However, a survey in *Demography* indicates that 95 percent of partnered male homosexual and 78 percent of partnered lesbian households do *not* have children.[7] This would mean that the one million children presumed to be living in homosexual households would be divided among the 15,000 (5 percent of 304,148) male homosexual and 65,000 (22 percent of 297,061) lesbian households that actually have children. This would result in an astounding 12.5 children per gay and lesbian family.

The cases highlighted by the media to generate sympathy for homosexual adoption typically feature "two-parent" homosexual households. Of course, some children are also being raised by a natural parent who identifies himself or herself as homosexual and lives alone. Nevertheless, the hypothetical calculations above give some indication of how absurdly inflated most of the estimates are concerning the number of children being raised by homosexuals. Far from being the proven success that some claim, homosexual parenting remains a relatively rare phenomenon.

Implications for Homosexual Parenting

Demands that homosexuals be accorded the right to . . . adopt children fit into the gay agenda by minimizing the differences between homosexual and heterosexual behavior in order to make homosexuality look as normal as possible. However, as already shown, only a small minority of gay and lesbian households have children. Beyond that, the evidence also indicates that comparatively few homosexuals choose to establish households together—the type of setting that is a prerequisite for the rearing of children. Consider the following:

- HRC claims that the U.S. population of gays and lesbians is 10,456,405, or 5 percent of the total U.S. population over 18 years of age.[8] The best available data supports a much lower estimate for those who engage in same-sex sexual relations.[9] However, assuming the higher estimate for the purposes of argument, this would indicate that *only 8.6 percent* of homosexuals (1,202,418 out of 10,456,405) choose to live in a household with a person of the same sex.

- HRC asserts that "30 percent of gay and lesbian people are living in a committed relationship in the same residence."[10] Assuming HRC's own figures, that would mean over three million gays and lesbians are living in such households, which, as shown above, is a wildly inflated estimate over the census figures. It is worth noting that the HRC claim amounts to a tacit admission that 70 percent of gays and lesbians choose not to live in committed relationships and establish households together.
- HRC claims that the numbers of gay and lesbian households were "undercounted" by the census. However, if true, it would represent an unprecedented, massive undercount of 260 percent on the part of the U.S. Census Bureau.

The census figures indicate that only a small minority of gays and lesbians have made the lifestyle choice that is considered a fundamental requisite in any consideration regarding adoption, and only a small percentage of those households actually have children. The evidence thus does not support the claim that significant numbers of homosexuals desire to provide a stable family setting for children.

The Nature of Homosexual "Committed Relationships"

Gay activists admit that the ultimate goal of the drive to legitimize homosexual marriage and adoption is to change the essential character of marriage, removing precisely the aspects of fidelity and chastity that promote stability in the home. They pursue their goal heedless of the fact that such households are unsuitable for the raising of children:

- Paula Ettelbrick, former legal director of the Lambda Legal Defense and Education Fund, has stated, "Being queer is more than setting up house, sleeping with a person of the same gender, and seeking state approval for doing so. . . . Being queer means pushing the parameters of sex, sexuality, and family, and in the process transforming the very fabric of society."[11]
- According to homosexual writer and activist Michelangelo Signorile, the goal of homosexuals is to redefine the term *monogamy*.

For these men, the term "monogamy" simply doesn't necessarily mean sexual exclusivity. . . . The term "open relationship" has for a great many gay men come to have one specific definition: A relationship in which the partners have sex on the outside often, put away their resentment and jealousy, and discuss their outside sex with each other, or share sex partners.[12]

- The views of Signorile and Ettelbrick regarding marriage are widespread in the homosexual community. According to the *Mendola Report,* a mere 26 percent of homosexuals believe that commitment is most important in a marriage relationship.[13] . . .

Even those who support the concept of homosexual "families" admit to their unsuitability for children:

- In their study in *Family Relations,* L. Koepke et al. observed, "Even individuals who believe that same-sex relationships are a legitimate choice for adults may feel that children will suffer from being reared in such families."[14]
- Pro-homosexual researchers J. J. Bigner and R. B. Jacobson describe the homosexual father as "socioculturally unique," trying to take on "two apparently opposing roles: that of a father (with all its usual connotations) and that of a homosexual man." They describe the homosexual father as "both structurally and psychologically at social odds with his interest in keeping one foot in both worlds: parenting and homosexuality."[15]

In truth, the two roles are fundamentally incompatible. The instability, susceptibility to disease, and domestic violence that is disproportionate in homosexual relationships would normally render such households unfit to be granted custody of children. However, in the current social imperative to grant legitimacy to the practice of homosexuality in every conceivable area of life, such considerations are often ignored.

But children are not guinea pigs to be used in social experiments in redefining the institutions of marriage and family. They are vulnerable individuals with vital emotional and developmental needs. The great harm done by denying them both a mother and a father in a committed marriage will not easily be reversed, and society will pay a grievous price for its ill-advised adventurism.

Notes

1. Liz Winfeld, "In a Family Way," *Denver Post,* November 28, 2001.
2. Marilyn Elias, "Doctors Back Gay "Co-Parents," *USA Today,* February 3, 2002.
3. "Chapter 4: Second-Parent Adoption," in *The Family* (Human Rights Campaign, 2002). . . .
4. Ibid.
5. Bob Egelko, "Court Clarifies Decision on Adoptions," *San Francisco Chronicle,* November 22, 2001. The decision is under review by the California Supreme Court.
6. "PCT 14: Unmarried-Partner Households by Sex of Partners" (U.S. Census Bureau: Census 2000 Summary File 1).
7. Dan Black et al., "Demographics of the Gay and Lesbian Population in the United States: Evidence from Available Systematic Data Sources," *Demography* 37 (May 2000): 150.

8. David M. Smith and Gary J. Gates, "Gay and Lesbian Families in the United States: Same-Sex Unmarried Partner Households," *Human Rights Campaign* (August 22, 2001): 2.

9. Dan Black et al., "Demographics of the Gay and Lesbian Population," "4.7 percent of men in the combined samples have had at least one same-sex experience since age 18, but only 2.5 percent of men have engaged in exclusively same-sex sex over the year preceding the survey. Similarly, 3.5 percent of women have had at least one same-sex sexual experience, but only 1.4 percent have had exclusively same-sex sex over the year preceding the survey." (p. 141.)

10. Ibid.

11. Paula Ettelbrick, quoted in William B. Rubenstein, "Since When Is Marriage a Path to Liberation?" *Lesbians, Gay Men, and the Law,* (New York: The New Press, 1993), pp. 398, 400.

12. Michelangelo Signorile, *Life Outside* (New York: HarperCollins, 1997), p. 213.

13. Mary Mendola, *The Mendola Report* (New York: Crown, 1980), p. 53.

14. L. Koepke et al., "Relationship Quality in a Sample of Lesbian Couples with Children and Child-free Lesbian Couples," *Family Relations* 41 (1992): 228.

15. Bigner and Jacobson, "Adult Responses to Child Behavior and Attitudes Toward Fathering," Frederick W. Bozett, ed., *Homosexuality and the Family* (New York: Harrington Park Press, 1989), pp. 174, 175.

POSTSCRIPT

Should Lesbian and Gay Individuals Be Allowed to Adopt Children?

Parenting is an area that has so many unknown factors, influences, and outcomes. Two-parent, high-income families sometimes have children who grow up with emotional and/or behavioral problems. Single parents can raise healthy, well-adjusted children. Some heterosexual couples raise children effectively, and some do not; some lesbian or gay couples raise children effectively, and some do not.

Although there is much research exploring correlations between economic health, number of parents, and other factors, literature reviewing the connections between a parent's sexual orientation and her or his ability to parent remains inconclusive. There are studies maintaining that children need to be raised by a married, heterosexual couple, and there are studies asserting that a same-sex couple can do just as effective a job.

There is also insufficient information about homosexuality itself and the effects that having a lesbian, gay, or bisexual parent may or may not have on a child. The lack of information and plethora of misinformation breed fear. In at least two countries, depending on the official(s) involved in screening for the adoption, the prospective parents may be required to provide proof that they are heterosexual. When people are afraid, they want to protect—in this case, people who do not understand the basis of sexual orientation feel they need to protect children. In doing so, they sometimes make decisions that are not always in the best interest of the child. For example, in 1996, a divorced heterosexual couple living in Florida was battling over custody of their 11-year-old daughter. The male partner had recently completed an eight-year prison sentence for the murder of his first wife and had married his third. His ex-wife, however, had since met and partnered with a woman. A judge determined that the man and his new wife would provide a more appropriate home for the child than the child's mother because she was in a relationship with another woman. In the end, the judge believed that the child would do best in a home with a mother and a father, even though the father was convicted of second-degree murder and accused of sexually molesting his daughter from his first marriage.

How do you feel about this? If you feel that heterosexual couples are more appropriate parents than same-sex couples, how would the fact that one of the heterosexual partners had committed a capital crime affect your opinion?

Sometimes, we argue for what we think "should be" in a given situation. A challenge arises when comparing the "should be" to the "is"—what we think is best as opposed to the reality. If you feel that heterosexual married couples make the best parents, what should be done with those same-sex couples who are providing a loving, stable home for their children? Would it be best to leave the child where she or he is, or do you think the child would be better off removed from her or his existing family structure and placed with a heterosexual couple? Clearly, this is a discussion and debate that will continue as more and more same-sex couples not only adopt but also have biological children of their own.

ISSUE 13

Should Private Sexual Acts between Gay and Lesbian Couples Be Legal?

YES: Anthony Kennedy, excerpts from Majority Opinion, *Lawrence v. Texas,* U.S. Supreme Court (2003)

NO: Antonin Scalia, excerpts from Dissenting Opinion, *Lawrence v. Texas,* U.S. Supreme Court (2003)

ISSUE SUMMARY

YES: Anthony Kennedy, Associate Justice of the Supreme Court of the United States, was appointed to the Court by President Reagan in 1988. In this case, Kennedy is writing for a six-member majority that overturns a previous case, *Bowers v. Hardwick. Bowers* is overturned by Kennedy's opinion, therefore striking down state antisodomy laws.

NO: Antonin Scalia, Associate Justice of the Supreme Court of the United States, was appointed to the Court by President Reagan in 1986. Scalia writes that there are no constitutional protections from discrimination based on sexual orientation and that state sodomy laws should be upheld.

Antisodomy laws have been found throughout Western civilization dating back to the Middle Ages, a time during which the belief became common that nonprocreative sex was immoral. The legacy of these morals is still evident in American society today. Throughout of American history, homosexuality has been regarded as morally wrong and therefore has often been illegal. Many nineteenth- and twentieth-century religious readers and psychologists regarded homosexuality as a mental illness.

In 1948, Dr. Alfred Kinsey published the groundbreaking book *Sexual Behavior in the Human Male*, which was followed with the 1953 publication of another groundbreaking book, *Sexual Behavior in the Human Female*. In both texts, the longest chapters were specifically about homosexuality. Kinsey's work had a significant impact in challenging American sexual morality, and he was particularly concerned about the discrimination faced by those who were lesbian, gay, and bisexual, a population that at the time was largely regarded as sex criminals. His work, though widely read at the time, did not have an immediate widespread impact on public perceptions of those who were lesbian, gay, or bisexual. In fact, Kinsey's books were published at the onset of the Lavender Scare, a period in which it was official U.S. policy to fire lesbian and gay federal employees.

The American Psychological Association removed homosexuality from its list of mental disorders in 1973. Coming out of the closet became increasingly common, and challenges to state antisodomy laws were practically inevitable. In 1986, the U.S. Supreme Court ruled in *Bowers v. Hardwick* to uphold state antisodomy laws.

In 2003, the Supreme Court heard a similar antisodomy case with *Lawrence v. Texas*. Prior to *Bowers* and *Lawrence*, the Supreme Court had three times ruled in favor of a nonprocreative right to sex. In the 1965 case of *Griswold v. Connecticut,* the Supreme Court ruled that married couples have the right to have access to contraception. *Eisenstadt v. Baird* (1972) extended this same right to unmarried couples. In 1973, the Supreme Court ruled in *Roe v. Wade* that women have a constitutional right to obtain an abortion. This right has been upheld in subsequent Supreme Court cases. Although each of these cases deals with nonprocreative sexual behaviors, they address neither sodomy nor homosexuality.

Lawrence v. Texas began when John Lawrence, who was not getting along with his neighbor, was engaged in consensual sex in his residence with another man, Tyron Garner. Lawrence's neighbor called the police with a false report of a burglary in Lawrence's residence. The police, having legal grounds to enter Lawrence's residence based on the phone call, entered and found Lawrence and Garner having sex. Lawrence and Garner were arrested, and the police charged them with violating Texas's antihomosexual conduct law. For having been caught engaging in consensual sex in a private residence, both men were found guilty, spent a night in prison, and were fined $200.

Lawrence and Garner appealed their conviction, claiming that their constitutional rights had been violated. Explicit in their argument was a challenge to the constitutional reasoning behind *Bowers v. Hardwick*, essentially arguing that *Bowers* had been wrongly decided and should be overturned. In 2003, *Lawrence v. Texas* reached the Supreme Court of the United States.

Review the legal framework section of the Introduction that examines Original Intent and Living Constitution. The opinions in this case are clear examples of these concepts. Try to identify which opinion is written from an Original Intent perspective and which is written from a Living Constitution perspective.

YES ←   Anthony Kennedy

Majority Opinion, *Lawrence v. Texas*

Liberty protects the person from unwarranted government intrusions into a dwelling or other private places. In our tradition the State is not omnipresent in the home. And there are other spheres of our lives and existence, outside the home, where the State should not be a dominant presence. Freedom extends beyond spatial bounds. Liberty presumes an autonomy of self that includes freedom of thought, belief, expression, and certain intimate conduct. The instant case involves liberty of the person both in its spatial and more transcendent dimensions.

The question before the Court is the validity of a Texas statute making it a crime for two persons of the same sex to engage in certain intimate sexual conduct.

In Houston, Texas, officers of the Harris County Police Department were dispatched to a private residence in response to a reported weapons disturbance. They entered an apartment where one of the petitioners, John Geddes Lawrence, resided. The right of the police to enter does not seem to have been questioned. The officers observed Lawrence and another man, Tyron Garner, engaging in a sexual act. The two petitioners were arrested, held in custody overnight, and charged and convicted before a Justice of the Peace.

The complaints described their crime as "deviate sexual intercourse, namely anal sex, with a member of the same sex (man)." It provides: "A person commits an offense if he engages in deviate sexual intercourse with another individual of the same sex." The statute defines "[d]eviate sexual intercourse" as follows:

"(A) any contact between any part of the genitals of one person and the mouth or anus of another person; or

"(B) the penetration of the genitals or the anus of another person with an object."

We granted certiorari, (2002), to consider three questions:

"1. Whether Petitioners' criminal convictions under the Texas 'Homosexual Conduct' law– which criminalizes sexual intimacy by same-sex couples, but not identical behavior by different-sex couples–violate the Fourteenth Amendment guarantee of equal protection of laws?

"2. Whether Petitioners' criminal convictions for adult consensual sexual intimacy in the home violate their vital interests in liberty and privacy protected by the Due Process Clause of the Fourteenth Amendment?

Majority Opinion: Lawrence v. Texas, 539 U. S 558 (2003)

"3. Whether *Bowers* v. *Hardwick,* (1986), should be overruled?"

The petitioners were adults at the time of the alleged offense. Their conduct was in private and consensual.

We conclude the case should be resolved by determining whether the petitioners were free as adults to engage in the private conduct in the exercise of their liberty under the Due Process Clause of the Fourteenth Amendment to the Constitution. For this inquiry we deem it necessary to reconsider the Court's holding in *Bowers*.

There are broad statements of the substantive reach of liberty under the Due Process Clause; but the most pertinent beginning point is our decision in *Griswold* v. *Connecticut* (1965).

In *Griswold* the Court invalidated a state law prohibiting the use of drugs or devices of contraception and counseling or aiding and abetting the use of contraceptives. The Court described the protected interest as a right to privacy and placed emphasis on the marriage relation and the protected space of the marital bedroom.

"It is true that in *Griswold* the right of privacy in question inhered in the marital relationship. . . . If the right of privacy means anything, it is the right of the *individual*, married or single, to be free from unwarranted governmental intrusion into matters so fundamentally affecting a person as the decision whether to bear or beget a child."

The opinions in *Griswold* and *Eisenstadt* were part of the background for the decision in *Roe* v. *Wade* (1973). As is well known, the case involved a challenge to the Texas law prohibiting abortions, but the laws of other States were affected as well. Although the Court held the woman's rights were not absolute, her right to elect an abortion did have real and substantial protection as an exercise of her liberty under the Due Process Clause. The Court cited cases that protect spatial freedom and cases that go well beyond it. *Roe* recognized the right of a woman to make certain fundamental decisions affecting her destiny and confirmed once more that the protection of liberty under the Due Process Clause has a substantive dimension of fundamental significance in defining the rights of the person.

In *Carey* v. *Population Services Int'l,* (1977), the Court confronted a New York law forbidding sale or distribution of contraceptive devices to persons under 16 years of age. Although there was no single opinion for the Court, the law was invalidated. Both *Eisenstadt* and *Carey*, as well as the holding and rationale in *Roe*, confirmed that the reasoning of *Griswold* could not be confined to the protection of rights of married adults. This was the state of the law with respect to some of the most relevant cases when the Court considered *Bowers* v. *Hardwick*.

The facts in *Bowers* had some similarities to the instant case. A police officer, whose right to enter seems not to have been in question, observed Hardwick, in his own bedroom, engaging in intimate sexual conduct with another adult male. The conduct was in violation of a Georgia statute making it a criminal offense to engage in sodomy. One difference between the two cases is that the Georgia statute prohibited the conduct whether or not the participants were of the same sex, while the Texas statute, as we have seen, applies only to participants of the same sex. Hardwick was not prosecuted, but he brought an action in federal court to declare the state statute invalid. He alleged he was a practicing homosexual and that the criminal prohibition violated rights guaranteed to him by the Constitution. The Court, in an opinion by Justice White, sustained the Georgia law.

The Court began its substantive discussion in *Bowers* as follows: "The issue presented is whether the Federal Constitution confers a fundamental right upon homosexuals to engage in sodomy and hence invalidates the laws of the many States that still make such conduct illegal and have done so for a very long time." That statement, we now conclude, discloses the Court's own failure to appreciate the extent of the liberty at stake. To say that the issue in *Bowers* was simply the right to engage in certain sexual conduct demeans the claim the individual put forward, just as it would demean a married couple were it to be said marriage is simply about the right to have sexual intercourse. The laws involved in *Bowers* and here are, to be sure, statutes that purport to do no more than prohibit a particular sexual act. Their penalties and purposes, though, have more far-reaching consequences, touching upon the most private human conduct, sexual behavior, and in the most private of places, the home. The statutes do seek to control a personal relationship that, whether or not entitled to formal recognition in the law, is within the liberty of persons to choose without being punished as criminals.

This, as a general rule, should counsel against attempts by the State, or a court, to define the meaning of the relationship or to set its boundaries absent injury to a person or abuse of an institution the law protects. It suffices for us to acknowledge that adults may choose to enter upon this relationship in the confines of their homes and their own private lives and still retain their dignity as free persons. When sexuality finds overt expression in intimate conduct with another person, the conduct can be but one element in a personal bond that is more enduring. The liberty protected by the Constitution allows homosexual persons the right to make this choice.

Having misapprehended the claim of liberty there presented to it, and thus stating the claim to be whether there is a fundamental right to engage in consensual sodomy, the *Bowers* Court said: "Proscriptions against that conduct have ancient roots." In academic writings, and in many of the scholarly *amicus* briefs filed to assist the Court in this case, there are fundamental criticisms of the historical premises relied upon by the majority and concurring opinions in *Bowers*. We need not enter this debate in the attempt to reach a definitive historical judgment, but the following considerations counsel against adopting the definitive conclusions upon which *Bowers* placed such reliance.

At the outset it should be noted that there is no longstanding history in this country of laws directed at homosexual conduct as a distinct matter. Beginning in colonial times there were prohibitions of sodomy derived from the English criminal laws passed in the first instance by the Reformation Parliament of 1533. The English prohibition was understood to include relations between men and women as well as relations between men and men. Nineteenth-century commentators similarly read American sodomy, buggery, and crime-against-nature statutes as criminalizing certain relations between men and women and between men and men. The absence of legal prohibitions focusing on homosexual conduct may be explained in part by noting that according to some scholars the concept of the homosexual as a distinct category of person did not emerge until the late 19th century. Thus early American sodomy laws were not directed at homosexuals as such but instead sought to prohibit nonprocreative sexual activity more generally. This does not suggest approval of homosexual conduct. It does tend to show that this particular form of conduct was not thought of as a separate category from like conduct between heterosexual persons.

Laws prohibiting sodomy do not seem to have been enforced against consenting adults acting in private. A substantial number of sodomy prosecutions and convictions for which there are surviving records were for predatory acts against those who could not or did not consent, as in the case of a minor or the victim of an assault. As to these, one purpose for the prohibitions was to ensure there would be no lack of coverage if a predator committed a sexual assault that did not constitute rape as defined by the criminal law. Thus the model sodomy indictments presented in a 19th-century treatise addressed the predatory acts of an adult man against a minor girl or minor boy. Instead of targeting relations between consenting adults in private, 19th-century sodomy prosecutions typically involved relations between men and minor girls or minor boys, relations between adults involving force, relations between adults implicating disparity in status, or relations between men and animals.

To the extent that there were any prosecutions for the acts in question, 19th-century evidence rules imposed a burden that would make a conviction more difficult to obtain even taking into account the problems always inherent in prosecuting consensual acts committed in private. Under then-prevailing standards, a man could not be convicted of sodomy based upon testimony of a consenting partner, because the partner was considered an accomplice. A partner's testimony, however, was admissible if he or she had not consented to the act or was a minor, and therefore incapable of consent. The rule may explain in part the infrequency of these prosecutions. In all events that infrequency makes it difficult to say that society approved of a rigorous and systematic punishment of the consensual acts committed in private and by adults. The longstanding criminal prohibition of homosexual sodomy upon which the *Bowers* decision placed such reliance is as consistent with a general condemnation of nonprocreative sex as it is with an established tradition of prosecuting acts because of their homosexual character.

The policy of punishing consenting adults for private acts was not much discussed in the early legal literature. We can infer that one reason for this was the very private nature of the conduct. Despite the absence of prosecutions, there may have been periods in which there was public criticism of homosexuals as such and an insistence that the criminal laws be enforced to discourage their practices. But far from possessing "ancient roots," American laws targeting same-sex couples did not develop until the last third of the 20th century. The reported decisions concerning the prosecution of consensual, homosexual sodomy between adults for the years 1880–1995 are not always clear in the details, but a significant number involved conduct in a public place.

It was not until the 1970's that any State singled out same-sex relations for criminal prosecution, and only nine States have done so. Post-*Bowers* even some of these States did not adhere to the policy of suppressing homosexual conduct. Over the course of the last decades, States with same-sex prohibitions have moved toward abolishing them.

In summary, the historical grounds relied upon in *Bowers* are more complex than the majority opinion and the concurring opinion by Chief Justice Burger indicate. Their historical premises are not without doubt and, at the very least, are overstated.

It must be acknowledged, of course, that the Court in *Bowers* was making the broader point that for centuries there have been powerful voices to condemn homosexual conduct as immoral. The condemnation has been shaped by religious beliefs, conceptions of right and acceptable behavior, and respect for the traditional family. For many persons these are not trivial concerns but profound and deep convictions accepted as ethical and moral principles to which they aspire and which thus determine the course of their lives. These considerations do not answer the question before us, however. The issue is whether the majority may use the power of the State to enforce these views on the whole society through operation of the criminal law. "Our obligation is to define the liberty of all, not to mandate our own moral code." *Planned Parenthood of Southeastern Pa.* v. *Casey.*

Chief Justice Burger joined the opinion for the Court in *Bowers* and further explained his views as follows: "Decisions of individuals relating to homosexual conduct have been subject to state intervention throughout the history of Western civilization. Condemnation of those practices is firmly rooted in Judeo-Christian moral and ethical standards." As with Justice White's assumptions about history, scholarship casts some doubt on the sweeping nature of the statement by Chief Justice Burger as it pertains to private homosexual conduct between consenting adults. In all events we think that our laws and traditions in the past half century are of most relevance here. These references show an emerging awareness that liberty gives substantial protection to adult persons in deciding how to conduct their private lives in matters pertaining to sex.

In 1955 the American Law Institute promulgated the Model Penal Code and made clear that it did not recommend or provide for "criminal penalties for consensual sexual relations conducted in private." It justified its decision on three grounds: (1) The prohibitions undermined respect for the law by penalizing conduct many people engaged in; (2) the statutes regulated private conduct not harmful to others; and (3) the laws were arbitrarily enforced and thus invited the danger of blackmail. Other States soon followed.

In *Bowers* the Court referred to the fact that before 1961 all 50 States had outlawed sodomy, and that at the time of the Court's decision 24 States and the District of Columbia had sodomy laws. Justice Powell pointed out that these prohibitions often were being ignored, however. Georgia, for instance, had not sought to enforce its law for decades.

The sweeping references by Chief Justice Burger to the history of Western civilization and to Judeo-Christian moral and ethical standards did not take account of other authorities pointing in an opposite direction. A committee advising the British Parliament recommended in 1957 repeal of laws punishing homosexual conduct. Parliament enacted the substance of those recommendations 10 years later.

Of even more importance, almost five years before *Bowers* was decided the European Court of Human Rights considered a case with parallels to *Bowers* and to today's case. An adult male resident in Northern Ireland alleged he was a practicing homosexual who desired to engage in consensual homosexual conduct. The laws of Northern Ireland forbade him that right. He alleged that he had been questioned, his home had been searched, and he feared criminal prosecution. The court held that the laws proscribing the conduct were invalid under the European Convention on Human Rights. Authoritative in all countries that are members of the Council of Europe (21 nations then, 45 nations now), the decision is at odds with the premise in *Bowers* that the claim put forward was insubstantial in our Western civilization.

In our own constitutional system the deficiencies in *Bowers* became even more apparent in the years following its announcement. The 25 States with laws prohibiting the relevant conduct referenced in the *Bowers* decision are reduced now to 13, of which 4 enforce their laws only against homosexual conduct. In those States where sodomy is still proscribed, whether for same-sex or heterosexual conduct, there is a pattern of nonenforcement with respect to consenting adults acting in private. The State of Texas admitted in 1994 that as of that date it had not prosecuted anyone under those circumstances.

Persons in a homosexual relationship may seek autonomy for these purposes, just as heterosexual persons do. The decision in *Bowers* would deny them this right.

The . . . post-*Bowers* case of principal relevance is *Romer* v. *Evans* (1996). There the Court struck down class-based legislation directed at homosexuals as a violation of the Equal Protection Clause. *Romer* invalidated an amendment to Colorado's constitution which named as a solitary class persons who were homosexuals, lesbians, or bisexual either by "orientation, conduct, practices or relationships," and deprived them of protection under state antidiscrimination laws. We concluded that the provision was "born of animosity toward the class of persons affected" and further that it had no rational relation to a legitimate governmental purpose.

As an alternative argument in this case, counsel for the petitioners and some *amici* contend that *Romer* provides the basis for declaring the Texas statute invalid under the Equal Protection Clause. That is a tenable argument, but we conclude the instant case requires us to address whether *Bowers* itself has continuing validity. Were we to hold the statute invalid under the Equal Protection Clause some might question whether a prohibition would be valid if drawn differently, say, to prohibit the conduct both between same-sex and different-sex participants.

Equality of treatment and the due process right to demand respect for conduct protected by the substantive guarantee of liberty are linked in important respects, and a decision on the latter point advances both interests. If protected conduct is made criminal and the law which does so remains unexamined for its substantive validity, its stigma might remain even if it were not enforceable as drawn for equal protection reasons. When homosexual conduct is made criminal by the law of the State, that declaration in and of itself is an invitation to subject homosexual persons to discrimination both in the public and in the private spheres. The central holding of *Bowers* has been brought in question by this case, and it should be addressed. Its continuance as precedent demeans the lives of homosexual persons.

The stigma this criminal statute imposes, moreover, is not trivial. The offense, to be sure, is but a class C misdemeanor, a minor offense in the Texas legal system. Still, it remains a criminal offense with all that imports for the dignity of the persons charged. The petitioners will bear on their record the history of their criminal convictions. Just this Term we rejected various challenges to state laws requiring the registration of sex offenders. We are advised that if Texas convicted an adult for private, consensual homosexual conduct under the statute here in question the convicted person would come within the registration laws of a least four States were he or she to be subject to their jurisdiction. This underscores the consequential nature of the punishment and the state-sponsored condemnation attendant to the criminal prohibition. Furthermore, the Texas criminal conviction carries with it the other collateral consequences always following a conviction, such as notations on job application forms, to mention but one example.

The foundations of *Bowers* have sustained serious erosion from our recent decisions in *Casey* and *Romer*. When our precedent has been thus weakened, criticism from other sources is of greater significance. In the United States criticism of *Bowers* has been substantial and continuing, disapproving of its reasoning in all respects, not just as to its historical assumptions. The courts of five different States have declined to follow it in interpreting provisions in their own state constitutions parallel to the Due Process Clause of the Fourteenth Amendment.

To the extent *Bowers* relied on values we share with a wider civilization, it should be noted that the reasoning and holding in *Bowers* have been rejected elsewhere. The European Court of Human Rights has followed not *Bowers* but its own decision in *Dudgeon* v. *United Kingdom*. Other nations, too, have taken action consistent with an affirmation of the protected right of homosexual adults to engage in intimate, consensual conduct. The right the petitioners seek in this case has been accepted as an integral part of human freedom in many other countries. There has been no showing that in this country the governmental interest in circumscribing personal choice is somehow more legitimate or urgent.

The rationale of *Bowers* does not withstand careful analysis. In his dissenting opinion in *Bowers* Justice Stevens came to these conclusions:

"Our prior cases make two propositions abundantly clear. First, the fact that the governing majority in a State has traditionally viewed a particular practice as immoral is not a sufficient reason for upholding a law prohibiting the practice; neither history nor tradition could save a law prohibiting miscegenation from constitutional attack. Second, individual decisions by married persons, concerning the intimacies of their physical relationship, even when not intended to produce offspring, are a form of

"liberty" protected by the Due Process Clause of the Fourteenth Amendment. Moreover, this protection extends to intimate choices by unmarried
as well as married persons."

Justice Stevens' analysis, in our view, should have been controlling in
Bowers and should control here.

Bowers was not correct when it was decided, and it is not correct today.
It ought not to remain binding precedent. *Bowers* v. *Hardwick* should be and
now is overruled.

The present case does not involve minors. It does not involve persons
who might be injured or coerced or who are situated in relationships where
consent might not easily be refused. It does not involve public conduct or
prostitution. It does not involve whether the government must give formal
recognition to any relationship that homosexual persons seek to enter. The
case does involve two adults who, with full and mutual consent from each
other, engaged in sexual practices common to a homosexual lifestyle. The petitioners are entitled to respect for their private lives. The State cannot demean
their existence or control their destiny by making their private sexual conduct
a crime. Their right to liberty under the Due Process Clause gives them the full
right to engage in their conduct without intervention of the government. "It
is a promise of the Constitution that there is a realm of personal liberty which
the government may not enter." The Texas statute furthers no legitimate state
interest which can justify its intrusion into the personal and private life of the
individual.

Had those who drew and ratified the Due Process Clauses of the Fifth
Amendment or the Fourteenth Amendment known the components of liberty
in its manifold possibilities, they might have been more specific. They did not
presume to have this insight. They knew times can blind us to certain truths
and later generations can see that laws once thought necessary and proper in
fact serve only to oppress. As the Constitution endures, persons in every generation can invoke its principles in their own search for greater freedom.

The judgment of the Court of Appeals for the Texas Fourteenth District
is reversed, and the case is remanded for further proceedings not inconsistent
with this opinion.

It is so ordered.

Antonin Scalia

Dissenting Opinion, *Lawrence v. Texas*

Most of the rest of today's opinion has no relevance to its actual holding—that the Texas statute "furthers no legitimate state interest which can justify" its application to petitioners under rational-basis review. Though there is discussion of "fundamental proposition[s]," and "fundamental decisions," *ibid.* nowhere does the Court's opinion declare that homosexual sodomy is a "fundamental right" under the Due Process Clause; nor does it subject the Texas law to the standard of review that would be appropriate (strict scrutiny) if homosexual sodomy *were* a "fundamental right." Thus, while overruling the *outcome* of *Bowers,* the Court leaves strangely untouched its central legal conclusion: "[R]espondent would have us announce ... a fundamental right to engage in homosexual sodomy. This we are quite unwilling to do." Instead the Court simply describes petitioners' conduct as "an exercise of their liberty"—which it undoubtedly is—and proceeds to apply an unheard-of form of rational-basis review that will have far-reaching implications beyond this case.

(1) A preliminary digressive observation with regard to the first factor: The Court's claim that *"Planned Parenthood* v. *Casey, supra,* "casts some doubt" upon the holding in *Bowers* (or any other case, for that matter) does not withstand analysis. As far as its holding is concerned, *Casey* provided a *less* expansive right to abortion than did *Roe, which was already on the books when Bowers was decided.* I have never heard of a law that attempted to restrict one's "right to define" certain concepts; and if the passage calls into question the government's power to regulate *actions based on* one's self-defined "concept of existence, etc.," it is the passage that ate the rule of law.

(2) *Bowers,* the Court says, has been subject to "substantial and continuing [criticism], disapproving of its reasoning in all respects, not just as to its historical assumptions." Exactly what those nonhistorical criticisms are, and whether the Court even agrees with them, are left unsaid, although the Court does cite two books. Of course, *Roe* too (and by extension *Casey)* had been (and still is) subject to unrelenting criticism, including criticism from the two commentators cited by the Court today.

The Dissenting Opinion: Lawrence v. Texas, 539 U. S 558 (2003)

(3) That leaves, to distinguish the rock-solid, unamendable disposition of *Roe* from the readily overrulable *Bowers,* only the third factor. "[T]here has been," the Court says, "no individual or societal reliance on *Bowers* of the sort that could counsel against overturning its holding … ." *Ante,* at 16. It seems to me that the "societal reliance" on the principles confirmed in *Bowers* and discarded today has been overwhelming. Countless judicial decisions and legislative enactments have relied on the ancient proposition that a governing majority's belief that certain sexual behavior is "immoral and unacceptable" constitutes a rational basis for regulation. We ourselves relied extensively on *Bowers* when we concluded, in *Barnes* v. *Glen Theatre, Inc.* (1991), that Indiana's public indecency statute furthered "a substantial government interest in protecting order and morality." State laws against bigamy, same-sex marriage, adult incest, prostitution, masturbation, adultery, fornication, bestiality, and obscenity are likewise sustainable only in light of *Bowers'* validation of laws based on moral choices. Every single one of these laws is called into question by today's decision; the Court makes no effort to cabin the scope of its decision to exclude them from its holding. See *ante,* at 11 (noting "an emerging awareness that liberty gives substantial protection to adult persons in deciding how to conduct their private lives *in matters pertaining to sex*" (emphasis added)). The impossibility of distinguishing homosexuality from other traditional "morals" offenses is precisely why *Bowers* rejected the rational-basis challenge. "The law," it said, "is constantly based on notions of morality, and if all laws representing essentially moral choices are to be invalidated under the Due Process Clause, the courts will be very busy indeed."

Texas Penal Code (2003) undoubtedly imposes constraints on liberty. So do laws prohibiting prostitution, recreational use of heroin, and, for that matter, working more than 60 hours per week in a bakery. But there is no right to "liberty" under the Due Process Clause, though today's opinion repeatedly makes that claim. The Fourteenth Amendment *expressly allows* States to deprive their citizens of "liberty," so long as "due process of law" is provided:

"No state shall … deprive any person of life, liberty, or property, *without due process of law.*"

Our opinions applying the doctrine known as "substantive due process" hold that the Due Process Clause prohibits States from infringing *fundamental* liberty interests, unless the infringement is narrowly tailored to serve a compelling state interest. We have held repeatedly, in cases the Court today does not overrule, that *only* fundamental rights qualify for this so-called "heightened scrutiny" protection—that is, rights which are " 'deeply rooted in this Nation's history and tradition,' " All other liberty interests may be abridged or abrogated pursuant to a validly enacted state law if that law is rationally related to a legitimate state interest.

Bowers held, first, that criminal prohibitions of homosexual sodomy are not subject to heightened scrutiny because they do not implicate a "fundamental right" under the Due Process Clause. Noting that "[p]roscriptions against that conduct have ancient roots," *id.*, at 192, that "[s]odomy was a criminal offense at common law and was forbidden by the laws of the original 13 States when they ratified the Bill of Rights," and that many States had retained their

NO / Antonin Scalia   **225**

bans on sodomy, *Bowers* concluded that a right to engage in homosexual sodomy was not " 'deeply rooted in this Nation's history and tradition,'"

The Court today does not overrule this holding. Not once does it describe homosexual sodomy as a "fundamental right" or a "fundamental liberty interest," nor does it subject the Texas statute to strict scrutiny. Instead, having failed to establish that the right to homosexual sodomy is " 'deeply rooted in this Nation's history and tradition,' " the Court concludes that the application of Texas's statute to petitioners' conduct fails the rational-basis test, and overrules *Bowers'* holding to the contrary, "The Texas statute furthers no legitimate state interest which can justify its intrusion into the personal and private life of the individual."

The Court's description of "the state of the law" at the time of *Bowers* only confirms that *Bowers* was right. The Court points to *Griswold* v. *Connecticut* (1965). But that case *expressly disclaimed* any reliance on the doctrine of "substantive due process," and grounded the so-called "right to privacy" in penumbras of constitutional provisions *other than* the Due Process Clause. *Eisenstadt* v. *Baird* (1972), likewise had nothing to do with "substantive due process"; it invalidated a Massachusetts law prohibiting the distribution of contraceptives to unmarried persons solely on the basis of the Equal Protection Clause. Of course *Eisenstadt* contains well known dictum relating to the "right to privacy," but this referred to the right recognized in *Griswold*—a right penumbral to the *specific* guarantees in the Bill of Rights, and not a "substantive due process" right.

Roe v. *Wade* recognized that the right to abort an unborn child was a "fundamental right" protected by the Due Process Clause. The *Roe* Court, however, made no attempt to establish that this right was " 'deeply rooted in this Nation's history and tradition' "; instead, it based its conclusion that "the Fourteenth Amendment's concept of personal liberty ... is broad enough to encompass a woman's decision whether or not to terminate her pregnancy" on its own normative judgment that anti-abortion laws were undesirable. We have since rejected *Roe*'s holding that regulations of abortion must be narrowly tailored to serve a compelling state interest.

After discussing the history of antisodomy laws, the Court proclaims that, "it should be noted that there is no longstanding history in this country of laws directed at homosexual conduct as a distinct matter." This observation in no way casts into doubt the "definitive [historical] conclusion" on which *Bowers* relied: that our Nation has a longstanding history of laws prohibiting *sodomy in general*—regardless of whether it was performed by same-sex or opposite-sex couples:

"It is obvious to us that neither of these formulations would extend a fundamental right to homosexuals to engage in acts of consensual sodomy. Proscriptions against that conduct have ancient roots. *Sodomy* was a criminal offense at common law and was forbidden by the laws of the original 13 States when they ratified the Bill of Rights. In 1868, when the Fourteenth Amendment was ratified, all but 5 of the 37 States in the Union had *criminal sodomy laws*. In fact, until 1961, all 50 States outlawed *sodomy*, and today, 24 States and the District of Columbia continue to provide criminal penalties for *sodomy* performed in private and between consenting adults. Against this background, to claim that a right to engage in such conduct is 'deeply rooted in this Nation's history and tradition' or 'implicit in the concept of ordered liberty' is, at best, facetious."

It is (as *Bowers* recognized) entirely irrelevant whether the laws in our long national tradition criminalizing homosexual sodomy were "directed at homosexual conduct as a distinct matter." Whether homosexual sodomy was prohibited by a law targeted at same-sex sexual relations or by a more general law prohibiting both homosexual and heterosexual sodomy, the only relevant point is that it *was* criminalized—which suffices to establish that homosexual sodomy is not a right "deeply rooted in our Nation's history and tradition." The Court today agrees that homosexual sodomy was criminalized and thus does not dispute the facts on which *Bowers actually* relied.

Next the Court makes the claim, again unsupported by any citations, that "[l]aws prohibiting sodomy do not seem to have been enforced against consenting adults acting in private." *Ante*, at 8. The key qualifier here is "acting in private"—since the Court admits that sodomy laws *were* enforced against consenting adults (although the Court contends that prosecutions were "infrequent"). I do not know what "acting in private" means; surely consensual sodomy, like heterosexual intercourse, is rarely performed on stage. If all the Court means by "acting in private" is "on private premises, with the doors closed and windows covered," it is entirely unsurprising that evidence of enforcement would be hard to come by. (Imagine the circumstances that would enable a search warrant to be obtained for a residence on the ground that there was probable cause to believe that consensual sodomy was then and there occurring.) Surely that lack of evidence would not sustain the proposition that consensual sodomy on private premises with the doors closed and windows covered was regarded as a "fundamental right," even though all other consensual sodomy was criminalized. There are 203 prosecutions for consensual, adult homosexual sodomy reported in the West Reporting system and official state reporters from the years 1880–1995. There are also records of 20 sodomy prosecutions and 4 executions during the colonial period. *Bowers'* conclusion that homosexual sodomy is not a fundamental right "deeply rooted in this Nation's history and tradition" is utterly unassailable.

Realizing that fact, the Court instead says: "[W]e think that our laws and traditions in the past half century are of most relevance here. These references show *an emerging awareness* that liberty gives substantial protection to adult persons in deciding how to conduct their private lives *in matters pertaining to sex*" (emphasis added). Apart from the fact that such an "emerging awareness" does not establish a "fundamental right," the statement is factually false. States continue to prosecute all sorts of crimes by adults "in matters pertaining to sex": prostitution, adult incest, adultery, obscenity, and child pornography. Sodomy laws, too, have been enforced "in the past half century," in which there have been 134 reported cases involving prosecutions for consensual, adult, homosexual sodomy. In relying, for evidence of an "emerging recognition," upon the American Law Institute's 1955 recommendation not to criminalize " 'consensual sexual relations conducted in private,' " the Court ignores the fact that this recommendation was "a point of resistance in most of the states that considered adopting the Model Penal Code." Gaylaw 159.

In any event, an "emerging awareness" is by definition not "deeply rooted in this Nation's history and tradition[s]," as we have said "fundamental right" status requires. Constitutional entitlements do not spring into existence because some States choose to lessen or eliminate criminal sanctions on certain behavior. Much less do they spring into existence, as the Court seems to believe, because *foreign nations* decriminalize conduct. The *Bowers* majority opinion *never* relied on "values we share with a wider civilization," but rather rejected the claimed right to sodomy on the ground that such a right was not " 'deeply rooted in *this Nation's* history and tradition'" (emphasis added). *Bowers'* rational-basis holding is likewise devoid of any reliance on the views of a "wider civilization." The Court's discussion of these foreign views (ignoring, of course, the many countries that have retained criminal prohibitions on sodomy) is therefore meaningless dicta. Dangerous dicta, however, since "this Court . . . should not impose foreign moods, fads, or fashions on Americans."

I turn now to the ground on which the Court squarely rests its holding: the contention that there is no rational basis for the law here under attack. This proposition is so out of accord with our jurisprudence—indeed, with the jurisprudence of *any* society we know—that it requires little discussion.

The Texas statute undeniably seeks to further the belief of its citizens that certain forms of sexual behavior are "immoral and unacceptable," *Bowers*—the same interest furthered by criminal laws against fornication, bigamy, adultery, adult incest, bestiality, and obscenity. *Bowers* held that this *was* a legitimate state interest. The Court today reaches the opposite conclusion. The Texas statute, it says, "furthers *no legitimate state interest* which can justify its intrusion into the personal and private life of the individual" (emphasis addded). The Court embraces instead Justice Stevens' declaration in his *Bowers* dissent, that "the fact that the governing majority in a State has traditionally viewed a particular practice as immoral is not a sufficient reason for upholding a law prohibiting the practice." This effectively decrees the end of all morals legislation. If, as the Court asserts, the promotion of majoritarian sexual morality is not even a *legitimate* state interest, none of the above-mentioned laws can survive rational-basis review.

Finally, I turn to petitioners' equal-protection challenge, which no Member of the Court save Justice O'Connor, *ante*, at 1 (opinion concurring in judgment), embraces: On its face §21.06(a) applies equally to all persons. Men and women, heterosexuals and homosexuals, are all subject to its prohibition of deviate sexual intercourse with someone of the same sex. To be sure, §21.06 does distinguish between the sexes insofar as concerns the partner with whom the sexual acts are performed: men can violate the law only with other men, and women only with other women. But this cannot itself be a denial of equal protection, since it is precisely the same distinction regarding partner that is drawn in state laws prohibiting marriage with someone of the same sex while permitting marriage with someone of the opposite sex.

The objection is made, however, that the antimiscegenation laws invalidated in *Loving* v. *Virginia* (1967), similarly were applicable to whites and blacks alike, and only distinguished between the races insofar as the *partner* was concerned. In *Loving*, however, we correctly applied heightened scrutiny, rather than the usual rational-basis review, because the Virginia statute was "designed to maintain White Supremacy." A racially discriminatory purpose is always sufficient to subject a law to strict scrutiny, even a facially neutral law that makes no mention of race. No purpose to discriminate against men or women as a class can be gleaned from the Texas law, so rational-basis review applies. That review is readily satisfied here by the same rational basis that satisfied it in *Bowers*—society's belief that certain forms of sexual behavior are "immoral and unacceptable." This is the same justification that supports many other laws regulating sexual behavior that make a distinction based upon the identity of the partner—for example, laws against adultery, fornication, and adult incest, and laws refusing to recognize homosexual marriage.

Justice O'Connor argues that the discrimination in this law which must be justified is not its discrimination with regard to the sex of the partner but its discrimination with regard to the sexual proclivity of the principal actor.

"While it is true that the law applies only to conduct, the conduct targeted by this law is conduct that is closely correlated with being homosexual. Under such circumstances, Texas' sodomy law is targeted at more than conduct. It is instead directed toward gay persons as a class."

Of course the same could be said of any law. A law against public nudity targets "the conduct that is closely correlated with being a nudist," and hence "is targeted at more than conduct"; it is "directed toward nudists as a class." But be that as it may. Even if the Texas law *does* deny equal protection to "homosexuals as a class," that denial *still* does not need to be justified by anything more than a rational basis, which our cases show is satisfied by the enforcement of traditional notions of sexual morality.

Justice O'Connor simply decrees application of "a more searching form of rational basis review" to the Texas statute. The cases she cites do not recognize such a standard, and reach their conclusions only after finding, as required by conventional rational-basis analysis, that no conceivable legitimate state interest supports the classification at issue. Nor does Justice O'Connor explain precisely what her "more searching form" of rational-basis review consists of. It must at least mean, however, that laws exhibiting " 'a ... desire to harm a politically unpopular group'" are invalid *even though* there may be a conceivable rational basis to support them.

This reasoning leaves on pretty shaky grounds state laws limiting marriage to opposite-sex couples. Justice O'Connor seeks to preserve them by the conclusory statement that "preserving the traditional institution of marriage" is a legitimate state interest. But "preserving the traditional institution of marriage" is just a kinder way of describing the State's *moral disapproval* of same-sex couples. Texas's interest in §21.06 could be recast in similarly euphemistic terms: "preserving the traditional sexual mores of our society." In the jurisprudence Justice O'Connor has seemingly created, judges can validate laws by characterizing them as "preserving the traditions of society" (good); or invalidate them by characterizing them as "expressing moral disapproval" (bad).

Today's opinion is the product of a Court, which is the product of a law-profession culture that has largely signed on to the so-called homosexual agenda, by which I mean the agenda promoted by some homosexual activists directed at eliminating the moral opprobrium that has traditionally attached to homosexual conduct. I noted in an earlier opinion the fact that the American Association of Law Schools (to which any reputable law school *must* seek to belong) excludes from membership any school that refuses to ban from its job-interview facilities a law firm (no matter how small) that does not wish to hire as a prospective partner a person who openly engages in homosexual conduct.

One of the most revealing statements in today's opinion is the Court's grim warning that the criminalization of homosexual conduct is "an invitation to subject homosexual persons to discrimination both in the public and in the private spheres." It is clear from this that the Court has taken sides in the culture war, departing from its role of assuring, as neutral observer, that the democratic rules of engagement are observed. Many Americans do not want persons who openly engage in homosexual conduct as partners in their business, as scoutmasters for their children, as teachers in their children's schools, or as boarders in their home. They view this as protecting themselves and their families from a lifestyle that they believe to be immoral and destructive. The Court views it as "discrimination" which it is the function of our judgments to deter. So imbued is the Court with the law profession's anti-anti-homosexual culture, that it is seemingly unaware that the attitudes of that culture are not obviously "mainstream"; that in most States what the Court calls "discrimination" against those who engage in homosexual acts is perfectly legal; that proposals to ban such "discrimination" under Title VII have repeatedly been rejected by Congress.

Let me be clear that I have nothing against homosexuals, or any other group, promoting their agenda through normal democratic means. Social perceptions of sexual and other morality change over time, and every group has the right to persuade its fellow citizens that its view of such matters is the best. That homosexuals have achieved some success in that enterprise is attested to by the fact that Texas is one of the few remaining States that criminalize private, consensual homosexual acts. But persuading one's fellow citizens is one thing, and imposing one's views in absence of democratic majority will is something else. I would no more *require* a State to criminalize homosexual acts—or, for that matter, display *any* moral disapprobation of them—than I would *forbid* it to do so. What Texas has chosen to do is well within the range of traditional democratic action, and its hand should not be stayed through the invention of a brand-new "constitutional right" by a Court that is impatient of democratic change. It is indeed true that "later generations can see that laws once thought necessary and proper in fact serve only to oppress," and when that happens, later generations can repeal those laws. But it is the premise of our system that those judgments are to be made by the people, and not imposed by a governing caste that knows best.

One of the benefits of leaving regulation of this matter to the people rather than to the courts is that the people, unlike judges, need not carry

things to their logical conclusion. The people may feel that their disapprobation of homosexual conduct is strong enough to disallow homosexual marriage, but not strong enough to criminalize private homosexual acts—and may
legislate accordingly. The Court today pretends that it possesses a similar freedom of action, so that that we need not fear judicial imposition of homosexual
marriage, as has recently occurred in Canada (in a decision that the Canadian
Government has chosen not to appeal). At the end of its opinion—after having
laid waste the foundations of our rational-basis jurisprudence—the Court says
that the present case "does not involve whether the government must give formal recognition to any relationship that homosexual persons seek to enter."
Do not believe it. More illuminating than this bald, unreasoned disclaimer is
the progression of thought displayed by an earlier passage in the Court's opinion, which notes the constitutional protections afforded to "personal decisions relating to *marriage*, procreation, contraception, family relationships,
child rearing, and education," and then declares that "[p]ersons in a homosexual relationship may seek autonomy for these purposes, just as heterosexual
persons do" (emphasis added). Today's opinion dismantles the structure of
constitutional law that has permitted a distinction to be made between heterosexual and homosexual unions, insofar as formal recognition in marriage is
concerned. If moral disapprobation of homosexual conduct is "no legitimate
state interest" for purposes of proscribing that conduct, and if, as the Court
coos (casting aside all pretense of neutrality), "[w]hen sexuality finds overt
expression in intimate conduct with another person, the conduct can be but
one element in a personal bond that is more enduring," what justification
could there possibly be for denying the benefits of marriage to homosexual
couples exercising "[t]he liberty protected by the Constitution," Surely not the
encouragement of procreation, since the sterile and the elderly are allowed to
marry. This case "does not involve" the issue of homosexual marriage only if
one entertains the belief that principle and logic have nothing to do with the
decisions of this Court. Many will hope that, as the Court comfortingly assures
us, this is so.

The matters appropriate for this Court's resolution are only three: Texas's prohibition of sodomy neither infringes a "fundamental right" (which the
Court does not dispute), nor is unsupported by a rational relation to what the
Constitution considers a legitimate state interest, nor denies the equal protection of the laws. I dissent.

POSTSCRIPT

Should Private Sexual Acts between Gay and Lesbian Couples Be Legal?

Lawrence and Garner won the case, and anti-sodomy laws were struck down in the remaining states that had them. Lawrence's neighbor was charged with making a false report to the police. *Lawrence v. Texas* is beginning to be regarded as a landmark Supreme Court case. Although this case was a significant victory for those who advocate for lesbian, gay, and bisexual rights, many students are stunned to find that, until recently, sodomy was illegal in many states. It may be interesting to research the history of antisodomy laws in your state.

How would you assess how the political climate has changed since 2003, when this decision was issued? In what ways was Justice Scalia correct and in what ways was he incorrect with the changes he said this decision could lead to?

In the five years since this case was heard in 2003, the Supreme Court has turned down every case appealed to it dealing with the topic of sexual orientation. However, a significant number of cases dealing with sexual orientation have been decided in state courts. In 2003, same-sex marriage was prohibited in all 50 states and the District of Columbia. As this book reaches publication, same-sex marriage is permitted in six states (Connecticut, Iowa, Maine, Massachusetts, New Hampshire, and Vermont).

New York and Washington, DC, though they do not permit same-sex marriages within their jurisdictions, will recognize same-sex marriages that are performed in any of the states in which it is legal. Additionally, there are states, such as New York, New Jersey, California, and Rhode Island, that have active movements working to ensure that same-sex marriage rights are extended to their states. It is possible that in the 10 years that follow *Lawrence v. Texas,* the states that permit same-sex marriage will have grown from 0 percent to over 20 percent.

In addition to states extending equal marital rights, many large corporations are instituting the equivalent in the workplace. According to the Human Rights Campaign's 2009 Corporate Equality Index, 259 companies employing more than 9 million employees prohibit discrimination based on sexual orientation and gender identity, while providing domestic partner benefits to their employees. These companies, when operating in states that deny lesbian and gay couples the right to marry, treat same-sex couples just as they treat married, heterosexual couples.

Some of the states that permit same-sex marriage have done so through state court order, while others have done so through legislative action. The case of *Lawrence v. Texas* did not serve as cited precedent in any of these state court decisions. However, this chapter demonstrates how quickly societal values have changed on this topic in, historically speaking, a relatively short period of time.

Based on what you learned from reading this chapter, what might be some topics for future Supreme Court cases at the federal level that will be related to sexual orientation? For what types of topics might *Lawrence v. Texas* be a particularly pertinent precedent?

Internet References . . .

American Association of Sex Educators, Counselors, and Therapists

The American Association of Sex Educators, Counselors, and Therapists is a not-for-profit, interdisciplinary professional organization whose members share an interest in promoting understanding of human sexuality and healthy sexual behavior.

http://www.aasect.org

American Association for Marriage and Family Therapy

The American Association for Marriage and Family Therapy (AAMFT) is the professional association for the field of marriage and family therapy. The AAMFT facilitates research, theory development and education, and develops standards for graduate education and training, clinical supervision, professional ethics, and the clinical practice of marriage and family therapy. Their Web site also features a search engine for finding a licensed marriage/family therapist.

http://www.aamft.org

The Rape, Abuse, and Incest National Network

The Rape, Abuse, and Incest National Network is the nation's largest antisexual assault organization, operating the National Sexual Assault Hotline, offering educational information and resources, and advocating for effective policies to reduce the incidence of sexual assault.

http://www.rainn.org

Men Can Stop Rape

Men Can Stop Rape (formerly Men's Rape Prevention Project) works to empower male youth and the institutions that serve them to work as allies with women in preventing rape and other forms of "men's violence." Through awareness-to-action education and community organizing, the organization seeks to promote gender equity and build men's capacity to be strong without being violent.

http://www.mencanstoprape.org

The American Red Cross

The American Red Cross, founded in 1881 by Clara Barton, is the nation's "premier emergency response organization." In addition to domestic disaster relief, the Red Cross also offers services in the following areas: community services that help the needy; support and comfort for military members and their families; the collection, processing, and distribution of lifesaving blood and blood products; educational programs that promote health and safety; and international relief and development programs.

http://www.redcross.org

Twenty-First-Century Sexuality Issues

*A*s times change, cultural beliefs about many things change. Nowhere is this more prevalent than in the discussion about romantic and sexual relationships. Technology, in particular the Internet, has added new dimensions to intimate relationships that were unimaginable even 15 short years ago. The media continue to depict images of what "ideal" relationships should look like. The discussions and debates surrounding how we conduct ourselves in relationships are rooted deeply in how we were raised, our spiritual and cultural values and beliefs, and our past experiences with relationships. They are also dramatically affected by current messages that bombard us from all factions of society. This section offers a look at three questions that are asked primarily within the context of heterosexual relationships:

- Is Cybersex "Cheating"?
- Are Open Relationships Healthy?
- Is Pornography Harmful to Teenagers?
- Are Statutory Rape Laws Effective at Protecting Minors?

ISSUE 14

Is Cybersex "Cheating"?

YES: Susan A. Milstein, from "Any Way You Slice It . . . Cheating Is Cheating," written for *Taking Sides: Family and Personal Relationships* (2009)

NO: Crystal Bedley, from "Cybersex as Relationship Enhancer," written for *Taking Sides: Family and Personal Relationships* (2009)

ISSUE SUMMARY

YES: Susan Milstein is a certified health education specialist and a certified sexuality educator. She is an associate professor in the Department of Health Enhancement at Montgomery College in Maryland, as well as the lead consultant for Milstein Health Consulting. Milstein contends that while it is difficult to create a universal definition of cheating, the majority of people feel that cybersex outside of a primary relationship is cheating.

NO: Crystal Bedley argues that the anonymous nature of cybersex means that it is not cheating.

What is your definition of infidelity? Does it include flirting? Phone sex? "Sexting"? If you are in a committed relationship, does your significant other have the same definition? Too often, couples fail to have this conversation. In the event that this conversation occurs, they may find that they have significantly different definitions of what is monogamy as well what is infidelity. This divergence in definitions can lead to significant conflict within a relationship. The differences may very well be vast without even raising the topic of cybersex.

Infidelity is a common occurrence in American society. Most people know someone who has been unfaithful. In 2008, national headlines were full of famous Americans who had been unfaithful to their spouses: Eliot Spitzer, John Edwards, Alex Rodriguez, and Peter Cook, Christie Brinkley's former husband and in 2009 we seen Mark Sanford and David Letterman—all of these cases involved real life, in-person affairs.

However, cybersex is creating new types of headlines among the powerful. Recently a conservative Congressman from Florida was caught sending sexually explicit text messages to teenage pages working in Washington, DC. The scandal destroyed his political career. Although this case did not involve the question of whether this behavior constituted cheating, it raised a national dialogue regarding the expected norms related to virtual sex.

Infidelity dates as far back in human history as marriage. Sometimes infidelity is sanctioned by society or the spouse, but it is typically forbidden. Infidelity can lead to marital breakups, creating great stress and instability in people's lives. It is highly unlikely that you could guarantee your anonymity when practicing in-person infidelity.

Cyberspace has fundamentally altered the landscape for meeting others, particularly for anonymous sexual encounters. Now, without leaving one's home and with minimal risk of meeting someone one knows, a person can have written, spoken, or streaming video cybersex with different people at any time. Indeed, one can log on at any time and find a significant number of people looking to meet someone.

In fact, there is not even a need to be yourself. Online, people change their hair color, height, weight, eye color, sexual history, age, race, and gender. It is possible to have cybersex with a level of anonymity that cannot be realized in person. Online, people can live out their sexual fantasies without fear of rejection from someone they care about and without anyone even knowing who they are. With the opportunity for sexually explicit virtual meetings, the personal risk of being identified recedes.

Cybersex has created a new dimension, a potential form of twenty-first-century infidelity, depending on one's definition of infidelity. This is new terrain that presents a unique set of challenges. The lines of what is cheating may be difficult to draw with new technology. Even if you determine that certain scenarios are off-limits, temptation to stray is virtually omnipresent when in the privacy of your own residence.

Before reading this chapter, write down your definition of infidelity. Compile a list of what types of cybersex, if any, are regarded as being unfaithful. Does anything on your list surprise you? While reading, examine the ways in which the authors' assessment compares and contrasts with your values. What are some ways in which your beliefs were supported? What are some ways in which they were challenged? Additionally, what are the generational differences, if any, of views of cybersex and infidelity?

YES ←

Susan A. Milstein

Virtual Liaisons: Cybersex Is Cheating

Consider the following behaviors: flirting with a coworker, engaging in intimate phone calls or sending love letters to someone other than your partner, looking at sexually explicit images while masturbating, having a one-night stand. Would any of these behaviors be cheating?

You may have answered "yes" to none, some, or all of these behaviors, whereas your partner's answers may have been very different. For this reason, defining cheating can be difficult. Many couples may never take the time to sit down and discuss what behaviors they consider to be cheating but feel betrayed nonetheless when certain lines are crossed. The lines of what is considered cheating may become even more blurred when the actions in question take place online.

Enter the world of cybersex.

What Is Cybersex?

There is no single definition of cybersex. It is a broad term that may be used to encompass a variety of behaviors, including different methods of communication that happen online like love letter e-mails or instant messages. Sex, Etc. (http://www.sexetc.org/) defines cybersex as "Sexual encounters that take place entirely via the Internet." This would include going on a virtual "date" in a chat room that may involve one or both people masturbating in real life. These dates may happen simply by typing on a keyboard, or they may include the use of webcams and microphones.

Meeting for cybersex can take place in a multitude of places, including chat rooms, inside online games like World of Warcraft, or inside the virtual world of Second Life. Thanks to webcams, Skype, and Googlechat, you don't necessarily need a specific site like a chat room to meet, you just need the time, the technology, and another person. The definition of cybersex will continue to evolve as technology changes, and for some the new definition will include the use of teledildonics.

For some people, the use of teledildonics with a person other than a significant other crosses yet another boundary in the world of cybersex and infidelity.

So What Is Cheating?

Many of us associate sexual infidelity with the word "cheating." It involves having sexual contact with someone other than your partner. How much sexual contact is required for it to be cheating will vary from one person's definition to another. It may extend beyond sexual intercourse to include oral sex or kissing, but regardless of how much contact is involved, most of us usually think of something physical when we think of cheating. But, there's more to it than that. Online or offline, cheating on a significant other may involve physical acts, which is called sexual infidelity, or it may involve emotional infidelity (Whisman & Wagers, 2005).

Emotional infidelity occurs when someone is spending time with, giving attention to, or falling in love with someone other than their partner (Shackelford, LeBlanc, and Drass, 2000; Whitty and Quigley, 2008). Regardless of whether it is emotional or sexual infidelity, violating the bounds of one's relationship can lead to anger, jealousy, hurt, resentment, and potentially the ending of the relationship.

Subotnik and Harris (2005) describe four different types of affairs one might see in offline relationships. The first type is the serial affair, where there are a string of one-night stands or affairs that lack both an emotional connection and commitment. The second type of affair is the fling, which can be seen in one-night stands. The other two types of affairs are the romantic love affair and the long-term affair. These two affairs are similar in that there is a deep emotional component to each. One thing that differentiates these two affairs is the amount of time that is invested in each. All of these types of affairs can be carried out online through cybersex, and like offline affairs, can have a tremendous negative impact on relationships.

Then there's the emotional affair, or what Glass and Staeheli (2003) describe as the "extramarital emotional involvement" (p. 35). This emotional involvement consists of three components: emotional intimacy, secrecy, and sexual chemistry. All three of these components may happen during cybersex, whether it's a one-time "date" in a chat room or an affair which is taking place solely online.

As with offline affairs, relationships where cybersex has occurred face many challenges. The affair may lead to conflict and a decision to separate or divorce as a result of the online cheating (Docan-Morgan and Docan, 2007; Schneider, 2000; Young, Griffin-Shelley, Cooper, O'Mara, and Buchanan, 2000). The partner who was cheated on may feel a host of emotions including betrayal, abandonment, and shame (Schneider, 2000). Part of the healing process for the partner who was cheated on through cybersex involves learning to cope with what happened and trying to find closure (Maheu and Subotnik, 2001).

Cybersex and Cheating

Research is showing that people do believe that cybersex is cheating and that it can have a negative impact on relationships. One study found that 33 percent of respondents felt that cybersex of any kind was cheating. If certain circumstances occurred, for instance, the use of webcams, or having cybersex repeatedly with the same person, then the number increased to 58 percent (McKenna, Green, and Smith, 2001).

One researcher, Monica Whitty, has completed a number of studies looking at which specific cybersex behaviors people believe constitute infidelity. What she has not been able to do is come up with one list of cybersex behaviors that everyone agrees is cheating. But this is to be expected. If you look back at the behaviors at the beginning of this article, you'll see why one list of "cheating behaviors" will probably never exist for cybersex or for offline behaviors. What her research has shown is that there are many who believe that cybersex is infidelity and that it can have just as much of a negative impact on a relationship as cheating that is done offline (Whitty, 2003, 2005).

The research previously mentioned was done using respondents' opinions based on hypothetical situations. It would be easy to say that what someone says in a hypothetical situation may be different from what that person would say if faced with the same situation in real life. This may be true in that people who have found out that their partners had been engaging in cybersex might be more likely to say that they feel like they were cheated on.

When looking at studies that involved people who had direct experience with cybersex, you can see the negative impact that it has on people and their relationships. One study found that the offline partners of those engaging in cybersex reported feeling hurt, abandoned, and betrayed (Schneider, 2000). In another study, one-quarter of the people surveyed who were engaging in cybersex admitted that it had affected their primary relationship (Underwood and Findlay, 2004).

Given the findings of these studies, it should come as no surprise that therapists are seeing the impact of cybersex among their clients. In one study, a majority of marriage and family therapists reported having clients where cybersex was a problem, and 16 percent of the therapists reported that cybersex was the primary reason why the couple was in therapy (Goldberg, Peterson, Rosen, and Sara, 2008). And this is just the beginning, as the number of people affected seems to be increasing. In the two years prior to the survey, more than half of the therapists said their cybersex caseload had increased (Goldberg, Peterson, Rosen, and Sara, 2008).

Cybersex Is Cheating

We know that people who are involved in committed relationships are having cybersex. In a survey done in 1998, almost 85 percent of people who reported that they were engaging in online sexual activity were either married or in a committed relationship (Maheu and Subotnik, 2001).

We also know that cybersex is viewed by many as cheating and that it can have the same long-term negative impact on relationships that offline infidelity has.

So what's the bottom line? If what one person is doing is going outside the bounds of his or her relationship, then it's cheating, and it doesn't matter if it's in a hotel room or a chat room.

References

T. Docan-Morgan and C. A. Docan, "Internet Infidelity: Double Standards and the Differing Views of Women and Men," *Communication Quarterly* (vol. 55, no. 3, 2007).

S. P. Glass and J. C. Staeheli, J. C., *"Not 'Just Friends.' Rebuilding Trust and Recovering Your Sanity after Infidelity* (New York: Free Press, 2003).

P. D. Goldberg, B. D., Peterson, K. H. Rosen, and M. L. Sara, "Cybersex: The Impact of a Contemporary Problem on the Practices of Marriage and Family Therapists," *Journal of Marital and Family Therapy* (vol. 34, no. 4, 2008).

M. M. Maheu, and R. B. Subotnik, *Infidelity in the Internet. Virtual Relationships and Real Betrayal* (Naperville, IL: Sourcebooks, Inc., 2001).

K. Y. A. McKenna, A. S. Green, and P. K. Smith, "Demarginalizing the Sexual Self," *The Journal of Sex Research* (vol. 38, no. 4, 2001).

J. P. Schneider, "Effects of Cybersex Addiction on the Family: Results of a Survey," *Sexual Addiction & Compulsivity* (vol. 7, 2000).

Sex, Etc., "Cyber Sex" (n.d.). Retrieved March 15, 2009, from http://www.sexetc. org/glossary/1148

T. K. Shackelford, G. J. LeBlanc, and E. Drass, "Emotional Reactions to Infidelity," *Cognition & Emotion* (vol. 14, no. 5, 2000).

R. B. Subotnik and G. G. Harris, *"Surviving Infidelity. Making Decisions, Recovering from the Pain* (Avon, MA: Adams Media, 2005).

H. Underwood and B. Findlay, "Internet Relationships and Their Impact on Primary Relationships," *Behaviour Change* (vol. 21, no. 2, 2004).

M. A. Whisman and T. P. Wagers, "Assessing Relationship Betrayals," *Journal of Clinical Psychology* (vol. 61, no. 11, 2005).

M. T. Whitty, "Pushing the Wrong Buttons: Men's and Women's Attitudes toward Online and Offline Infidelity," *CyberPsychology and Behavior* (vol. 6, no. 6, 2003).

M. T. Whitty, "The Realness of Cybercheating. Men's and Women's Representations of Unfaithful Internet Relationships," *Social Science Computer Review* (vol. 23, no. 1, 2005).

M. T. Whitty and L-L. Quigley, "Emotional and Sexual Infidelity Offline and in Cyberspace," *Journal of Marriage and Family Therapy* (vol. 34, no. 4, 2008).

K. S. Young, E. Griffin-Shelley, A. Cooper, J. O'Mara, and J. Buchanan, "Online Infidelity: A New Dimension in Couple Relationships with Implications for Evaluation and Treatment," *Sexual Addiction & Compulsivity* (vol. 7, 2000).

Crystal Bedley

→ **NO**

Virtual Reality: Cybersex Is Not Cheating

As the Internet continues to expand and evolve, so do the possibilities for engaging in sexual encounters online. From chat rooms, to social networking sites, to virtual boy/girlfriends, new technologies are shaping the ways in which desires can be explored and indulged. Couples must navigate these new technologies to determine the role(s) that virtual encounters may or may not play in their relationships. Some people might enjoy engaging in cybersex, whereas their partners may not; some couples may enjoy engaging in cybersex together, whereas others may not. To understand whether a particular cybersex act is a form of cheating, therefore, one must take into account the nature of the relationship. Ultimately, whether cybersex is a form of cheating depends largely on both the interpersonal dynamics of the couple *and* the intentions and perceptions of the cybersex participant.

The term "interpersonal dynamics" refers to the nature of the relationship between the two romantic partners. More specifically, interpersonal dynamics shape how partners come to agree or disagree about the meanings of particular acts (e.g., whether cybersex is a form of cheating). Importantly, the ways in which couples negotiate their relationships, especially when each partner has different expectations, shape how both partners will interpret particular behaviors. For example, few people would argue that if both partners agree to participate in cybersex together that their shared action is a form of cheating. Moreover, if one partner communicates to the other partner that she or he would like to engage in cybersex and the other partner consents, then most would agree that the partners are being faithful to one another. Each of these examples demonstrates how the interpersonal dynamics of the couple determine whether cybersex is cheating. The ways partners choose to communicate with one another and the decisions they reach are critical for understanding whether cybersex is cheating or an expression of sexual desires. If both partners share an understanding of cybersex as an expression of sexual desire that does not constitute cheating, then it is clear that cybersex is not cheating. By the same token, if both partners believe the act of cybersex is cheating, then there is no reason to draw a different conclusion.

In contrast, if a partner deceives the other partner in order to engage in cybersex, one could argue that in this context, cybersex is an act of infidelity. Because relationships are built on mutual trust (among other factors), deception not only serves to destabilize the relationship but also becomes the framework for interpreting the cybersex act as an act of cheating. Importantly, recent research suggests that deception and emotional unavailability are primary reasons why partners view cybersex as equivalent to adultery (Schneider, 2003). In these cases, it is clearer that cybersex is an act of infidelity.

Although there are a variety of ways to engage in cybersex, when it comes to interpreting cybersex as cheating, traditionally the virtual form of the sex act is often inconsequential, trumped by the emotional toll paid by the partners involved in the relationship. Consider the following example:

> Shannon and Kendall are in a long-term committed relationship. Neither partner has been physically or emotionally intimate with anyone outside of the relationship. One day, Kendall decides to participate in a mutual masturbation session with an anonymous person he meets in a chat room. Minutes later Shannon walks into Kendall's office and witnesses the masturbation session. Devastated by what she sees, Shannon feels that Kendall has cheated. From Shannon's perspective, Kendall's online session is a form of cheating because of the sexual intimacy Kendall shared with the other person. From Kendall's perspective, Shannon is overreacting. Kendall believes that because cybersex does not involve physical contact, it is not cheating. So, Kendall views the cybersex act as a way of exploring one's fantasies in a safe environment.

This scenario illustrates the notion that the same act (in this case, the act of participating in a mutual masturbation session) can be interpreted in different and sometimes conflicting ways. For this reason, I argue that the individual perceptions of each partner are important to understanding whether cybersex should be considered cheating. The expression "individual perceptions" refers to the beliefs and/or attitudes of a person, which shape how the individual will interpret a particular behavior. Unlike interpersonal dynamics, which involve a negotiated agreement (or disagreement) about the meanings attributed to particular acts, individual perceptions are those beliefs held by each individual about the meanings attributed to particular acts, *regardless* of the beliefs of one's partner. To clarify the distinction between individual perceptions and interpersonal dynamics using the current example, it is clear that Kendall's individual perception is that the cybersex act is not a form of cheating, whereas Shannon's perception is that it is cheating. The interpersonal dynamics of the couple can be described as a disagreement over the cybersex act because each partner's perceptions are at odds with the other's.

Because partners can have differing perceptions of the same act, it is critical to also consider each partner's perception of cybersex to understand whether the cybersex is a form of infidelity. On the one hand, let's assume Shannon is not emotionally hurt by the act of masturbation alone but rather is hurt that Kendall transgressed upon an important moral boundary in their relationship, namely that partners are to remain sexually faithful to one another. On the other hand, Kendall does not see cybersex as cheating because the cybersex was used only to facilitate masturbation. Because masturbation has never been considered an act of cheating throughout the course of their relationship, Kendall believes that cybersex is merely another form of masturbation. Therefore, Kendall's perception of cybersex as masturbation reinforces the belief that Kendall is remaining sexually faithful to Shannon. Undoubtedly, Shannon and Kendall have differing views about the same act. If Shannon and Kendall cannot come to an agreement about whether or not the online mutual masturbation session was indeed an act of cheating, then whose perception helps us to best understand whether this act of cybersex is a form of cheating?

Traditionally, the perceptions of the partner not involved in the act of cybersex determine whether the act is considered cheating. In other words, if the partner not involved in the act of cybersex believes cybersex is cheating, then it is cheating.

But why should the perceptions of the partner prevail over the perceptions of the cybersex participant? The short answer is that they should not. Instead, whether an act of cybersex is cheating depends primarily not only on the intentions of the person who engages in cybersex but also on how this person perceives the cybersex act. I am arguing that rather than privilege the perceptions of the person not directly involved in the cybersex act, one must focus instead on the cybersex participant. Specifically, it is important to take into account both the intentions *and* perceptions of the cybersex participant in order to determine whether an act of cybersex is a form of infidelity.

To demonstrate the significance of one's intention in relation to the cybersex act, it is helpful to think about the following contrasting examples. In the first example, the cybersex participant intends to seek sexual and/or emotional pleasure from a person who is outside of the participant's relationship. The person may feel guilty for engaging in cybersex because she believes that she is being unfaithful given the nature of the cybersex encounter (e.g., cybersex acts that foster emotional and/or sexual intimacy). In this case, because the cybersex participant's intentions and perceptions of her behavior are adulterous, then this act should be interpreted as cheating. Even if a cybersex encounter does not begin with adulterous intentions, if during the course of the encounter the cybersex participant's intentions and/or perceptions of the act change, then the act could still be considered cheating. For many cybersex participants, however, this is not the reality of their experience. To state this point differently, many people who engage in cybersex do not engage in cybersex in order to cheat on their partners. Because people often do not engage in cybersex to harm their relationship, it is important to consider other intention/perception understandings of the cybersex act.

Now consider the case of a person who engages in cybersex with the sole intention of having an orgasm. It is important to point out that this person is not engaging in deceptive behavior in order to take part in the cybersex act. In this case, the cybersex participant is not looking to create an emotional connection with another person but instead is seeking out a stimulating aid for the purpose of masturbating. This person could choose to watch a pornographic movie, for instance, but instead chooses a chat room for arousal. In fact, an in-depth interview study of cybersex participants found that these participants often "equated participation in chat rooms with watching a movie or reading a novel" (Mileham, 2007, p. 16). Therefore, not only does the person involved in the cybersex act intend to engage in masturbation (a sexual act that is not generally considered to be a form of cheating), his perception of the experience is the same. Specifically, the cybersex participant perceives the cybersex act as an act of masturbation, not infidelity. From this perspective, I argue that the cybersex participant did not cheat on his partner because he did not intend to cheat, nor did he perceive the act as cheating.

For those who still remain skeptical as to whether cybersex is cheating, it is critical to understand the implications of this position. If someone believes that, although the cybersex participant thinks he is simply masturbating, he is actually cheating on his partner, then where can we draw the distinction between other forms of masturbation and cheating? Is the person who masturbates to a racy magazine cheating on her partner? Moreover, how do we make sense of situations where a person's mind wanders during sex? Is one cheating if he thinks of someone other than his partner during sex? Clearly, neither of these cases seems to constitute cheating. Skeptics must be aware that if the intentions and the perceptions of the cybersex participant are overlooked, then a variety of sex acts should also be considered alternative forms of cheating. Yet, if these masturbatory acts were all considered cheating, many of us would have to acknowledge that we've cheated on our partners!

By privileging the perceived "victim's" individual perceptions of the cybersex act above the intentions and perceptions of the cybersex participant, one is more likely to conclude that cybersex is cheating. It has been my aim to question this traditional bias to suggest that many of the acts typically considered cheating are vastly more complicated. By highlighting the intentions and perceptions of the cybersex participant, it becomes clear that many cybersex acts are not necessarily acts of infidelity. Oftentimes, cybersex is used to sexually enrich the lives of those who take part, which can ultimately benefit a relationship rather than destroy it.

References

B. L. A. Mileham, "Online Infidelity in Internet Chat Rooms: An Ethnographic Exploration," *Computers in Human Behavior* (vol. 23, 2007), 11–13.

J. Schneider, The Impact of Compulsive Cybersex Behaviours on the Family," *Sexual and Relationship Therapy* (vol. 18, no. 3, 2003), 329–354.

POSTSCRIPT

Is Cybersex "Cheating"?

Have you ever hid something from your significant other that you feared would make him or her jealous? Maybe texting an ex? Visiting a strip club? Going out to a platonic dinner with someone you find attractive? Although none of these incidents are physical sexual encounters with another person, many people will conceal these encounters out of fear that their significant other will regard them as being unfaithful in the relationship. Each incident described has some degree of emotional or physical interaction. In contrast, cybersex can be nonphysical and anonymous. Because it involves reduced risk of exposure and regular access to virtual sexual encounters, cybersex creates a new set of boundaries to be negotiated in a relationship.

Cybersex potentially changes the ways in which trust is extended within a relationship. While access to anonymous sexual encounters may be a threatening prospect to many, there is a fundamental question that must be asked and evaluated, which has not changed despite the virtual world of sexual relations:

What is a healthy relationship?

Write down what you consider to be the most important qualities of a healthy relationship. Then rank how important the different qualities are. This should provide a larger perspective related to cybersex and infidelity. Whether or not Internet use is considered, the qualities of healthy relationships should remain constant.

Once you have identified your views about sexual infidelity and cybersex, are you ready to talk about your criteria with a significant other? How might you respond to answers that may differ from yours? Specifically, weigh whether you can negotiate if you have decidedly different values related to cybersex and infidelity. How much are you willing to compromise your beliefs? What are your expectations related to how your significant other will compromise his or her beliefs?

If you are in a relationship that lacks equality or fails to respectfully communicate, you may find that this conversation is difficult to have. If you are in a relationship of equality and mutual respect, this conversation is far easier, provided that you and your partner feel comfortable having frank conversations about sexuality. Keep in mind that it is normal to struggle when having such conversations. It might be a good idea to acknowledge this at the start of such a conversation and not to be too hard on yourself if the conversation is challenging.

Melanie Davis, an expert on communicating about sexuality within families and relationships, advises a person do the following in starting this conversation: "The first thing is for the person who wants to bring up the conversation to define the purpose of the conversation. Is it just idle curiosity, or is there some sort of fear? Or is there a need to disclose something? That can help you get into the right frame of mind. If you think your partner is cheating on you, it might come across as accusing the person, and that is never an effective way to start a conversation. The other thing to consider is where you're going to have the conversation. It is probably not a conversation you want to have in the middle of a crowded restaurant. If you fear what will be disclosed, you might want to have the conversation in the presence of a counselor or a therapist who can help guide the conversation."

Davis adds, "Sometimes you just want to test the waters conversationally. A good way to do that it to remark about a TV show or an article that you read, something that can get you to that conversation in a neutral way."

Once these conversations begin, you may find that they are likely to get easier, provided you have a cooperative and supportive partner. If these conversations cannot occur, it may not be surprising if people get hurt when they lack a full understanding of each other's boundaries and the rationale behind them.

ISSUE 15

Are Open Relationships Healthy?

YES: Donald Dyson, from "Seeing Relationships Through a Wider Lens: Open Relationships As A Healthy Option," written for *Taking Sides: Family and Personal Relationships* (2009)

NO: Stanley Kurtz, from "Here Come the Brides: Plural Marriage Is Waiting in the Wings," *The Weekly Standard* (December 26, 2005)

ISSUE SUMMARY

YES: Donald Dyson is assistant professor of human sexuality education at Widener University and the national co-chair of the conference for the American Association of Sexuality Educators, Counselors and Therapists. Dyson argues that there are essential qualities of a healthy relationship and that an open relationship can be successful.

NO: Stanley Kurtz, a writer and senior fellow at the Ethics and Public Policy Center, argues that allowing for same-sex marriage will create a slippery slope, eventually leading to plural marriages. Kurtz contends that such marriages prove destructive to the institution of marriage itself.

During the nineteenth century, the U.S. Congress outlawed polygamy. Although all citizens of the United States were affected by this, the intent was to target members of the Church of Latter-Day Saints, otherwise known as Mormons. In fact, in order for Utah to join the union, the state first had to adopt antipolygamy laws.

In the late 1870s, George Reynolds, a Mormon resident of Utah, was arrested for having multiple wives. He was convicted and sentenced to two years in prison and was fined $200. Reynolds challenged his conviction, and the case, *Reynolds v. United States,* reached the Supreme Court of the United States.

The Court ruled to uphold antipolygamy and antibigamy laws, stating: "Polygamy has always been odious among the northern and western nations of Europe, and, until the establishment of the Mormon Church, was almost exclusively a feature of the life of Asiatic and of African people."

The bizarre, and frankly racist, choice of words in the Supreme Court opinion seemingly blames people of color, who were largely banned from the

Mormon Church at that time, for white, Mormon polygamy. Aside from this language, this decision provides case law in addition to already existing statutory law stating that there is no right to plural marriages.

Although polygamy is illegal in the United States today, sex outside of a primary relationship—including sex outside of marriage—occurs to a significant degree. Over the course of a heterosexual marriage, an estimated 24 percent of husbands and 18 percent of wives have sex outside of marriage. The temptation to have sex outside of marriage is clearly significant, and the practice is fairly common. These statistics reflect the frequency of sex outside of marriage *without* the permission of one's spouse.

The difference between infidelity and an open relationship is that in an open relationship, sex occurs outside of the marriage or relationship with the consent of one's partner or spouse. Open relationships have been referred to as wife swapping, swinging, and "the lifestyle." Wife swapping is perhaps the most misappropriated phrase. First, it implies that all open relationships are inherently heterosexual. Second, it indicates that men possess the power and that women are commodities being traded.

Heterosexual women in open relationships are often in high demand. Women in such relationships often find that they have a significant amount of power. In fact, in some relationships, the man might push to experiment with swinging only to find that he does not care for it after seeing how sought-after his partner is by other men.

It is a challenge to find open relationships represented positively in television or film. A number of major American cities have swingers clubs that typically cater to heterosexual couples and single women. Due to the stigma associated with open relationships, most people within them work to conceal this from friends, family, and acquaintances.

Although open relationships exist, the majority of Americans believe that sex outside of marriage is morally wrong and destructive. These individuals typically regard sexual intimacy and emotional intimacy as inseparable. They will often voice concerns that open relationships are bound to threaten the stability of a person's marriage or committed relationship.

When reading these articles, give some thought to historical factors that influence sexual morality today. Examine how your value system affects your reaction to these articles.

YES

Donald Dyson

Seeing Relationships Through a Wider Lens: Open Relationships As A Healthy Option

Introduction: The Current Cultural Context for Relationships

There are many ways in which human beings have learned to organize their daily relationships. People sometimes have family with whom they are very close; they have layers of social circles in which they operate, have friends, and good friends, and intimate friends (some of whom may also be lovers). People have lovers and spouses; they have husbands and wives; they have partners and playmates. Each of these relationships involves a unique level of intimacy, the level of which is usually determined by the unique natures of the individuals involved.

Often, when people think of ideal relationship structures, they initially think of the types of relationships with which they are most familiar, or to which they have been most exposed. In Western cultures such as the United States, that relationship structure is most often a heterosexual, monogamous, married couple. In fact, so strong is the bias toward this one type of relationship structure, the questions of multiple partners or alternatives to monogamy are rarely discussed or considered.

Pile on top of this unquestioned assumption the cultural and clinical bias we see attached to sexual activity outside of a monogamous pair bond. When one even considers sex with someone other than a primary partner, immediately the words "infidelity" and "cheating" spring to mind. Connected to those words are the culturally constructed ways in which people are supposed to respond to such things: anger, jealousy, hurt, rage. Indeed such behaviors have many iconic images attached to them, including throwing a partner's belongings onto the front yard or cutting the partner's face out of pictures from a photo album.

Almost never does one instantly consider the possibility that the couple has agreed to a relationship style different from the monogamous monopoly. In the Clinton/Lewinsky scandal of the 1990s, in which Hillary Clinton was seen by some as a devoted wife who "stood by her man," and by others as a weak woman who should have divorced her husband for cheating on her—few considered the possibility that then-President Clinton and his wife might have had a different relationship style. Instead, people wondered why Mrs. Clinton remained with her spouse and conjectured that the President must have been a sex addict of some sort. This type of knee-jerk reaction clearly illustrates the monogamist (assuming that everyone is or should be monogamous) cultural bias in which we now live.

Add to this the prevailing cultural myth of "The One." This myth creates the expectation that somewhere, out there in the wide world, there is just one special person (think of the idea of a "soulmate") that is waiting for each of us. That person will meet all of our emotional, physical, intellectual, social, and sexual needs. That person will be the "yin" to our "yang." That one special person will become a person's "better half." That one individual, somewhere out there in the world, will "complete" another person. With every Disney movie supporting this romanticized ideal, how can we, as a culture, *not* believe that such a "One" exists?

Consider, then, where this leaves us. We are culturally programmed to consider only traditional, pair-bonded relationships that without question include sexual monogamy. We are taught that the proper response to sex outside of a committed relationship is cheating and should be punished or at least pathologized. We are brainwashed with the myth of "The One"; taught to believe that we must find that person within the billions of people in the wide world. In essence, people today are taught from early childhood to hold the highest of standards for potential partners, believing that this special person must be everything to them. Is it any wonder that the divorce statistics for traditional marriage relationships are so high?

One Possible Scenario: Consider This

The author's first experience with a couple who had an open relationship was in meeting a heterosexually married couple in their 60s. After a 30-year relationship, when they were in their 50s, the wife in the couple was diagnosed with a degenerative illness—one they were told would result in a loss of sensation in her sexual organs. In addition, the medicine that she took to slow the progression would result in a decrease in her interest in sex. Given this inevitability, the couple looked for viable alternatives. Neither wanted to end their marriage; they were both still very much in love. They also continued to enjoy an active sex life, which was very important to both of them.

How could they resolve their dilemma? Was the wife to ask the husband to give up sex entirely for the rest of his life? Was the husband to foreswear sexual activity of any kind out of a grand gesture for his wife—a promise that would have been ripe for building resentment and bitterness?

This couple chose to open their relationship. The result was wonderful for both of them. They continued to be happy for 10 years after, and may still be enjoying the love they have nurtured for decades.

Alternatives: What Options Exist?

In reality, there are many "lifestyles" that people have adopted and adapted over time to suit their intimacy needs. In his 1985 work, Dr. William R. Stayton identified 17 different types of relationships. These included traditional monogamy, serial monogamy, singlehood, single parenthood, child-free marriage, polyamory, polyfidelity, open marriage, group marriage, swinging, synergamy, communal living, cohabitation/trial marriage, family clusters, secret affair, celibate monogamy, and lifelong celibacy/chastity.

Of those 17, polyamory, polyfidelity, open marriage, group marriage, swinging, synergamy, family clusters, and secret affairs are relevant to this discussion. Briefly:

- Polyamory is often a general term used to describe all forms of multipartner relating.
- Polyfidelity is a form of group relationship where all the members agree to be faithful within their group and commit to exist as a family.
- Open marriage is when the primary couple agrees to engage in sexual activities with others outside of the dyad. In these situations, couples usually make agreements that dictate the nature of relationships and sexual activities that would be deemed acceptable outside of the primary relationship.
- Group marriage usually includes three or more people who agree to "marry" each other.
- Swinging is often a couple's experience and includes the practice of having sexual relationships with others, sometimes in groups, and is founded upon responsible, consensual sexual relating.
- Synergamy is when one or both people involved in a couple have an additional intimate relationship outside of that pair. This arrangement often includes the establishment of more than one household and the full involvement of the individual in more than one family system.
- Family clusters include multiple family systems that are interdependent in social, relational, financial, and sometimes sexual functioning.

Secret affairs are relevant here because it is this type of "open relationship" that is most practiced in our current cultural milieu. Current statistics estimate that between 45 and 50 percent of married women and between 50 and 60 percent of married men engage in extramarital sex at some point during their relationships (Atwood and Schwartz, 2002). Although this type of relationship is the most common, it is also the most damaging. It is estimated that 60 to 65 percent of divorces result from secret affairs. In addition, the betrayal of trust, the lack of communication, and the resulting deceptions are often considered to be the most harmful outcomes of these experiences.

The Argument: Why Are Open Relationships Healthy?

With all of these options giving context to the argument, it must be acknowledged that no matter the specifics of the lifestyle or relationship choice, it is the practice of a relationship that makes any of them healthy or unhealthy. It is the behavior of the people involved that has the greatest effect on the relative healthiness of any given relationship style.

Whether checking dating and relationship Web sites, looking through marriage encounter brochures, perusing the outlines of pre-cana marriage classes, or flipping through the pages of *The Complete Idiot's Guide to a Healthy Relationship* (Kuriansky, 2001), each source includes three basic requirements for healthy and long-lasting relationships: trust, honesty, and communication. Although some sources include additional components, the universality of these three is striking.

Let us consider these three in reverse order, beginning with communication. The skills of good communication are the stuff of workshops, lesson plans, relationship and marriage seminars, and countless books and articles. These skills include using direct language, "I" statements, and active listening, among others. What is critically important here, though, is that these skills are not dependent on the type of relationship in which they are used. The same skills work effectively in conversations with one's parents, one's coworkers, and with one's sexual and relationship partners.

Good communication in open relationships is no different from good communication in monogamous ones. Instead, because of the many complexities inherent in dyadic communication, including significant others, those complexities increase exponentially. As a result of this explosion, open relationships might offer individuals increased opportunities for intimacy as well as challenges to honing their communication skills.

Add to these multiple complexities the sensitive nature of the topics about which the individuals involved are communicating. Conversations are occurring about intimacy needs, sexual desires and fantasies, and personal preferences, as well as limitations, jealousy, attraction, and so much more. Many couples never brave these waters. For people involved in open relationships, they are necessary and sometimes daily conversations.

This level of communication leads directly into the next aspect of healthy relationships: honesty. As individuals broach subjects such as sexual desires, jealousies, and possibilities, the need for and reliance upon honesty increases. In the context of loving relationships, people can begin to express not only the ways that they feel fulfilled by a partner, but also the wants and needs that they are experiencing that are not being met by their primary partner. They can be honest about their sexual and emotional attractions to others. These are topics that are often avoided by other couples for fear of hurting one another or for fear of reprisals for having these types of feelings.

In this way, the honesty required within open relationships can be a very healthy benefit to the relationship overall. Secret keeping and lying take energy. So does honest communication. When practiced with strong communication, most would choose the latter over the former.

Finally, the practice of open and honest communication requires a significant degree of vulnerability. As individuals express their wants and needs, their often secret desires and attractions, as well as their jealousy or fears of loss, the resulting vulnerability is incredibly acute. When this vulnerability is met with equal honesty and care, and when good communication is present and practiced, the result is a significant increase in trust and intimacy between the partners.

Trust, or the reliance upon the strength, integrity, ability, and surety of a person, is certainly a cornerstone of healthy relationships. It is usually built, bit by bit, within the shared experiences of vulnerability and care experienced by people within their relationships. In the context of open relationships, this trust is discussed, explored, and tested in ways that many in monogamous relationships never openly experience. As people practice honesty in their relationships, discuss sexual boundaries and limitations, acknowledge and explore their own desires, and allow their partners to do the same, that trust can increase and the bonds between people can become stronger.

Summary

No type of relationship, in and of itself, is inherently or unequivocally healthy or unhealthy. It is the practice of relationships that give them their subjective qualification. Healthy relationships require effective, open communication; honesty; and trust. Open relationships can, indeed, be characterized by all of those things, thus characterizing them as healthy.

In addition, open relationships may offer some specific benefits. They can release individuals and relationships from the unspoken specter of monogamy. That is not to say that couples who discuss alternative relationship structures and choose monogamy are less healthy or self-aware. Instead, it demonstrates that the discussion and intentional choices related to monogamy are opportunities for growth and increased intimacy.

Open relationships also have the power to allow individuals to be less "perfect" within their relationships and more human in their strengths and shortcomings. The pressure to be someone's "everything" and the resulting disappointment and resentment when that individual falls short of those expectations have surely been the demise of many potentially wonderful relationships. Exploring options for individuals to have their wants and needs met outside of a dyadic relationship might well be the healthiest thing within a given relationship.

As people express their intimacy needs, their sexual fantasies, and their desires, they practice honesty in ways that many others never do. This exploration and reflection allow individuals to build increased levels of sexual awareness and self-awareness that have the potential to benefit not only themselves, but also all of their current and future partners.

And finally, open relationships by necessity include the constant practice of good communication skills. The opportunities to practice talking about all aspects of the relationship increase skills that are easily transferable to other situations. Healthy and honest communication is a benefit to every relationship. Open relationships are not a paradigm to be compared and contrasted with traditional monogamous ones. Instead, they are a paradigm all their own and should be measured against standards for good relationships, not monogamy.

For more information about open relationships, consider *Loving More: The Polyfidelity Primer,* by Ryam Nearing (PEP Publishing, 1992); or *The Ethical Slut,* by Dossie Easton and Catherine A. Liszt (Greenery Press, 1998).

References

J. D. Atwood, and L. Schwartz, "Cyber-Sex: The New Affair Treatment Considerations," *Journal of Couple and Relationship Therapy* (vol. 1, no. 3, 2002).

J. Kuriansky, *The Complete Idiot's Guide to Healthy Relationships,* 2nd ed. (Fort Smith, AZ: Alpha Books, 2001).

W. R. Stayton, "Alternative Lifestyles: Marital Options," in D. C. Goldberg and P. J. Fink, eds., *Contemporary Marriage: Special Issues in Couples Therapy* (Homewood, IL: Dorsey, 1985).

Stanley Kurtz

Here Come the Brides: Plural Marriage Is Waiting in the Wings

On September 23, 2005, the 46-year-old Victor de Bruijn and his 31-year-old wife of eight years, Bianca, presented themselves to a notary public in the small Dutch border town of Roosendaal. And they brought a friend. Dressed in wedding clothes, Victor and Bianca de Bruijn were formally united with a bridally bedecked Mirjam Geven, a recently divorced 35-year-old whom they'd met several years previously through an Internet chatroom. As the notary validated a *samenlevingscontract*, or "cohabitation contract," the three exchanged rings, held a wedding feast, and departed for their honeymoon.

When Mirjam Geven first met Victor and Bianca de Bruijn, she was married. Yet after several meetings between Mirjam, her then-husband, and the De Bruijns, Mirjam left her spouse and moved in with Victor and Bianca. The threesome bought a bigger bed, while Mirjam and her husband divorced. Although neither Mirjam nor Bianca had had a prior relationship with a woman, each had believed for years that she was bisexual. Victor, who describes himself as "100 percent heterosexual," attributes the trio's success to his wives' bisexuality, which he says has the effect of preventing jealousy.

The De Bruijns' triple union caused a sensation in the Netherlands, drawing coverage from television, radio, and the press. With TV cameras and reporters crowding in, the wedding celebration turned into something of a media circus. Halfway through the festivities, the trio had to appoint one of their guests as a press liaison. The local paper ran several stories on the triple marriage, one devoted entirely to the media madhouse.

News of the Dutch three-way wedding filtered into the United States through a September 26 report by Paul Belien, on his Brussels Journal website. The story spread through the conservative side of the Internet like wildfire, raising a chorus of "I told you so's" from bloggers who'd long warned of a slippery slope from gay marriage to polygamy.

Meanwhile, gay marriage advocates scrambled to put out the fire. M.V. Lee Badgett, an economist at the University of Massachusetts, Amherst, and research director of the Institute for Gay and Lesbian Strategic Studies, told a sympathetic website, "This [Brussels Journal] article is ridiculous. Don't be fooled—Dutch law does not allow polygamy." Badgett suggested that Paul Belien had deliberately mistranslated the Dutch word for "cohabitation contract" as "civil union," or even "marriage," so as to leave the false impression that the triple union had more legal weight than it did. Prominent gay-marriage advocate Evan Wolfson, executive director of Freedom to Marry, offered up a detailed legal account of Dutch cohabitation contracts, treating them as a matter of minor significance, in no way comparable to state-recognized registered partnerships.

In short, while the Dutch triple wedding set the conservative blogosphere ablaze with warnings, same-sex marriage advocates dismissed the story as a silly stunt with absolutely no implications for the gay marriage debate. And how did America's mainstream media adjudicate the radically different responses of same-sex marriage advocates and opponents to events in the Netherlands? By ignoring the entire affair.

Yet there is a story here. And it's bigger than even those chortling conservative websites claim. While Victor, Bianca, and Mirjam are joined by a private cohabitation contract rather than a state-registered partnership or a full-fledged marriage, their union has already made serious legal, political, and cultural waves in the Netherlands. To observers on both sides of the Dutch gay marriage debate, the De Bruijns' triple wedding is an unmistakable step down the road to legalized group marriage.

More important, the De Bruijn wedding reveals a heretofore hidden dimension of the gay marriage phenomenon. The De Bruijns' triple marriage is a bisexual marriage. And, increasingly, bisexuality is emerging as a reason why legalized gay marriage is likely to result in legalized group marriage. If every sexual orientation has a right to construct its own form of marriage, then more changes are surely due. For what gay marriage is to homosexuality, group marriage is to bisexuality. The De Bruijn trio is the tip-off to the fact that a connection between bisexuality and the drive for multipartner marriage has been developing for some time.

As American gay-marriage advocates were quick to point out, the cohabitation contract that joined Victor, Bianca, and Mirjam carries fewer legal implications and less status than either a registered partnership or a marriage—and Dutch trios are still barred from the latter two forms of union. Yet the use of a cohabitation contract for a triple wedding is a step in the direction of group marriage. The conservative and religious Dutch paper *Reformatorisch Dagblad* reports that this was the first known occurrence in the Netherlands of a cohabitation contract between a married couple and their common girlfriend. . . .

So the use of cohabitation contracts was an important step along the road to same-sex marriage in the Netherlands. And the link between gay marriage and the De Bruijns' triple contract was immediately recognized by the Dutch. The story in *Reformatorisch Dagblad* quoted J.W.A. van Dommelen, an attorney opposed to the De Bruijn union, who warned that the path from same-sex cohabitation contracts to same-sex marriage was about to be retraced in the matter of group marriage.

Van Dommelen also noted that legal complications would flow from the overlap between a two-party marriage and a three-party cohabitation contract. The rights and obligations that exist in Dutch marriages and Dutch cohabitation contracts are not identical, and it's unclear which arrangement would take precedence in case of a conflict. "The structure is completely gone," said Van Dommelen, as he called on the Dutch minister of justice to set up a working group to reconcile the conflicting claims of dual marriages and multipartner cohabitation contracts. Of course, simply by harmonizing the conflicting claims of dual marriages and triple cohabitation contracts, that working group would be taking yet another "small step" along the road to legal recognition for group marriage in the Netherlands.

The slippery-slope implications of the triple cohabitation contract were immediately evident to the SGP, a small religious party that played a leading role in the failed battle to preserve the traditional definition of marriage in the Netherlands. SGP member of parliament Kees van der Staaij noted the substantial overlap between marriage rights and the rights embodied in cohabitation contracts. Calling the triple cohabitation contract a back-door route to legalized polygamy, Van der Staaij sent a series of formal queries to Justice Minister Piet Hein Donner, asking him to dissolve the De Bruijn contract and to bar more than two persons from entering into cohabitation contracts in the future.

The justice minister's answers to these queries represent yet another small step—actually several small steps—toward legal and cultural recognition for group marriage in the Netherlands. To begin with, Donner reaffirmed the legality of multipartner cohabitation contracts and pointedly refused to consider any attempt to ban such contracts in the future. Donner also went so far as to assert that contracts regulating multipartner cohabitation can fulfill "a useful regulating function" (also translatable as "a useful structuring role"). In other words, Donner has articulated the rudiments of a "conservative case for group marriage."

The SGP responded angrily to Donner's declarations. In the eyes of this small religious party, Donner had effectively introduced a form of legal group marriage to the Netherlands. A party spokesman warned of an impending legal mess—especially if the De Bruijn trio, or others like them, have children. The SGP plans to raise its objections again when parliament considers the justice department's budget.

It's not surprising that the first English-language report was a bit unclear as to the precise legal status and significance of the triple Dutch union. The Dutch themselves are confused about it. One of the articles from which Paul Belien drew his original report is careful to distinguish between formal marriage and the cohabitation contract actually signed by Victor, Bianca, and Mirjam. Yet the very same article says that Victor now "officially" has "two wives."

Even Dutch liberals acknowledge the implications of the De Bruijn wedding. Jan Martens, a reporter and opinion columnist for *BN/DeStem,* the local paper in Roosendaal, wrote an opinion piece mocking opposition to group marriage by religious parties like the SGP. Noting the substantial overlap between cohabitation contracts and marriage, Martens said he agreed with the SGP that the De Bruijn triple union amounts to a "short-cut to polygamy." Yet Martens emphasized that he "couldn't care less if you have two, three, four, or sixty-nine wives or husbands."

Minority religious parties and their newspapers excepted, this mixture of approval and indifference seems to be the mainstream Dutch reaction so far.

Not only has Justice Minister Donner articulated the beginnings of a conservative case for group marriage, but Green Party spokesman Femke Halsema, a key backer of gay marriage, has affirmed her party's support for the recognition of multipartner unions. The public has not been inclined to protest these developments, and the De Bruijn trio have been welcomed by their neighbors. . . .

When it comes to marriage, culture shapes law. (It's a two-way street, of course. Law also influences culture.) After all, Dutch same-sex marriage advocates still celebrate the foundational role of symbolic gay marriage registries in the early 1990s. Although these had absolutely no legal status, the publicity and sympathy they generated are now widely recognized as keys to the success of the Dutch campaign for legal same-sex unions and ultimately marriage. How odd, then, that American gay-marriage advocates should respond to the triple Dutch wedding with hair-splitting legal discourses, while ignoring the Dutch media frenzy and subsequent signs of cultural acceptance—for a union with far more legal substance than Holland's first symbolic gay marriages. Despite the denials of gay-marriage advocates, in both legal and cultural terms, Victor, Bianca, and Mirjam's triple union is a serious move toward legalized group marriage in the Netherlands.

Given the stir in Holland, it's remarkable that not a single American mainstream media outlet carried a story on the triple Dutch wedding. Of course the media were all over the Dutch gay marriage story when they thought the experiment had been a success. In late 2003 and early 2004, in the wake of the Supreme Court's *Lawrence v. Texas* decision, which ruled sodomy laws unconstitutional, and looming gay marriage in Massachusetts, several American papers carried reports from the Netherlands. The common theme was that Holland had experienced no ill effects from gay marriage, and that the issue was no longer contentious. . . .

Although the triple Dutch union has been loosely styled "polygamy," it's actually a sterling example of polyamory. Polyamorists practice "responsible nonmonogamy"—open, loving, and stable relationships among more than two people (see "Beyond Gay Marriage: The Road to Polyamory," *The Weekly Standard,* August 4/August 11, 2003). Polygamous marriages among fundamentalist Mormons or Muslims don't depend on a blending of heterosexuality and bisexuality. Yet that combination perfectly embodies the spirit of polyamory. And polyamorists don't limit themselves to unions of one man and several women. One woman and two men, full-fledged group marriage, a stable couple openly engaging in additional shifting or stable relationships—indeed, almost any combination of partner-number and sexual orientation is possible in a polyamorous sexual grouping.

Polyamorists would call the De Bruijn union a "triad." In a polyamorous triad, all three partners are sexually connected. This contrasts with a three-person "V," in which only one of the partners (called the "hinge" or "pivot") has a sexual relationship with the other two. So the bisexuality of Bianca and Mirjam classifies the De Bruijn union as a polyamorous bisexual triad. In another sense, the De Bruijn marriage is also a gay marriage. The Bianca-Mirjam component of the union is gay, and legalized gay marriage in Holland has clearly helped make the idea of a legally recognized bisexual triad thinkable. . . .

The germ of an organized effort to legalize polyamory in the United States can be found in the Unitarian Church. Although few realize it, the Unitarian Church, headquartered in Boston, played a critical role in the legalization of same-sex marriage in Massachusetts. Julie and Hillary Goodridge, lead plaintiffs in *Goodridge v. Department of Public Health,* were married at the headquarters of the Unitarian Universalists in a ceremony presided over by the Reverend William G. Sinkford, president of the Unitarian Universalist Association. Hillary Goodridge is program director of the Unitarian Universalist Funding Program. And Unitarian churches in Massachusetts played a key role in the struggle over gay marriage, with sermons, activism, and eventually with marriage ceremonies for same-sex couples. Choosing a strongly church-affiliated couple like the Goodridges as lead plaintiffs was an important part of the winning strategy in the *Goodridge* case.

It's a matter of interest, therefore, that an organization to promote public acceptance of polyamory has been formed in association with the Unitarian Church. Unitarian Universalists for Polyamory Awareness (UUPA) was established in the summer of 1999. At the time, the news media in Boston carried reports from neighboring Vermont, where the soon-to-be-famous civil unions case was about to be decided. And the echo effect of the gay marriage battle on the polyamory movement goes back even further. The first informal Unitarian polyamory discussion group gathered in Hawaii in 1994, in the wake of the first state supreme court decision favorable to same-sex marriage in the United States.

"Our vision," says UUPA's website, "is for Unitarian Universalism to become the first poly-welcoming mainstream religious denomination." Those familiar with Unitarianism's role in the legalization of gay marriage understand the legal-political strategy implicit in that statement. UUPA's political goals are spelled out by Harlan White, a physician and leading UUPA activist, on the society's website. Invoking the trial of April Divilbiss, the first American polyamorist to confront the courts, White says, "We are concerned that we may become the center of the next great social justice firestorm in America."

White maintains that American polyamorists are growing in number. An exact count is impossible, since polyamory is still surrounded by secrecy. Polyamorists depend on the Internet to connect. Even so, says White, "attendance at conferences is up, email lists and websites are proliferating, and poly support groups are growing in number and size." As for the Unitarian polyamorists, their email list has several hundred subscribers, and the group has put on well-attended workshops at Unitarian General Assemblies since 2002. And although the number of open polyamorists is limited, some Unitarian ministers already perform "joining ceremonies" for polyamorous families. . . .

Shortly after the second article appeared, UUA president Sinkford circulated a statement among Unitarians acknowledging that press interest in Unitarian polyamory had "generated a great deal of anxiety" among the church's leadership. "Many of us are concerned that such press coverage might impair our ability to witness effectively for our core justice commitments." Sinkford appeared to be expressing a concern that had been stated more baldly in the original *Chronicle* article. According to the *Chronicle,* many of the students and faculty at the Unitarians' key west-coast seminary, Starr King School for the Ministry, in Berkeley, see the polyamory movement as a threat to the struggle for same-sex marriage.

In other words, Unitarians understand that moving too swiftly or openly to legitimize polyamory could validate the slippery-slope argument against same-sex marriage. So with news coverage prematurely blowing the cover off the Unitarians' long-term plan to legalize polyamory, President Sinkford took steps to hold UUPA at arm's length. Sinkford issued a public "clarification" that distanced the church from any formal endorsement of polyamory, yet also left room for the UUPA to remain a "related organization." . . .

The other fascinating angle in the *San Francisco Chronicle*'s coverage of the Unitarian polyamorists was the prominence of bisexuality. Most members of UUPA are either bisexual or heterosexual. One polyamorist minister who had recently come out to his congregation as a bisexual treated polyamory and bisexuality synonymously. "Our denomination has been welcoming to gays and lesbians and transgendered people," he said. "Bisexuals have not received the recognition they deserve." In other words, anything less than formal church recognition of polyamory is discrimination against bisexuals.

Two developing lines of legal argument may someday bring about state recognition for polyamorous marriage: the argument from polyamory, and the argument from bisexuality. In a 2004 law review article, Elizabeth F. Emens, of the University of Chicago Law School, offers the argument from polyamory (see "Monogamy's Law: Compulsory Monogamy and Polyamorous Existence," *New York University Review of Law & Social Change*). Polyamory is more than the mere practice of multiple sexual partnership, says Emens. Polyamory is also a disposition, broadly analogous to the disposition toward homosexuality. Insofar as laws of marriage, partnership, or housing discriminate against polyamorous partnerships, maintains Emens, they place unfair burdens on people with "poly" dispositions. Emens takes her cue here from the polyamorists themselves, who talk about their "poly" inclinations the way gays talk about homosexuality. For example, polyamorists debate whether to keep their poly dispositions "in the closet" or to "come out."

Emens's case for a poly disposition was inspired by the radical lesbian thinker Adrienne Rich, who famously put forward a "continuum model" of lesbianism. Rich argued that all women, lesbian-identified or not, are in some sense lesbians. If women could just discover where they fall on the "lesbian continuum," then even those women who remain heterosexually identified would abandon any prejudice against homosexuality.

Following Rich, Emens argues that all of us have a bit of "poly" inside. By discovering and accepting our own desires for multiple sexual partners, then even those who remain monogamous would abandon their prejudice against polyamorists. Of course some people fall at the extreme ends of these continuums. Some folks are intensely monogamous, for example. But by the same token, others are intensely polyamorous. Whether for biological or cultural reasons, says Emens, some folks simply cannot live happily without multiple simultaneous sexual partners. And for those people, Emens argues, our current system of marriage is every bit as unjust as it is for homosexuals. . . .

The second legal strategy available to the polyamorists is the argument from bisexuality. No need here to validate anything as novel-sounding as a "polyamorous disposition." A case for polyamory can easily be built on the more venerable orientation of bisexuality. While no legal scholar has offered such a case, the groundwork is being laid by Kenji Yoshino, a professor at Yale Law School and deputy dean for intellectual life.

Yoshino's 2000 *Stanford Law Review* article "The Epistemic Contract of Bisexual Erasure" has a bewildering title but a fascinating thesis. Yoshino argues that bisexuality is far more prevalent than is usually recognized. The relative invisibility of bisexuality, says Yoshino, can be attributed to the mutual interest of heterosexuals and homosexuals in minimizing its significance. But according to Yoshino, the bisexuality movement is on the rise and bound to become more visible, with potentially major consequences for the law and politics of sexual orientation.

Defining bisexuality as a "more than incidental desire" for partners of both sexes, Yoshino examines the best available academic studies on sexual orientation and finds that each of them estimates the number of bisexuals as equivalent to, or greater than, the number of homosexuals. Up to now, the number of people who actively think of themselves as bisexuals has been much smaller than the number who've shown a "more than incidental" desire for partners of both sexes. But that, argues Yoshino, is because both heterosexuals and homosexuals have an interest in convincing bisexuals that they've got to make an all-or-nothing choice between heterosexuality and homosexuality.

Heterosexuals, for example, have an interest in preserving norms of monogamy, and bisexuality "destabilizes" norms of monogamy. Homosexuals, notes Yoshino, have an interest in defending the notion of an immutable homosexual orientation, since that is often the key to persuading a court that they have suffered discrimination. And homosexuals, adds Yoshino, have an interest in maximizing the number of people in their movement. For all these reasons and more, Yoshino argues, the cultural space in which bisexuals might embrace and acknowledge their own sexual identity has been minimized. Yoshino goes on to highlight the considerable evidence for the recent emergence of bisexuality as a movement, and predicts that in our current cultural climate—and given the numerical potential—bisexuality activism will continue to grow.

In addition to establishing the numerical and political significance of bisexuality, Yoshino lays down an argument that could easily be deployed to legalize polyamory: "To the extent that bisexuals are not permitted to express their dual desires, they might fairly characterize themselves as harmed." Yet Yoshino does not lay out a bisexual defense of polyamory. Instead Yoshino attacks—rightly—the stereotype that treats all bisexuals as nonmonogamous. Yet the same research that establishes the monogamous preferences of many bisexuals also confirms that bisexuals tend toward nonmonogamy at substantially higher rates than homosexuals. (See Paula C. Rust, "Monogamy and Polyamory: Relationship Issues for Bisexuals" in Firestein, ed., *Bisexuality: The Psychology and Politics of an Invisible Minority*.) That fact could easily be turned by a bisexuality rights movement into an argument for legalized polyamory. . . .

In 2004, the *Journal of Bisexuality* published a special double issue on polyamory, also released as the book *Plural Loves: Designs for Bi and Poly Living*. It's clear from *Plural Loves* that the polyamory movement now serves as the de facto political arm of the bisexual liberation struggle. As one contributor notes, "the large number of bi people in the poly movement provides evidence that bisexuality is one of the major driving forces behind polyamory. In other words, polyamory was created and spread partly to satisfy the need for bisexual relationship structures. . . . [T]he majority of poly activists are also bisexual. . . . Poly activism is bi activism. . . . The bi/poly dynamic has the potential to move both communities towards a point of culture-wide visibility, which is a necessary step on the road to acceptance."

Clearly, visibility and acceptance are on the rise. This past summer, the *Baltimore Sun* featured a long, friendly article on the polyamorists' national conference, held in Maryland. In September, the *New York Times* ran a long personal account of (heterosexual) polyamory in the Sunday Styles section. But the real uptick in public bisexuality/polyamory began with the October 2005 release in New York of the documentary *Three of Hearts: A Postmodern Family*.

Three of Hearts is the story of the real-life 13-year relationship of two men and a woman. Together for several years in a gay relationship, two bisexual-leaning men meet a woman and create a threesome that produces two children, one by each man. Although the woman marries one of the men, the entire threesome has a commitment ceremony. The movie records the trio's eventual breakup, yet the film's website notes their ongoing commitment to the view that "family is anything we want to create." . . .

Of course, many argue that true bisexuality does not exist. In this view—held by a variety of people, from some psychiatrists to certain pro-gay-marriage activists—everyone is either heterosexual or homosexual. From this perspective, so-called bisexuals are either in confused transition from heterosexuality to homosexuality, or simply lying about their supposedly dual sexual inclinations. Alternatively, it's sometimes said that while female bisexuality does exist, male bisexuality does not. A recent and controversial study reported on by the *New York Times* in July 2005 claimed to show that truly bisexual attraction in men might not exist.

Whatever view we take of these medical/psychiatric/philosophical controversies, it is a fact that a bi/poly rights movement exists and is growing. Whether Koen Brand and Bianca and Mirjam de Bruijn are "authentic" bisexuals or "just fooling themselves," they are clearly capable of sustaining polyamorous bisexual V's and triads for long enough to make serious political demands. *Three of Hearts* raises questions about whether the two men in the triangle are bisexual or simply confused gays. But with two children, a 13-year relationship, and at one time at least a clear desire for legal-ceremonial confirmation, the *Three of Hearts* trio is a harbinger of demands for legal group marriage. Public interest in the De Bruijn triangle has already raised the visibility and acceptance of polyamorous bisexuality in the Netherlands. For legal-political purposes, acceptance is what matters. And given Yoshino's numerical analysis, the growth potential for self-identifying bisexuals is substantial.

Americans today respond to gay and bisexual friends and family members in a variety of ways. Despite stereotypical accusations of "homophobia," the traditionally religious generally offer a mixture of compassion and concern. Many other Americans, conservative and liberal alike, are happy to extend friendship, understanding, and acceptance to gay and bisexual relatives and acquaintances. This heightened social tolerance is a good thing. Yet somehow the idea has taken hold that tolerance for sexual minorities requires a radical remake of the institution of marriage. That is a mistake.

The fundamental purpose of marriage is to encourage mothers and fathers to stay bound as a family for the sake of their children. Our liberalized modern marriage system is far from perfect, and certainly doesn't always succeed in keeping parents together while their children are young. Yet often it does. Unfortunately, once we radically redefine marriage in an effort to solve the problems of adults, the institution is destined to be shattered by a cacophony of grown-up demands.

The De Bruijn trio, Koen Brand, the Unitarian Universalists for Polyamory Awareness, the legal arguments of Elizabeth Emens and Kenji Yoshino, and the bisexual/polyamory movement in general have been launched into action by the successes of the campaign for gay marriage. In a sense, though, these innovators have jumped too soon. They've shown us today—well before same-sex marriage has triumphed nationwide—what would emerge in its aftermath.

Liberals may now put behind-the-scenes pressure on the Dutch government to keep the lid on legalized polyamory for as long as the matter of gay marriage is still unsettled. The Unitarian polyamorists, already conflicted about how much recognition to demand while the gay marriage battle is unresolved, may be driven further underground. But let there be no mistake about what will happen should same-sex marriage be fully legalized in the United States. At that point, if bisexual activists haven't already launched a serious campaign for legalized polyamory, they will go public. It took four years after the full legalization of gay marriage in the Netherlands for the first polyamory test case to emerge. With a far larger and more organized polyamory movement in America, it might not take even that long after the nationalization of gay marriage in the United States.

It's easy to imagine that, in a world where gay marriage was common and fully accepted, a serious campaign to legalize polyamorous unions would succeed—especially a campaign spearheaded by an organized bisexual-rights movement. Yet win or lose, the culture of marriage will be battered for years by the debate. Just as we're now continually reminded that not all married couples have children, we'll someday be endlessly told that not all marriages are monogamous (nor all monogamists married). For a second time, the fuzziness and imperfection found in every real-world social institution will be contorted into a rationale for reforming marriage out of existence.

POSTSCRIPT

Are Open Relationships Healthy?

Sometimes the concept of open relationships is addressed in a cursory way by the popular media:

- On one episode of the sitcom *King of Queens,* Doug and Carrie, a married couple featured in the show, both agree that they can have sex outside of their marriage with their dream person if the opportunity arises. They have to tell each other who that person is. Carrie shares first, disclosing a famous celebrity. Doug agrees to her choice, then shares his choice: a woman he works with. Amid laughter, Carrie refuses to accept his choice.
- On an episode of the cable series *Entourage,* Vincent Chase, a fictional Hollywood star, meets a woman in public and has sex with her in a nearby hotel room. He asks her whether they can see each other again. She explains she is engaged and can only do this once. She and her fiance both have a list of famous people they are allowed to have sex with.

Despite these examples from popular television shows, monogamy is treated as such a universal value that a significant number of readers may have never heard of polyamory or open relationships before reading this chapter. What are some of the reasons that people are hesitant to discuss alternatives to monogamy? What is the impact, positive or negative, of this silence on individual relationships?

This chapter specifically asks whether open relationships are healthy. Is there a universal definition for what is emotionally healthy regarding sexual partners? Specifically, is monogamy a universal value that should be practiced in all relationships? Is polyamory a universal value that should be practiced in all relationships? What, if anything, would you regard as a standard relationship model that all couples should aspire to? Is sex outside of marriage cheating if your spouse approves of it? What kind of communication is necessary to ensure that people are being honest about their feelings?

Aside from the diverse views of polyamory between Dyson and Kurtz, this chapter exposes fundamentally different philosophies. Dyson argues that open relationships can be positive. The argument portrays the impact of open relationships as self-contained to the individuals involved rather than assuming that such an arrangement will have a single, universal impact on all relationships. In contrast, Kurtz contends that any redefinition of marriage will be the start of a slippery slope that will ultimately affect everyone by causing the institution of marriage itself to disintegrate.

What is your response to Dyson's argument that the impact depends on the individual relationship? What is your response to Kurtz's argument that same-sex marriage will lead to polyamory? Is the progression as inevitable as he contends? What are some other factors that influence your views related to monogamy and polyamory?

What do their views reveal about their position on the Political Ideology Continuum examined in the Introduction to this book? How do your views on this topic compare and contrast with other relationship issues raised in this book? The truth is that many people in open relationships are traditionally conservative and many people committed to lifetime monogamy are quite liberal.

Regardless of the conclusion that you reach, this chapter should help readers understand that one cannot make an assumption that relationship monogamy is a universal value. It is well advised for the reader to talk with a significant other at one point about his or her views on monogamy and relationships.

ISSUE 16

Is Pornography Harmful to Teenagers?

YES: Wayne Grinwis, from "Is Pornography Harmful to Teenagers? Yes!" written for *Taking Sides: Family and Personal Relationships* (2009)

NO: Justin A. Sitron, from "Why Porn Is Not Harmful to Teens," written for *Taking Sides: Family and Personal Relationships* (2009)

ISSUE SUMMARY

YES: Wayne Grinwis, has been a sexual health educator for Planned Parenthood for 15 years. He is also adjunct professor in the Department of Health at West Chester University. Grinwis credits Andrea Daniels for help with this article. Grinwis argues that pornography is all right for adults, but for teenagers it can create unrealistic expectations about sex, provide a negative and inaccurate sexuality education, and increase sexual violence against women.

NO: Justin Sitron, is assistant professor of Education at Widener University. Sitron argues that pornography has no negative impact on teenagers and, in fact, has potential benefits. Sitron contends that Internet pornography can be helpful in providing teens an opportunity to see real bodies, a chance to learn about sex from seeing rather than doing, and an open door for communication with parents.

T he First Amendment to the U.S. Constitution states, "Congress shall make no laws . . . abridging the freedom of speech." Although this amendment is written as an absolute, there are limitations to speech that are known as unprotected speech, including libel, slander, seditious speech, and obscenity. It is the latter form of unprotected speech that is the focus of this chapter, as obscenity is often thought of as synonymous with pornography.

In the United States, federal censorship of obscene materials began with the Tariff Act of 1842. Although prosecutions were initially limited, the American middle class grew following the Civil War. Many social reformers believed that the United States too often failed to apply proper moral values, thus leading to social problems. Antivice societies were formed and worked to create laws regarding labor, prison reform, temperance, welfare, and obscenity. By 1873, the United States had a federal anti-obscenity law, often referred to as the Comstock Law.

During this time, anti-obscenity laws were designed to protect three groups who were considered to be particularly vulnerable: women, the lower classes, and children. Today, women and the so-called lower classes are not considered groups that deserve legal protection, though the primary audience for pornographic pictures and films today is men.

A challenge that has existed regarding censorship has been to determine specifically what is obscenity. In 1973, The Supreme Court of the United States provided the following standard for evaluating whether or not materials are pornographic in the case of *Miller v. California:*

1. That the average person, applying contemporary standards, would find a work, taken as a whole, appeals to the prurient interest
2. Whether the work depicts or describes, in a patently offensive way, sexual conduct specifically defined to be offensive and "hard core" by the applicable state law.
3. That the work, taken as a whole, lacks serious literary, artistic, political, or scientific value.

Therefore, there exists a legal standard of how to define pornography and legal precedent that pornography is regarded as unprotected speech. Additionally, there is legal precedent that children do not have the right to have access to pornography. As a result, the federal government sought to create new censorship policies in the face of children's access to pornography online.

Congress passed and President Clinton signed into law both the Communications Decency Act of 1996 and the Child Online Protection Act of 1998. Each of these laws was struck down by the Supreme Court. The Supreme Court did not challenge the fact that pornography can be censored for children. However, it also said that there was no mechanism to limit children's access to online pornography without also limiting adults' access to pornography. When censoring unprotected speech, in this case children's access to pornography, laws cannot be so broad that they also censor protected speech, in this case adults' access to pornography.

With limited means for government censorship, controlling access to pornography becomes almost entirely the domain of parents and children. The access to sexually explicit materials that exists is unprecedented in human history. Children today have more access to sexually produced materials than ever before. Previously, parents were urged to leave their computer in a common space in their house. Today, however, few families buy desktop computers, opting instead for a portable laptop. In fact, many children access the Internet whenever they want, wherever they want, via their IPhone, BlackBerry, or another portable device.

This chapter examines the debate over the impact of pornography on teenagers. The conclusions that one reaches should have significant implications in what teenagers should be taught by their parents about pornography.

YES ←

Wayne Grinwis

Is Pornography Harmful to Teenagers?

There are some who would argue that pornography has no acceptable audience or any valid place, even for entertainment purposes, in a healthy relationship. In this mindset, pornography might even be considered harmful and its effects wide-reaching enough to encapsulate every age group who may be attracted to the lure of a little adult fantasy. High school students, grandparents, Baby Boomers, Gen Xers—all would fall victim to its inappropriate ideals if we were to place a general label of "harmful"—a sort of "Mr. Yuck" sticker for grown-ups, if you will—onto pornography. I am unable to do such a thing. In the right setting and with the right frame of mind, pornography can be a pleasurable addition to an adult individual's or couple's sexual life.

When speaking of teenagers, however, the term *harmful* may well apply. Without the proper maturity and level of experience, navigating through the very adult world of relationships and sex, most teens simply do not possess the necessary tools needed for their first foray into fantasy, and many of the themes found in a good deal of easily accessible pornography may actually be harmful to their adolescent development.

Access to Pornography

Before we can examine pornography's harmful effects on teenagers, we must first discuss the specifics of what pornography actually is. Former Supreme Court Justice Potter Stewart said, in discussing a potential definition of pornography, "I know it when I see it" (*Jacobellis v. Ohio,* 1964). That statement, albeit somewhat glib, brings to mind a serious thought: In the high-tech, ever-evolving cyber-realm that young people today inhabit, they are inundated with more varied forms of pornography than ever before, stumbling upon sites that they probably shouldn't and gaining access to those deemed "adult-only" by easily tiptoeing around safeguards as flimsy as a few keystrokes and the honor system.

In the past, teens had to seek out pornography by obtaining and viewing magazines (*Playboy* and *Hustler* are among the more tame periodicals), locating old VHS films or DVDs not hidden quite carefully enough in their own homes, or watching soft-core versions of these films on cable (good 'ol' "Skinemax"—an informal reference to occasional late-night viewing opportunities on Cinemax—has long been a favorite). However, tech-savvy young people have more opportunities than ever before to satisfy their sensual cravings. In recent years, pornographic-like activity has been added to some video games (*Grand Theft Auto,* one of the most popular video games among this demographic, is rife with sexual content), and then, of course, there is the ever-pervasive Internet, which, to many teens, is just as tangible a home as the concrete structures they inhabit with their family members. Although the onetime estimate that over 80 percent of Internet sites are pornographic was proven false (Godwin, 2003), recent estimates are that 12 percent of all Web sites are porn and that a quarter of all search engine requests are for porn (Ropelato, 2003). Even if someone were trying to avoid this type of explicit sexual material, it would only be the über-diligent who would succeed in avoiding pornography on the Internet, and it is important to note that not all teenage exposure to pornography is intentional; contact may be unintended—stumbled upon when receiving emails advertising porn sites or even through the simple act of employing an Internet search (Bryan, 2009). For those who do take the time to seek out pornography, their fingers don't have far to travel on their computer keyboards. From things as basic as still pictures to home videos of sexual encounters, from monthly subscription services to "fetish" sites, thousands upon thousands of hours of porn can easily be found online.

It is true that most adult sites stipulate that a viewer must be "18 to enter;" however, age is often established by a simple mouse click stating that the visitor is, indeed, the required age or by asking the visitor to enter in his or her birthdate. Young people can handle the simple math of subtracting a few years from the date on which they were born in order to appear age-appropriate for viewing.

Now that we have determined the ease with which pornography can be viewed and before we begin to examine the harmful effects of pornography on teenagers, we must first establish the gender of which we speak. Do we mean male teens or female? The simple answer is both. Although teens actively seeking out and viewing pornography are predominantly male, girls are also affected by the messages boys receive.

But all of this—the pervasive and easily accessible nature of pornography—is not in and of itself proof positive of its harmful nature when speaking in terms of teens. We must now begin to dig deeper to unearth the negative effects that exposure to an adult-oriented fantasy world has upon adolescent development by examining pornography's fostering of unrealistic expectations when it comes to sexual encounters and body image, its role as an unqualified sexuality educator, and its bent toward violence.

Unrealistic Expectations

How many times has this happened to you? You're in your office making copies, perhaps scantily clad and probably glistening a little from the heat of the copier, and in walks a very attractive member of the opposite sex, who immediately begins complimenting your body and undressing you. Moments later you are in the throes of passion, with the copier working overtime capturing fantasy, flipbook-worthy images of all that is happening on it.

This has never happened to you? Then clearly you are not living in the world of pornography.

Most teenagers lack the abstract processing skills that advise them that the incidents and images displayed in pornography are not representative of most adults' sex lives. Teens exposed to what the pornography industry and, indeed, its consumers ordain as "sexy" or "passionate" or "hot," and who lack the aforementioned skills, eventually begin to think that the sexual acts displayed are necessary to have the desired adjectives listed above become attributes of their own lives.

This is especially true when it comes to body image. Average people, who are endowed in a very average way, are not typically stars of the pornographic industry, or at least not pre–surgical alteration. As teenagers watch pornography, they cannot help but make comparisons to the unrealistic images they see and, consequently, may begin to find themselves and perhaps their own partners less attractive. As if being a teenager and dealing with hormonal changes and body image insecurities weren't difficult enough, now teenagers are comparing pornographic superstars to their own developing, young bodies and those of their partners.

However, it is not body image alone that suffers through the consumption of pornography. Oftentimes a teen's view of the sex act itself becomes skewed in an unrealistic and unhealthy way, especially when pornography becomes the educator through which he or she learns about sex.

Pornography as Education

Where do young people actually learn to have sex? Comprehensive sexuality education, although widely favored in this country (despite the current trend of abstinence-only education), doesn't include demonstrations or lessons on how to engage in the act of having sex. Likewise, most parents surely don't advise their children on the virtues and techniques of making love. When people lose their virginity, one hopes the experience will happen with a partner whom they are able to feel comfortable with and who will accept their genuine selves. In an ideal situation, one inexperienced partner should be able to say to the other: "I don't really know what I'm doing!" However, sad truth though it may be, that is not usually the case. Many times, people lose their virginity with someone they've just met, or when they've been drinking or using drugs, or with someone they care about but with whom they aren't completely intimate—in other words, not someone with whom they can allow themselves to be completely vulnerable. That leaves pornography as the most viable sexual education tool.

We've already established that pornography sets up unrealistic expectations, and that most certainly poses a problem when people are modeling their sex life after knowledge—albeit knowledge that has no basis in reality—gleaned from pornography and when they lack any other alternative. But consider the advantages film has over real life. What appears to the viewer as a 15-minute sexual encounter may have taken eight hours to film, incorporated multiple camera angles to find the best view of the bodies, and required extensive editing in order to make it work—all advantages that the fantasy world of pornography has over typical sexual experiences.

This leads us to our last concern: Besides the unrealistic expectations created by viewing and utilizing pornography, even inadvertently, as an educational tool, the simple, yet serious fact is that pornography can contribute to greater acceptance of sexual violence. This is because much of pornography is based around images and incidents that are degrading toward women, exhibit misogynistic attitudes, and largely focus on the pleasure of the male as its utmost goal.

Sexual Violence

Pornography is rarely about love, intimacy, tenderness, and affection. It is about sex. People don't view pornography to feel closer to themselves or their partner emotionally. They view it for the purpose of arousal and, oftentimes, use it as an impetus for masturbation or intercourse. As previously stated, viewers of pornography are predominantly male, and because of this and of its aforementioned purpose, pornography often objectifies women—props who become a means to an end, with an end most likely translating into male orgasm.

In much of the pornographic world, women are there to serve men and to be dominated by them, the ideas of sexual arousal and power becoming intertwined in a way that can be processed cognitively by an adult but not by a teenager whose emotions and hormones so often overrule any rational thought (Peter and Valkenburg, 2007). Think of the underlying meaning of a porn staple, "the money shot," where the male subject in a pornographic film ejaculates onto his partner, expressing his regard for her with an action devoid of any feeling or affection. If this doesn't model the idea that women are objects, then what does?

The fact is, young men who view pornography are more likely to have negative perceptions of women and be more accepting of violence toward them (Jensen and Okrina, 2004). This is not to say that all men who view pornography will engage in an act of sexual assault, but viewing pornography certainly contributes to a misogynistic culture, a culture where men feel entitled to view and treat women as sexual objects, and in that type of culture, men are more inclined to take advantage of women and, indeed, have an easier time justifying sexual violence.

Although adult men may have the internal processing skills to understand that what they see in porn is not an accurate portrayal of how men should treat women, teenage boys often have not developed that capacity. When they continually see a man belittle a woman in pornography—either emotionally or physically—they view that attitude as acceptable. This is especially true if young men view porn with their friends, as the pack mentality increases the support for this notion—further proof that no good can come of inappropriate sexual content coupled with immaturity.

Conclusion

A healthy sexual appetite is normal and can be expressed in myriad ways. For adults, viewing pornography with a partner can be a fun and "inspiring" experience, but it requires maturity to keep it in the proper context.

Though youth has its advantages, it also has its limitations. Young men and women who are just beginning to develop as sexual beings should take care to learn from examples of loving, mature, and healthy relationships. Pornography does not provide the proper model for any of these and is more likely to prove harmful to teens than advantageous in any way. A healthy sex life is not teeming with unrealistic expectations or fraught with an underlying sense of violence or disrespect. Teenagers whose sexual education is informed through the dark, sensual world of pornography are sure to come to the opposite conclusion, and their relationships will only suffer because of it.

References

C. Bryan, "Adolescence, Pornography, and Harm," *Trends and Issues in Crime and Criminal Justice* (vol. 368, 2009).

M. Godwin, *Cyber Rights: Defending Free Speech in the Digital Age* (Cambridge, MA: MIT Press, 2003).

Jacobellis v. Ohio, 378 U.S. 184, 197 (1964).

R. Jensen and D. Okrina, *Pornography and Sexual Violence* (2004). Retrieved March 14, 2009, from National Online Resource Center on Violence Against Women, http://new.vawnet.org/Assoc_Files_VAWnet/AR_PornAndSV.pdf.

J. Peter and P. M. Valkenburg, "Adolescents' Exposure to a Sexualized Media Environment and Their Notions of Women as Sex Objects," *Sex Roles* (vol. 56, 2007).

J. Ropelato, *Internet Pornography Statistics* (2003). Retrieved March 22, 2009, from Top Ten Reviews, http://www.internet-filter-review.toptenreviews.com/internet-pornography-statistics.html.

Justin A. Sitron → **NO**

Why Porn Is Not Harmful to Teens

The question about whether pornography is harmful is something that has been on the minds of researchers, parents, and others for decades (Malamuth, Addison, and Koss, 2000). Since the invention of the Internet, the question has become more and more popular as access to pornography has become as easy as pressing the keys on a keyboard and clicking a mouse. While years ago most people had to go to a bookstore, video store, or adult sex shop to access pornography, now one does not even need to leave one's home or even pay for it. With much more explicit cable television programming and the advent of the Internet, accessing pornography for teens is as easy as finding out the answers to a question on their geography homework (and, the teens might say, infinitely more interesting!). Some researchers even have shown that some youth who access porn do so unintentionally (Sabina, Wolak, and Finkelhor, 2008; Ybarra and Mitchell, 2005).

The question about whether pornography is harmful, dangerous, or leads to aggressive sexual behavior has been studied in adults with varying results (e.g., Fukui and Westmore, 1994; Kutchinsky, 1991). Quite simply, some researchers have found that it makes men more aggressive, whereas others find that it does not. Malamuth, Addison, and Koss (2000) conclude in their meta-analysis of such studies that ". . . for the majority of American men, pornography exposure (even at the highest levels assessed here) is not associated with high levels of sexual aggression" (p. 85). So why the big concern about teens having access to porn?

While in recent years there is growing interest in the effects of online pornography on youth here has been little research done to date (Sabina, Wolak, and Finkelhor, 2008). In maintaining my position that porn is not harmful to people—teen and adult alike—I need to describe the context in which pornography exists. By and large, the opposing viewpoint—that pornography is harmful to teens—comes from a place of fear; fear of sex and sexual pleasure that has been a part of American society since before the word "American" even existed (Klein, 2006).

The sexual value system that prevails in the United States sees sex as St. Augustine of Hippo saw it after his conversion from a period of lust and sexual promiscuity to a Christian man of high morals—sexual behaviors are only appropriate between a man and a woman, within the confines of marriage, and for procreative purposes. This same values system is one that leaves out something that has become a part of American mainstream media in recent years with sex therapists and relationship counselors on America's talk shows, like *Oprah, Tyra Banks,* and *Dr. Phil,* among others, as well as the nightly news: sexual pleasure. Sexual pleasure is a part of pornography, whether it is something that filmmakers aim to represent on the screen or it is being experienced by pornography's viewers. It is a part of sexual expression and sexual behaviors. If it were not, our culture would not be spending as much time discussing it—and certainly nowhere nearly as much money on it—as it does.

In a society that values sex for reproduction rather than for sexual pleasure and an individual's right to ecstasy and self-fulfillment, the very idea that our teenagers might be experiencing pleasure or witnessing others doing so incites an even more pronounced fear. Certainly, these fearful individuals speculate, indulgent pleasure can only have one outcome—danger or harm. Therefore, the idea of consuming pornography is reserved for the lowest members of society—criminals, prevents, sex maniacs, and so on. Those who aim for achieving the greater good by being successful in our careers, raising families, and experiencing a sense of spiritual satisfaction wouldn't allow ourselves to stoop to self-satisfying physical pleasure. It is far too much of a distraction and therefore not valued.

Varying media, when relating stories about the Internet, frequently discuss either the wealth of information that it offers or the dangers of its use. Sutter (2000) connects the statements I make above with a recurring fear of humanity since its very first scholars: "The furor over Internet pornography follows the classic pattern of moral panic throughout the ages. From Plato's concerns regarding the 'dramatic poets' effects on the young to the 1980s 'video nasties' scare, to screen violence and internet pornography in the 1990s and beyond: the contexts change but the arguments are consistent" (p. 338). So, I ask that we reconsider the question and begin to explore the panic from a new angle: an angle that begs us to ask what the harmful effects of the panic itself may be.

The panic in which our society engages around the harmfulness of pornography, as I mentioned before, is about the assumption that sexual pleasure is harmful and therefore something from which teens must be protected. Consider this short scenario:

> A parent and 10-year-old child are sitting around the living room, and perhaps the child is sitting on the floor playing with a toy while the parent is flipping through prime-time television. After flipping through the channels, the parent decides on a favorite love story. Although the story itself is over the child's head, the child is otherwise occupied. As the story progresses, the child begins to watch and ends up captivated until the parent switches the channel, which sparks protest in the child because the story was so engaging. The parent's response is, "Go back to playing with your toys, I want to watch something else." What sparked the change of channel? The two main characters engaged in a kiss that transformed into the removal of clothing and rolling in the sheets. No nudity. No words between the characters of any kind, just a romantic ballad in the background and two people beginning to kiss passionately and remove clothing.

Although the child in the story objects to the channel being changed, the parent does nothing to engage the child in a discussion about why the channel was changed or what was going on in the story before the flick of the remote. The message that is entirely implicit in this situation is that kissing and the touching of naked bodies between two adults is not something a child should see. If something suitable for prime-time television is too harmful for children, the mainstream thinking would certainly hold that pornography is harmful as well, if not more so.

I disagree. I posit here that there are benefits to teens watching pornography: (1) Internet pornography offers teens an opportunity to see real bodies; (2) pornography offers an opportunity for teens to learn by watching rather than by doing; and (3) pornography opens doors for communication.

Internet Pornography Offers Teens an Opportunity to See Real Bodies

The days of pornography being only accessible in commercially produced formats (DVD, VHS, film, etc.) are gone. Such content has been described by researchers as being responsible for promoting artificial and unrealistic body types in women and men alike. Certainly, this is not a phenomenon left to the pornography industry alone; producers of mainstream film, television, and video all contribute to the perpetuation of unrealistic body types as more beautiful than that of the average viewer. Why, then, should pornography be held to a higher standard than any other type of media?

On the Internet, there is a multitude of sites where Internet users can generate their own original video content and post it on Web sites for others to see. A visitor to sites like XTube.com and bigbeautifulwomen.com can see a variety of different film clips that include a diversity of body types, sexual orientations, gender, body hair levels, and sexual behaviors ranging from the most mainstream to fetishes. Such a site can build a sense of self-esteem for individuals who might never have seen other people whose nude bodies are like their own.

Pornography Offers an Opportunity for Teens to Learn by Watching Rather Than by Doing

Howard Gardner's (1983) theory of multiple intelligences, which articulates the varying ways in which people express their learning styles, has had a great impact on the ways in which educators approach teaching students. Two of the intelligence styles are kinesthetic, which learns best by physically doing and/or handling something, and visual, which prefers seeing. Teens who match either of these two learning styles may be able to use pornography as a substitute for actual sexual behaviors. Although the kinesthetic learners might be motivated naturally to engage in sex, they may find watching it or masturbating while watching it to be a learning experience. They can understand what they do and don't find arousing; they can learn about their own bodies and what feels and does not feel good. Pornography, and any sexually explicit material for that matter, can actually serve as an excellent teaching tool. Considering that no one has ever gotten pregnant or acquired a sexually transmitted infection from masturbation, one might go so far as to argue that teens who view porn might be able to maintain a decision to remain abstinent longer than teens who do not.

In addition to pornography serving as a tool for varied learning styles, it also serves as a medium through which to portray sexual behaviors. There are few educational venues for teens to see sex in this way. Sexuality, as it is taught in schools, is taught very much separate from the rest of the human body, often even in a different set of classes from other body parts and their functions. Sexual health and reproduction are usually a stand-alone unit in a health class or biology class. The focus of such education is on how the parts work, what their purpose is (procreation) and how to avoid disease. So, although the body parts (uterus, vagina, ovaries, penis, testicles, prostate, etc.) are explained, and often their functions described, all of it is done as if they are detached organs from the rest of the body and without discussion of pleasure.

From a learning standpoint, adolescents and teens are concrete learners—they must be have very specific, straightforward examples to support teaching in order for that teaching to resonate. Talking hypothetically about sexual behaviors is often much more challenging for a teenager to understand than seeing an actual representation of it. Pornography provides teens with that representation.

Pornography Opens Doors for Communication

Finally, pornography offers us, as adults, an opportunity to engage young people in conversations about sexuality. If we engage in conversations with young people about sexuality, sexual bodies, and sexual pleasure, we provide teens with valuable lessons. Pornography as a medium, therefore, becomes neutral, neither good nor bad. It is merely another teachable moment for educators and parents alike.

Realistically speaking, the context in which pornography is viewed is the complicated and potentially troubling component. Sure, some pornography depicts stereotypical sexual behaviors, unrealistic body types, and even behaviors that some perceive to be violent or degrading, but this all presents just as many challenges for teens as it does for adults. Viewing pornography, if not done critically and with discussion, may leave the viewer with misconceived notions of sexual behavior and pleasure. The problems with pornography are cultural and social and can only be further understood and framed appropriately with teens if adults are willing to engage teens in a discussion—a discussion that may even include watching pornography together. Adults sometimes expect that they can control their children's lives, their exposure to the world, and their behaviors. The reality is that while many parents take action to censor their children's Internet access, friends, and media viewing, children who aim to find pornography will always be able to do so. In addition, as mentioned earlier, even children who do not aim to find or view pornography sometimes come upon it unwittingly. The irony of the situation is that enough studies have been done to demonstrate that adolescents and children are sexual, whether alone or with someone else, and even without engaging in sexual behavior, they have fantasies and think about it. As most adults who work with children and teens will tell you, when adults are not present, sex is something teens talk about.

If adults and children don't discuss sex and sexuality, then where are the models for adults to discuss it as well? Pornography, whether viewed in secret, in groups, or with adults present, opens the door for young people to talk about sex and their feelings about it and to find out what important adults in their lives think about it. Pornography presents an opportunity to raise many questions, if the questions are allowed to be asked. Openly discussing sexuality can bring a lot of potential benefits to teens as they age. To consider the ramifications of a culture where sex is taboo, one only needs to read through a chapter in a text on the treatment of sexual dysfunctions. So many of the problems that adults face with the expression of their sexuality have their roots in their lives as children, teenagers, and young adults—times in their lives when sex was not discussed openly, positively, or in constructive ways. Rather than predispose our teens to a future with sexual dysfunction and a fear of finding support around their sexuality, why not begin conversations about sex when young people naturally want to have them?

If our answer to the question posed as the title of this section—Is viewing pornography harmful to teens?—is "yes," we begin on a misguided, thorny path of protecting children and teens from pornography, sexual pleasure, and sex in general by shutting and locking the doors to learning and communication. On the other hand, if the answer is "no," doors open to begin a dialogue about pornography, its use, misuse, benefits, and detriments, and an invaluable conversation can begin between adults and children about healthy sexual expression.

References

A. Fukui and B. Westmore, "To See or Not to See: The Debate over Pornography and Its Relationship to Sexual Aggression," *Australian and New Zealand Journal of Psychiatry* (vol. 28, 1994).

M. Klein, *America's War on Sex* (New York: Praeger Publishers: 2006).

B. Kutchinsky, "Pornography and Rape: Theory and Practice? Evidence from Crime Data in Four Countries Where Pornography Is Easily Accessible," *International Journal of Law and Psychiatry* (vol. 14, 1991).

N. M. Malamuth, T. Addison, and M. Koss, "Pornography and Sexual Aggression: Are There Reliable Effects and Can We Understand Them?" *Annual Review of Sex Research* (vol. 11, 2000).

C. Sabina, J. Wolak, and D. Finkelhor, "The Nature and Dynamics of Internet Pornography Exposure for Youth," *CyberPsychology & Behavior* (vol. 11, 2008).

G. Sutter, "'Nothing New Under the Sun': Old Fears and New Media," *International Journal of Law and Information Technology* (vol. 8, 2000).

M. L. Ybarra and K. J. Mitchell, "Exposure to Internet Pornography Among Children and Adolescents: A National Survey," *CyberPsychology & Behavior* (vol. 8, 2005).

POSTSCRIPT

Is Pornography Harmful to Teenagers?

Pornography is one of the most controversial issues addressed in this volume. What are some of the ways in which these articles reinforced your value system? What are some of the ways in which these articles challenged your value system? How did it feel when your value system was challenged?

In some sections of this chapter, Grinwis and Sitron addressed the same issue but cited different research, therefore reaching different conclusions. For example, Grinwis stated that pornography can lead to sexual violence and stated this in part by citing research published by the National Online Resource Center on Violence Against Women. In contrast, Sitron argued that the research is divided but that a meta-analysis published in the *Annual Review of Sex Research* found no association between pornography and "high levels of sexual aggression." What are some ways that you can examine these resources to determine which research you think is accurate?

Students may find important research topics raised in this chapter. That can include topics that were specifically examined in this chapter as well as other issues not specifically examined. What are some related topics that are important to address?

For example, Sitron's article cites the significant amount of amateur pornography uploaded onto the Internet when he addresses the diversity of body images available online. A separate issue to consider, particularly for young people, are issues of consent for uploading photographs and video online. One significant technological difference for teenagers today as compared to generations past involves the degree of access to photo and video cameras. Here are some questions to be considered:

- What are some of the ways, if any, that teenagers today feel pressure to photograph and record themselves hooking up?
- How does seeing amateur pornography online influence discussions or actual behavior with teenagers about recording themselves when hooking up?
- How can teenagers ensure that their pictures or videos will never be posted online without their consent?
- Have teenagers had experiences being recorded without first giving consent?
- Does consent to be recorded mean that there is consent to show the footage to others?
- Sometimes amateur footage is seen by millions of people. How might others seeing amateur pornography featuring someone they know

possibly affect that person's college admissions? College scholarships? Job prospects? Familial relationships?

- In short, what are the rights of people featured in amateur pornography available online?

Beyond these questions, middle and high school students need to know that some teenagers are being prosecuted for creating child pornography when recording themselves engaged in sexual activities before they have reached the age of 18. Crimes that teenagers are charged with can range from public indecency to the creation of child pornography, possession of child pornography and distribution of child pornography. Some of these young people have been convicted of felonies, sentenced to long prison terms and will be required to register as sex offenders after their release.

Today, teenagers do not just have access to pornography but also the ability to create pornography with greater ease than ever before. While it is important to research the impact of viewing pornography of teenagers, it is also necessary to conduct more research to better understand the ways in which the creation of amateur pornography may be affecting the young people involved.

ISSUE 17

Are Statutory Rape Laws Effective at Protecting Minors?

YES: Sherry F. Colb, from "The Pros and Cons of Statutory Rape Laws," CNN.com (February 11, 2004)

NO: Marc Tunzi, from "Curbside Consultation: Isn't This Statutory Rape?" *American Family Physician* (May 1, 2002)

ISSUE SUMMARY

YES: Sherry F. Colb, columnist and law professor, uses a case study involving a statutory rape case to raise concerns about whether rape and assault cases would be prosecuted sufficiently without statutory rape laws. Although not perfect, statutory rape laws can be assets in such rape cases as when the older partner denies the rape occurred or denies responsibility for a resulting pregnancy or infection.

NO: Marc Tunzi, a family physician, believes that statutory rape laws are ineffective because people can get around them too easily. These laws, he argues, require that an otherwise healthy relationship between two people of different ages be criminalized solely because there is some kind of sexual activity involved. As a result, medical and other licensed professionals do not want to break up these relationships that, in their professional opinion, are not problematic based on just the age difference between the two partners.

The term "rape" refers to forced sexual contact between two people that usually involves the insertion of a penis or inanimate object into another person's vagina, anus, or mouth. Rape is against the law in every state in the United States and usually results in heavy penalties on the rapist.

Statutory rape laws say that sexual behavior between two people where one individual is below a certain age is against the law, even if there was no force involved. These laws, which were originally created to protect adolescent girls from predatory adult males, are different in every state. The age at which a person is considered legally able to engage in sexual behavior, called the "age of consent," is different in every state, too. Most state laws are no longer restricted to a female victim and male perpetrator; they now apply to couples of any gender combination, including same-sex relationships. Most recently, the media has carried news of former schoolteacher Mary Kay Letourneau, an adult who was convicted of statutory rape for having a sexual relationship with an adolescent student. Even though the two claimed then (and maintain now) that they were in love, the law said that this relationship was illegal, and Ms. Letourneau went to prison.

People who support statutory rape laws argue that in any relationship where there is a significant age difference, the older of the two people has an inherent power advantage over the younger. Even if the younger partner agrees to have sex, statutory rape law supporters argue, that person was not old enough to make a well-thought-out decision—and may have been coerced emotionally, even if not physically. What an older partner has can be very seductive—power, money, a job, a car, and more. These tangible things, they argue, play a powerful role in a younger person's decision-making process. In addition, it is quite flattering for a 14-year-old to have a 24-year-old person interested in her or him. One wonders, however, what a 24-year-old could possibly have in common, developmentally and experientially, with a 14-year-old. Statutory rape laws are designed, in part, to keep these types of unequal relationships from becoming sexual in nature.

Others disagree, saying that statutory rape laws are ineffective, judgmental, patronizing, and sexist. Opponents to statutory rape laws argue that adolescents and teenagers are able to make their own decisions about their sexual behavior, even if their partner is older. Opponents maintain that relationships are about much more than sexual behavior, and that if a relationship is otherwise healthy and loving, penalizing the couple for their age difference does more to ruin lives than save them. There are young men, they argue, who have gone to jail because the parents of their younger partners learned that they were having sex and wanted to punish them. As a result, these young men have a jail sentence on their records forever, solely because of an age difference.

What do you think about statutory rape laws? Do they protect, or do they discriminate? Do you think that an adult has more power than a teenager just because she or he is older? If so, is this power strong enough that the adolescent or teen could not say whether she or he wanted to have sex with that adult? What are some of the inherent problems with a significant age difference in a relationship? What are some of the positive things that can happen from two people of different ages having a relationship?

In the following selections, Sherry F. Colb takes the side of the victim, arguing that statutory rape laws, although inherently imperfect, do much more good than harm. For the number of young adolescents who claim they were forced to have sex (particularly by a known assailant), when the situation is often a simple matter of believing one person over the other, statutory rape laws give young rape victims a voice. Dr. Marc Tunzi raises the concern that other health professionals have: how statutory rape laws affect health professionals' guarantee of confidentiality and informed consent to their patients. These laws, he argues, are discriminatory against young men (because these cases most commonly involve an older male partner and a younger female partner), condescending to young women, and sometimes culturally disrespectful if there is a value that early sexual relationships are appropriate within the couple's particular cultural group.

YES

Sherry F. Colb

The Pros and Cons of Statutory Rape Laws

A 10-Year Sentence for Marcus Dwayne Dixon

Recently, the Georgia Supreme Court heard arguments in *Dixon v. State*. The case involves the conviction of Marcus Dwayne Dixon for statutory rape and aggravated child molestation. (Dixon was acquitted of rape and several other charges.)

Statutory rape is sex between an adult and a minor, while aggravated child molestation also involves an injury. At the time of his offense, Dixon was an 18-year-old high school football player who had sex with a 15-year-old female classmate. The aggravated child molestation statute mandates a ten-year minimum sentence, and Dixon challenges the harshness of the resulting penalty.

The case has attracted claims of racism, because the victim was a white girl and the convict an outstanding African-American student with a football scholarship to Vanderbilt.

One provocative underlying (though unstated) question that has contributed to the notoriety of this case is whether the law can legitimately send teenagers to prison for having sex with other teenagers, in the absence of force. Because every state has a statutory rape law in some form, this case presents a challenge to a long and continuing tradition of criminal laws that confine men for what could be consensual sex with minors who are close to the age of majority.

Such liability is controversial in a number of ways, but it also has some benefits that are often overlooked by critics, thus leaving us with a difficult dilemma that admits of no easy answers.

Statutory rape laws have a checkered past. A primary purpose was to guard the virginity of young maidens against seduction by unscrupulous cads. To give up one's "virtue" to a man who was unwilling to pay with his hand in marriage was foolish and presumptively a product of youthful, poor judgment.

Such laws had more to do with preserving female virginity than with the force and violence that define rape. One sign of this is the fact that a man could (and in some states still can) defend himself against statutory rape charges by proving that his victim was already sexually experienced prior to their encounter (and thus not subject to being corrupted by the defendant).

Justifications for Statutory Rape Laws

Despite their unsavory beginnings, however, some feminists have favored these laws as well. Progressive women supported such statutes mainly as measures to help combat the sexual abuse of young girls.

Though a statutory rape charge would not require proof of force or coercion, feminists observed, young girls were (and may continue to be) especially vulnerable to being raped by the adults in their lives. In one study, for example, 74 percent of women who had intercourse before age 14 and 60 percent of those who had sex before age 15 report having had a forced sexual experience.

In addition, prosecutors attempting to prove rape in court have historically faced significant burdens, such as corroboration requirements premised on the complaining witness's presumptive lack of credibility.

For many years, legal thinkers like 18th-century British jurist Sir Matthew Hale were convinced that rape "is an accusation easily to be made and hard to be proved, and harder to be defended by the party accused, though never so innocent." Thus, rape law did not provide a reliable or efficacious vehicle for addressing most sexual violence, and it continues to be of limited utility for acquaintance rapes. . . .

For this reason too, feminists may have viewed statutory rape laws as a godsend. As long as there was sexual intercourse and an under-age victim, the jury could convict. And more importantly, that possibility itself might deter real sexual abuse.

Is Statutory Rape Just Rape Without Proof of One Element?

Viewing statutory rape laws as salutary in this way does raise a serious problem, however. In *In Re Winship,* the U.S. Supreme Court required that prosecutors prove every element of a crime beyond a reasonable doubt before a conviction can be constitutionally valid. Removing the "force" element of rape and leaving only intercourse and age might seem to amount, from some perspectives, to a presumption that the force element of rape is established, without the prosecutor's having to prove it and without the defense even having the option of affirmatively disproving it.

Such a presumption allows for the possibility that a fully consensual sexual encounter will be prosecuted and punished as rape. Some might understandably believe that this unfairly subjects essentially innocent men to unduly harsh treatment, simply in the name of deterring other, unrelated men from engaging in very different and far more culpable sorts of conduct.

Responses to Concerns About Prosecuting Consensual Sex

There are two potential responses to this concern. First, at some level, we might have doubts about the competence of a minor to "consent," in a meaningful way, to sexual activity. Because of her youth, the minor might not fully appreciate the full physical and emotional implications of her decision (including the possibility of offspring for which she will likely have little means of support).

Of course, many adults might also fall into this category, and the decision to treat intercourse as distinctive in this way may simply represent a revival of the old view that maidens should be protected from the corruption of their virtue. Why, otherwise, should girls who are sexually attracted to men be considered the men's victims rather than participants in arguably unwise and socially costly but mutually gratifying activity?

Another response to the concern about innocent men is more in keeping with feminist concerns. It is that when sexual activity with a minor is truly consensual, the activity is unlikely, at least in modern times, to be prosecuted. In other words, to the extent that statutory rape is truly a consensual and therefore victimless crime in a particular case, it is highly unlikely to generate a criminal action.

In the Dixon case, for example, the 15-year-old victim claimed that the defendant "tracked her down in a classroom trailer that she was cleaning as part of her duties in an after-school job, asked if she was a virgin, grabbed her arms, unbuttoned her pants, and raped her on a table." This description renders the statutory rape and aggravated child molestation prosecution something other than the state targeting consensual activity for unduly harsh punishment.

Though Dixon was acquitted on the rape charge, that fact does not rule out the possibility of sexual assault. It means only that the jury was not convinced beyond a reasonable doubt that Dixon forced the 15-year-old girl to have sex against her will.

The normative question, then, becomes this: Is the likelihood that consensual sex will be punished by imprisonment sufficient to override the benefits of statutory rape legislation in facilitating the fight against actual sexual abuse of young adults?

Is Convicting in the Absence of Force Unacceptable?

One reaction to this question is that even the theoretical possibility of convicting in a case of consensual sex is unacceptable and unconstitutional. Prosecutors and juries, on this reasoning, should not have the option of finding a person guilty in the absence of force, regardless of how unlikely they are to exercise that option. Consensual sex is not criminal, period.

The assumptions underlying this reaction, however, though understandable, are at odds with other areas of the criminal law. Consider drug laws. Possession of a large quantity of narcotics is regularly treated as a far more serious offense than possession of a smaller quantity. One reason is that the first is viewed as possession with the intent to distribute (that is, drug dealing), while the second is thought to be consistent with personal use. Since legislators and others view dealing as much more harmful than mere possession, the penalties are accordingly more severe.

Yet possession of a large quantity of drugs, though highly suggestive, is not necessarily accompanied by an intent to distribute. A person might, for example, possess large amounts of drugs to avoid having to risk apprehension or sources drying out, through repeated purchases.

Suppose the drug statute did require proof of intent to distribute. If so, then the judge would, on request, have to instruct the jury that the bare fact of quantity alone is enough for a conviction only if the jury draws the inference, beyond a reasonable doubt, that the defendant intended distribution. Without such a finding of intent, the jury would have to acquit.

With the statute providing instead that quantity is the sole element, however, intent becomes legally irrelevant. As a result, even a prosecutor and jury who know that the defendant is simply saving up for an anticipated heroin shortage rather than planning to deal drugs can convict the defendant of the more serious felony without giving rise to any grounds for appeal.

By crafting a statute without an "intent to distribute" element, in other words, legislators target distribution without requiring its proof (or even allowing for its disproof). One might characterize this as an end-run around the constitutional requisite of proving every element of guilt beyond a reasonable doubt.

The same "end run" accusation can be leveled against statutory rape laws. Young girls may represent a substantial portion of rape victims, perhaps because they are vulnerable and have not yet become sufficiently suspicious of the people around them. In most cases, moreover, a truly consensual encounter with a minor will probably not be brought to a prosecutor's attention or trigger the prosecutorial will to punish.

As with drug possession laws, then, the omission of a requirement that would pose proof problems might generally serve the interests of justice, despite appearances to the contrary.

Consensual Sex with Minors
Is Not a Fundamental Right

What permits legislatures the discretion to enact such laws, ultimately, is the fact that (like drug possession), consensual sex with minors is not a constitutionally protected activity. Even if it is victimless, sex with a minor may be criminalized and punished severely without resort to a force requirement. Indeed, it once was punished routinely in this way because of misogynist concerns about preserving female purity.

In modern times, though, when consensual sex among teenagers is generally understood to be both common and profoundly different from the crime of rape, there might still be a role for statutory rape laws in protecting young girls from actual rapists, through deterrence and through the real possibility of retribution.

Racism Raised in the Dixon Case

A remaining concern is the worry about racism specifically, and discrimination more generally, that arises whenever officials are vested with a large amount of discretion. In Dixon's case, one witness testified that the victim said that the sexual intercourse in question was consensual but that she claimed it was rape to avoid the wrath of her violent, racist father. This testimony may have given rise to reasonable doubt in the jury on the rape charges.

In easing the burden of proof at trial by eliminating the requirement of proving force, then, the law does permit unscrupulous prosecutors and complainants to bring charges on the basis of what is truly victimless behavior.

One does wonder, though, why a girl would tell a violent and racist father about a sexual encounter with a black man in the first place, rather than simply keeping the information from him, if the encounter were actually consensual.

Are Statutory Rape Laws Worth Their Cost?

In short, the crime of statutory rape may have originated from repressive and misogynist conceptions of sexuality. Nonetheless, it has (and may always have had) redeeming characteristics, even from an enlightened perspective that takes into account the realities of prosecuting rape and of women's equality. It makes it easier, for example, to prosecute and thus to deter real rapists who count on jury skepticism about acquaintance rape allegations.

Still, reducing burdens of proof relies a great deal on trust—in victims and in prosecutors—that the omitted element will truly be present when cases come to trial. If and when that trust is misplaced, . . . a grave injustice can result.

Marc Tunzi → **NO**

Curbside Consultation:
Isn't This Statutory Rape?

Case Scenario

Several pregnant teenagers in my practice are underage and have boyfriends older than 18. Isn't this statutory rape? Some of these patients are immigrants who prefer to keep a low profile, not calling the attention of local authorities to themselves or their boyfriends. In most cases, the sex is consensual, and the teens involved don't particularly care about legal fine points. However, I do, because I have often seen older boyfriends disappear, becoming "deadbeat dads." If I reported these young men, maybe they would be forced to fulfill their obligations. On the other hand, reporting them might disrupt a potentially viable relationship. What is my obligation?

Commentary

"Isn't this statutory rape?" our colleague asks. The answer is . . . "maybe." Statutory rape laws were first enacted to protect minors from older predators. States differ considerably in the legal definition of statutory rape.[1] For example, in California, where my practice is located, the age of consent for lawful sexual relationships is 18. If the age difference between the adult and the minor victim is more than three years, the charge is a felony; if three years or less, it is a misdemeanor. In Hawaii, the age of consent is 14. In other states, the age of consent ranges from 15 to 18 years, and many states have associated provisions that specify the level of offense depending on age differences and other factors.

Consideration of the legal fine points of statutory rape requires knowledge of specific state laws. Most states require that health care providers report injuries related to criminal violence regardless of the age of the victim, and four states (California, Colorado, Kentucky, and Rhode Island) require health professionals to report domestic violence.[2] While reporting violent injuries is a well-accepted practice, there continues to be controversy about domestic violence laws (for example, what if the victim doesn't want the abuse reported?). Most experts, however, believe that unreported domestic violence simply breeds more violence and that it should be reported in most cases.

Whether statutory rape is considered violence may depend on the consent of the minor involved. From a strictly legal standpoint, minors are unable to give consent, which is exactly the reason statutory rape laws exist. However, in the majority of statutory rape cases, minors have given consent (legally or not) to having sex, limiting any potential criminal charge to that of domestic violence rather than the more serious charge of child abuse.

In fact, whether health care professionals are required to report consensual statutory rape to authorities really depends on whether the specific state considers it a type of child sexual abuse, which is reportable in all states. Unfortunately, laws on mandatory statutory rape reporting are confusing and often do not appear to be enforced even where they exist.[3-5] California child abuse law requires health practitioners and other child-related professionals to report statutory rape only when the adult is 21 years or older and the minor is younger than 16 years.[6] California law also specifically states that "the pregnancy of a minor does not, in and of itself, constitute a reasonable suspicion of child abuse."[6]

Many people believe that enforcing statutory rape laws will decrease the teen pregnancy rate and the number of young families needing public support because of "deadbeat dads." In fact, part of the 1996 federal welfare reform law specifically directed state and local governments to develop and enforce strict measures against statutory rape for those very reasons. California's response was a multimillion-dollar vertical prosecution program that allows the same prosecutor and investigator to remain on a case from beginning to end, while other states have developed their own programs.[4]

Even though more statutory rape convictions have resulted from these efforts, there is no real evidence that any of the programs have been the effective deterrents that Congress intended. In fact, there are still a lot of 16- and 17-year-olds on my hospital's labor and delivery unit. What these laws may have influenced is the unwillingness of pregnant teens to seek early prenatal care. While knowledge of statutory rape laws does not appear to prevent adult–minor relationships from occurring, fear of these laws may keep some young women from seeking prenatal care as a means of protecting their boyfriends from incarceration or deportation. Many professionals who work with pregnant adolescents are beginning to collect evidence supporting this concern.[1,4]

Another issue for family physicians is that statutory rape laws seem to conflict with the law as it applies to our practice and our understanding of informed consent for adolescents in other situations. Many teens have the capacity to participate in their own health care decision-making, even regarding serious and terminal illnesses. For example, teens are specifically able to consent for contraception, STD treatment, and pregnancy care in nearly all cases. The only illegality may be actually having sex.

The problem is that not all teens and situations are the same. Some teens are much more mature than others of the same age and are as able to consent to sexual activity just as an 18- to 20-year-old could. At the same time, I think all of us would question a relationship between even the most mature 15-year-old and a 25- or 30-year-old. My own experience is that many teens of 16 and 17 know the emotions and consequences of having intercourse just as well as many teens of 18 and 19. In some of my Latina patients, becoming sexually active at a young age seems culturally acceptable and, at times, even encouraged within their culture. I, however, discourage it quite strongly. The question is whether enforcing laws against it is the right approach.

What is the right thing for a family physician to do when caring for a patient who has been involved in statutory rape (as defined by state law)? Not all young men are "deadbeat dads"—many work and are as responsible and dedicated to their partners and children as older men with older partners. Removing a source of financial and emotional support by incarcerating a young man in this situation would probably not help the young woman and her baby; in fact, it might possibly harm them.

If criminal violence has been involved, it must be reported to authorities. If domestic violence has been involved and the victim is a minor, I would report it as a case of child abuse even if the state does not have a mandatory domestic violence reporting law. If it is not violence, given the fact that mandatory statutory rape reporting laws are confusing and not necessarily enforced, I believe that a physician should report only after carefully considering several factors.

How mature is the minor? Is he or she in school and responsible in other matters? Does the minor have the capacity to consent to intercourse? Is she or he using contraception? Does the minor understand the consequences of pregnancy?

Is the couple's relationship truly consensual? What is the couple's age difference? Are they 16 and 36 (an older predator), or are they 16 and 19? Is the adult partner using physical or other power to take advantage of the minor?

If the patient is a pregnant minor, is her adult male partner emotionally and financially responsible and supportive? Is this a potential family in the making, or has the man already abandoned the patient?

Family physicians will probably not report most cases to authorities, believing instead that building patient trust and making appropriate referrals to social services and other allied health professionals are the right things to do for the patient and family involved.

References

1. Donovan P. Can statutory rape laws be effective in preventing adolescent pregnancy? Family Planning Perspectives 1997; 29:30–4, 40.

2. Rodriguez MA, McLoughlin E, Nah G, Campbell JC. Mandatory reporting of domestic violence injuries to the police. JAMA 2001; 286:580–583.

3. Madison AB, Feldman-Winter L, Finkel M, McAbee GN. Commentary: Consensual adolescent sexual activity with adult partners—conflict between confidentiality and physician reporting requirements under child abuse laws. Pediatrics 2001; 107(2). . . .

4. Oliveri R. Statutory rape law and enforcement in the wake of welfare reform. Stanford Law Review 2000; 52:463–508.

5. Leiter RA, ed. National survey of state laws. 2d ed. Detroit-Gale, 1999; 313–30.

6. California Penal Code section 261.5 (Unlawful sexual intercourse with a minor) and California Penal Code sections 11165.1 and 11166 (Child Abuse and Neglect Reporting Act).

POSTSCRIPT

Are Statutory Rape Laws Effective at Protecting Minors?

The combination of age and sexuality is a sensitive subject in many cultures and societies. In the United States, we have many double standards about the age difference between sexual and romantic partners and the gender of the people involved in the relationship. An older man with a much younger woman is much more commonplace than an older woman with a much younger man. An adult male pursuing a teenage girl is seen as a predator, while an adult female doing the same is seen as much less threatening. Even in some court cases, judges have dismissed charges in cases where the older partner was female and the younger one male. It is as if the law does not see an adolescent girl as being able to consent, but a younger male is simply "coming of age" by being sexual with an older partner. In our mainstream society's eyes, an adolescent girl has lost something by being sexual so young; she has shown poor judgment and has been taken advantage of by this terrible older male. An adolescent male in the same situation with an adult woman, however, is often seen as having gained from the relationship—respect and experience. These assumptions are as prejudicial to boys as they are to girls.

What about same-gender relationships? In the well-known play, "The Vagina Monologues," a 15-year-old girl talks about her first sexual experience with an adult woman in town. The description is very loving, empowering, and positive. But isn't this statutory rape? Would anyone be applauding this coming-of-age story if the 15-year-old girl had done the exact same things with a 30-year-old man?

There are far too many unhealthy and abusive relationships in the United States. People bring different things to their relationships, including different levels of power. In some cases, age brings power with it; in others, money and experience; race or ethnicity; physical ability—the examples can continue almost endlessly. The questions that remain are these: In what way can people have healthy, respectful, equal relationships given the inherent power differences that are there? To what extent can and should personal relationships be governed by law? As you read in Issue 10, there used to be laws dictating whether people of different races could marry (and, implicitly, be sexual together). In what ways is it different to govern who can be sexual together based on the ages of the people involved?

Contributors to This Volume

EDITOR

DR. DAVID M. HALL is the author of *Allies at Work: Creating a Lesbian, Gay, Bisexual, and Transgender Inclusive Work Environment.* He is a distinguished corporate diversity trainer and college instructor, having taught graduate courses in The History and Ethics of Human Sexuality, Sexuality and Law, Addressing LGBTQ Issues in School, and other related topics. His long list of clients includes JP Morgan Chase, Merck, the U.S. Department of Energy, PSE&G, The Hershey Company, and The University of Pennsylvania. Dr. Hall is a recipient of teaching and humanitarian awards at the national, state, and local levels.

AUTHORS

SUE ALFORD is the director of public information services at Advocates for Youth, providing editorial oversight for the organization's publications and Web sites, and researching and writing documents for the organization. She is the author of *Science & Success: Sex Education and Other Programs That Work to Prevent Teen Pregnancy, HIV, & Sexuality Transmitted Infections* (Advocates for Youth, 2003) as well as *Science & Success in Developing Countries* (in press).

CRYSTAL BEDLEY has taught Introduction to Sociology, Deviance, and Research Methods at Rutgers University. Her current research focuses on the construction and maintenance of multiracial identities.

RACHEL L. BERGERON is an assistant clinical professor of psychiatry at the Yale University School of Medicine.

JOAN BISKUPIC is the Supreme Court correspondent for *USA Today*. She has also served as the Supreme Court reporter for *The Washington Post* and the legal affairs writer for *Congressional Quarterly*. The author of several reference books, she recently completed a biography of retired Justice Sandra Day O'Connor.

JEANNE BROOKS-GUNN is Virginia and Leonard Marx Professor of Child Development and Education at Teachers College, Columbia University. As a developmental psychologist, Brooks-Gunn serves as consultant to and trainer of in-house researchers, faculty, and students in areas of child development. Brooks-Gunn is a member of the National Advisory Committee of the Institute for Research on Poverty, an advisory board member of Substance Abuse and Sex of the National Center on Addiction and Substance Abuse, and a senior faculty affiliate of the Joint Center on Poverty Research, Northwestern University/University of Chicago.

SARAH WERTHAN BUTTENWIESER has published articles in numerous magazines, including *Brain Child, Bitch,* and *New England Watershed*. She has been a regular contributor to *Mothers Movement Online, Literary Mama,* and *Mamazine*.

B. CHERTIN is on the faculty of health science at Ben-Gurion University in Jerusalem, Israel.

SHERRY F. COLB is a professor at Rutgers Law School in Newark, New Jersey, where she has taught courses in criminal procedure, evidence, mental health law, and feminist legal studies. She has published articles in a variety of law reviews, covering such areas as Fourth Amendment privacy, Fourteenth Amendment liberty from physical confinement, and the role of personal character in criminal culpability.

TERESA STANTON COLLETT is a professor of law at University of St. Thomas School of Law in Minneapolis, Minnesota, and has taught courses in property; professional responsibility; legal limits of medical decision making; constitutional law; church-state relations; and religion, law, and ethics. Recent publications relating to family issues include *Recognizing Same-Sex Marriage: Asking for the Impossible, Seeking Solomon's Wisdom: Judicial Bypass* *of Parental Involvement in a Minor's Abortion Decision,* and *Independence or Interdependence? A Christian Response to Liberal Feminism.*

TIMOTHY J. DAILEY is a senior research fellow at the Center for Marriage and Family Studies at the Family Research Council (FRC), where he specializes in "issues threatening the institutions of marriage and the family." His experience includes college-level instruction both at home and abroad, including several years in Israel teaching the historical, geographical, and archaeological background of the Bible.

NORMAN DANIELS is the Goldthwaite Professor of Philosophy at Tufts University. He is a former senior fellow at the NIH Clinical Bioethics Center and coauthor of *Setting Limits Fairly: Can We Learn to Share Medical Resources?*

DONALD DYSON is a professor at Widener University, Center for Social Work Education. He is also a researcher for the New Jersey Department of Health and Senior Services.

AMICUR FARKAS is the director of the Urology Department at Shaare Zedek Medical Center. Farkas is also on the faculty of health science at Ben-Gurion University in Jerusalem, Israel.

MARC GERMAIN is a physician who is currently medical director of microbiology and epidemiology, for Héma-Québec and associate professor of social and preventive medicine at Laval University, also in Quebec.

EZRA E. H. GRIFFITH is the deputy chair for clinical affairs and professor of psychiatry and African-American studies in the psychiatry department at the Yale University School of Medicine.

WAYNE GRINWIS has been a sexual health educator for Planned Parenthood for 15 years. He is also an adjunct professor in the department of health at West Chester University of Pennsylvania.

IRITH HADAS-HALPREN is director of the radiology and imaging department at Shaare Zedek Medical Center and is on the faculty of health science at Ben-Gurion University in Jerusalem, Israel.

WEN-JUI HAN is an associate professor at the Columbia University School of Social Work, where she focuses on such topics as social welfare policy, with an emphasis on children and families; the effects of maternal employment and child care on children's cognitive and behavior outcomes; the impact of welfare reform and child care subsidies on families; work schedules and child care use of low-income and welfare families; and child care issues facing immigrant families.

LESLIE DOTY HOLLINGSWORTH is an associate professor in the University of Michigan's School of Social Work. She is a certified social worker in Michigan, a clinical member of the American Association of Marriage and Family Therapists, and a member of the National Association of Social Workers, the Academy of Certified Social Workers, the National Council on Family Relations, and the Society for Social Work and Research.

THE HUMAN RIGHTS CAMPAIGN (HRC) is the country's largest gay and lesbian organization, providing a national voice on gay and lesbian issues. HRC effectively lobbies Congress, mobilizes grass-roots action in diverse communities, invests strategically to elect a fair-minded Congress, and increases public understanding through innovative education and communication strategies.

CHRIS JEUB is the founder and president of Training Minds Ministry, which works to provide educational opportunities to families participating in speech and debate. He previously worked as an editor and freelance writer for Focus on the Family and as a public school teacher.

ANTHONY KENNEDY is an associate justice of the U.S. Supreme Court. He received his LL.B. from Harvard Law School in 1961 and worked for law firms in San Francisco and Sacremento, California, until he was nominated by President Gerald Ford to the U.S. Court of Appeals for the Ninth Circuit in 1975. He was nominated by President Ronald Reagan to the Supreme Court in 1988.

STANLEY KURTZ is a contributing editor to the *National Review Online* and a fellow at the Hoover Institution. His writings have also appeared in *Policy Review, The Wall Street Journal,* and *Commentary.* He received his Ph.D. in social anthropology from Harvard University and later taught at Harvard, and was also a Dewey Prize lecturer in psychology at the University of Chicago.

BRIDGET E. MAHER is a policy analyst in the Center for Marriage and Family Studies at the Family Research Council (FRC), where she researches, writes, and offers expert commentary on the issues of marriage, divorce, cohabitation, adoption, family structure, and abstinence.

MARY B. MAHOWALD is a professor at the Pritzker School of Medicine at the University of Chicago. She is the author of *Women and Children and Health Care: An Unequal Majority; Disability, Difference, Discrimination: Perspectives on Justice in Bioethics and Public Policy;* and *Genes, Women, Equality.*

PAUL MCHUGH is the director of the department of psychiatry and behavioral sciences and the Henry Phipps professor of psychiatry at the Johns Hopkins University School of Medicine, the psychiatrist-in-chief of the Johns Hopkins Hospital, and co-chairman of the ethics committee of the American College of Neuropsychopharmacology.

SUSAN A. MILSTEIN received her Ed.D. in human sexuality education from Widener University and is a certified health education specialist in the department of health enhancement, exercise science and physical education at Montgomery College. Professor Milstein was named "Emerging Professional" in the field of sexology by the Society for the Scientific Study of Sexuality at the 50th anniversary national conference. She has also appeared as a guest speaker on NPR's Bryant Park Project, in their spot "The Tough Task of Teaching Sex Ed."

PLANNED PARENTHOOD FEDERATION OF AMERICA, INC., is the world's oldest and largest voluntary reproductive health care organization. Founded by Margaret Sanger in 1916 as America's first birth control clinic, Planned Parenthood believes in the fundamental right of each individual, throughout the world, to manage his or her fertility, regardless of the individual's income, marital status, race, ethnicity, sexual orientation, age, national origin, or residence.

LARA RISCOL is a freelance writer who explores societal conflicts and controversies surrounding sexuality and family. Her published works have appeared in *The Nation, Salon, AlterNet,* and other media outlets, and she is working on a book called *Ten Sex Myths That Screw America*. She is also a member of the Society for the Scientific Study of Sexuality and the American Association of Sexuality Educators, Counselors and Therapists (AASECT).

JOHN A. ROBERTSON is the Vinson and Elkins Chair at the University of Texas School of Law at Austin. He served as a professor at the University of Wisconsin Law School and as the Russell Sage Fellow in Law and Social Science at Harvard Law School. He is the author of two books in bioethics, *The Rights of the Critically Ill* and *Children of Choice: Freedom and the New Reproductive Technologies*. He currently serves as the chair of the Ethics Committee of the American Society for Reproductive Medicine.

BOB ROEHR is a biomedical and freelance writer with a focus on HIV and infectious disease, who is based in Washington, DC. He serves on the Council of Public Representatives (COPR), an advisory body to the director of the National Institutes of Health.

ALLYSON SANDAK has been a sexuality educator and trainer for a decade as well as an adjunct professor at Montclair State University. She is also the editor of Contemporary Sexuality, a publication of the American Association of Sexuality Educators, Counselors and Therapists (AASECT).

MARK V. SAUER is the vice chair of academic affairs at Columbia University Medical Center in the Department of Obstetrics and Gynecology. Dr. Sauer also chairs Sloane Hospital's medical ethics committee.

ANTONIN SCALIA is an associate justice of the U.S. Supreme Court. He taught law at the University of Virginia, the American Enterprise Institute, Georgetown University, and the University of Chicago before being nominated to the U.S. Court of Appeals by President Ronald Reagan in 1982. He served in that capacity until he was nominated by Reagan to the Supreme Court in 1986.

GRAHAM SHER, the chief executive officer of Canadian Blood Services, is an expert in the field of transfusion science who was directly involved in the evolution of Canada's blood system. Dr. Sher has taught at the University of Toronto, served as the medical director of blood transfusion services at the Toronto Hospital/Princess Margaret Hospital, and was a staff physician in the Hematology/Oncology Division at the Toronto Hospital.

JUSTIN A. SITRON is an assistant professor of education at Widener University. He is also a certified sex educator and specialist in cross-cultural sexuality. He has presented at conferences of international and national organizations in cross-cultural sensitivity and sexuality issues.

PETER SPRIGG is the director of the Center for Marriage and Family Studies at the Family Research Council (FRC), having been senior director of culture studies for two years prior to his appointment. He oversees FRC's efforts to analyze and influence our culture as it relates to "marriage and family structure; education; human sexuality and the homosexual agenda; religion in public life; and the arts and entertainment." He also serves as executive editor of the monthly e-mail newsletter *Culture Facts*.

CARSON STRONG is a professor in the department of human Values and ethics at the University of Tennessee College of Medicine in Knoxville.

WILLIAM J. TAVERNER is editor of the *American Journal of Sexuality Education* and director of the Center for Family Life Education. He has coauthored numerous sexuality education manuals and is the author of *Taking Sides: Human Sexuality.*

MARC TUNZI is director of the Family Practice Residency Program at Natividad Medical Center, Salinas, California, and associate clinical professor of family and community medicine at the University of California, San Francisco, School of Medicine. He received his medical degree from the University of California, San Diego, School of Medicine.

THOMAS M. VANDER VEN is an associate professor in the sociology department at Ohio University, specializing in the areas of crime and delinquency; work, family, and crime; criminological theory; and the sociology of social problems.

JANE WALDFOGEL is professor of social work and public affairs at the Columbia University School of Social Work, and a research associate at the Centre for Analysis of Social Exclusion at the London School of Economics. Dr. Waldfogel currently is a member of the National Academy of Science's Committee on Family and Work Policies and the author of *The Future of Child Protection: How to Break the Cycle of Abuse and Neglect* (Harvard University Press, 1998).